*Under the General Editorship of
Taylor W. Meloan,
University of Southern California
Houghton Mifflin Adviser in Marketing*

Readings in

HOUGHTON MIFFLIN COMPANY • BOSTON

SAMUEL V. SMITH

RICHARD H. BRIEN

JAMES E. STAFFORD

University of Houston

Marketing Information Systems

A NEW ERA IN

MARKETING RESEARCH

New York • Atlanta • Geneva, Ill. • Dallas • Palo Alto

Copyright © 1968 by Samuel V. Smith, Richard H. Brien and James E. Stafford

The selections reprinted in this book are used by permission of and special arrangement with the proprietors of their respective copyrights. All rights reserved. No part of this work may be reproduced or transmitted in any form or by any means, electronic or mechanical, including photocopying, recording, or by any information storage or retrieval system, without permission in writing from the publisher.

Printed in the U.S.A.

Editor's Introduction

Too many in marketing still regard success in the field to be essentially rooted in art. At best such decision making is based upon experience or intuition; at worst, upon guess estimate or hunch. Without negating the value of perception and judgment, marketing has reached the stage where it is possible to quantify decision making through systems oriented flows of internally generated data and externally gathered information. But such inputs are valueless unless they are organized and used to provide for more insightful analyses of the key variables involved in formulating marketing strategies.

This book synthesizes literature germane to business information and intelligence systems, and relates it to marketing planning and strategy formulation. Selections are also included which stress the embryonic state of information systems development, plus the pitfalls involved in managing such networks and utilizing data emanating from them. Currently marketers are faced with an explosion of information. It is evident that this data flow will continue to grow in the future. Used intelligently it can enhance managerial effectiveness immeasurably.

TAYLOR W. MELOAN
University of Southern California

Preface

The need for a book devoted to marketing information systems became increasingly apparent to us during a recent review of our marketing courses. Although some very fine recently published marketing books make reference to systems or to information flows, nowhere could we find material that exposes the student to the significance and implications of the information system concept in a complete, organized manner.

This book may be used as a supplementary book in a marketing research course, as a readings book in the introductory course, or as the foundation material for a course in marketing information systems.

Here is the organization of the book. The first section starts with an introductory overview of the subject written by the editors. The next section covers basic concepts in system analysis and proceeds from there to implications for business and marketing management in general. Next, the role of information in marketing planning is discussed, including comparison of the traditional market research approach with certain new approaches to information management. The previous sections lead logically to the fourth section which is devoted to the emergence of marketing information systems. This deals with the design and implementation of informational systems as well as with problems that have arisen in efforts to apply the concept. This section concludes with a summary of the state of the art today and a forecast.

We wish to express our appreciation for the cooperation of the many publishers and authors who permitted us to incorporate their material into the plan of the book. We also are indebted to Dean Ted R. Brannen of the College of Business Administration at the University of Houston who made available faculty time and secretarial assistance in order that this project be completed.

Samuel V. Smith
Richard H. Brien
James E. Stafford

University of Houston

Contents

Editor's Introduction   v

Preface   vii

PART ONE: Introduction   1

    1 / *Marketing Information Systems: An Introductory Overview*   1
       SAMUEL V. SMITH
       RICHARD H. BRIEN
       JAMES E. STAFFORD

    2 / *A Design for the Firm's Marketing Nerve Center*   14
       PHILIP KOTLER

PART TWO: Systems Analysis: Some Basic Concepts   31

    A: The Nature of Systems
      3 / *The Nature of Systems*   34
        STANFORD L. OPTNER

    B: The Systems Concept in Business Management
      4 / *Systems Theory and Management*   44
        RICHARD A. JOHNSON
        FREMONT E. KAST
        JAMES E. ROSENZWEIG

5 / *The Manager's Job: A Systems Approach*   57
SEYMOUR TILLES

C: The Systems Concept in Marketing Management

6 / *Systems Approach to Marketing*   72
LEE ADLER

D: The Systems Concept in Information Management

7 / *Communications and Systems Concepts*   93
RICHARD A. JOHNSON
FREMONT E. KAST
JAMES E. ROSENZWEIG

8 / *Information Flows and the Coordination of Business Functions*   110
DAVID BENDEL HERTZ

PART THREE: *The Role of Information in Marketing Planning*   125

A: Nature of the Marketing Planning Process

9 / *The Role of Planning in Marketing*   127
WENDELL R. SMITH

10 / *The Application of Operating Control Systems to Marketing*   133
CARLOS R. VEST

B: Information in the Marketing Plan: The Traditional Research Approach

11 / *The Role of Research in Marketing Management*   148
HARRY ROBERTS

12 / *Phasing Research Into the Marketing Plan*   162
LEE ADLER

C: The Modern Information Explosion

13 / *Will Managers Be Overwhelmed by the Information Explosion?*   178
HOWELL M. ESTES

14 / *Information Becomes a Hot Item*   187
BUSINESS WEEK

15 / *The Thrust of Information Technology on Management*   191
OLIVER W. TUTHILL

16 / *Marketing Intelligence Systems: A DEW Line for Marketing Men*   204
BUSINESS MANAGEMENT

17 / *Information Systems in Marketing*   209
BELDEN MENKUS

PART FOUR: The Emergence of Marketing Information Systems   217

A: The Design of Information Systems

18 / *Better Management of Market Information*   219
KENNETH P. UHL

19 / *Marketing Intelligence for Top Management*   229
WILLIAM T. KELLEY

20 / *Information Flow and Decentralized Decision Making in Marketing*   238
GERALD S. ALBAUM

21 / *Organization Structure and Its Underlying Theory of Buyer Behavior*   253
JOHN A. HOWARD

B: The Implementation of Information Systems

22 / *Information Processing Model of Executive Decisions*   259
JOHN A. HOWARD
WILLIAM M. MORGENROTH

23 / *Computers Begin to Solve the Marketing Puzzle*   272
BUSINESS WEEK

24 / *A Reporting System for Marketing and Sales*   287
LIONEL E. GRIFFITH

25 / A Corporate Information System for
Distribution Management 294
ALLAN D. DALE
RICHARD J. LEWIS

26 / "Some Day I'm Going to Have a Little
Black Box on My Desk" 304
SALES MANAGEMENT

C: Problems with Information Systems

27 / Keys to a Management Information
System in Your Company 312
ADRIAN McDONOUGH

28 / Some Organizational Problems Which Arise
as the Result of Large-Scale Information
Systems 323
EMANUEL KAY

29 / The Total Systems MYTH 330
W. M. A. BROOKER

D: The State of the Art

30 / The Marketing Executive and Management
Information Systems 341
ARNOLD E. AMSTUTZ

31 / Marketing Management and the Computer 357
SALES MANAGEMENT

32 / The Corporate CIA-A Prediction of
Things to Come 368
WILLIAM R. FAIR

33 / How to Build A Marketing
Information System 384
DONALD F. COX
ROBERT E. GOOD

PART ONE

Introduction

Marketing Information Systems: An Introductory Overview — 1

SAMUEL V. SMITH
RICHARD H. BRIEN
JAMES E. STAFFORD

INTRODUCTION

This collection of readings from recent literature in marketing, organization, and information technology is something of a chronicle of the early impact of the "Communications Revolution" and the "Age of Information" on marketing management. Business enterprise in the United States is caught in an ironic dilemma: our economic system generates a massive volume of data daily, or even hourly, and the rate of information generated appears to be increasing exponentially, yet most managers continue to complain that they have insufficient, inappropriate, or untimely information on which to base operating decisions.

In 1958, Adrian McDonough observed: "Half the cost of running our economy is the cost of information. No other field offers such concentrated room for improvement as does information analysis."[1] Today, a decade

---

[1] "Today's Office—Room for Improvement," *Dun's Review and Modern Industry*, Vol. 73, No. 3 (September, 1958), p. 50.

later, the need for efficient information management is even greater, perhaps especially for marketing management since its job is to match the firm's products with dynamic markets. It is our belief, however, that the problem of generating adequate decision information for marketing must, and now *can,* be seen from a broader perspective than previously has been the case. In seeking to establish a new outlook on a matter it is often helpful to cast the problem in new terms. The new perspective from which we shall launch this inquiry is that of "managerial systems." The process of developing timely, pertinent decision data for marketing management can now, we think, be characterized more meaningfully, if somewhat prematurely, as the functioning of a "marketing information system" rather than simply as "marketing research."

UP FROM MARKETING RESEARCH

To put marketing information systems in perspective relative to marketing research, it is helpful to begin with the notion of "the marketing concept."

The marketing concept has two coextensive dimensions—one philosophical, the other operational.[2] Probably the most famous exposition of the concept belongs to Theodore Levitt who says it represents management's definition of the role of the enterprise "not as producing products but as providing customer creating value satisfaction."[3] As a management philosophy, then, the marketing concept argues that the needs, wants, and value-attitudes of consumers should be the common focus of all marketing decisions, indeed of all business decisions, made by the firm. Only such a common focus can provide the unity of purpose and cohesion of effort necessary for success in today's complex, intensely competitive markets.

At the operating level, the marketing concept emphasizes the importance of integrating and coordinating the many functional decision areas of marketing in order to develop the optimal method of serving profitable opportunities in the market place. The formulation of a marketing program or "marketing mix" typically involves the integration of four major strategic areas: product planning, pricing, distribution, and promotion. In addition to integrating these aspects of the marketing mix, the marketing concept involves coordinating the entire marketing process with the other major areas of the enterprise: production, finance, accounting, statistical control, and personnel.[4]

---

[2] Samuel V. Smith, "Managerial Aspects of Marketing," in Ross M. Trump, ed., *Essentials of Marketing Management* (Boston: Houghton Mifflin Company, 1966), pp. 1–2.

[3] "Marketing Myopia," *Harvard Business Review,* Vol. 38, No. 4 (July–August, 1960), p. 56.

[4] Martin L. Bell, *Marketing: Concepts and Strategy* (Boston: Houghton Mifflin Company, 1966), p. 13.

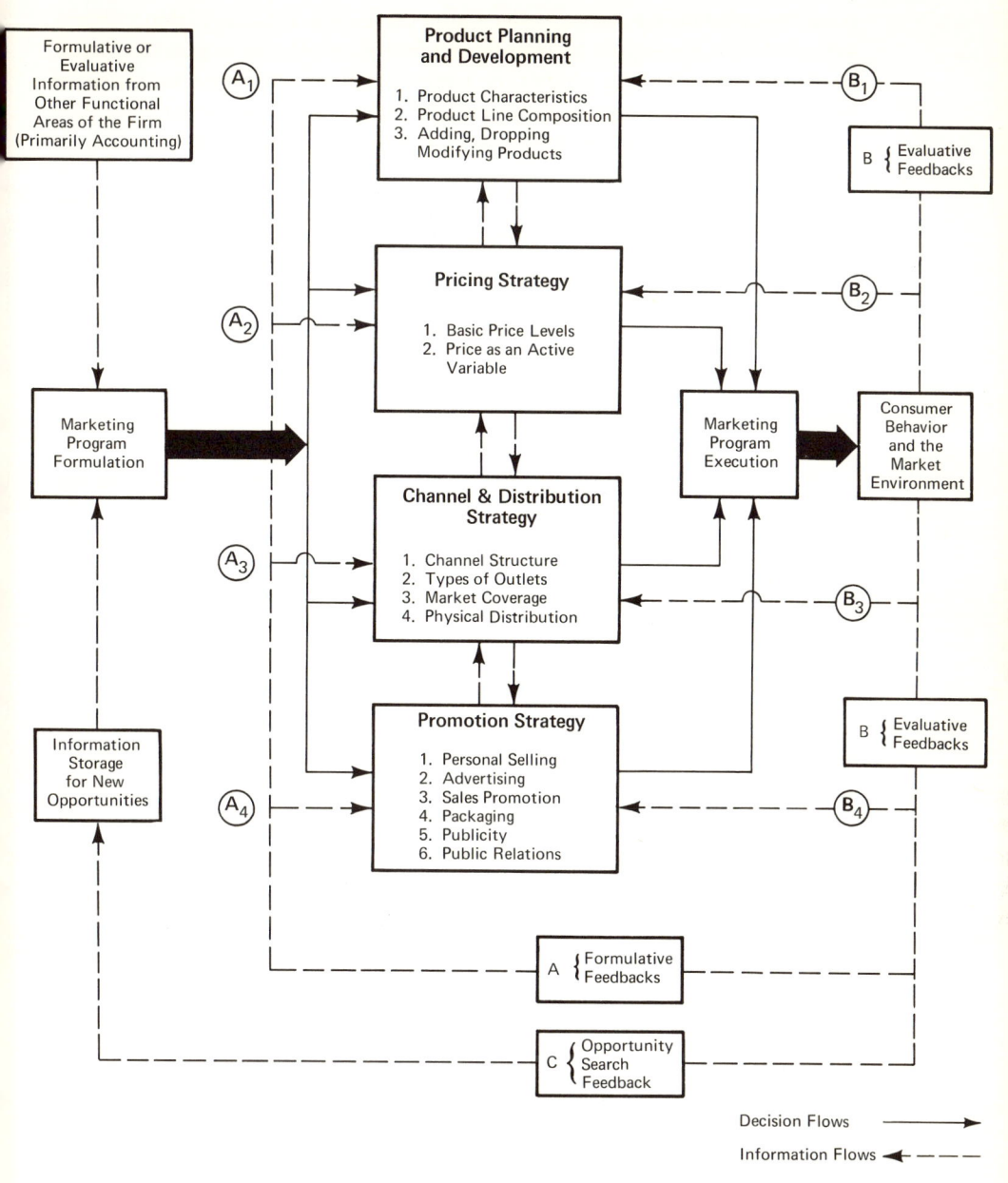

Figure 1. **The Marketing Management Process and Information Flow**

Where does marketing research fit into this view of marketing management? If the marketing concept really is an operative doctrine in a given firm, the answer is fairly clear. Research attempts to identify and analyze causal relationships in order to sharpen decision making in the functional areas of marketing. (See Figure 1.)

Research findings serve at the outset as a basis for establishing objectives and formulating an apparently optimal plan. At this stage the role of research essentially is to predict the results of alternative business decisions (e.g., a "penetration" price versus a "skimming" price or information dissemination through salesmen rather than through advertising). (See the *A* feedbacks in Figure 1.)

If the research effort extends full cycle, periodic post hoc studies are conducted to evaluate the execution of specific aspects or phases of the marketing program (*B* feedbacks, Figure 1). In this role, research provides the basis for control, modification, or redirection of the overall program.

Notice that formulative and evaluative information can also come *from inside the firm,* notably from the accounting department. This information flow typically is not considered part of "marketing research." It will be our contention later, however, that it definitely is a part, in fact a very integral part, of a marketing information system.

Research can also help in anticipating new profit opportunities for the firm in the form of new products or services.[5] (*C* feedbacks, Figure 1.) In many U.S. industries, especially consumer goods industries, the rate of product innovation, the rate of new product failure, and the cost of new product failure are all extremely high—and still rising. To survive in such dynamic markets the firm must try to develop a sensitivity to changes, either in behavior or in the conditions that influence behavior, and create opportunities for successful new products.

Of course it is meaningless to talk of a new product without considering at the same time the related marketing decisions (the rest of that product's marketing mix) that will have to be made. This consideration brings us back to the formulative role of research (the *A* feedbacks) and suggests that marketing research ought really to be a coordinating agent. Each marketing decision must be thought of as an input in a dynamic system and research as an agent to assist in phasing the inputs.[6] The common philosophy of the decision inputs is the profitable satisfaction of consumer needs or wants; thus, we are back to the marketing concept and the package seems reasonably complete. In fact, if marketing research and the marketing concept had this kind of relationship in widespread practice, the case for marketing information systems would be considerably weakened.

Unfortunately, though a great deal has been written about the marketing concept, a recent survey by Martin Bell reveals that there is still considerable confusion and wide divergence of opinion regarding the definition and

---

[5] See Chester R. Wasson, "What Is 'New' About a New Product?," *Journal of Marketing,* Vol. 25, No. 1 (July, 1960), pp. 52–56.

[6] Richard H. Brien and James E. Stafford, "The Myth of Marketing in Banking," *Business Horizons,* Vol. 10, No. 1 (Spring, 1967), p. 72.

managerial implications of the concept.[7] The inquiry was conducted among executives of the member companies of the American Marketing Association "to discover the currently accepted meaning of the term 'marketing concept.'"[8] Disappointingly, about one-third of the responses were so vague they defied classification while many others were traditional or sales-oriented in character, failing to cite customer-orientation and integrated decision-making as important aspects of the marketing concept.

With such a narrow view of the marketing concept being held by many firms within the A.M.A. itself, it is not difficult to understand why marketing research has evolved somewhat "by fits and starts" and why it falls considerably short of being a complete marketing information system. A widely used definition of marketing research is "the systematic gathering, recording, and analyzing of data about problems relating to the marketing of goods and services."[9] Unfortunately, the research procedure has tended to be unsystematic, to emphasize data collection per se instead of the development of decision-pertinent information, and to concern itself with isolated problems almost on an ad hoc basis. According to Joseph W. Newman:

> It is common, for example, for some researchers to see research as being the application of certain techniques—those techniques which they know how to apply. Great emphasis has been given to the technicalities, and this has affected the thinking of business executives as well as researchers. As a result, management tends to equate surveys and research and to ask about such things as sample size and cost before clarifying what it really wants to learn.
>
> The main point is that many people in both research and management have been thinking too narrowly. Our emphasis has been on details or parts of research—and not on research itself. There is a widespread failure to visualize a continuing process of inquiry in which executives are helped to think more effectively.[10]

Addressing precisely the same point, Lee Adler observes that the narrow, traditional notion of marketing research is rapidly becoming obsolete because:

> ... it leads to dreary chronicles of the past rather than focusing on the present and shedding light on the future. It is particularistic, tending to concentrate on the study of tiny fractions of a

---

[7] Bell, p. 10.

[8] *Ibid.*

[9] *Marketing Definitions: A Glossary of Marketing Terms,* Committee on Definitions of the American Marketing Association, Ralph S. Alexander, Chairman (Chicago: American Marketing Association, 1960), pp. 16–17.

[10] "Put Research Into Marketing Decisions," *Harvard Business Review,* Vol. 40, No. 2 (March-April, 1962), p. 106.

marketing problem rather than on the problem as a whole. It lends itself to assuaging the curiosity of the moment, to fire-fighting, to resolving internecine disputes. It is a slave to technique.[11]

TOWARD MARKETING INFORMATION SYSTEMS

Both Newman and Adler, in criticizing the deficiencies of traditional marketing research, have resorted to new terminology to describe what they think should succeed it. To emphasize that there should be a great deal more to research than data gathering technique, Newman employs the term "research resources," which he says, "refers to ways of thinking, theories, knowledge, and skills, as well as methodology."[12]

> Research resources will change over time as progress is made. What remains constant is the concept of careful search to generate a flow of ideas and information which will help executives make better decisions.[13]

Adler alleges that although some new life has recently been breathed into the term "marketing research" (no doubt by a person such as Newman, who does not scrap the term altogether), the narrow perpsective it typically has represented is not appropriate for the systems approach to marketing management. "The role of the systems approach is to help evolve a *marketing intelligence* system tailored to the needs of each marketer. Such a system would serve as the ever-alert nerve center of the marketing operation."[14]

The "nerve center" concept is the theme, also, of Philip Kotler's article which immediately succeeds this introductory overview and which drafts "a blueprint for an organizational unit that promises to improve the accuracy, timeliness, and comprehensiveness of executive marketing information services."[15]

> This unit is a generalization of the marketing research department into something infinitely more effective known as the Marketing Information and Analysis Center (MIAC). MIAC will function as the marketing nerve center for the company and will not only provide instantaneous information to meet a variety of executive needs but also will develop all kinds of analytical and decision aids for executives—ranging from computer forecasting programs to complex simulations of the company's markets.[16]

---

[11] "Systems Approach to Marketing," *Harvard Business Review*, Vol. 45, No. 3 (May–June, 1967), p. 110.

[12] Newman, p. 106.

[13] *Ibid.*

[14] Adler, p. 110.

[15] "A Design for the Firm's Marketing Nerve Center," *Business Horizons*, Vol. 9, No. 3 (Fall, 1966), p. 70.

[16] *Ibid.*

Despite minor variations in terminology, it is clear that Newman, Adler, and Kotler are all talking about a common concept. We prefer the term "marketing information system," defined as follows:

> A structured, interacting complex of persons, machines and procedures designed to generate an orderly flow of pertinent information, collected from both intra- and extra-firm sources, for use as the bases for decision-making in specified responsibility areas of marketing management.

It will be helpful to take a closer look at the essential components of the definition: first, *a structured, interacting complex*. The important notion here is that the marketing information system is a carefully developed master plan for information flow, with explicit objectives and a home in the formal organization. Successful information systems will not evolve spontaneously within the organization, nor will they result if their creation is left exclusively to information technicians. Cox and Good, in the final article in this book, point out that a characteristic common to each of the companies that so far have had success with their marketing information systems is the *support of top management*.[17]

A marketing information system is a structured, interacting complex of *persons, machines, and procedures*.

> Sophisticated systems require the coordinated efforts of many departments and individuals, including:
>
> Top management
> Marketing management, brand management
> Sales management
> New products groups
> Market research personnel
> Control and finance departments
> Systems analysts and designers
> Operations researchers, statisticians, and model builders
> Programmers
> Computer equipment experts and suppliers.[18]

It is clear that in traditional management terms both line and staff personnel inevitably will be involved in any marketing information system. Decision makers will have to be a great deal more precise in specifying their information needs, and a complete crew of new information specialists will be called upon to satisfy them.

---

[17] Donald F. Cox and Robert E. Good, "How to Build a Marketing Information System," originally published in *Harvard Business Review*, Vol. 45, No. 3 (May–June, 1967), p. 149.

[18] *Ibid.*

What is not clear, what in fact is the greatest deterrent to the more rapid and widespread application of the information systems concept, is the determination of the most effective organizational arrangement for implementing and administering the system. The question, like many others in the area of organization, is not generically answerable; each firm's system will have to be tailor-made. The relative merits of four approaches to the organization problem are discussed in the Cox and Good article.

One of the major factors that makes it meaningful to talk of information systems is the tremendous improvement since World War II in information handling *technology and machinery*. The building of the first primitive computer, only some twenty-two years ago, has been designated the beginning of a revolution in the information sciences.[19] Frederic G. Withington of Arthur D. Little, Inc., discusses the relationship between computers and information systems:

> The study of information systems . . . is not the study of computers. It is the study of how the organization communicates and processes information to maximize the effectiveness of management and further the objectives of the organization. *In fact, however, most organizations never devoted great attention to their information systems until they began to consider the use of computers.* The flexibility and power of the new tool, as well as its great cost, has caused many managers to think for the first time of formally planning their information flows and processing functions.[20]

Computers have been applied on a relatively limited scale in marketing, despite the fairly widely held opinion that their potential is perhaps greater there than in most other major functional areas of business.[21] The discussion of computers in marketing in this book will be much more concerned with the relatively non-technical, but crucial, questions of their general role in information systems and the state of the art of their application than with the mechanics of specific hardware-software combinations.

Business information systems include many machines other than the computer, of course, and some of them promise to have an impact on future systems that will rival the influence of the computer. In particular, data

---

[19] Howell M. Estes, "Will Managers Be Overwhelmed By The Information Explosion?," article number 18 in this book, originally published in *Armed Forces Management* (December, 1966), pp. 75–84.

[20] *The Use of Computers In Business Organizations* (Reading, Mass.: Addison-Wesley, 1966), p. 3. Our italics.

[21] See, for example, Richard F. Neuschel, quoted in E. B. Weiss, "The Communications Revolution and How It Will Affect All Business and All Marketing," a special issue reprinted from *Advertising Age* (Chicago: Advertising Publications, Inc., 1966), p. 22.

copying, storage, and retrieval machines are working revolutionary magic on information processing.

It is estimated that in 1966 some half a million duplicating machines spewed out 400 billion copies.[22] At the same time, a new document storage system was developed, permitting the storage of up to 500,000 single-page documents on a single 7,200 foot reel of videotape. This means that roughly 20,000 articles or chapters from books could be stored on one reel with a retrieval time measured in seconds.[23] Statistics such as these, and the somewhat staggering realization that they represent a relatively crude level of achievement, suggest dramatically enough that information management has entered a new era.

But the physical capacity to generate and process fantastic volumes of data is an asset only if the types of data to be gathered and the sources from which they are to be elicited are carefully prescribed. Our definition of a marketing information system alleged that it is *designed to generate an orderly flow of pertinent information, collected from both intra- and extra-firm sources.*

Internal information includes fundamental records of costs, shipments, and sales and any analyses of these that can be made to measure the firm's performance (distribution cost analysis, market shares by product and region, and the like). The computer, and the more progressive accounting departments that see their role as the provision of management information rather than as simply "scorekeeping," have been two of the most important contributors to the integration of such data, on a regular basis, into the marketing information flow.

In a look at current "computerized marketing,"[24] E. B. Weiss points to the following examples, among others:

> Lever Bros. now gets computerized monthly reports on 3,000 key customers the first week of the month—*20 days earlier* than before. These reports show how each account has done in comparison with the previous year. They show the percentage, item by item, each account takes of the total Lever Bros. market zone volume. Another figure shows how this percentage has changed since the previous year in comparison with the general market trend. These reports enable salesmen to provide customers with a relative measure of customer performance. The system also provides brand management with daily tabulations for each brand and package size by geographic district.
>
> Lever Bros. now contemplates a management market information system that will integrate Lever Bros. sales data with consumer records. "One of these days," predicts a Lever executive, "we'll be

---

[22] Weiss, p. 14.
[23] *Ibid.*, p. 13.
[24] *Ibid.*

able to put Nielsen or similar statistics into the computer and get a *decision-making* tool that's *far broader* than one restricted to our own sales data."

One of the more advanced "total systems" in marketing is the Pillsbury Company's "Management Information System." Pillsbury is linked by Teletypewriter from Minneapolis to 128 sales offices, warehouses, etc. Every day, orders are transmitted over the network to headquarters. At 5 p.m. every day, Pillsbury's computers analyze the day's orders. By 8 a.m. the next morning, marketing management has a complete sales analysis and inventory position of the business as of closing time the day before!

Pillsbury is developing a systems program that will more accurately analyze trade promotion expenditures. The object—to pinpoint whether Pillsbury has received adequate additional volume from each promotion and from each account to balance out the promotional expense.

In three branches of Pillsbury's grocery products division, salesmen are "mark sensing" their call reports—using special computer data sheets that are mailed into Minneapolis headquarters each night and electronically recorded the next morning by an optical scanner. This will wind up as a combination sales reporting and in-store checking system that will provide a realistic product-movement picture at the retail level.

This computerized analysis covers 324 items of basic sales information accumulated in on-the-spot reports of investigators checking in-store impact, frontings, shelf positions, displays, etc. How often these retail checks must be made, how many stores must be covered to make the survey valid, are still unanswered questions. However, Pillsbury hopes to have the program operational in about two years.

Once the necessary data have been fed into the computer, Pillsbury plans to experiment with the reorganization of salesmen's time—Pillsbury has 16 different classifications of salesmen. (Pillsbury has already found out their coverage is less regular than had been assumed.)

General Mills aims to obtain a more rational analysis of product movement *at retail*—a largely uncharted area. General Mills has concluded that taking its information system closer to the consumer will lead to a more realistic evaluation of marketing programs.

For the longer term, General Mills contemplates a computer-based data system that will analyze products monthly, in terms of current profitability and projected annual profit-and-loss compared with operating target. The system will show cumulative profit by item, whether it is above or below target and how much, whether the current trend is better or worse than previously reported, and for how long the trend has been evident. This, obviously, involves market trend spotting and tracking.

Its computerized information system will eventually diagnose problems covering such areas as delivery schedules, profit margins, rate of expenditures on consumer advertising and promotion, etc.

The most important notion in these examples is that there must be a timely, basic data flow to chart the firm's progress and raise warning signals when there is a marketing malfunction. Such a framework will make additional data needs much clearer, allowing special supplementary information to be collected, as needed, from external sources through surveys, panels, or experiments.

Such an approach will help assure that any data gathered are *pertinent*. It is perhaps a more grievous sin to collect unnecessary or redundant information than it is to fail to collect any data at all about a particular matter. Superfluous information costs money to develop and wastes decision makers' time; it represents a serious misallocation of managerial resources. Remember that our definition specified that the data generated were to be used as *the bases for decision making in specified responsibility areas of marketing management*.

When Ralph Cordiner was president of General Electric, he observed that:

> It is an immense problem to organize and communicate the information required to operate a large, decentralized organization . . . This deep communication problem is not solved by providing more volume of data for all concerned, by faster accumulation and transmittal of conventional data, by wider distribution of previously existing data, or by holding more conferences. Indeed, the belief that such measures will meet the . . . (management information) challenge is probably one of the great fallacies in business and managerial thinking.
>
> What is required, instead, is a far more penetrating and orderly study of the business in its entirety to discover what specific information is needed at each particular position in view of the decisions to be made there.[25]

Thus the questions of the types of data the information system is to generate and the sources from which it is to elicit the data really can be answered only in the framework of a careful designation of the organizational decision-structure and the specification of the information requirements for the decision process. In fact, according to many organizational theorists, information processing and decision making are inseparable in practice. A

---

[25] Ralph J. Cordiner, *New Frontiers for Professional Managers* (New York: McGraw-Hill Book Company, 1956), quoted in Richard F. Neuschel, *Management by System* (New York: McGraw-Hill Book Company, 1960), p. 208.

decision occurs only on "the receipt of some kind of communication, it consists of a complicated process of combining communications from various sources and it results in the transmission of further communications."[26]

Mr. Paul Funk, executive vice-president of McCann/ITSM, contends that information management *is* the basic business of business:

> Only by putting together an over-all construction of the total marketing process; only by identifying—and in most instances by visualizing—interrelationships, information flows, concurrent and sequential work patterns and critical decision points can one truly grasp control of the bewildering and complex range of activities engaged in by the present-day major corporation.[27]

The pursuit of marketing information systems, then, involves really much more than expanding and automating the data gathering process. It is an inextricable part of the larger pursuit of more efficient forms and methods of organization for marketing management.

WE ARE RUNNING LATE

There is ample evidence that marketing decision making is becoming more complex, making the need for a systematic approach to information management all the greater.

The rate of change in the environmental parameters of business is increasing. Social and cultural patterns, generally considered quite stable, are now highly dynamic and promise to become even more so. This is true in both the quantitative (i.e., demographic, socioeconomic) sense and the qualitative (i.e., value system) sense. We can observe significant shifts within and among traditionally defined "social classes" and we also are experiencing attempts to establish entire new subcultures (the "hippies" are preeminent at this writing).

The political-legal environment for business grows increasingly activist as the attempt to manage macroeconomic conditions is stepped up. And our burgeoning technology makes ever more real the promises—and the threats—of the nuclear age.

That same technology has given us an ability to produce in excess of our current apparent ability to consume (in any sort of a reasonable pattern), intensifying competition for the individual firm as well as raising additional value questions.

---

[26] John T. Dorsey, Jr., "A Communication Model for Administration," *Administrative Science Quarterly* (December, 1957), p. 309, quoted in John M. Pfiffner and Frank O. Sherwood, *Administrative Organization* (Englewood Cliffs, N. J.: Prentice-Hall, Inc., 1960), p. 305.

[27] "Why Industrial Marketers Aren't Using Computers," *Industrial Marketing* (November, 1966), pp. 88–89.

There is also a growing complexity of the areas which have to be managed, largely a function of the tendency toward larger scale enterprise.

> Everyone in commerce, industry, engineering, science, the professions and government feels the force with which the growth curves are pulling apart. The things we have to manage are growing geometrically, while our knowledge of how to manage seems to increase only arithmetically at best. Thus, there is more to manage, and more information to manage it with—but, by some new form of math, "more plus more" seems to add up to less in the way of control.[28]

The "laws" concerning the effect of increasing scale in production seem much less applicable with regard to marketing. If increased marketing takes the firm across existing frontiers, be they geographic, economic, or social (or, more likely, all three), the information needs of the enterprise are substantially compounded. It is highly likely that the most crucial constraint currently imposed on the growth of international marketing is the dearth of decision-information.

But perhaps the most compelling argument for marketing information systems is the "Information Explosion" itself. "The world's accumulation of knowledge has presumably doubled in the past decade. It will double again in the next decade."[29]

> Information, including management information, is growing by the microsecond and even the nanosecond.[30] We cannot turn off the flow. We had therefore better learn to control it—and we are already running late.[31]

THE PLAN OF THE BOOK

The other article in Part I is Philip Kotler's previously mentioned discussion of a design for MIAC, the firm's marketing information and analysis center. It has been placed in the introduction to bring into clearer focus the promise—and some of the problems—of systemic information management.

Part II consists of a progression of articles dealing with basic concepts in systems analysis. The first article analyzes the "pure" systems concept, the next two apply the concept to management of the business enterprise, and the next refines the area of analysis to the systems concept in marketing. The final group of papers in Part II formally introduces the relation between systems theory and information management (although it has been raised in some of the previous articles).

---

[28] Estes, p. 77.
[29] Weiss, p. 5.
[30] A nanosecond is one billionth of a second.
[31] Estes, p. 84.

The crucial role of information in marketing planning and decision making is the topic of Part III. The discussion first centers in the nature of the marketing planning process, then reviews the traditional, "marketing research" approach to the generation of decision-information for use in planning. The third groups of papers outlines further the dimensions of the "Information Explosion," reinforcing our conclusion that there is, in fact, an urgent need for systemic information management in marketing. A further discussion of that need is offered in the final section of Part III.

The fact that the last major segment of the book, Part V, is entitled "The Emergence of Marketing Information Systems," reflects the nascent state of the art. The first collection of papers deals with the design of information systems, the second group with the implementation or execution of the designs. To dampen excessive, premature optimism about the future of marketing information systems, the third section in Part IV recognizes some of the major problems that information systems face.

The final section takes inventory. It assesses the state of the art, reminding us, as was stated at the outset of this introductory overview, that this book chronicles only the *early* impact of the "Communications Revolution" and the "Age of Information" on marketing management. Upon completing the readings collected here, the marketing student should become more sensitive to the demands of the new era of marketing information.

2   A Design for the Firm's Marketing Nerve Center*

PHILIP KOTLER

The author drafts a blueprint for expanding and upgrading the traditional marketing research department into a vastly more comprehensive marketing information and analysis center.

As company operations expand in size and complexity, company executives grow further removed from first-hand contact with the scenes of marketing action. They have to rely increasingly on second-hand information for their picture of what is happening in the marketplace, and, on the basis of highly fragmented and typically tenuous information, must make decisions that have profound consequences. The company's effective-

*Reprinted from **Business Horizons,** national quarterly publication of the Graduate School of Business, Indiana University, Vol. 9, No. 3 (Fall, 1966), pp. 63–74.

ness in the marketplace is increasingly at the mercy of the executive's marketing information.

It is hard to find executives who are satisfied with the quality of their marketing information. Their complaints fall into a number of categories:

There is too much marketing information of the wrong kind, and not enough of the right kind.

Marketing information is so dispersed throughout the company that a great effort is usually necessary to locate simple facts.

Important information is sometimes suppressed by other executives or subordinates, for personal reasons.

Important information often arrives too late to be useful.

Information often arrives in a form that leaves no idea of its accuracy, and there is no one to turn to for confirmation.

Despite these serious complaints, few companies have taken the trouble to consider basic alternatives to their present marketing information arrangements. They are surprisingly slow to take advantage of new information-management concepts and technology. The typical attitude seems to be that important marketing information eventually flows to the right executives, that each executive can gather best the information he needs, and that a system of information management carries the danger of manipulation.

My work with companies convinces me that these premises are wrong. Key executives are often abysmally ignorant of important marketing developments; they do not always make optimal use of existing information; and they frequently distort information in passing it on. A systematic solution to these problems is absolutely necessary if executives are to make effective and swift marketing decisions in an age characterized by intensifying competition, frequent product change, and complex and shifting customer wants.

The literature on total management information systems is singularly uninformative on the specific subject of marketing, and, while a small handful of progressive companies are conducting their own experiments, these are either undisclosed or revealed in a form too fragmentary to provide concrete guidance. This article will present a coherent view of the major concepts and design steps in developing a modern marketing information system.

PRESENT INADEQUACIES

The marketing information requirements of the modern executive have changed radically in the postwar period while the basic information arrangements have remained essentially the same.

On the one hand, the firm is involved in many more markets and products than ever before; the competitors are able to move more swiftly and deftly; and the environment of surrounding law, technology, economics, and culture is undergoing faster change.

On the other hand, executives must still hunt for their information from highly dispersed sources within and outside the company. The marketing research department typically supplies only a fraction of what is needed. The executive must also seek and receive information from the controller, the research and development department, the long-range corporate planning department, the legal department, the economic research department, and other parts of the company. He must supplement these findings by scanning hundreds of salesmen and dealer reports, and by reading half a dozen magazines and newspapers for possible items of significance. In short, he is on a perpetual information safari.

The marketing research department's primary obligations are to conduct special field studies, generate some routine reports and analyses of current sales, and send occasional clippings that might interest particular executives. On the other hand, it does not actively search for all sorts of marketing intelligence that might be needed by executives; it does not typically develop computer programs to aid in marketing analysis and decision making; and it generally does not render information evaluation, indexing, storage, and retrieval services, which would be the mark of a real information center. The marketing research department generally lacks—both in spirit and form—a conception of itself as the total information arm of the modern marketing executive.

One aspect of the insufficiency of information arrangements is dramatized in a planned experiment by Albaum. Albaum set out to study how well information flowed from the customers of a large decentralized company through company salesmen to company executives. He arranged with a sample of company customers to pass on six fabricated pieces of market information to company salesmen. The intelligence told of the changing requirements of customers, the building of a new factory by a competitor, the price being quoted by a competitor, the availability of a new material that might be used in making the product, and the development of a competitive product made from a new material. Clearly, all of these constitute useful marketing information in the right hands. Albaum wanted to discover how far, how fast, and how accurately this information would travel within the company.

Of the six pieces of market information, only two ever traveled beyond the company salesmen! For one reason or another, the majority of the salesmen chose not to pass on their intelligence to anyone in their company. Of the two reports that reached company executives, one arrived in three days but was seriously distorted; the other arrived in about ten days in fairly accurate form, although its usefulness could have been impaired by its tardiness.[1]

---

[1] Gerald S. Albaum, "Horizontal Information Flow: An Exploratory Study," *Journal of the Academy of Management,* VII (March, 1964), pp. 21–33.

Three Information Problems

Albaum's report suggests that at least three different problems arise in an unmanaged information system. They are information disappearance: the salesmen may forget to relay information, may not know who can use it, or may purposely suppress it for personal reasons; information delay: intelligence takes longer than necessary to travel from the original relay point to the decision center; information distortion: the message becomes distorted in the process of being encoded, transmitted and decoded many times. The likelihood of disappearance, delay, and distortion tends to increase with the number of relay points between the source and the final decision center.

Attempts at Correction

There are signs here and there that a few companies have recognized that these problems are sufficiently serious to warrant the development of new concepts and innovations. One such company is Du Pont:

> ... DuPont is moving toward marketing information centers. Basically, it means storing in a computer a great deal of information about specific markets, your position and your competitor's in those markets, the vehicles which cover the markets, etc. When the time comes to make a move, all this information is at your fingertips, so you're working on facts, not hunches.[2]

Monsanto is another company that is taking steps to put marketing information on a technologically advanced footing. Wherever feasible, the computer has been harnessed to supply rapid information and complex marketing analysis. Computer programs have been developed to help the executive select the best warehouse from which to ship an order, the best means of shipment, and the best allocation of customer sales effort. Computer programs are also available to generate sales forecasts, customer profitability studies, analyses of sales call effectiveness, and pricing proposals.[3]

In addition, United Air Lines recently commissioned the Univac Division of Sperry Rand Corporation to build a $56 million on-line computerized system designed to provide United with a totally integrated reservations, operations, and management information capability. Applications will range from passenger reservations, complete name record storage, crew and aircraft scheduling, and flight and meal-planning data to air freight and cargo loading information.

---

[2] Malcolm McNiven, "An Interview with Malcolm McNiven," *Sales Management* (April 19, 1963), p. 42.

[3] William A. Clark, "Monsanto Chemical Company: A Total Systems Approach to Marketing," in Alan D. Meacham and Van B. Thompson, eds., *Total Systems* (Detroit: American Data Processing Inc., 1962), pp. 130–142.

Retailing is also showing signs of innovation in the area of marketing information. The Chicago department store of Carson Pirie Scott & Company recently installed an in-store system that enables its retail personnel to check a customer's credit in a matter of seconds by dialing the customer's number on a phone. The computer returns a spoken answer, either authorizing the sale or giving other instructions. Giant retailers are also experimenting with computerized inventory-ordering systems, direct computer lines to suppliers, and improved sales analysis systems.

Other companies, such as the Hotpoint Division of General Electric, the Mead Paper Company of Dayton, Ohio, and General Mills, are known to be developing a total systems approach to their marketing information needs. But these companies still number only a handful. Other companies are interested but lack a comprehensive understanding of the marketing information problem or how to proceed to solve it.

THE MAJOR INFORMATION FLOWS

Every company is involved in three distinct marketing information flows (see Figure 1a). The first, the marketing intelligence flow, is the flow of information from the environment to relay points within the firm. Information on dealers, competitors, customers, government actions bearing on marketing, prices, advertising effectiveness, and so forth would be considered marketing intelligence. The second, the internal marketing information flow, is the flow between relay points within the firm. This includes intelligence as it flows through the company and internally generated reports germane to marketing. The third, or marketing communications flow, is the flow of information from the firm outward to the environment. It consists of both straight information and product and company promotion. The importance of marketing communications cannot be overemphasized but, as an outward information flow, it will not concern us here.

The Marketing Intelligence Flow

The flow of information known as marketing intelligence consists of salient facts about institutions and developments in the environment that affect the company's opportunities and performance. Figure 1b shows the nine major institutions in the environment that the firm monitors for marketing intelligence. It represents an elaboration of the marketing intelligence flow in Figure 1a.

Marketing intelligence is a broad term, embracing raw data, summary statistics, qualitative inferences, expert and lay opinions, impressions, and even rumors. Examples include figures showing that a certain important customer is beginning to divert some of his purchases to competitors; rumors that a competitor is developing a substantially improved product; and a survey indicating that many customers are dissatisfied with the service provided by the manufacturer's representative.

Each item constitutes marketing intelligence since it has potential action implications for one or more marketing executives in the firm. Information

1a. Three Marketing Information Flows

1. Marketing Intelligence (Inward Information Flow)
2. Internal Marketing Information (Inner Information Flow)
3. Marketing Communications (Outward Information Flow)

1b. Major Sources of Marketing Intelligence

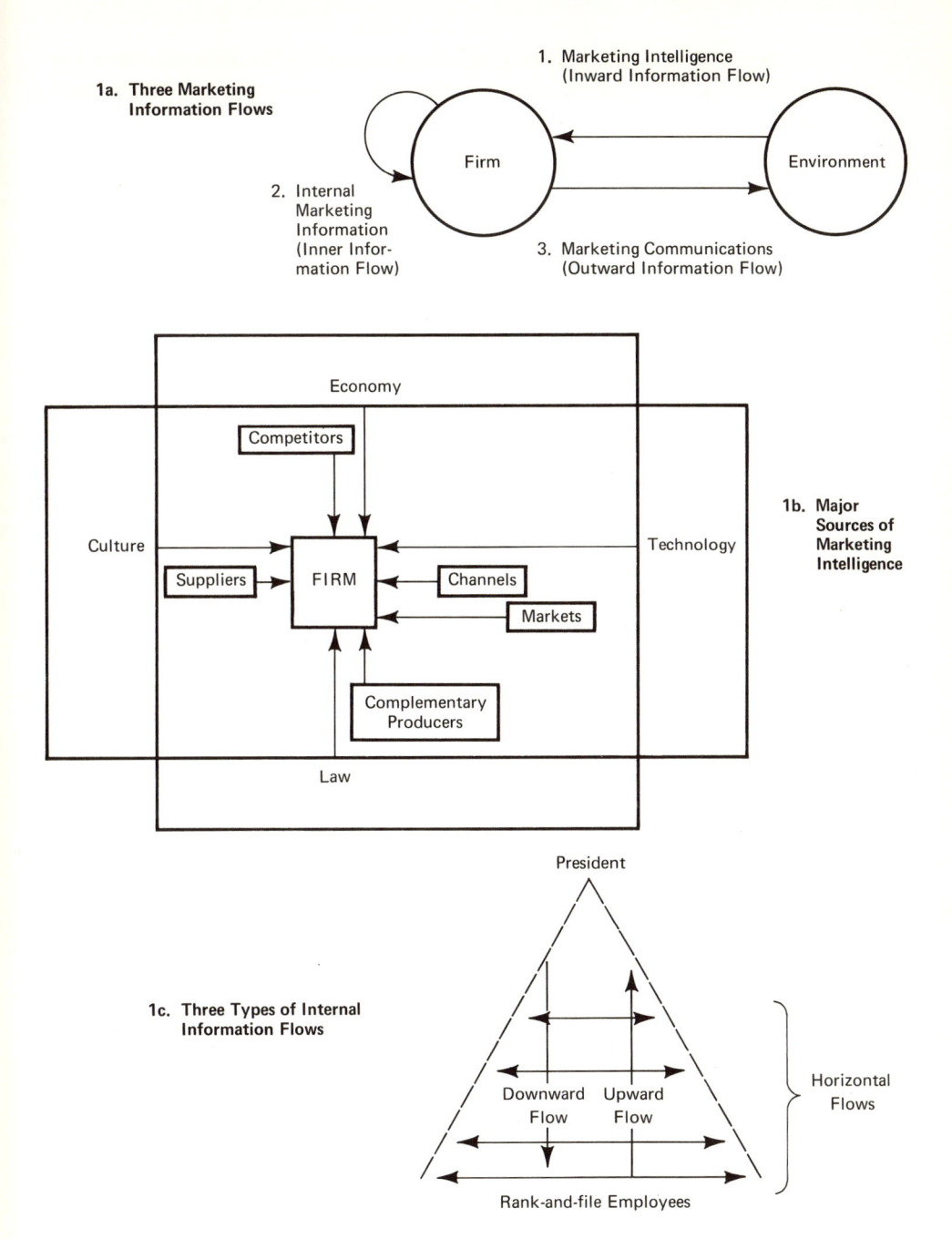

Economy, Culture, Technology, Law, Competitors, Suppliers, Channels, Markets, Complementary Producers → FIRM

1c. Three Types of Internal Information Flows

President — Rank-and-file Employees; Downward Flow, Upward Flow, Horizontal Flows

Figure 1. **What is Meant by Marketing Information**

about a wavering customer is useful intelligence to a district sales manager, although it would be trivial to the new product manager. Reports about a competitor's development of a new product would be useful to the new

A Design for the Firm's Marketing Nerve Center

product manager, and information about customer dissatisfaction with the manufacturer's representative would be useful to the trade relations manager.

The idea of marketing intelligence comes from the military. The high level military decision maker is usually far removed from the battlefield and therefore totally dependent upon second-hand information in directing the battle. He requires continuous data on the current position of his troops, the occurrence and outcomes of skirmishes, and the plans of the enemy. He needs hunches and rumors as well as hard facts.

The marketing executive is in an analogous situation. He fights for terrain (markets) with allies (channels) against an enemy (competitors) for a prize (sales). Because he is remote from the battle scenes, he needs reports on the positions and effectiveness of his salesmen, on the resistances they are encountering, and on the activities of competitors. He needs current and accurate facts as well as some of the talk and gossip of the marketplace.

Marketing intelligence varies in its availability. Information about broad characteristics of the market—such as the number of buyers or their geographical dispersion—is the easiest to obtain. The information is public and often can be drawn routinely from secondary sources—government and trade associations. Information about present and potential customer preferences and attitudes is a little more difficult to acquire. Generally, it does not exist in published form, and, since it may have to be gathered as primary information, its value must be considered carefully in relation to its cost. Most difficult to collect is information related to the marketing expenditures and plans of competitors. Such facts are tightly controlled for security reasons. The firm that wants it may have to develop an industrial espionage unit within the marketing intelligence unit. This, however, raises fundamental issues in business ethics.

The Internal Information Flow

A crucial point about marketing intelligence is that it must reach the right executive to be useful; the information must flow not only to the firm but through it. The internal flow is made up of downward, upward, and horizontal flows. The three are illustrated in Figure 1c where a pyramid form of organization is assumed. The downward flow consists of communications from higher company officials to subordinates. The upward flow consists of requisitioned as well as unsolicited information moving from lower to higher levels in the organization. The horizontal flow consists of information passing among company employees who occupy approximately the same levels.

In the typical company, these internal flows are left to take place in a natural unmediated way. It is assumed that employees generally will know where to find needed information within the company and will receive vital intelligence from others in the company as a matter of course. But these assumptions about the free flow of internal information in an unmanaged communications system are not justified, as Albaum's earlier cited study shows.

EXAMINING INFORMATION NEEDS

At least three steps must be taken by the company that is serious about a total systems approach to marketing information. The first step is to appoint a responsible committee; the second is for this committee to develop studies of present information arrangements and needs. Third, the committee must design the new system on the basis of its studies and carry out its gradual implementation.

The Committee

Responsibility for the quality of marketing information should rest ultimately with the vice-president of marketing and his top ranking executives. This group must define the objectives that are to guide the supply of marketing information; it is also their responsibility to review the workings of the system and to institute desirable reforms.

These same men, however, are not equipped with either the time or training to play a first-hand role in studying, designing, or implementing the improved system. The actual work must be done by a special team usually consisting of the following personnel: the marketing research director, the economic research director, a company sales force executive, a representative from the long-range corporate planning office, a representative from the controller's office, a company computer center specialist, and a company operations researcher (see Figure 2). Each man is on this committee, either because of his special concern for the quality of marketing information or because of his special skills in helping design efficient information systems.

Committee Studies

At its initial meetings, the committee will want to develop a consensus on broad objectives regarding the marketing information system and a general strategy for improvement. It will find, however, that substantial information is lacking on the present system, and that information must be collected. Two studies in particular will loom large in the future recommendations of this committee.

Internal Information Flow Characteristics. Elementary study of the flow of basic information through the company often leads to substantial improvements. For example, what happens after the receipt of a customer purchase order? How long does the customer credit check take? What procedures are used to check inventory, and how long does this take? How soon does manufacturing hear of new stock requirements? How long does it take for sales executives to learn of daily or weekly total sales?

Ringer and Howell reported a study of one company's order routing, which resulted in cutting down the elapsed time between the receipt of an

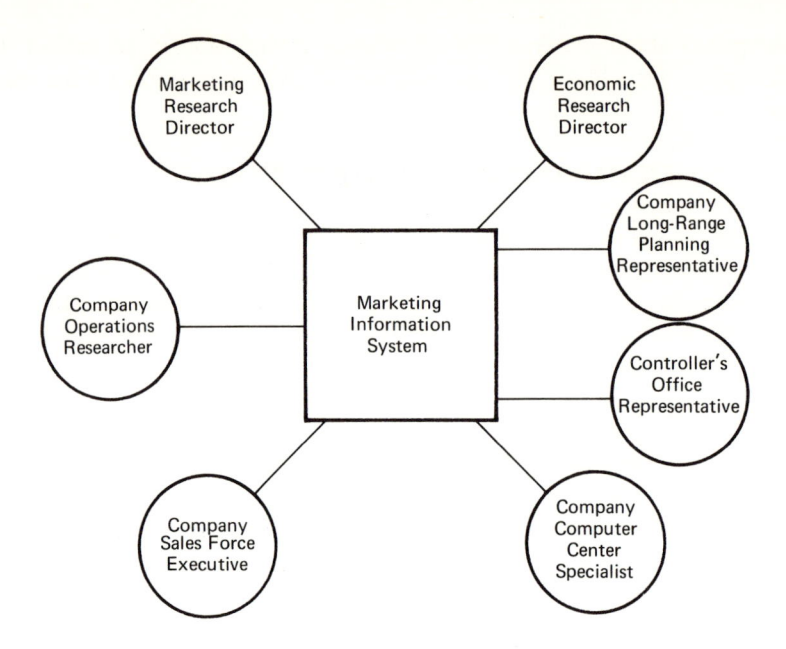

Figure 2. **The Marketing Information Systems Committee**

order and the issuance of the order to be filled from sixty-two hours to thirty hours without any change in costs.[4] Evans and Hague showed how advanced information flow charting techniques could be used to describe and improve interoffice and intraoffice information flows.[5]

The effect of information delays on marketing and manufacturing efficiency has been studied most intensively by Forrester at M.I.T. Using stimulation techniques, Forrester is able to show how various delays in the processing and transmission of information lead to marketing decisions that often accentuate production fluctuations beyond those caused by forecasting errors and resource immobilities. His technique enables an estimate to be made of the cost-benefit effects of proposed alterations in the speed of information transmission through the organization.[6]

Executive Marketing Information Needs. The committee also will want direct feedback from executives on their satisfactions and dissatisfactions with current marketing information. Sampling of a small but representative group of executives from different levels and parts of the organization is adequate. The purpose is not to find out individual needs at this stage since information appetites and decision-making styles differ from

[4] Jurgen F. Ringer and Charles D. Howell, "The Industrial Engineer and Marketing," in Harold Bright Maynard, ed., *Industrial Engineering Handbook* (2d ed.; New York: McGraw-Hill Book Co., Inc., 1963), pp. 10, 102–103.

[5] Marshall K. Evans and Lou R. Hague, "Master Plan for Information Systems," *Harvard Business Review* (January–February, 1962), pp. 92–104.

[6] Jay W. Forrester, "Advertising—A Problem in Industrial Dynamics," *Harvard Business Review* (March–April, 1959), pp. 100–110.

1. What types of decisions are you regularly called upon to make?
2. What types of information do you need to make these decisions?
3. What types of information do you regularly get?
4. What types of special studies do you periodically request?
5. What types of information would you like to get which you are not now getting?
6. What information would you want daily? weekly? monthly? yearly?
7. What magazines and trade reports would you like to see routed to you on a regular basis?
8. What specific topics would you like to be kept informed of?
9. What types of data analysis programs would you like to see made available?
10. What do you think would be the four most helpful improvements that could be made in the present marketing information system?

Figure 3. **Sample Questionnaire for Determining Marketing Information Needs**

executive to executive. Rather, the purpose is to determine how the information needs of product managers, territorial sales managers, customer account executives, advertising managers, salesmen, and other types of executives differ from each other.

Executive attitudes can be surveyed in a number of ways, including interoffice mail or the telephone. The best technique, however, is through personal interviews. Figure 3 suggests the major types of executive responses sought. The questionnaire covers the executive's information sources, attitudes, needs, and suggestions. The questions are stated mainly in an open-end fashion to encourage more involvement and frankness on the part of executives. Results will be more difficult to tabulate, but open-end surveys lead to deeper insights into the problem being studied.

Developing a Long-Range Plan

The studies of the present information flows and executives' needs provide the basis for developing a long-range plan for improving the marketing information system. The committee will not accept all suggestions because the value of additional or faster information must always be measured against the costs of providing it. The committee's task is to rate the various information needs against their probable contributions to better decision making and control. The resulting long-range plan would be submitted to the executive committee for comment and approval, and would be implemented in a series of steps over a number of years.

THE MARKETING INFORMATION AND ANALYSIS CENTER

This section will describe a blueprint for an organizational unit that promises to improve the accuracy, timeliness, and comprehensiveness of executive marketing information services. This unit is a generalization of the marketing research department into something infinitely more effective

```
      Information        Information        Information
      Gathering          Processing         Utilization
```

THE MARKETING INFORMATION AND ANALYSIS CENTER

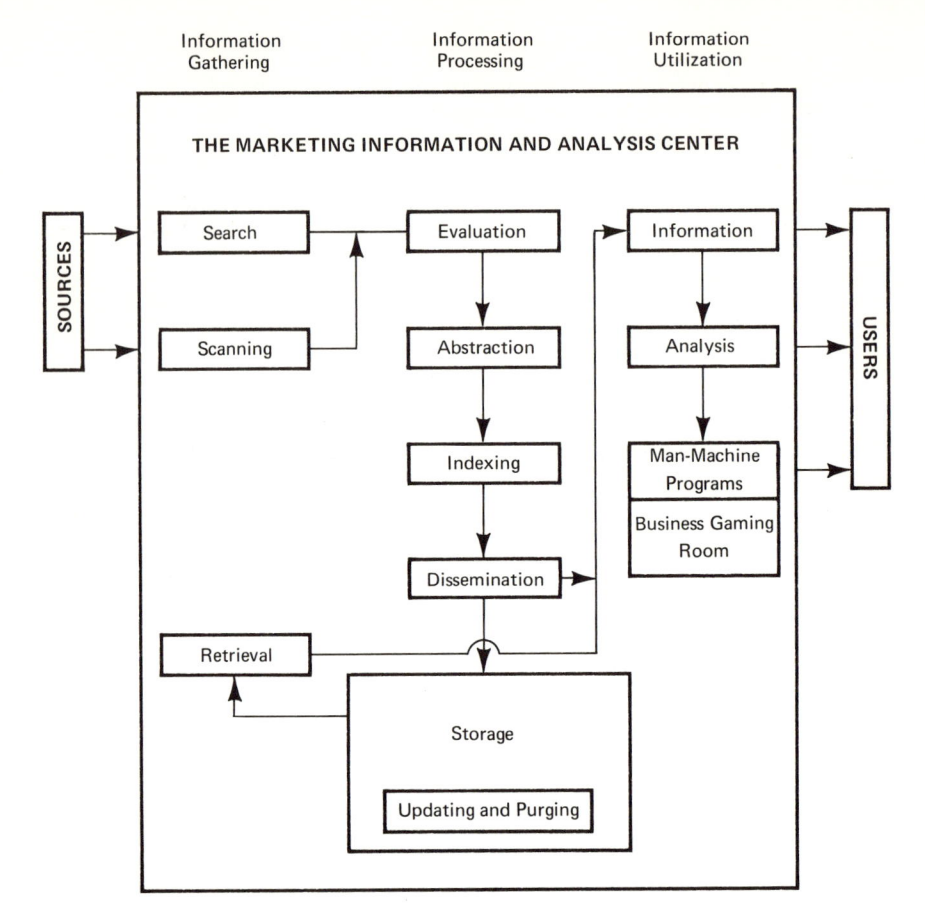

```
SOURCES → [Search] → [Evaluation] → [Information] → USERS
          [Scanning]   ↓             ↓
                       [Abstraction] [Analysis]
                       ↓             ↓
                       [Indexing]    [Man-Machine Programs]
                       ↓             [Business Gaming Room]
                       [Dissemination]
          [Retrieval] ←
                ↑
                [Storage]
                [Updating and Purging]
```

Figure 4. **A Schematic Diagram of MIAC's Information Services**

known as the Marketing Information and Analysis Center (MIAC). MIAC will function as the marketing nerve center for the company and will not only provide instantaneous information to meet a variety of executive needs but also will develop all kinds of analytical and decision aids for executives—ranging from computer forecasting programs to complex simulations of the company's markets.

The concept of this center can be understood best if we view its functions as being completely user oriented. It is designed to meet the total planning, implementational, and control needs of the modern marketing executive. Figure 4 shows the flow of marketing information from ultimate sources to and through MIAC to those who use this information. The ultimate sources consist of parties outside the firm, such as customers, dealers, suppliers, and competitors (see Figure 1b), and parties inside the firm, such as the accounting department, the economic and forecasting department, and the field sales force. The ultimate users consist of company executives, such as product managers, sales force managers, advertising managers, traffic managers, and production scheduling personnel. The MIAC stands between these two groups and performs over a dozen different services to enhance and expedite the marketing information and decision-making process. These information services break down into three major types: gathering, processing, and utilization.

Information Gathering

Gathering involves the effort to develop or locate information sought by company executives or deemed to be relevant to their needs. This function is made up of three constituent services.

The first is search, which is activated by requests for specific marketing information. Search projects can range from quick "information please" inquiries to large-scale field marketing studies. Marketing research departments traditionally spend a substantial portion of their time in search activity.

The second information gathering service is scanning. This describes MIAC's responsibility for assembling general marketing intelligence. Intelligence specialists in MIAC will regularly scan newspapers, magazines, trade journals, special reports, and specific individuals to uncover any developments that might have import for one or more company executives. This partially relieves executives from the necessity to scan endless reams of written material for the sake of finding only a few items of interest. Because executives have overlapping information interests, the centralization of this function and its delegation to MIAC is likely to save considerable executive time. Its effectiveness, however, depends on how well MIAC personnel really understand the differing and specific information needs.

The third information gathering service is retrieval. When the needed information is already on file, the problem is to locate the information efficiently and speedily. This depends on the extent to which MIAC adopts advanced information storage and retrieval techniques, such as computer systems, microfilm devices, display consoles, and the like.

Information Processing

MIAC will also offer a variety of processing services designed to enhance the over-all quality of the information. Five major services can be distinguished.

The first service is evaluation. One or more MIAC staffers trained in techniques of data validation would offer a technical opinion as to how much confidence might be placed in a piece of information. The amount of confidence depends upon how the information was gathered, the size of the sample, the reliability of the source, and other considerations that the data evaluator would immediately recognize as pertinent. This service would offset the tendency to treat all information as equally valid. The data evaluator may show that a particular consumer panel market share figure may vary 20 per cent from the true value (at the 95 per cent confidence level), and that a magazine readership estimate may vary by as much as 50 per cent from the true figures. These opinions on the reliability and credibility of information will temper executive judgments in making decisions.

A second important service is information abstraction. Marketing information comes to MIAC in highly discursive forms. Many executives do not want to read pages and pages of reports to get a kernel of information. Trained abstractors on MIAC's staff condense and edit incoming information; they may omit important material, but this risk must be balanced against the gains accruing from a service that sharpens up information and supplies the executive with an immediate sense of what is relevant.

A third important service is that of indexing the information. This involves devising a set of descriptors that will permit its efficient classification for storage and retrieval purposes, and a ready identification of which executives might be interested in it. For example, information about a proposed merger of two supermarket chains in California might be assigned the descriptors "supermarkets," "mergers," and "California," so that marketing executives interested in either supermarkets, mergers, or California would find this information readily. Developing a good indexing system is the key to the rapid dissemination of marketing information among the right parties and to its easy retrieval.

Dissemination is a fourth important information processing service. Dissemination involves getting information to the right people in the right form in the shortest feasible time. Among the devices used are periodic newsletters, telephone calls, teletype services, and interconnected company computers. Companies are experimenting with new and bolder dissemination procedures, as the following two examples show.

A large chemical company compiles during the week news of special interest to its salesmen, records the news on magnetic tapes, and sends the tapes to them. Each salesman's car is equipped with a tape recorder, and the salesmen pass many otherwise idle driving hours assimilating relevant marketing and company information.

A large supermarket chain is considering the idea of preparing up-to-the-minute reports of news affecting store operations, which its managers around the country can dial into.

MIAC's final information processing service is that of storage. Every company must find an efficient way to store and compress the mountains of information that come in yearly; otherwise, it is storage without utility. Executives should be able to put their fingers on past sales figures, costs, dealer data, and other information with minimum effort. The engineering of an efficient system is a problem for the technicians. Each company must determine the economically desirable life of different types of information so that it can be periodically updated and purged.

Information Utilization

MIAC must offer more than information gathering and processing services if it is to add substantial leverage to the executive's planning and control capabilities. The executive basically needs three types of staff assistance.

His first need is for information itself. Under this heading fall periodic reports, special market studies, and general marketing intelligence. We have seen how MIAC represents an improved vehicle for these services over the traditional marketing research department.

The second major need is for assistance in analysis. In this connection, MIAC's staff would include research specialists in statistical analysis, econometric analysis, psychometric analysis, and operations research, as well as research generalists to gauge needs and interpret results. These analysts would assist the decision maker in formulating problems and developing models for a solution. They would be able to specify the data needed and analyze the gathered data for important relationships and parameters. In this way, complex marketing decisions such as dropping a price, revising sales territories, or increasing the advertising expenditure level can be preevaluated and postevaluated through the scientific analysis of available data. These analysts would also help make periodic analyses of distribution costs, sales trends, expense records, and product and salesman performances.

The third major need of the executive is for computer programs, which will enhance his power to make decisions and to control operations. Future management gains in decision-making effectiveness will depend on the development of "man-computer" systems of decision making. Cohen and Miller have defined this type of system in the following way:

> . . . it makes use of mathematical models (processed by a computer) to arrive at many decisions, but requires management to monitor these decisions and make others that are less subject to programming. The computer not only relieves the firm of much clerical work in handling and compiling the data, but it permits the use of mathematical techniques for optimizing certain decisions which involve large quantities of data and numerous calculations. Where models are not available, the computer often can produce information, from data on hand, to permit more efficient decisions.[7]

The nature of this new and growing service area is best conveyed by several examples.

> A large paper company is developing a computer hookup among its plants and warehouses, which will permit salesmen to obtain quick answers to customers' questions concerning how soon they might receive the goods if they placed an order. The inquiry is entered at a console and transmitted to the central computer system where a determination is made as to whether the item is in

---

[7] Kalman J. Cohen and Merton H. Miller, "Management Games, Information Processing, and Control," *Management International,* III (1963), p. 168.

stock. If it is in stock, the computer indicates how long it would take to schedule its production and ship it to the customer. The salesman can give the customer his answer in a number of minutes.

At a large chemical company, an executive can have a statistical demand analysis made for any product or product item by entering its past sales into the console. The computer program selects the economic and other variables (from a set of 200), which are most highly correlated with the product's past sales and prints out the resulting demand equation.

At a large packaged food company, sales executives get weekly reports on deliveries to retail trade with a red asterisk after those figures showing unusual variances from norms. The red asterisks alert the executives to look into these situations and determine if any special measures are needed.

A large department store is experimenting with a computer program that can make ordering, pricing, and markdown decisions on some staple items and thus free buyers' time for the less routine decisions.

A major advertising agency uses the computer to develop an initial media plan, which will optimize on the clients' objectives, given the available information and constraints. The computer's proposed plan is then refined by changing certain assumptions or information, or by modifying it according to more intangible considerations.

A large chemical company uses a computer program to help evaluate each new product's promise at any point in its development. The executive enters the best information at his disposal regarding probable price, advertising, size of market, competitive strength, cost of development, and so forth, and the computer prints out possible rates of return and their respective probabilities.

A major electrical manufacturer uses a large and complex computer model of the company's markets for one of its products to pretest the likely effects of alternative trade promotions on competitors, customers, and final sales.

All of these are contemporary examples of the possibilities that lie in the exploitation of the man-machine interface. The ultimate implication is the development of a business gaming room, as part of MIAC, where information comes in continuously on field operations, and is evaluated, indexed, abstracted, and disseminated; important developments leads to speedily arranged executive meetings to decide on marketing defensive or offensive actions. Information can be retrieved instantly as the meeting progresses, and the executives can pretest proposed moves on a simulation model of the relevant markets.

There is considerable evidence that executives are dissatisfied with the quality and quantity of their marketing information. Contemporary information systems are usually inadequate to supply the information and analysis needed by marketing and other company executives to respond rapidly and optimally to changing opportunities and challenges. Only a handful of companies are presently pioneering an assortment of innovations, which promise to synthesize one day into the outlines of a new and more effective marketing information system.

A look at the nature and types of information flows provides perspective on planning an improved system. The plan of attack for an organization serious about improving its system calls for the formation of a systems committee, studies of present information flows and executive information needs, and a long-range plan for progressive improvement of the information services. The nerve center of such a system, MIAC, carries out information gathering, processing, and utilization services, which go far beyond those observed in traditional marketing research departments.

The description of MIAC is more a blueprint for the future than a feasible system for the present. Marketing information systems cannot be overhauled overnight. Yet present systems can be guided to evolve in the direction of this blueprint. Difficult questions have to be answered concerning the proper relation between MIAC and other company information centers; the proper relation between MIAC and grass roots marketing research efforts by company personnel; the proper administrative arrangements within MIAC; the cost of MIAC; and so forth.

It must also be asked what the dangers may be in the centralized management of marketing information, and whether this system could make a fetish of information, causing more to be gathered than is economically justifiable. There are no general answers to these questions. They call for inventiveness and good judgment on the part of individual firms. The only judgment to be ventured here is that companies now have it within their power to make substantial improvements in their marketing information system—and can ill afford to neglect them.

PART TWO

Systems Analysis: Some Basic Concepts

Undeniably, there is a vogue in the terminology we use to analyze business management. This fashion in words stems largely from the great amount of borrowing we do from other disciplines in our effort to make business analysis more scientific. To be sure, there almost always is something to recommend the new phraseology; in fact, the rate of change of fashionable terminology may be taken as a crude index of the vigor of the discipline.

Unfortunately, along with their fresh contributions to the body of knowledge, the new terms often bring a rather intimidating mystique. Such has been the case with the "systems" concept. It has roots in the natural and physical sciences, in engineering and the military; and more recently it has become inextricably enmeshed with the exotic jargon of computer technology. What it means in essence and how it can be applied to business management seems to have gotten unduly obscured, perhaps by its multiple derivations.

As we shall use it, that is, to apply to human decision making, systems analysis probably originated in the development of optimal attack and defense patterns during World War II.[1] In this military

---

[1] Lee Adler, "The Systems Approach to Marketing," **Harvard Business Review,** Vol. 45, No. 3 (May–June, 1967), p. 112.

context, the RAND Corporation has defined the systems approach in a fashion which seems equally appropriate for business strategists:

> An inquiry to aid a decision-maker choose a course of action by systematically investigating his proper objectives, comparing quantitatively where possible the costs, effectiveness, and risks associated with the alternative policies or strategies for achieving them, and *formulating additional alternatives if those examined are found wanting.*[2]

The systems approach to decision making, then, involves looking at the objectives, resources and constraints of organized behavior patterns as sets of interacting variables. In the business system, as in the military, decisions must be made to solve complex problems under uncertain conditions. In that situation, the role of systems analysis is "to specify a closed operating network in which the components will work together so as to yield the optimum balance of economy, efficiency and risk minimization."[3]

Applying the concept to marketing (which may be thought of as a subsystem in the larger total-enterprise management system), one must view the making of marketing decisions as an integrated, ongoing administrative process. Carlos Vest, of General Learning Corporation, has borrowed the simple module or "black-box" concept from computer systems to demonstrate the basic structure of the marketing system[4]:

Control

Input   Processor   Output

Feedback

Output. It should not seem strange to the student of marketing to begin a discussion of the components of the marketing system with output, since he knows that all marketing behavior is purposeful or goal-oriented. The purpose of marketing is to identify, stimulate and serve profitable opportunities in the marketplace, and the firm's basic output is the products and services it creates to do

---

[2] Quade, E. S., editor, **Analysis for Military Decisions** (Santa Monica, California, The RAND Corporation, 1964), p. 4, quoted in Adler.

[3] Adler, p. 112.

[4] "The Application of Operating Control Systems to Marketing," John S. Wright and Jac L. Goldstucker, editors, **New Ideas for Successful Marketing** (Chicago: American Marketing Association, 1966), pp. 95–99.

so. Additional outputs are the messages the firm sends to the marketplace regarding its products.

Processor. The processor of the module is marketing administration itself since, "in all cases of systems analysis, the system under study is, by definition, the processor."[5] We are concerned here with the structure of the marketing organization—the design of the human machinery necessary to execute the marketing function and accomplish marketing objectives. Within the marketing processor is a complex series of subsystems including those for making decisions regarding pricing, distribution and channel management, advertising, selling, sales servicing and the like.

Control. All systems operate within the constraints imposed by a set of environmental parameters. These parameters are known collectively as control in the simple module. The principal marketing environments might be cultural, social, political-legal, economic and technological (external) and enterprise objectives and resources (internal).

Input. One particular input may be considered the *sine qua non* of the marketing system: the product idea. It serves as the point of initiation and remains the focal point of the marketing process, from input as an idea to output as a tangible product offering. There are other important inputs in the marketing system, however.

Feedback. To get the product from ideation to marketplace in a fashion that will accomplish the system's goals typically requires additional input in the form of information. This information may come from linked systems within the firm, especially accounting, or it may come from those persons who have received the initial outputs, through the feedback loop. The formal process of developing feedback traditionally has been called marketing research.

The purpose of the readings in this section of the book will be to develop further the systems concept, placing special emphasis on business and marketing systems and the role of information in them.

---

[5] Vest, p. 98.

A   The Nature of Systems

3   The Nature of Systems*

STANFORD L. OPTNER

The author discusses the "nature" of the systems concept, defines the elements of such systems, differentiates among various classes of systems, and, finally, describes how a total system must be viewed as a collection of complementary sub-systems.

WHAT IS A SYSTEM?

A general definition of a system is that it is an on-going process. Thus, any thing in motion, in process, or in a state of change could be defined as a system. This definition is not incorrect, but merely incomplete. There are systems (telephone systems, radio communication, etc.) that would not be included under the above definition because they lack "motion" in a conventional sense. A more complete and inclusive general definition would describe a system as a set of objects with a given set of relationships between the objects and their attributes. In a more specific form, the foregoing system elements would be defined as follows:

> *Objects* are the parameters of systems; the parameters of systems are input, process, output, feedback-control, and a restriction. Each system parameter may take a variety of values to describe a system state.
>
> *Attributes* are the properties of object parameters. A property is the external manifestation of the way in which an object is known, observed, or introduced in a process. Attributes characterize the parameters of systems, making possible the assignment of a value and a dimensional description. The attributes of objects may be altered as a result of system operation.

---

*From **Systems Analysis For Business And Industrial Problem Solving** (Englewood Cliffs, Prentice-Hall, Inc., 1965), pp. 26–36. Used by permission of Prentice-Hall Book Company.

Relationships are the bonds that link objects and attributes in the system process. Relationships are postulated among all system elements, among systems and subsystems, and between two or more subsystems. Relationships may be characterized as first order, when they are functionally necessary to each other. Symbiosis, a first-order example, is the necessary relationship of dissimilar organisms; for example a plant and a parasite. Relationships may be characterized as second order if they are complementary, adding substantially to system performance when present, but not functionally essential. Synergy is a second-order relationship. Synergistic relationships are those where the co-operative action of independent agencies taken together produce total effects greater than the sums of their effects taken independently. Relationships may be characterized as third-order when they are either redundant or contradictory. *Redundance* describes a state whereby the system contains superfluous objects. A *contradictory* condition exists when the system contains two objects, which, if one is true, the other by definition is false.

A system, condition, situation, or state is postulated to describe a set of objects, attributes, and relationships. A *postulated* proposition is one which is put forth hypothetically, as a tentative statement.

From the foregoing definitions of a system, the postulate of a system malfunction is generated. To account for system failure, which may take a wide variety of forms, the *system malfunction* is defined as a change in first-, second- or third-order relationship of objects and attributes, such that the system passes its critical point. In passing the critical point, one or more of the system objects is altered, setting up new relationships, and hence new outputs. The term *critical* is defined as the change in system parameter, where a property crosses a threshold and assumes a finite value of a different order. Critical levels result from wide variations in the properties of parameters (system objects) outside the range provided through system design. The concept of a system malfunction is postulated to provide a general term to describe a variety of system failures that occur when the system is required to operate outside its design limits.

The term *process,* employed repeatedly in defining the on-going state of systems, is defined as the totality of components encompassed by all objects, attributes, and relationships to produce a given result. Processes may be mental (thinking, planning, learning), mental-motor (testing, writing, constructing) or mechanical (operating, functioning). Processes apply to men or machines and their combined activities. Systems may be identified by their processors or processes. No system, within the definition of this presentation, may be said to exist without a process.

PHYSICAL AND ABSTRACT SYSTEMS

Systems may be categorized through their similarities and dissimilarities. Physical systems deal with hardware, equipment, machinery and, in general, real objects or artifacts. These systems may be contrasted with abstract systems. In the latter, symbols represent attributes of objects that may not be known to exist, except in the mind of the investigator. Concepts, plans, hypotheses, and ideas under investigation may be described as abstract systems.

Within the categories of physical and abstract systems, the on-going process may be seen at many levels. The component processes necessary to the operation of a total system are known as *subsystems*. Subsystems in turn may be further described as more detailed subsystems. The hierarchy of systems or the number of subsystems are dependent only upon the intrinsic complexity of the total system. It is conceivable therefore, that some systems may contain an infinite variety of processes. Conversely, other systems contain a finite, limited number of processes. At each identifiable process the analyst may stipulate a system. Systems may operate simultaneously, in parallel, or in series without any restrictions other than those imposed by design or the real world.

Each system may be said to exist within a specific environment. Systems exist within, and are conditioned by, the environment. The first condition of this environment is the boundary within which the system is said to operate. *Environment* is defined as a set of all objects, within some specific limit, that may conceivably have bearing upon the operation of the system.

The business systems analyst cannot conduct unlimited research in an attempt to understand all conditions that have impact upon system operation. The concept of a *boundary* prescribes a limitation within which the objects, attributes, and their relationships are adequately explained and manageable. Systems and their boundaries may be defined simply if the objects are absolute or finite in nature. Physical systems can be described most conveniently in quantitative, performance terms. Abstract systems, however, may not be as easily defined in finite terms. All systems operate within a given environment and a given boundary.

The study of systems may take one of two basic courses, process analysis, or final outcome analysis. In the first, the system may be studied as a number of intimately related subsystems. This microscopic view of the world generates the process type of analysis. In a process-oriented analysis, the analyst defines the intermediate outputs of systems. He then studies the means by which they are introduced into serially-related processes for subsequent processing. In process analysis, there are many alternatives or options that qualify as intermediate solutions. Process analysis is frequently associated with real-world problems and physical systems.

Juxtaposed to process analysis is final-outcome analysis, which provides a macroscopic view. Under this method, the system is treated as a whole. The analyst is more concerned with the overriding, end results than the intermediate results. In outcome-oriented analysis, there is no certain knowledge of all the intermediate outputs. Thus, there may be no means to establish the basis on which all of the processes are united in the total system operation.

The goal of the investigator is to make a model of his system, be it physical or abstract. He further attempts to understand the system as an on-going process, given the objects, attributes, and relationships that are combined in the system operation. The model may be mathematical, if the investigator can apply quantitative properties to his problem. If the problem is both quantitative and qualitative in nature, the model may be less rigorous and be no more complex than a system or data processing flow chart. The model maker seeks to reproduce in some "miniature" or manageable form, the real-world operations of the system under study.

If a model is an accurate replica or representation of the real world, it may be termed special purpose. Special purpose models may be brought to bear upon most problems with some calculable expectation of success. General purpose models approximate the real world with something less than the subjectivity and substantive content of the special purpose model. It follows that solutions derived by general purpose models are general in nature; in the same way, solutions derived by special purpose models are special purpose in nature. Neither are applicable to their opposite category of solutions without carefully stated assumptions.

Systems may be centralized or decentralized. In a centralized system, one element or one major subsystem plays a dominant role that may override the other system components. In this arrangement of systems and subsystems, the major subsystem is central to the operation. The minor subsystems are satellite to the central operation. In a decentralized system, the converse may be true; major subsystems are of approximately equal value. Rather than being arranged around a central subsystem as satellites, the major subsystems are serially arranged. Otherwise they may be arranged in parallel, each providing both unique and isomorphic (superficially similar) outputs. In both centralized and decentralized systems, inputs and outputs may be prescribed. Conceptually, both types of systems may be in existence in the physical and abstract systems categories.

NATURAL AND MAN-MADE SYSTEMS

The second major systems category separates systems according to their origin. Natural systems are defined as those growing out of natural processes. Climate and terrain are typical natural systems. Man-made systems are those in which man has made a contribution to the on-going process either through objects, attributes, or relationships. Natural and man-made systems may also be physical or abstract.

Quantitative description of natural processes may be made through physical systems when they are linked to finite occurrences. Natural systems are macroscopic and not subject to easy management. Natural systems may be stable over long periods of time, since they tend to operate within defined limits, however broad. Some natural systems are called *adaptive*. These are the systems in which there is a constant readjustment to new environmental inputs. Weather fronts are an example of an adaptive system.

Open systems are typical of those found in the natural category. An open system trades its materials or energies with the environment in a regular and understandable manner. Most business activities are conducted in an environment of an open system. Opposed to this are *closed* systems, which operate with relatively little interchange of either energy or materials with the environment. In the business world, the best example of a partly-closed system would be a monopoly whose processes and products are protected by patents and other capabilities; these competitive advantages may enable it to operate in a less open fashion.

Man-made systems have some, but not all, of the foregoing characteristics. The man-made system may reproduce, in a controlled environment, the natural conditions that are not manageable in the real world. The military establishment and the government are also open systems. Each of these has wide interchange with its environment; in this case the public, the laws of the land, and private enterprise. Man-made systems are closed when they are designed for invariant input and statistically predictable output. Such systems are also characterized as completely structured. In a closed system, the objects and relationships are combined in ways not found in natural systems. Completely structured, invariant output systems exist under laboratory conditions or under circumstances where the role of physical objects dominates system operation. The objective in business system design is to move toward a closed system through feedback-control.

Man-made systems may also be adaptive. This commonly occurs when man must introduce input, process it, and deliver output. An adaptive system is one in which there is a continuous learning or *self-organizing* process in motion. In adaptive systems, the range of input may be wide and the processor may be required to deal with uncertain input. Man's machines have not been learning machines. Considerable effort is being expended at this time to teach machines to learn from previous experience. The classic example of the learning machine is the automatic computer. In a special sense, the computer is capable of "reading" its intermediate results and taking subsequent (adaptive) steps along previously defined paths. Man has programmed the machine to test all of the options that may be open to it at any stage of processing. The machine may repeat the programmed steps as many times as there are new sets of conditions that have been introduced. This is known as the iterative (repetitive) loop. The technology of computer processing may ultimately make it possible for machines to carry the adaptive process beyond the horizons that man has stipulated through programming instructions.

Systems may be further characterized as having random properties. These exist in both the natural and man-made categories. *Randomness* describes a condition of statistically unstable input or output. In a random system, input is not predictable and the system operation takes place within more widely defined limits. Adaptive systems may be designed to cope with a random condition. However, man typically attempts to restrict randomness in an effort to design simple systems. When randomness is among the important conditions of a problem, it may be relegated to one specific area of subsystem activity. This is done to restrict the unstable objects, attributes, and relationships in ways which minimize their impact on other, more stable subsystems.

One of the principal goals in system design is to reduce system failure at some cost. Only man-made systems respond to this restriction with any statistical accuracy; where natural systems are concerned, the objects may not be manageable, hence the relationships are random and unstable (i.e., unpredictable). Man expresses these uncertain situations through estimates of a probability of occurrence.

Natural systems are structured through the interplay of environmental forces. The quality of structure is achieved when a set of system objects are organized into something approaching an adaptive operation. Man-made systems, however, can be structured only by man. When man designs the system, one of the principal goals is to reduce human failure, as it may contribute to system malfunction. The systems analyst may be called upon to design a system that exists in a random, ill-structured state. His objective may be to reorganize it so it may operate as a well-structured open system, with the capability of adapting to a given range of inputs in a predetermined fashion. System malfunction is conditioned in part by the extent to which structure is achieved in system design.

The foregoing types of systems may also be described as coarse and fine. The thermostat is a physical, man-made system that can be designed to accept input in wide thermal gradients. In this case, its operation may be called *coarse*. The same physical system may also be designed to accept input within much narrower gradients and therefore be called *fine*. In man-made systems, the designer attempts to maintain a relatively consistent level of coarseness and fineness.

MAN-MADE SYSTEMS

In the man-machine system, the role of each component is defined. Either man or machine may be central to the operation. The system designer attempts to raise the quality of the human input to the level of the machine. As the power of the machine is increased, its role becomes more central, and that of the human, less central. The machine performs the function of processor with the human introducing the input. As the machine increases in flexibility, it may do many processing steps and provide more than one output. In special-purpose models that have been automated, it is possible to design a sensor (an instrument) capable of "reading" an ongoing process. This reading may be automatically transmitted to a central processor. The processor operates on this input and interprets some parameter property (i.e., characteristic), of the physical process. Thus, the role of the machine may be expanded to include the input function.

Man-machine systems operate through a range of capabilities and complements. Capabilities refer to the intrinsic abilities of men or equipment to perform system tasks. For example, a system requirement to take a reading every second from a heat-recording instrument cannot be performed effectively by man. Another example: If a machine is designated to sort on magnetic tape 300,000 records of 12 alphanumeric characters each, using 4,000 word memory, the effectiveness of the system would be low, cost would be high, and a very large amount of time would be consumed. Capabilities vary with requirements for speed, reliability, accuracy, and frequency of processing. The capability of a given system will ultimately rest upon its fitness to adapt to the condition it is required to service. It is possible that some systems may be overpowered, that is, possess far more capability than is required for system operation; the converse is also possible. The over- or under-powered system may be deficient in the man or machine category.

The *complements* (page 35) of systems vary in terms of numbers and *capabilities* of men or machines. Where capabilities reflect the relative "power" of system objects, complements reflect the quantities of objects brought to bear upon system operation. Complements may also be defined as the application of an "intensive" to a system. *Intensives* are defined as the amounts of capital, labor, materials, or equipment provided for system operation. Intensives are increased to augment the rate or effectiveness of system performance. One intensive may be increased without decreasing others; intensives may be varied "up or down," depending upon the intrinsic range of the parameter property. All system objects are defined as having both capabilities and complements that are described by parameter properties.

There are three basic distinctions to be drawn between men and machines: How they are the same; how they differ; and how the similarities and differences explain the best way to employ both, simultaneously, to best advantage.

Both men and machines are similar in that they both use languages. However, man's language takes three forms: thought, spoken, and written. The thought process is usually in the context of exploring and relating ideas. Spoken language focuses on asking or answering questions and verbalizing the thought process. The written process fixes the thought and spoken processes, which are too long, too complex, too minute, or too ill-structured to be totally held in memory.

The machine's language is a formal, systematic, logical, mathematically-based symbology. It has none of man's language forms; its own form may be characterized as automatic, programmed, and outcome-oriented. It is automatic because it may be energized to execute steps with or without human intervention. It is programmed in that it "thinks" along logically, preplanned lines. It selects alternatives in a patterned, iterative manner, each iteration being more or less identical. It is outcome-oriented in that its intermediate or ultimate solution objectives are derived without any capability to anticipate the objectives, but only to execute.

A first distinction between man and machines is that the language of man is different, providing flexible capabilities not possessed by machines.

Man may think a problem, speak it, and write it; he may solve it or merely state it in one of these stages. Machines cannot "invent" the problem about which to "think," unless the components of the problem are contained in the symbolically, logically programmed language. Unless the machine language contains the basic formula for attacking the problem, the problem may as well be unstated, since it cannot be processed. The design of self-organizing systems (automatic, programmed, self-modifying of all objects in a fully adaptive system) increases the flexibility of computational devices. However, severe restrictions on the adaptiveness of systems exist today and in the foreseeable future.

The properties of men and machines may be combined effectively: This is achieved when the iterative solution-deriving capabilities of the machine are coupled to the inductive-deductive capablities of man. The cost of a first solution via the computer may be high; the cost of successive solutions decreases steadily, although not always linearly.

Costs are dimensionally described by dollars, man-hours, pounds, or other quantitative yardsticks of kind. Costs may also be described as a period of time. Costs may be expressed by assigning values to qualitative expressions of effectiveness. Qualitatively, one system exceeds another in effectiveness when, for example, it sets up the condition for improved safety. The cost of improved safety may be measured, for example, by reduced speed on the highway, which is translated into longer duration of travel; the latter may be further measurable in terms of fewer trips per unit of time (week, month, year), although the cost per trip may remain constant. Fewer trips per unit of time may be translated, not into cost, but into a reduction in revenue and hence, profit or loss. Qualitative expressions of cost are more difficult to assess than quantitative costs. They become especially elusive when proposed or desired system states are in the future.

A second distinction between men and machines recognizes that men are fully adaptive and that machines are not. A machine solution is the end of the operation for the machine. The machine is dominated by its outcome-oriented program. Despite the number of iterations, the machine ultimately can do no more than complete its cycle, which results in an output. But for man, a solution is the means by which he makes steady improvements in adaptation to his environment; the solution finds utility. This points to another important advantage of combining men and machines in problem solving. Machines are fast and sure; they can speed up the problem-solving process, bringing improved environmental adaptation closer. Machines can examine a number of alternative solutions rapidly and systematically. Man can study the best of these solutions. He deduces their impact on environment, and applies the best solution to improve his relationship to the environment.

There is a third distinction between man and machines: Man can easily override the machine. He can discard all its solutions and substitute his own, which may be empirical or intuitive. In so doing, he may be forced to trade the machine's answers, which are unambiguous and precise, for a human solution, which is not necessarily of this quality. The power to override the machine is not reversible; that is, the reasonableness of the computer-derived solution is always subject to question. Although high confidence may be placed in the automated output, the machine is seldom, if ever, seen as the *ne plus ultra* (summit) of decision making. Today, the machine still serves man and man's intuition.

There is an argument for calling intuition a special case of logical analysis. Using the computer analogy, the mind of man has a large memory —larger than any machine conceived to date. It has a capacity to adapt far beyond that of software (programming) and hardware (equipment). Man's mind has, in addition, a special ability to suppress some experiences and select others for use in new situations. These special experience patterns may be structured into plans and models of action more flexible and complete than those that a machine could make.

Again the complementary relationship of men and machines emerges. Machines enable man to attack problems of greater magnitude than would otherwise be possible, were the machine's capabilities unavailable. Machines also make it possible for man to derive a wider range of solutions to a given problem. A large number of solutions would be unavailable without the benefit of machine capabilities. Man's recall of patterned experience, stimulated by the machine's derivation of solutions, appears to be an ideal combination of capabilities. This suggests that intuition, logically applied, may emerge as the more valuable tool as the problems to be solved become increasingly complex.

THE TOTAL SYSTEM

The total system consists of all the objects, attributes, and relationships necessary to accomplish an objective, given a number of constraints. The term *system* is most frequently employed in the sense of a total system. The objective of the total system defines the purpose for which all the system objects, attributes, and relationships have been organized. The constraints of the system are the limitations placed upon its operation. Constraints define the boundary of a system and make it possible to state explicitly the condition under which it is intended to operate.

An example of the total system is illustrated by the missile. The components of a missile system are (1) the missile, (2) the ground support equipment, (3) the spares and maintenance facilities, (4) the men and other material that make the system operable, (5) the command structure controlling its release, and (6) the targets. These six components of the missile system are its major subsystems. Each major subsystem has several contributing subsystems. Some of the contributing subsystems of the missile are: (1) nose cone, (2) propulsion, and (3 guidance. Each of these in turn is subdivided into major physical components which are also subsystems. Descriptions of systems must be expanded to include, not only all of the objects, but also all of the attributes and their relationships. For each object, there may be only one attribute, but there may be many relationships; the converse may also be true.

Information systems in business must be defined by the full scope of the complementary subsystems. For example, the objective to overhaul the material control subsystem of a company would involve (1) the subsystems to which material control was an input or an output, (2) the subsystems that were major components of material control, and (3) the elemental subsystems of each of the major components of (2), above. Such an assignment would require the analyst to work in the areas of manufacturing, purchasing, production control, accounting, engineering, and sales. Definition of the system (subsystems) under study is among the first tasks of the systems analyst.

The approach of studying problems in the business environment as a total system is essentially new. The concept of the total system enables the analyst to draw a wide, but complete, boundary around the problem under study. By defining the full scope of the system, the analyst attempts to attack the underlying problem. The underlying problem may have relationships over a wide set of objects. This makes it necessary to test alternative solutions iteratively. The objective is to determine the behavior of all system objects under varying conditions.

The problem-solving procedures to be explored rely upon systems concepts. Illustrating and analyzing problems as subsystems of a total system supplies the necessary condition that all parts of the problem are properly and functionally related. Viewing a problem as a system entails identification of problem parameters as system parameters. Each parameter must be further defined by its properties and relationships.

B The Systems Concept in Business Management

4 Systems Theory and Management*

RICHARD A. JOHNSON
FREMONT E. KAST
JAMES E. ROSENZWEIG

A fundamental account of "general systems theory" as it relates to management — the process whereby unrelated resources are integrated into a total system for the accomplishment of objectives.

The systems concept is primarily a way of thinking about the job of managing. It provides a framework for visualizing internal and external environmental factors as an integrated whole. It allows recognition of the function of subsystems, as well as the complex supersystems within which businessmen must operate. The systems concept fosters a way of thinking which, on the one hand, help to dissolve some of the complexity and, on the other, helps the manager to recognize the nature of complex problems and thereby to operate within the perceived environment. It is important to recognize the integrated nature of specific systems, including the fact that each system has both inputs and outputs and can be viewed as a self-contained unit. But it is also important to recognize that business systems are a part of larger systems—possibly industry-wide, or including several, maybe many, companies and/or industries, or even society as a whole. Further, business systems are in a constant state of change—they are created, operated, revised, and often eliminated.

What does the concept of systems offer to students of management and/or to practicing executives? Is it a panacea for business problems that will replace scientific management, human relations, management by objective, operations research, and many other approaches to, or techniques of,

---

*Adapted from **The Theory and Management of Systems** (New York: McGraw-Hill, 1967), pp. 3–16. Used by permission of McGraw-Hill Book Company.

44   *Systems Analysis: Some Basic Concepts*

management? Perhaps a word of caution is needed initially. Anyone looking for "cookbook" techniques will be disappointed. In this book we de not develop "ten easy steps" to success in management. Such approaches, while seemingly applicable and easy to grasp, are usually shortsighted and superficial. Fundamental ideas, such as the systems concept, are more difficult to comprehend, and yet they present an opportunity for a large-scale payoff.

In this section we shall develop a foundation for management by system. However, turning to aspects concerned primarily with business, it will be necessary to set the stage with certain introductory materials relating to systems in general and concerning an evolving body of knowledge called "general systems theory." This background material will provide the basis for relating systems theory to business and for the integration of systems concepts and management.

The discussion is centered on the following topics:

Systems Defined

General Systems Theory

Systems Theory for Business

Systems Concepts and Management

SYSTEMS DEFINED

A system is "an organized or complex whole; an assemblage or combination of things or parts forming a complex or unitary whole." The term *system* covers an extremely broad spectrum of concepts. For example, we have mountain systems, river systems, and the solar system as part of our physical surroundings. The body itself is a complex organism including the skeletal system, the circulatory system, and the nervous system. We come into daily contact with such phenomena as transportation systems, communication systems (telephone, telegraph, etc.), and economic systems.

A science often is described as a systematic body of knowledge; a complete array of essential principles or facts, arranged in a rational dependence or connection; a complex of ideas, principles, laws, forming a coherent whole. Scientists endeavor to develop, organize, and classify material into interconnected disciplines. Sir Isaac Newton set forth what he called the "system of the world." Other examples are "system of politics" and "system of theology." Two relatively well known works which represent attempts to integrate a large amount of material are Darwin's *Origin of the Species* and Keynes's *General Theory of Employment, Interest, and Money*. Darwin, in his theory of evolution, integrated all life into a "system of nature" and indicated how the myriad of living subsystems were interrelated. Keynes, in his general theory of employment, interest, and money, connected many complicated natural and man-made forces which make up an entire economy. Both men had a major impact on man's thinking because they were able to conceptualize interrelationships among complex phenomena and integrate them into a systematic whole. The word *system* connotes plan, method, order, and arrangement. Hence it is no wonder that scientists and researchers have made the term so pervasive.

The antonym of systematic is chaotic. A chaotic situation might be described as one where "everything depends on everything else," but where the connecting system is not understood. Since two major goals of science and research in any subject area are explanation and prediction, such a condition cannot be tolerated. Therefore there is considerable incentive to develop bodies of knowledge that can be organized into a complex whole, within which subparts or subsystems can be interrelated.

There is an obvious hierarchy of supersystems that can be created; that is, systems, systems of systems, and systems of systems of systems. For example, the universe is a system of heavenly bodies which includes many subsystems of stars called *galaxies*. Within one such galaxy, the Milky Way, there is the solar system, one of many planetary systems. Similarly, an organism is a system of mutually dependent parts each of which might include many subsystems. Human life is comprised of microorganisms which form larger systems that are subsystems of the organism as a whole.

While much research has been focused on the analysis of minute segments of knowledge, there has been increasing interest in developing larger frames of reference for synthesizing the results of such research. Thus attention has been focused more and more on overall systems as frames of reference for analytical work in various areas. Eddington describes this process as follows:

> From the point of view of the philosophy of science the conception associated with entropy must I think be ranked as the great contribution of the 19th century to scientific thought. It marked a reaction from the view that everything to which science need pay attention is discovered by microscopic dissection of objects. It provided an alternative standpoint in which the centre of interest is shifted from the entities reached by the customary analysis (atoms, electric potentials, etc.) to qualities possessed by the system as a whole, which cannot be split up and located—a little here and a little bit there. . . .
>
> We often think that when we have completed our study of *one* we know all about *two*, because "two" is "one and one." We forget that we still have to make a study of "and." Secondary physics is the study of "and"—that is to say, of organization.[1]

The problem of AND is a legitimate one for scientists. It is also legitimate for scientists to concentrate on individual parts in pushing back the frontiers of knowledge, leaving to others the task of integrating results. For managers,

---

[1] Sir Arthur Eddington, *The Nature of the Physical World,* University of Michigan Press, Ann Arbor, Mich., 1958, pp. 103–104.

however, the problem of AND is central. The essence of management is coordination; it is our contention that a similar synthesizing process can be useful for managers. Whereas managers have often focused attention on particular specialized areas, they may lose sight of the over-all objectives of the business and the role of their particular business in even larger systems. These indiviuals can do a better job of carrying out their own responsibilities if they are aware of the "big picture." It is the familiar problem of not being able to see the forest for the trees.

This disregard of the total system may be deliberate in the sense that departmental or subsystem managers are inclined to enhance their own performance at the expense of the total operation. However, it is more likely that such disregard is unintentional, resulting from the inability of decision makers in isolated segments to comprehend the interaction of their decisions with other segments of the business. The focus of systems management is on providing a better picture of the network of subsystems and interrelated parts which go together to form a complex whole.

Before proceeding to a discussion of systems theory for business, it will be beneficial to explore recent attempts to establish a general systems theory covering all disciplines or scientific areas.

GENERAL SYSTEMS THEORY [2]

General systems theory is concerned with developing a systematic, theoretical framework for describing general relationships of the empirical world. A broad spectrum of potential achievements for such a framework is evident. Existing similarities in the theoretical construction of various disciplines can be pointed out. Models can be developed which are applicable to many systems, whether physical, biological, behavioral, or social. An ultimate but distant goal will be a framework (or system of systems of systems) which will tie all disciplines together in a meaningful relationship.

One of the most important indications of the need for a general systems theory is the problem of communication between the various disciplines. Although there is similarity between general methods of approach—the scientific method—the results of research efforts are not often communicated across discipline boundaries. Hence conceptualizing and hypothesizing done in one area seldom carries over into other areas where it could conceivably point the way toward a significant breakthrough. Specialists do not seem to communicate with one another. For example:

---

[2] Two articles provide the basis for this section. The name first appeared in an article by Ludwig von Bertalanffy, "General System Theory: A New Approach to Unity of Science," *Human Biology,* December, 1951, pp. 303-361. Another discussion, and one more pertinent to the specific task at hand, was that of Kenneth Boulding, "General Systems Theory: The Skeleton of Science," *Management Science,* April, 1956, pp. 197-208.

Hence physicists only talk to physicists, economists to economists—worse still, nuclear physicists talk only to nuclear physicists and econometricians to econometricians. One wonders sometimes if science will not grind to a stop in an assemblage of walled-in hermits, each mumbling to himself words in a private language that only he can understand.[3]

Of course, the conflict of ideas and difficulties of communication are even greater between the various cultures—the scientific, the social sciences, and the humanistic. This conflict has been intensified during the twentieth century.[4]

On the brighter side there has been some development of interdisciplinary studies. Areas such as social psychology, biochemistry, astrophysics, social anthropology, economic psychology, and economic sociology have been developed in order to emphasize the interrelationships of previously isolated disciplines. More recently, areas of study and research have been developed which call on numerous subfields. For example, cybernetics, the science of communication and control, calls on electrical engineering, neurophysiology, physics, biology, and other fields. Operations research is often pointed to as a multidisciplinary approach to problem solving. Information theory is another discipline which calls on numerous subfields. Organization theory embraces economics, sociology, engineering, psychology, physiology, and anthropology. Problem solving and decision making are becoming focal points for study and research, drawing on numerous fields. Unfortunately the "new" cross-disciplines often create a jargon or "in" language that compounds the communication problem further.

With all these examples of interdisciplinary approaches, it is easy to recognize a surge of interest in larger-scale, systematic bodies of knowledge. However, this trend calls for the development of an overall framework within which the various subparts can be integrated. In order that the *interdisciplinary* movement may not degenerate into *undisciplined* approaches, it is important that some structure be developed to integrate the various separate disciplines while retaining the type of discipline which distinguishes them. One approach to providing an over-all framework (general systems theory) would be to pick out phenomena common to many different disciplines and to develop general models which would include such phenomena. A second approach would include the structuring of a hierarchy of levels of complexity for the basic units of behavior in the various empirical fields. It would also involve development of a level of abstraction to represent each stage.

We shall explore the second approach, a hierarchy of levels, in more detail since it can lead toward a system of systems which has application in

---

[3] Boulding, *op. cit.,* p. 198.

[4] C. P. Snow, *The Two Cultures and the Scientific Revolution,* Cambridge University Press, London, 1959.

most businesses and other organizations. The reader can undoubtedly call to mind examples of familiar systems at each level of the following model.

1. The first level is that of static structure. It might be called the level of *frameworks*. This is the geography and anatomy of the universe. . . . The accurate description of these frameworks is the beginning of organized theoretical knowledge in almost any field, for without accuracy in this description of static relationships no accurate functional or dynamic theory is possible.

2. The next level of systematic analysis is that of the simple dynamic system with predetermined, necessary motions. This might be called the level of *clockworks*. The solar system itself is of course the great clock of the universe from man's point of view, and the deliciously exact predictions of the astronomers are a testimony to the excellence of the clock which they study. . . . The greater part of the theoretical structure of physics, chemistry, and even of economics falls into this category.

3. The next level is that of the control mechanism or cybernetic system, which might be nicknamed the level of the *thermostat*. This differs from the simple stable equilibrium system mainly in the fact that the transmission and interpretation of information is an essential part of the system. . . . The homeostasis model, which is of such importance in physiology, is an example of a cybernetic mechanism, and such mechanisms exist through the whole empirical world of the biologist and the social scientist.

4. The fourth level is that of the "open system," or self-maintaining structure. This is the level at which life begins to differentiate itself from not-life: it might be called the level of the *cell*.

5. The fifth level might be called the genetic-societal level; it is typified by the *plant*, and it dominates the empirical world of the botanists.

6. As we move upward from the plant world towards the animal kingdom we gradually pass over into a new level, the "animal" level, characterized by increased mobility, teleological behavior, and self-awareness. Here we have the development of specialized information-receptors (eyes, ears, etc.) leading to an enormous increase in intake of information; we also have a great development of nervous systems, leading ultimately to the brain, as an organizer of the information intake into a knowledge structure or "image." Increasingly as we ascend the scale of animal life, behavior is response not to a specific stimulus but to an "image" or knowledge structure or view of the environment as a whole. . . . The difficulties in the prediction of the behavior of these systems arises largely because of this intervention of the image between the stimulus and the response.

7. The next level is the "human" level, that is, of the individual human being considered as a system. In addition to all, or nearly all, of the characteristics of animal systems man possesses self-consciousness, which is something different from mere-awareness. His image, besides being much more complex than that even of the

higher animals, has a self-reflective quality—he not only knows, but knows that he knows. This property is probably bound up with the phenomenon of language and symbolism. It is the capacity for speech—the ability to produce, absorb, and interpret *symbols,* as opposed to mere signs like the warning cry of an animal—which most clearly marks a man off from his humbler brethren.

8. Because of the vital importance for the individual man of symbolic images in behavior based on them it is not easy to separate clearly the level of the individual human organism from the next level, that of social organizations. . . . Nevertheless it is convenient for some purposes to distinguish the individual human as a system from the social systems which surround him, and in this sense social organizations may be said to constitute another level of organization. . . . At this level we must concern ourselves with the content and meaning of messages, the nature and dimensions of value systems, the transcription of images into historical record, the subtle symbolizations of art, music, and poetry, and the complex gamut of human emotion.

9. To complete the structure of systems we should add a final turret for transcendental systems, even if we may be accused at this point of having built Babel to the clouds. There are however the ultimates and absolutes and the inescapables and unknowables, and they also exhibit systematic structure and relationship. It will be a sad day for man when nobody is allowed to ask questions that do not have any answers.[5]

Obviously, the first level is most pervasive. Descriptions of static structures are widespread. However, this descriptive cataloguing is helpful in providing a framework for additional analysis and synthesis. Dynamic "clockwork" systems, where prediction is a strong element, are evident in the classical natural sciences such as physics and astronomy; yet even here there are important gaps. Adequate theoretical models are not apparent at higher levels. However, in recent years closed-loop cybernetic, or "thermostat," systems have received increasing attention. At the same time, work is progressing on open-loop systems with self-maintaining structures and reproduction facilities. Beyond the fourth level we hardly have a beginning of theory, and yet system description via computer models may foster progress even at these levels in the complex of general systems theory.

Regardless of the degree of progress at any particular level in the above scheme, the important point is the concept of a general systems theory. Clearly, the spectrum, or hierarchy, of systems varies over a considerable range. However, since the systems concept is primarily a point of view and a desirable goal, rather than a particular method or content area, progress can be made as research proceeds in various specialized areas but within a total system context. The important aspect of such a hierarchy of system con-

[5] Boulding, *op. cit.,* pp. 202–205.

cepts revolves around the critical element of communication. McGrath, Nordlie, and Vaughn express it as follows:

> Consequently, while scientists from many fields contribute to the area, and bring with them a wide range of scientific tools, the steps necessary to provide *all* applicable methods have not as yet been accomplished. This lack leads to less than optimal application of scientific tools, and to relatively ineffective communication among scientists from different fields working on similar problems, which in turn retards the rate of development of the system research field.
>
> The impetus for the present research program comes from recognition of the need for a more systematic catalogue of methods applicable to system research problems, in order to provide a basis for a common language of method by means of which system research scientists can intercommunicate more adequately.[6]

General systems theory provides for scientists at large a useful framework within which to carry out specialized activity. It allows researchers to relate findings and compare concepts with similar findings and concepts in other disciplines. The relationship between general systems theory and the development of functionalism in the social sciences is described by Martindale as follows:

> In the period since World War II, as Western society readjusted to the radical change in milieu that followed, with the attempt to return to something that looked like "normalcy," but in a permanently transformed world, the essential unity of the social sciences has been revealed through the flooding of the functionalistic point of view across the boundaries of the special disciplines. This point of view has had both theoretical and methodological dimensions. Theoretically, it consists in the analysis of social and cultural life from the standpoint of wholes or systems. Epistemologically, it involves analysis of social events by methods thought peculiarly adapted to the integration of social events into systems.
>
> The functionalistic point of view has been manifest in all the social sciences from psychology through sociology, political science, economics, and anthropology to geography, jurisprudence and linguistics. Most primary theoretical and methodological debates in postwar social science have centered on functionalism and alternatives to it.[7]

---

[6] Joseph D. McGrath, Peter G. Nordlie, and W. S. Vaughn, Jr., *A Systematic Framework for Comparison of System Research Methods,* Human Sciences Research, Inc., Arlington, Va., November, 1959, p. 2.

[7] Don Martindale, *Functionalism in the Social Sciences,* Monograph 5, American Academy of Political and Social Science, February, 1965, pp. viii–ix.

Although there are several connotations of the word *functionalism*, its most important aspect is the emphasis upon systems of relationship and the integration of parts and subsystems into a whole.[8] General systems theory and the functionalistic point of view (including dynamic equilibrium concepts from economics) offer a theoretical framework for the study of business organizations.

SYSTEMS THEORY FOR BUSINESS

An important aspect of general systems theory is the distinction between closed and open systems. An example of an open system is a living organism which is not a conglomeration of separate elements but a definite system, possessing organization and wholeness. An organism is an open system which maintains a constant state while the matter and energy which enter it keep changing (so-called "dynamic equilibrium"). The organism is influenced by, and influences, its environment and reaches a state of dynamic equilibrium in this environment. Such a description of a system adequately fits the typical business organization. The business organization is a manmade system whch has a dynamic interplay with its environment—customers, competitors, labor organizations, suppliers, government, and many other agencies. Furthermore, the business organization is a system of interrelated parts working in conjunction with each other in order to accomplish a number of goals, both those of the organization and those of individual participants.

At times scholars in the field of management have depicted organizations as smoothly running machines. This would coincide with Boulding's second level in the general systems theory, that of "clockwork" systems. Organizations were described as highly mechanistic and predictable, and the various resources available—men, material, and machines—were manipulated in just that way.

Another common analogy was the comparison of the organization to the human body, with the skeletal and muscle systems representing the operating line elements and the circulatory system as a necessary staff function. The nervous system stood for the communication system. The brain symbolized top-level management, or the executive committee. In this sense an organization was represented as a self-maintaining structure, one which could reproduce. Such an analysis hints at the type of framework which would be useful as a systems theory for business—one which is developed as a system of systems and which can focus attention at the proper points in the organization for rational decision making, from the standpoint both of the individual and of the organization.

---

[8] Robert K. Merton discusses various connotations of the word *function* in *Social Theory and Social Structure,* The Free Press of Glencoe, New York, 1957, pp. 20–22.

The scientific-management movement utilized the concept of a man-machine system but concentrated primarily at the shop level. The so-called "efficiency experts" attempted to establish procedures covering the work situation and providing an opportunity for all those involved to benefit—employees, managers, and owners. The human relationists, the movement stemming from the Hawthorne–Western Electric studies, shifted some of the focus away from the man-machine system per se to motivation and interrelationships among individuals in the organization. Recognition of the effect of interpersonal relationships, human behavior, and small groups resulted in a relatively widespread reevaluation of managerial approaches and techniques.

The concept of the business enterprise as a social system also has received considerable attention in recent years. The social-system school looks upon management as a system of cultural interrelationships. The concept of a social system draws heavily on sociology and involves recognition of such elements as formal and informal organization within a total integrated system. Moreover, the organization or enterprise is subject to external pressure from the cultural environment. In effect, the enterprise system is recognized as a part of a larger environmental system.

Over the years, mathematics has been applied to a variety of business problems, primarily internal. Since World War II, operations-research techniques have been applied to large, complex systems of variables. They have been helpful in shop scheduling, in freight-yard operations, cargo handling, airline scheduling, and other similar problems. Queuing models have been developed for a wide variety of traffic- and service-type situations where it is necessary to program the optimum number of "servers" for the expected "customer" flow. Management-science techniques have undertaken the solution of many complex problems involving a large number of variables. However, by their very nature, these techniques must structure the analysis by quantifying system elements and often narrowing and isolating the focus of attention. This process of abstraction frequently simplifies the problem and takes it out of the real world. The solution of the problem may not be applicable in the actual situation because it cannot be integrated.

Simple models of maximizing behavior no longer suffice in analyzing business organizations. The relatively mechanical models apparent in the "scientific management" era gave way to theories represented by the "human relations" movement. Emphasis has developed around "decision making" as a primary focus of attention, relating communication systems, organization structure, questions of growth, and questions of uncertainty. This approach recognizes the more complex models of administrative behavior and should lead to more encompassing systems that will provide the framework within which to fit the results of specialized investigations of management scientists.

The aim of systems theory for business is to facilitate better understanding in a complex environment; that is, if the system within which managers make decisions can be provided as a more explicit framework, then such decision making should be easier to handle. But what are the elements of this systems theory which can be used as a framework for integrated decision making? Will it require wholesale change on the part of organization structure and administrative behavior? Or can it be fit into existing situations? In general, the new concepts can be applied to existing situations. Organizations will remain recognizable. Simon makes this point when he says:

> 1. Organizations will still be constructed in three layers; an underlying *system* of physical production and distribution processes, a layer of programmed (and probably largely automated) decision processes for governing the routine day-to-day operation of the physical *system,* and a layer of nonprogrammed decision processes (carried out in a man-machine system) for monitoring the first-level processes, redesigning them, and changing parameter values.
> 2. Organizations will still be hierarchical in form. The organization will be divided into major subparts, each of these into parts, and so on, in familiar forms of departmentalization. The exact basis for drawing departmental lines may change somewhat. Product divisions may become even more important than they are today, while the sharp lines of demarcation among purchasing, manufacturing, engineering, and sales are likely to fade.[9]

We agree essentially with this picture of the future. However, we want to emphasize the notion of systems as set forth in several layers. This connotes basic horizontal organization cutting across typical departmental lines. Thus the systems that are likely to be emphasized in the future will develop from tasks, projects, or programs, and authority will be vested in managers whose influence will cut across traditional departmental lines. The focus of attention is likely to turn more and more to patterns of material, energy, and information flow throughout organizations. Identifying information-decision systems will provide a useful means of analysis and synthesis. These concepts will be developed more fully throughout this book.

SYSTEMS CONCEPTS AND MANAGEMENT

Management is the primary force within organizations which coordinates the activities of the subsystems and relates them to the environment. Management as an institution is relatively new in our society, stemming primarily from the growth in size and complexity of business since the industrial revolution. As Drucker says:

---

[9] Herbert A. Simon, *The New Science of Management Decision,* Harper & Row, Inc., New York, pp. 49–50 (italics by authors).

> The emergence of management as an essential, a distinct and a leading institution is a pivotal event in social history. Rarely, if ever, has a new basic institution, a new leading group, emerged as fast as has management since the turn of this century. Rarely in human history has a new institution proven indispensable so quickly; and even less often has a new institution arrived with so little opposition, so little disturbance, so little controversy. . . . Management, which is the organ of society specifically charged with making resources productive, that is, with the responsibility for organized economic advance, therefore reflects the basic spirit of the modern age. It is in fact indispensable—and this explains why, once begotten, it grew so fast and with so little opposition.[10]

Managers are needed to convert the disorganized resources of men, machines, and money into a useful and effective enterprise. Essentially, management is the process whereby these unrelated resources are integrated into a total *system for objective accomplishment*. A manager gets things done by working with people and physical resources in order to accomplish the objectives of the system. He coordinates and integrates the activities and work of others. To accomplish this task the manager should be aware of the danger of isolating problems. He should recognize relationships and the need to synthesize. According to Herbst:

> In dealing with practical problems, one cannot tease out separate psychological, economic, or technological aspects, for the problem nearly always involves working with a total, integrated organizational unit. For instance, in studying the functioning of a work group, we cannot isolate the observed structure of interaction relationships from the technological structure which determines the nature of the task to be done and the types of relationship required for task performance. Nor can we disregard the economic aspects of behavior either from the point of view of individual group members or in relation to the conditions for group survival. There is a need for the development of interstitial disciplines, among which social psychology, sociotechnical analysis, and socioeconomic theory are of special interest, since they demonstrate different ways in which bridging or unifying disciplines can be constructed and they provide the natural growing-points for the development of a unified approach.[11]

---

[10] Peter F. Drucker, *The Practice of Management,* Harper & Row, Inc., New York, 1954, pp. 3–4.

A general theory of management which has evolved in recent years focuses attention on the fundamental administrative processes which are essential if an organization is to meet its primary goals and objectives.[12] These basic managerial processes are required for any type of organization—business, government, educational, social, and other activities where human and physical resources are combined to meet certain objectives. Furthermore, these processes are necessary regardless of the specialized area of management—production, distribution, finance, and facilitating activities. Although the management process has been described in numerous ways, four basic functions have received general acceptance—planning, organizing, controlling, and communicating. They can be defined in terms of systems concepts as follows:

Planning

The managerial function of planning is one of selecting the organizational objectives and the policies, programs, procedures, and methods for achieving them. The planning function is essentially one of providing a framework for integrated decision making and is vital to every man-machine system.

Organizing

The organizing function helps to coordinate people and resources into a system so that the activities they perform lead to the accomplishment of system goals. This managerial function involves the determination of the activities required to achieve the objectives of the enterprise, the departmentation of these activities, and the assignment of authority and responsibility for their performance. Thus the organizing function provides the interconnection, or intertie, between the various subsystems and the total organizational system.

Control

The managerial function of control is essentially that of assuring that the various organizational subsystems are performing in conformance to the plans. Control is essentially the measurement and correction of activity of the subsystems to assure the accomplishment of the over-all plan.

Communication

The communication function is primarily one of the transfer of information among decision centers in the various subsystems throughout the organization. The communication function also includes the interchange of information with the environmental forces.

---

[11] P. G. Herbst, "Problems of Theory and Method in the Integration of the Behavioural Sciences," *Human Relations,* November, 1965, pp. 353–354.

[12] See, for example, Harold F. Smiddy and Lionel Naum, "Evolution of a 'Science of Managing' in America," *Management Science,* October, 1954, pp. 1–31 and Harold Koontz (ed.), *Toward a Unified Theory of Management,* McGraw-Hill Book Company, New York, 1964.

Although these four managerial functions are listed and described separately, they should not be considered as independent activities, nor is any exact time sequence implied. Adequate performance of each of these functions is dependent upon the performance of the other three. For example, effective communication and control depends to a major extent upon the adequacy of the organizational structure and the planning process. Thus the total management process involves coordinating all four of these activities in order to meet the over-all objectives of the system.

5 The Manager's Job: A Systems Approach*

SEYMOUR TILLES

The author sees the manager's job as defining the company as a system, establishing system objectives, creating formal sub-systems, and integrating the systemic hierarchy, as well as the systemic models.

"What does a manager do?" I once asked a group of foremen. Here are two typical answers I received:

"He's the guy who gives orders to people."

"He sits in a plush office at the corner of the building and drives a large automobile."

Naturally, when I related such answers to the top officials of the company, they were derisive. However, when I asked the executives to answer the question themselves, they did not do nearly as well. At least the foremen based their responses on reliable firsthand observation. The managers themselves could only provide responses that were nothing more than secondhand clichés. For example, they said that—

They "organize things"—but not one could remember who designed the existing structure, or explain how it contributed to the achievement of corporate objectives.

Their job is "getting things done," but there was little agreement concerning *which* things were meant.

At the end of the discussion, we were no closer to solving the riddle of the manager's job than when we began.

---

*Reprinted from **Harvard Business Review,** Vol. 41, No. 1 (January–February, 1963), pp. 73–81.

The question, "What does a manager do?" is a vital one. Its significance is recognized on both sides of the Iron Curtain. And yet we still lack an answer which would prove helpful to managers in deciding whether they are, in fact, doing what they ought to be doing.

The unfortunate results of not having a comprehensive concept of the manager's job is that many executives become so preoccupied with issues which are not really critical to their company's success that they ignore other issues of truly vital significance. One management team, for example, was justifiably proud of the data-processing system it had installed. Meanwhile, however, its labor relations had deteriorated to a point where a long strike made the high-speed computer output extremely dour reading. A second management group prided itself on its high return on investment and continuous dividend record. Meanwhile, however, competitors were ensuring the company's demise by plowing money into research.

Part of the problem of developing a comprehensive concept of the manager's job is that we do not yet have a theory which covers the whole expanse of the problem. One distinguished student of management recently put it this way:

> [The manager's] predicament is that he is an involved member of an open-ended system through which he is trying to secure results. So far as I know, no scientist has come up with a satisfactory theory of and for this predicament. Most theories I know tell him how to escape from rather than how to cope with it.[1]

Of course, we do have a lot of very good theories which explain limited aspects of management. Specifically:

Social scientists and personnel executives theorize that "the firm is really a *social system*." Starting from this point of view, they have developed a large body of knowledge concerning the manager's function in the social system.

Data-processing specialists, as well as company controllers, have been saying that "the firm may be considered as a *data-processing system* and *decision network*." From this theory they have accumulated a considerable amount of information about the manager's role in decision making.

Financial people hold that "the firm is really a system of funds flows." This concept has led them to compile a store of knowledge about the manager's use of financial resources.

How do we go about fusing all of these separate theories into a meaningful and integrated concept of the manager's job? In my opinion, the most promising approach to such a synthesis stems from the emerging field of

---

[1] F. J. Roethlisberger, talk given to the Harvard Business School Association, 32nd National Business Conference, Boston, June 8, 1962.

systems theory. Therefore, in this article, I will attempt (a) to describe the manager's job in systems terms, and (b) to show how the manager, once he understands the full range of his responsibilities as revealed by a systems approach, is enabled to do a better job.

SYSTEMS APPROACH

The basic notion of a system is simply that it is a set of interrelated parts. Thus, a molecule may be thought of as a system of atoms, a person as a system of organs, and a group as a system of individuals. Implicit in these concepts is a degree of "wholeness" which makes the whole something different from, and more than, the individual units considered separately.

While it is convenient to introduce the concept of a system as an entity in itself, any attempt to deal with actual systems, whether atoms, people, or companies, immediately reveals that such things do not exist in themselves. They are intimately connected with a wider variety of other units which cannot really be ignored if meaningful statements about systemic behavior are to be made.

Of course, we could say, "Let us look at the company as if it existed all by itself," but this has been the trouble with so many statements that have been made about management in the past. In fact, it is precisely because the concept of "system" involves an understanding of the relationships among things that it has so much to offer as a basis for thinking about the problems that face the general manager. For the general manager must constantly be concerned about how things relate to each other. This is true both of the relationship between his company and a wide variety of external entities (competitors, customers, government, and so on) and among groups within the company itself.

Suppose we turn now to an examination of just what the manager's job really is—if we look at it from a systems point of view. Considered this way, the manager's work divides into four basic tasks:

(1) Defining the company as a system.
(2) Establishing system objectives, which can be further broken down to:
   Identifying wider systems.
   Setting performance criteria.
(3) Creating formal subsystems.
(4) Systemic integration.

As with any other breakdown of the management task, the parts are really meaningless in themselves—for each aspect necessarily involves all the others. So I will ask readers to suspend their questions until each of these tasks has been individually discussed.

DEFINING THE COMPANY

One of the most common errors which general managers commit—especially in smaller companies—is that of equating (1) the notion of viewing things in their totality with (2) doing everything oneself. Both, however, are clearly incompatible. In fact, the strongest argument against failure to delegate is that it prevents the general manager from thinking about his primary responsibility: How do things all fit together? This, of course, leads to the question, "What is the company as a system?" While the answer to this may appear ridiculously simple from a conventional point of view, every systems engineer will testify that this is one of the most fundamental, and most difficult, issues to be resolved in any serious project. In management terms, this question may be further subdivided into two critical issues:

(1) Who is the company (the business as a group of people, or a social system)?
(2) What is the company (the business as an integrator of markets and products)?

Who Is the Company?

Systems theory contributes importantly to this seemingly academic question by saying: "Hold on a moment—don't just claim that the company consists of everyone on the payroll, period. The boundaries of a company are not so simply and narrowly defined." Chester Barnard, whose brilliant analysis of management is still a classic, showed that he recognized this long ago when he wrote:

> In industrial organizations the group is commonly regarded as "officers and employees," but from some points of view stockholders, the terms of whose participation are radically different, are included. At other times, or in other contexts, creditors, suppliers, and customers must be included. . . .[2]

Thus, when a company is defined from a systems point of view, no single group—customers, stockholders, or anybody else—is, for all purposes, considered to be the "insiders." There are times when it is tactically wise to include within the company's boundaries people who would never conventionally be thought of as being within it. The justification for this is quite simply that, since their cooperation is essential to the success of the enterprise, they should be explicitly included in any model of the real situation that is created. Otherwise, their significance may well be overlooked.

Two areas where this becomes particularly important are cost reduction and managerial assistance. Cost reduction can be achieved to a very limited extent if the scope of investigation is restricted only to those factors which are completely within a company's exclusive control. In many cases, the big payoff comes from cooperative action with individuals in other organizations. Thus:

[2] *The Functions of the Executive* (Cambridge, Harvard University Press, 1938), p. 69.

—After a careful analysis of its costs, one company concluded that one of the major cost reduction opportunities was in its relationship with suppliers. It therefore enlisted their cooperation and reduced its cost considerably.

—Another organization, a newspaper, found its operations hampered by the manner in which it received copy from some of its major advertisers. Joint action was instituted and resulted in both improved service to the customer and better efficiency of the paper.

Many organizations have a management team that includes individuals —auditors, lawyers, bankers, brokers, and a variety of other specialists— who never appear on the organization chart. In some cases, these outside experts are consulted with such regularity that they are really a part of the management system. In fact, the extent of the management system is frequently an indication of the manager's ability.

What Is the Company?

A highly important contribution the general manager makes to any company is, first, in getting it committed to a concept of itself; and, secondly, in forcing it to re-examine the appropriateness of that concept as conditions change.

As has been pointed out previously in an HBR article,[3] the company is essentially the device which integrates the customer's requirements and the products which will fulfill them economically. But once we have said this, the concept of the business has not been settled; in fact, it has barely begun to be recognized. Immediately many questions arise:

What customers are we interested in?
What specific customer needs do we wish to satisfy?
Which products will we include in our line?

These issues are intimately related to each other; answering one immediately limits the freedom with which we may answer the others. However, there has to be some consistency of pattern among the answers to these questions if the company is to operate successfully.

For example, the McGraw-Hill Publishing Company has built its magazine business around the concept of providing vocationally useful information to narrowly defined groups of readers. It therefore publishes such magazines as *Business Week, Chemical Engineering, Gasoline Retailer, American Machinist/Metalworking Manufacturing,* and *Textile World*. On one occasion it attempted to publish a general circulation periodical called *Science Illustrated*. This was not successful.

There are numerous other illustrations of this: the attempt of the publishers of *Playboy* to put out *Show Business Illustrated,* the effort of Packard Motors to introduce a small car, and the attempts of Underwood

---

[3] Theodore Levitt, "Marketing Myopia," HBR July–August 1960, p. 45.

and Royal McBee to enter the computer business. Each enterprise individually discovered that when it tried to go beyond some consistent pattern of customers, needs, and products—some definition of itself—it ran into trouble.

An organization is never finished dealing with the problem of self-definition. The caustic observation of Mark Twain about life being "just one damned thing after another" holds just as true for corporate affairs as for people. Take, for example, two organizations which are readily recognized as outstanding in their respective fields: International Business Machines and *The New York Times*. While each organization may be considered currently successful, each faces critical developments at present which will determine its future:

IBM, today the acknowledged leader in the field of data processing, is directly influenced by the tremendous technological developments sweeping the whole electronics industry. One result of this technological revolution has been to force IBM to integrate into the component field, after years of depending almost entirely on outside sources for supply of components. Thus, despite decades of success, this company is still in the process of redefining itself. This is not only the price of leadership; it is essential to survival. Like dinosaurs, modern corporations die when they become too big to change in the face of environmental demands.

The New York Times is one of the great newspapers of the world. Today the clear tendency in the United States for many reasons is for fewer and fewer newspapers. The combination of the movement of advertisers to television and the movement of readers to the suburbs has resulted in there being fewer and fewer newspapers each year. One result of this has been the appearance of newspapers which are no longer limited to a single community. The recent decision of *The New York Times* to publish a West Coast edition and an International edition may well make national or even international journalism the rule, rather than the exception. In any case, the *Times,* like IBM, has found that greatness does not provide immunity from a continuing concern with the issue: "What are we now, and what should we become?"

SETTING SYSTEM GOALS

The general state of the art of setting corporate objectives is an appalling one. By and large, the terms in which managers state their official aspirations are oversimplified deceptions: profit, market share, or return on investment. Each of these indicators still has great appeal to management, despite the extent to which scholars have rejected them as valid bases for performance evaluation.[4] Their appeal lies primarily in the fact that each one sounds simple, since its inherent ambiguities are not obvious; each can

---

[4] See, for example, Robert N. Anthony, "The Trouble with Profit Maximization," HBR November–December 1960, p. 126.

be expressed in numbers, and thereby endowed with an aura of objectivity and utility; and each one can be claimed to be a logical measure of past performance.

The trouble with these criteria is that they entice the general manager to focus his attention where it does not belong: on the company itself, rather than on the relationship between the firm and the broader systems of which it is a part. This is vividly reflected in the design of the information systems which ultimately produce the quantitative criteria listed above. Looking at these systems, one sees a great deal of money and effort devoted to analyzing what went on within the organization itself and very little, if anything, devoted to an analysis of environmental trends. Managers, too, frequently lose sight of the fact that corporate performance is the result of a company interacting with its environment, rather than the result of factors wholly within the company itself.[5]

The preoccupation with events taking place inside the company, rather than with the company's relationship to a wider environment, is reflected in many aspects of managerial action. For example, much that has been written about the relationship between managers and subordinates is quite misleading, because it has been built on an implicit assumption that the behavior of subordinates would be influenced only by the way the manager behaved toward them. Thus, the manager has been exhorted to be a "benevolent autocrat," a "participative leader," and a variety of other subordinate-oriented roles.

One advantage of a systems view of the manager's job is that it broadens the area of relationships that a manager properly should consider. It encourages him to think seriously about looking outward and upward, instead of being continually preoccupied with looking down the ladder at his subordinates. Many managers rivet their attention on their subordinates, despite the fact that meddling in the affairs of competent assistants is likely to do much more damage than good. Actually, the major contribution the general manager can make to his unit lies in the area of his relationship with individuals over whom he does *not* exercise direct control, his peers, his superiors, or persons who are completely outside the company—customers, stockholders, bankers, lawyers, politicians, or labor leaders. Without their cooperation, it is unlikely that the business will be successful.

Moreover, subordinates are likely to be influenced at least as much by a manager's attitude toward the environment as by his attitude toward them. The manager who is adventurous, entrepreneurial, dynamic—even though he may be discourteous to his employees—will generate fierce loyalties. And, conversely, the stagnant company which treats its employees well usually winds up with an executive team that is either incompetent, dissatisfied, or both. The following quote from a young executive about to switch jobs is typical:

[5] See Robert B. Young, "Keys to Corporate Growth," HBR November–December 1961, p. 51.

I have no complaint about being unfairly treated—he's been very fair about everything; and he pays me a pretty good salary. I just don't want to get tied down to a firm that isn't going anywhere.

Similarly, in the case of profit, it is not so much the reported profit itself that must be the focus of management's concern, but rather *what the reported figure implies for the company's relationships with the various systems of which it is a part.* One such system will be the network of investors and creditors who provide the organization with funds. Clearly, their confidence must be preserved, and they must be compensated for the risks they assume. However, profit is not an automatic indicator of the extent to which either is accomplished. Conversely, the business which says that its only objective is to enhance the stockholders' equity implies that no other system of which it is a part—neither market, nor community, nor nation—can be considered as deserving of equal priority.

Of course, the traditional significance which attaches to profit as a prerequisite for corporate survival is important. But for most companies it can well be claimed that the achievement of a reported profit is less a test of the quality of management than of how its funds are distributed.

It can be established that many companies have faced their most critical tests of survival in precisely those years when they were reporting the highest net profits in their history—mainly because these were being achieved at the price of not keeping up with competitors in research, equipment renewal, and management development.

If, then, criteria such as profit are to be rejected as the measures of performance, what will take their place? It follows from the preceding arguments that what must be substituted is *sets of criteria,* each corresponding to some wider system of which the company is a part. One implication of this is that the general manager must be concerned both with the identification of relevant wider systems and with an assessment of the relative obligation the organization owes each of them.

IDENTIFYING WIDER SYSTEMS

In order to survive, an organization must achieve what is called "symbiosis" (i.e., the mutually beneficial living together of two dissimilar organisms) with a variety of external systems, and it is the responsibility of the general manager to be concerned with all of these systems. The first step in discharging this responsibility is the identification of those broader or, to use a more technical term, those superordinate systems of which the company is a part. For example, we can think of an enterprise as being part of an industry, a community, a market, an economy, and a variety of other superordinate systems. But each of these systems is really only a nebulously defined abstraction, and yet each of these abstractions poses a set of highly significant issues for management.

Let us take the notion of an "industry," which may appear to be a fairly obvious an unambiguous superordinate or wider system. No doubt it once was—when specializations were clearly defined, broad, and stable—but not in today's changing world. Consider these examples:

Petroleum used to be quite a precise description of an industry. Today, the rapid advances in petrochemistry and the development of a variety of energy sources (from fuel cells to thermoelectricity) have presented petroleum companies with a greater variety of alternatives concerning industry definitions as well as more knotty problems of strategic choice. Now it is crucial for a petroleum company to decide whether it is in the petrochemical industry, or the petroleum industry, or both.

In the aircraft industry the necessity for redefining superordinate systems arises as missiles are rapidly replacing manned aircraft for military use. This is a dramatic illustration of the basic issue that confronts management in every industry.

Another important superordinate system involves the federal government. To an ever-increasing extent, the federal government and the individual firm have to be thought of as parts of the same system; the recent furor over steel pricing is an excellent example of this. But the tendency toward government and business being parts of the same system is apparent in numerous other aspects of business life, ranging from tariff policy and depreciation allowance to research expenditures and production contracts.

It is unfortunate that this issue of government and business has so often been posed in terms of freedom versus control. This point of view leads to conceptualizing the situation in terms of two antagonists—as only black and white. It is more in tune with the times to think of business and the federal government as part of the same system, and to explore the effect that each may have on the other by pursuing a particular course of action. Today in the free countries of Western Europe, joint government-industry activities are well advanced. Their experience has made clear that enlightened management can no longer refuse to accept the existence of the federal government within the same system as the company. Of course, approving the over-all system does not completely solve the question of the relationship between the parts of the system. But some consideration of that issue will benefit a business much more than will simply resenting "interference from Washington."

A final example of a superordinate system is that which embraces a business and the communities in which it operates. This issue appears in its most acute form when the company is large and the community small; for, under this set of circumstances, the mutual relationship between the two systems is apparent. Certainly the issue is most dramatic in this context, as has been demonstrated again and again in now nearly deserted New England textile communities and neglected Pennsylvania mining towns. However, from an ethical point of view, the issue over the relationship between the business and the community becomes no less significant merely because the relative size of each is different.

Superordinate system	Criteria
Stockholders	Price appreciation of securities
	Dividend payout
Labor force	Wage levels
	Stability of employment
	Opportunity
The market: consumers	Value given
The market: competitors	Rate of growth
	Innovation
Suppliers	Rapidity of payment
Creditors	Adherence to contract terms
Community	Contribution to community development
Nation	Public responsibility

Exhibit I. **Systems Criteria for Judging Company Performance**

Setting System Criteria

Once the broader systems of which the company is a part have been identified, some criteria must be adopted which will determine how well the company has performed with respect to each system. One set of performance criteria which reflects the broad range of management concern is shown in EXHIBIT I.

It should be clear, for example, from the criteria listed in EXHIBIT I that improved short-run payouts with respect to any particular system can only be achieved in three ways: (1) by immediately raising the level of performance of the whole organization, (2) by paying out now what might be saved for the future, or (3) by raising the payouts to one superordinate system at the expense of another. Consequently, the wise general manager should never be concerned with a *single* objective and with a single superordinate system. Rather, he must be concerned with a *set* of objectives; and thus the trade-off of one good against another is a critical aspect of his responsibility.

He must decide whether short-run profits (so dear to the "stockholder system") are obtained at the expense of long-range profits (within the same system) or at the expense of payouts to other systems. For example, short-run profits may stem from actions which will reduce the company's effectiveness in coping with future competition (the "market/competition system") or with future labor demands (the "labor system"). He must decide whether his company's contribution to the "nation system" is sufficient to warrant risks of loss to the "stockholder system." In short, he is concerned with how the organization relates to *all* who contribute to it; and unless he can formulate a meaningful set of objectives which cover all such relationships, he is in danger of running into difficulty in some area.

Many other sets of criteria are of course possible. However, each should be considered in terms of (1) which superordinate systems have been explicitly included, and (2) what criteria will best serve as reliable indicators of how well the company is achieving its objectives in relationship to the included systems.

CREATING SUBSYSTEMS

One of the most significant ways in which managerial ability expresses itself is in the creation and change of formal subsystems. The term "formal subsystem" is used here to refer to the officially established groups and entities which are created to carry on the company's activities. These include such units as divisions, departments, and regions which are reflected on the conventional organization chart. Also included are the committees, boards, and groups which have official status but are frequently not shown on the organization chart, despite the fact that decisions concerning which committees shall be established, what their membership will be, and how long they will be permitted to operate are at least as significant to the operation of a company as is its formal structure.

Thinking of the company as a set of formal subsystems offers two benefits:

(1) It focuses attention on the essential relatedness of activities carried on by specific individuals.
(2) It emphasizes the fact that to meet the particular requirements of a specific business, the subunits of which the organization is composed must be as carefully designed as the subunits of any other system.

One of the tragedies frequently suffered by people who fall in love with such traditional organizational techniques as job descriptions and organization charts is that after a while they become far more concerned with specialization than with coordination. Somehow the inevitable result of boxes and lines appears to be the *division* of tasks, rather than merely their *delineation*. As a result, the neat little lines on the chart, which were originally intended to be boundaries, always seem to become fences.

This is so universal and unfortunate a tendency that it would not be too wild a statement to claim that *most organizations would probably contribute enormously to their own progress if they burned their existing organization charts and manuals*. Then management would be free to think about how the employees might be grouped together to form meaningful systems, rather than being concerned with which particular bits and pieces of a total activity should be set aside as the exclusive preoccupation of a single individual.

Most serious company problems call for cooperative action, rather than for individual decisions. And yet not one job description in a hundred tells what an individual contributes to a broader system or how he cooperates with his colleagues. The net effect has been to hinder cooperation, stifle creativity, and restrict change. Indeed, it is not accidental that formal organizational arrangements are played down by those companies which are most dynamic and most creative.

This idea should not be construed to mean that organization charts of a different type might not prove to be of value and importance. However, if they are to be of more help than hindrance, charts should be drawn in terms of systems, rather than in terms of *individual components*. And they should be viewed as blueprints—as the expression of a design—and not as the photograph of a jungle.

When an engineer looks at formal organizational arrangements, he is immediately struck by how seldom such arrangements have been "designed" —in the sense of matching specific groups and structures to the objectives and resources of a particular business. In most companies, the organizational structure is merely the result of a haphazard process of evolution, and, as such, has no particular relationship to the needs, aspirations, or competencies of the people in it—and even less relationship to the company's external strategy.

Unfortunately, there are no ready rules for the design of a set of subsystems which will meet the requirements listed in EXHIBIT I. In the field of formal organization we are still very much at the level of amateur mechanics. At present, we know a good deal more about breaking tasks apart than about putting them together in new and imaginative ways. This task, then, is one which has to be performed by the effective chief executive on the basis of his own judgment and intuition, rather than as a result of a set of precise principles. The great managers have made impressive and lasting improvisations in this way.[6]

Systems Integration

The chief executive is the focal point of many different worlds. His desk is the point of contact between a bewildering variety of groups, issues, pressures, and values. His major responsibility, therefore, is to maintain some degree of *consistency* between the demands imposed by the many systems which are part of his organization's life. This is what is meant by systems integration, a process that involves two different kinds of activities: (1) the integration of the systemic hierarchy; (2) the integration of systemic models. Both of these are essential parts of the manager's job.

It cannot be emphasized enough that the essence of the manager's job is not simply that of understanding broader and broader superordinate systems, but rather of achieving some measure of integration between the

---

[6] See Alfred D. Chandler, *Strategy and Structure* (Cambridge, MIT Press, 1962); also James W. Culliton, "Age of Synthesis," HBR September–October 1962, p. 36.

broader superordinate systems and the smallest subsystems which form his organization. Thus, an economist or a market researcher on the corporate staff will certainly be more intimately concerned wit some broad superordinate system than the chief executive should be. But what distinguishes the executive's job from theirs is the range of systems which he must integrate. Specifically, the general manager must be able to:

Translate the broadest abstractions into the most detailed aspects of company operations.

See what implications major industry trends hold for the kind of worker recruitment that he expects to do over the next few years, for the kinds of machines he may expect to buy, and for the materials which may be available.

Translate the broad trends which are transmuting our society into specific decisions concerning new products, the development of salesmen, and many other detailed issues.

Recognize the strategic implications of the ostensibly humdrum event. For example:

A small shift in the market performance of a product may presage a major movement.

The introduction of a minor change in office methods can be the key to a whole data-processing installation.

A whole new social structure may eventually emerge from an act as seemingly insignificant as moving a coffee machine.

A second aspect of systemic integration is that concerning the various models of corporate life. A manager must understand thoroughly how an organization behaves if he is to influence it, and the key to such undering lies in an awareness of the various models which may be used to explain its operation. Such an awareness is not only essential to the manager's perception of the company; it is also essential to the manager's perception of himself.

What happens in an organization may often be explained by the use of a particular "model." For example, a company may be regarded as:

1. A *social system*—where the many and varied tools of the social scientists may be used to reveal the patterns and significance of the way the members behave.

2. An *economic system*—where the insights afforded by classical economics may be highly useful in explaining a wide range of occurrences.

3. A *data-processing system*—where a knowledge of information-handling technology is required in order to analyze communication needs.

Each of these analogies is extremely useful to the manager, for each is often the key to a valid explanation of what goes on inside the company. Consequently, the more models a manager can bring to bear on particular problems, the more he will be able to understand why specific events take place, and what he ought to do about them. Conversely, a manager may easily damage his organization by assiduously behaving in accordance with an inappropriate model. A frequent illustration of this is the reliance on economic incentives to remedy deficiencies in the social system.

This still happens often, despite the amount of research that has been done on the social determinants of output levels. One would think that more than 20 years after the publication of *Management and the Worker*[7] exclusive reliance on economic means to deal with performance would no longer be common. However, a panacea frequently resorted to by managers who wish to raise output is a sweetened bonus program for individuals. Here is one example:

A manufacturer of custom-built machinery, eager to improve output per man-hour, installed a wage incentive plan. All that it did was cost the company money, since the key individuals turned out to be highly skilled senior mechanics whose work could not be measured. Only by cancelling the incentive plan, by conscientiously improving communications within the plant, and by transferring greater responsibility to its foremen did the company begin to solve its problems. Its mistake, obviously, was that it was trying to cure ills in its social system by applying economic measures. If the top management of this company had considered a broader variety of models, it might well have avoided this costly error.

Of course, no single model or conceptual scheme embraces the whole breadth and complexity of reality, even though each in turn may be useful in particular instances. This is why management remains an art, for the practitioner must go beyond the limits of theoretical knowledge if he is to be effective. As soon as the manager begins to think "scientifically," he has already made an abstraction from reality. This abstraction may be based on economics, sociology, psychology, or engineering—but it is only a part of reality. The real challenge to the manager is to see and to understand the whole situation.

CONCLUSION

In this atomic age too many managers are thinking of themselves and of their companies in buggy-whip terms. They have a concept of management which rests on a point of view that has remained largely unchanged since it was formulated by Henri Fayol just after World War I. In the meantime, however, a deluge of important new ideas has swept across the business scene. Whole new fields of critical importance to management have emerged: cybernetics, integrated data processing, systems engineering, and a variety of others ranging from social psychology to Bayesian statistics.

---

[7] F. J. Roethlisberger and W. J. Dickson (Cambridge, Harvard University Press, 1939).

The impact of all these new ideas on management has been so fundamental that new ways of thinking about the manager's job are long overdue.

The modern manager needs a new approach to his job for three reasons:

1. He must have a way of thinking about management that permits him to take account of the tremendous amount of new knowledge that is appearing.
2. He has to have a framework that permits him to relate one specialty with another in his work.
3. He must be able to raise his sights above the hurly-burly of current in-company operations and understand how his company relates to its complex environment—to the other great systems of which it is a part.

A systems approach to management promises to do this, as I have tried to demonstrate in this article. I have also attempted to indicate the kinds of questions that come up when a manager tries to think of his job in systems terms. One of the most important of these is: "Have I been concerned with those things that I, as a manager, must be concerned with?" This is a very disconcerting question for a manager to ask. But if there is some suspicion that the answer is *no,* isn't it better for a manager to reach that conclusion himself?

C The Systems Concept in Marketing Management

6 Systems Approach to Marketing*

LEE ADLER

The author seeks to dispel some of the mystery and also the glamor which tend to surround the systems concept. He discusses the utilization of the concept in marketing, using case histories drawn from various industries.

More and more businessmen today recognize that corporate success is, in most cases, synonymous with marketing success and with the coming of age of a new breed of professional managers. They find it increasingly important not only to pay lip service to the marketing concept but to do something about it in terms of (a) customer orientation, rather than navel-gazing in the factory, (b) organizational revisions to implement the marketing concept, and (c) a more orderly approach to problem solving.

In an increasing number of companies we see more conscious and formal efforts to apply rational, fact-based methods for solving marketing problems, and greater recognition of the benefits these methods offer. While these benefits may be newly realized, there is nothing new about the underlying philosophy; in the parlance of military men and engineers, it is the systems approach. For, whether we like it or not, marketing is, by definition, a system, if we accept Webster's definition of systems as "an assemblage of objects united by some form of regular interaction or interdependence." Certainly, the interaction of such "objects" as product, pricing, promotion, sales calls, distribution, and so on fits the definition.

There is an expanding list of sophisticated applications of systems theory—and not in one but in many sectors of the marketing front. The construction of mathematical and/or logical models to describe, quantify, and evaluate alternate marketing strategies and mixes is an obvious case in

---

*Reprinted from **Harvard Business Review,** Vol. 45, No. 3 (May–June, 1967), pp. 105–118.

point. So, too, is the formulation of management information systems[1] and of marketing plans with built-in performance measurements of predetermined goals. But no less vital is the role of the systems approach in the design and sale of products and services. When J. P. Stevens Company color-harmonizes lines and bedspreads, and towels and bath mats, it is creating a product system. And when Avco Corporation sells systems management to the space exploration field, involving the marriage of many scientific disciplines as well as adherence to budgetary constraints, on-time performance, and quality control, it is creating a *service* system.

In this article I shall discuss the utilization of the systems concept in marketing in both quantitative and qualitative ways with case histories drawn from various industries. In doing so, my focus will be more managerial and philosophical than technical, and I will seek to dissipate some of the hocus-pocus, glamor, mystery, and fear which pervade the field. The systems concept is not esoteric or "science fiction" in nature (although it sometimes *sounds* that way in promotional descriptions). Its advantages are not subtle or indirect; as we shall see, they are as real and immediate as decision making itself. The limitations are also real, and these, too, will be discussed.

(Readers interested in a brief summary of the background and the conceptual development of the systems approach may wish to turn to the box on pages 88 and 89.)

PROMISING APPLICATIONS

Now let us look at some examples of corporate application of the systems approach. Here we will deal with specific parts or "subsystems" of the total marketing system. EXHIBIT I is a schematic portrayal of these relationships.

Products and Services

The objective of the systems approach in product management is to provide a complete "offering" to the market rather than merely a product. If the purpose of business is to create a customer at a profit, then the needs of the customer must be carefully attended to; we must, in short, study what the customer is buying or wants to buy, rather than what we are trying to sell.

In the consumer products field we have forged ahead in understanding that the customer buys nutrition (not bread), beauty (not cosmetics), warmth (not fuel oil). But in industrial products this concept has been slower in gaining a foothold. Where it has gained a foothold, it expresses itself in two ways: the creation of a complete product system sold (1) as a

---

[1] See, for example, Donald F. Cox and Robert E. Good, "How to Build a Marketing Information System," on page 145 of this issue.

SUBSYSTEMS

PRODUCT FUNCTIONS
- Packaging
- Pricing
- Brand Name

NEW PRODUCT DEVELOPMENT

DISTRIBUTION CHANNELS

PHYSICAL DISTRIBUTION

FIELD SALES

MARKETING INTELLIGENCE

MARKETING ADMINISTRATION
- Planning
- Budgeting
- Control
- Evaluation

ADVERTISING

SALES PROMOTION AND MERCHANDISING

PUBLICITY AND PUBLIC RELATIONS

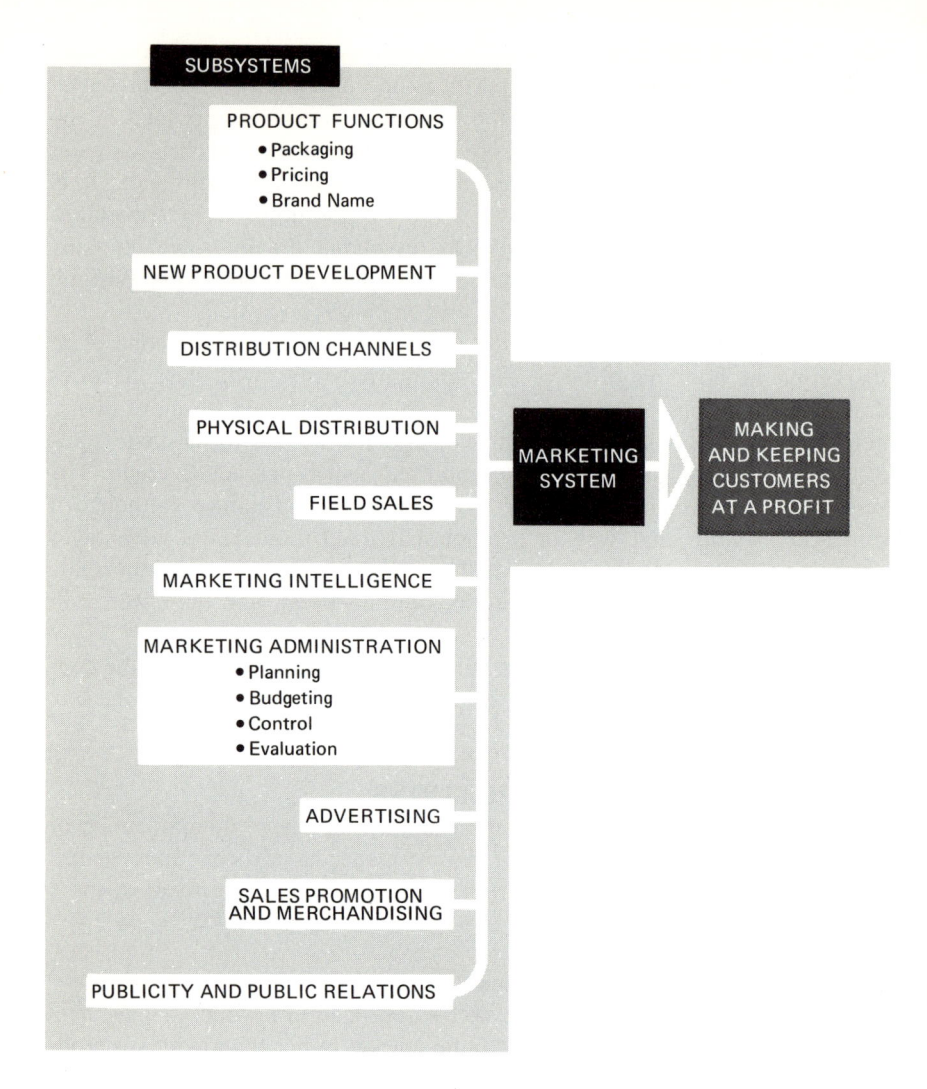

MARKETING SYSTEM ⇒ MAKING AND KEEPING CUSTOMERS AT A PROFIT

Exhibit I. **Marketing Subsystems and the Total System**

unit, or (2) as a component or components which are part of a larger consumption system.

Perhaps the most eloquent testimony to the workability and value of the systems approach comes from companies that have actually used it. For a good example let us turn to the case of The Carborundum Company. This experience is especially noteworthy because it comes from industrial marketing, where, as just indicated, progress with the systems concept has generally been slow.

Birth of the Concept. Founded in 1894, the company was content for many years to sell abrasives. It offered an extremely broad line of grinding wheels, coated abrasives, and abrasive grain, with a reputed capacity for 200,000 different products of varying type, grade, and formulation. But the focus was on the product.

In the mid-1950's, Carborundum perceived that the market for abrasives could be broadened considerably if—looking at abrasives through customers' eyes—it would see the product as fitting into *metal polishing, cleaning,* or *removal systems.* Now Carborundum is concerned with all aspects of abrading—the machine, the contact wheel, the workpiece, the labor cost, the overhead rate, the abrasive, and, above all, the customer's objective. In the words of Carborundum's president, W. H. Wendel:

> That objective is never the abrasive per se, but rather the creation of a certain dimension, a type of finish, or a required shape, always related to a minimum cost. Since there are many variables to consider, just one can be misleading. To render maximum service, Carborundum (must offer) a complete system.[2]

Organizational Overhaul. To offer such a system, management had to overhaul important parts of the organization:

(1) The company needed to enhance its knowledge of the total system. As Wendel explains:

> We felt we had excellent knowledge of coated abrasive products, but that we didn't have the application and machine know-how in depth. To be really successful in the business, we had to know as much about the machine tools as we did the abrasives.[3]

To fill this need, Carborundum made three acquisitions—The Tysaman Machine Company, which builds heavy-duty snagging, billet grinding, and abrasive cut-off machines; Curtis Machine Company, a maker of belt sanders; and Pangborn Corporation, which supplied systems capability in abrasive blast cleaning and finishing.

(2) The company's abrasive divisions were reorganized, and the management of them was realigned to accommodate the new philosophy and its application. The company found that *centering responsibility for the full system in one profit center* proved to be the most effective method of coordinating approaches in application engineering, choice of distribution channels, brand identification, field sales operations, and so forth. This method was particularly valuable for integrating the acquisitions into the new program.

(3) An Abrasives Systems Center was established to handle development work and to solve customer problems.

[2] "Abrasive Maker's Systems Approach Opens New Markets," *Steel,* December 27, 1965, p. 38.
[3] *Ibid.*

(4) Technical conferences and seminars were held to educate customers on the new developments.

(5) Salesmen were trained in machine and application knowledge.

Planning. A key tool in the systems approach is planning—in particular, the use of what I like to call "total business plans." (This treme care by the operating companies and divisions. Very specific objectives functions.) At Carborundum, total business plans are developed with extreme care by the operating companies and divisions. Very specific objectives are established, and then detailed action programs are outlined to achieve these objectives. The action programs extend throughout the organization, including the manufacturing and development branches of the operating unit. Management sets specific dates for the completion of action steps and defines who is responsible for them. Also, it carefully measures results against established objectives. This is done both in the financial reporting system and in various marketing committees.

Quantitative Methods. Carborundum has utilized various operations research techniques, like decision tree analysis and PERT, to aid in molding plans and strategies. For example, one analysis, which concerned itself with determining the necessity for plant expansion, was based on different possible levels of success for the marketing plan. In addition, the computer has been used for inventory management, evaluation of alternate pricing strategies for systems selling, and the measurement of marketing achievements against goals.

It should be noted, though, that these quantitative techniques are management tools only and that much of the application of systems thinking to the redeployment of Carborundum's business is qualitative in nature.

Gains Achieved. As a consequence of these developments, the company has opened up vast new markets. To quote Carborundum's president again:

> Customers don't want a grinding wheel, they want metal removed. . . . The U.S. and Canadian market for abrasives amounts to $700 million a year. But what companies spend on stock removal—to bore, grind, cut, shape, and finish metal—amounts to $30 billion a year." [4]

Illustrating this market expansion in the steel industry is Carborundum's commercial success with three new developments—hot grinding, an arborless wheel to speed metal removal and cut grinding costs, and high-speed conditioning of carbon steel billets. All represent conversions from nonabrasive methods. Carborundum now also finds that the close relationship with customers gives it a competitive edge, opens top customer management doors, gains entree for salesmen with prospects they had never been able to "crack" before. Perhaps the ultimate accolade is the company's re-

---

[4] "Carborundum Grinds at Faster Clip," *Business Week,* July 23, 1966, pp. 58, 60.

port that customers even come to the organization itself, regarding it as a consultant as well as a supplier.

Profitable Innovation

The intense pressure to originate successful new products cannot be met without methodologies calculated to enhance the probabilities of profitable innovation. The systems approach has a bearing here, too. EXHIBIT II shows a model for "tracking" products through the many stages of ideation, development, and testing to ultimate full-scale commercialization. This diagram is in effect a larger version of the "New Product Development" box in EXHIBIT I.

Observe that this is a logical (specifically, sequential), rather than numerical, model. While some elements of the total system (e.g., alternate distribution channels and various media mixes) can be analyzed by means of operations research techniques, the model has not been cast in mathematical terms. Rather, the flow diagram as a whole is used as a checklist to make sure "all bases are covered" and to help organize the chronological sequence of steps in new product development. It also serves as a conceptual foundation for formal PERT application, should management desire such a step, and for the gradual development of a series of equations linking together elements in the diagrams, should it seem useful to experiment with mathematical models.

Marketing Intelligence

The traditional notion of marketing research is fast becoming antiquated. For it leads to dreary chronicles of the past rather than focusing on the present and shedding light on the future. It is particularistic, tending to concentrate on the study of tiny fractions of a marketing problem rather than on the problem as a whole. It lends itself to assuaging the curiosity of the moment, to fire-fighting, to resolving internecine disputes. It is a slave to technique. I shall not, therefore, relate the term *marketing research* to the systems approach—although I recognize, of course, that some leading businessmen and writers are breathing new life and scope into the ideas referred to by that term.

The role of the systems approach is to help evolve a *marketing intelligence* system tailored to the needs of each marketer. Such a system would serve as the ever-alert nerve center of the marketing operation. It would have these major characteristics:

Continuous surveillance of the market.
A team of research techniques used in tandem.
A network of data sources.
Integrated analysis of data from the various sources.
Effective utilization of automatic data-processing equipment to distill mountains of raw information speedily.
Strong concentration not just on reporting findings but also on practical, action-oriented recommendations.

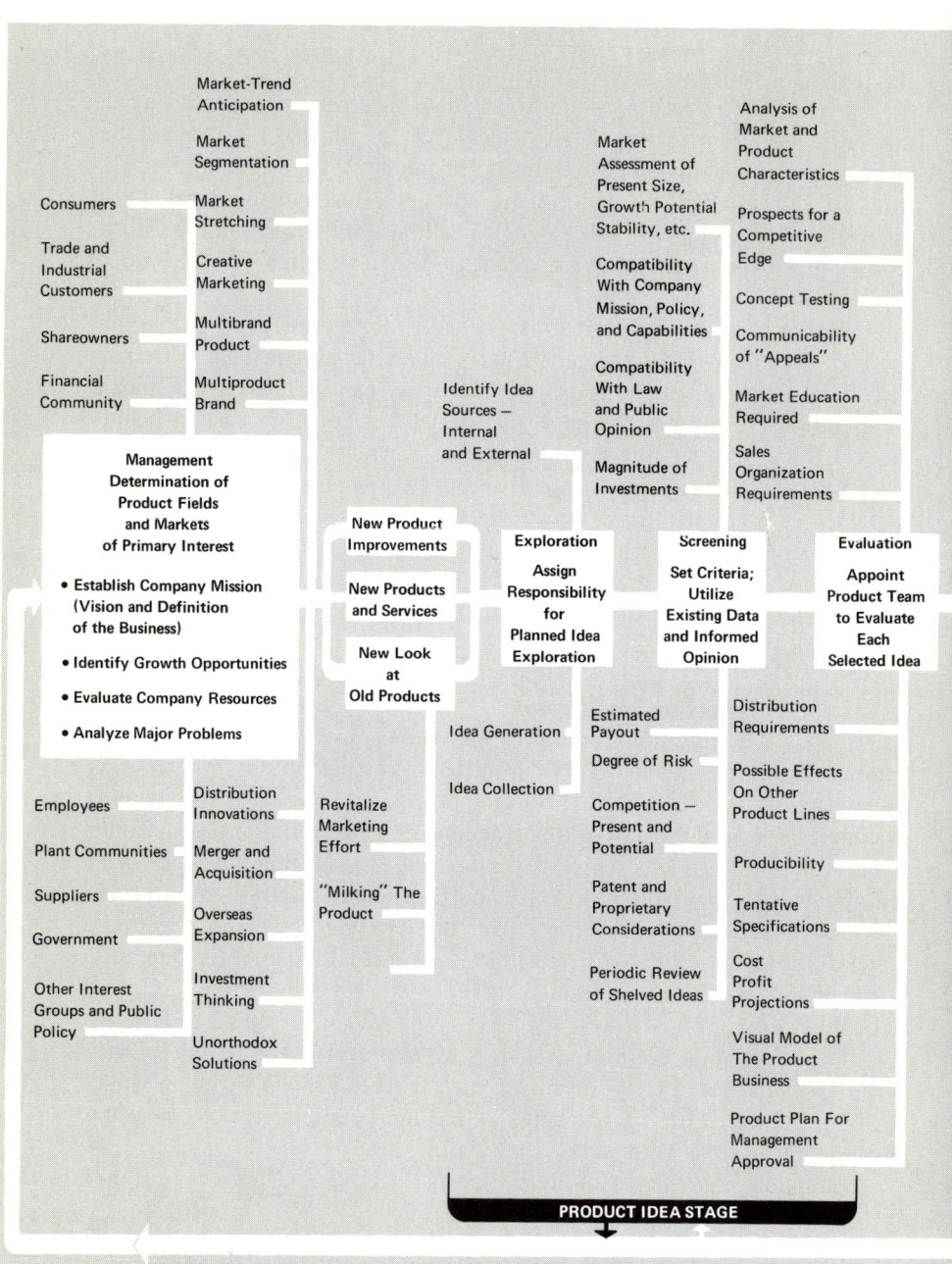

	Market-Trend Anticipation				Analysis of Market and Product Characteristics
	Market Segmentation		Market Assessment of Present Size, Growth Potential Stability, etc.		
Consumers	Market Stretching				Prospects for a Competitive Edge
Trade and Industrial Customers	Creative Marketing		Compatibility With Company Mission, Policy, and Capabilities		Concept Testing
Shareowners	Multibrand Product				Communicability of "Appeals"
Financial Community	Multiproduct Brand	Identify Idea Sources — Internal and External	Compatibility With Law and Public Opinion		Market Education Required
Management Determination of Product Fields and Markets of Primary Interest			Magnitude of Investments		Sales Organization Requirements
		New Product Improvements	**Exploration**	**Screening**	**Evaluation**
• Establish Company Mission (Vision and Definition of the Business)		New Products and Services	Assign Responsibility for Planned Idea Exploration	Set Criteria; Utilize Existing Data and Informed Opinion	Appoint Product Team to Evaluate Each Selected Idea
• Identify Growth Opportunities		New Look at Old Products			
• Evaluate Company Resources			Estimated Payout		Distribution Requirements
• Analyze Major Problems			Degree of Risk		
					Possible Effects On Other Product Lines
Employees	Distribution Innovations	Revitalize Marketing Effort	Idea Collection		
Plant Communities	Merger and Acquisition		Competition — Present and Potential		Producibility
Suppliers	Overseas Expansion	"Milking" The Product	Patent and Proprietary Considerations		Tentative Specifications
Government					
Other Interest Groups and Public Policy	Investment Thinking		Periodic Review of Shelved Ideas		Cost Profit Projections
	Unorthodox Solutions				Visual Model of The Product Business
					Product Plan For Management Approval

PRODUCT IDEA STAGE

NOTE: This flow diagram was developed by Paul E. Funk, President, and the staff of McCann/ITSM, Inc.

Exhibit II. **Work Flow and Systems Chart for Management of New Products**

Development and Test Stage

Product (and Production) Testing
- Continue Market Studies To Enhance Product Salability
- Engineering Studies and Prototype Development
- Laboratory Testing and Quality Control Studies
- Check With Salesmen and Key Customers
- Product Design and Lab Testing
- Package Design and Container Engineering
- Release Designs for Pilot Production
- Production Development
- Pilot Production
- Check Government Codes and Opinion Trends
- Conduct Tests of Performance of Product in Use
- Conduct Tests of Product Durability
- Test Quality Control System
- Test Production System and Establish Production Costs
- Get Outside Professional Evaluation
- Start Technical Service Development
- Improve Product Design and Freeze Specifications
- Prepare Report and Recommendation for Management Approval

Marketing Communications Development
- Advertising Concepts
- Media Selection
- Product Literature
- Budget Determination
- Sales Promotion
- Merchandising
- Shows and Exhibits

Market Testing
- Determination of Criteria for Success and Test Design
- Customer Response to Product Line — Reasons for Buying and Not Buying
- Packaging and Methods of Shipment
- Price Structures
- Trade Response to Product Line
- Effectiveness of Communications Tools
- Media Effectiveness and Mix
- Effectiveness of Sales Methods
- Technical Service Effectiveness
- Distribution Patterns
- Distribution Negotiations
- Optimum Product Characteristics, Product-Line Mix, and Marketability
- Optimum Marketing Mix
- National Projections of Marketing Cost Levels, Sales, and Profits
- Preparation of Report and Recommendations

Full Scale Commercialization

Building Production Capacity and Inventories
- Modifications of Product Line, Production Process, and Marketing Mix Completed
- Production Facilities Completed
- Warehousing Points and Shipping Patterns
- Inventory Levels
- Quality Control System Operative
- Production-Data Processing System Operative

Readying The Sales Force and Distribution
- Determination of Numbers, Backgrounds, and Kinds of Men
- Sales Recruiting Program
- Sales Training Program
- Sales Aids Program
- Sales Incentive Programs
- Regional Distribution and Territories
- Sales Data and Inquiry Processing Operative

Full-Scale Introduction
- Measurement Systems Operative for All Elements of the Marketing Mix
- Integrated Data Processing Systems Operative
- Anticipate Competitive Countermoves
- Kick-Off Sales Meeting
- Preview Presentations to Key Trade Customers
- Trade Press Conference
- Trade Communications Program Launched
- Trade-Show Exhibit
- Introduction to Trade Completed
- General Press Conference
- Consumer Communications Program Launched
- Introduction Monitored

Measurement and Evaluation
- Product Design Evaluated
- Product Quality Evaluated
- Product Name and Symbol Evaluated
- Packaging Evaluated
- Pricing Policy Evaluated
- Inventory System Evaluated
- Distribution Pattern Evaluated
- Sales Organization Evaluated
- Technical Service Evaluated
- Communications Tools and Mix Evaluated
- Overall Marketing Mix Evaluated
- Sales Cost, and Profit Forecasts Evaluated
- Business Evaluation Report Prepared for Management Review

Systems Approach to Marketing

Concept in Use. A practical instance of the use of such an intelligence system is supplied by Mead Johnson Nutritionals (division of Mead Johnson & Company), manufacturers of Metrecal, Pablum, Bib, Nutrament, and other nutritional specialties. As Exhibit III shows, the company's Marketing Intelligence Department has provided information from these sources:

A continuing large-scale consumer market study covering attitudinal and behavioral data dealing with weight control.

Nielsen store audit data, on a bimonthly basis.

A monthly sales audit conducted among a panel of 100 high-volume food stores in 20 markets to provide advance indications of brand share shifts.

Supermarket warehouse withdrawal figures from Time, Inc.'s new service, Selling Areas-Marketing, Inc.

Salesmen's weekly reports (which, in addition to serving the purposes of sales management control, call for reconnaissance on competitive promotions, new product launches, price changes, and so forth).

Advertising expenditure data, by media class, from the company's accounting department.

Figures on sales and related topics from company factories.

Competitive advertising expenditure and exposure data, supplied by the division's advertising agencies at periodic intervals.

A panel of weight-conscious women.

To exemplify the type of outputs possible from this system, Mead Johnson will be able, with the help of analyses of factory sales data, warehouse withdrawal information, and consumer purchases from Nielsen, to monitor transactions at each stage of the flow of goods through the distribution channel and to detect accumulations or developing shortages. Management will also be able to spot sources of potential problems in time to deal with them effectively. For example, if factory sales exceed consumer purchases, more promotional pressure is required. By contrast, if factory sales lag behind consumer purchases, sales effort must be further stimulated.

Similarly, the company has been able to devise a practical measurement of advertising's effectiveness in stimulating sales—a measurement that is particularly appropriate to fast-moving packaged goods. By relating advertising outlays and exposure data to the number of prospects trying out a product during a campaign (the number is obtained from the continuing consumer survey), it is possible to calculate the advertising cost of recruiting such a prospect. By persisting in such analyses during several campaigns, the relative value of alternative advertising approaches can be weighed. Since measurement of the sales, as opposed to the communications, effects of promotion is a horrendously difficult, costly, and chancy process, the full significance of this achievement is difficult to exaggerate.

IRREGULARLY SCHEDULED REPORTS

ADVERTISING PRETESTS

SPECIAL CONSUMER
STUDIES
- Marketing Opportunities
- Tests of Concepts
- Product Placements

PRODUCT QUALITY TESTS

GOVERNMENTAL AND TRADE
INFORMATION

BIMONTHLY OR QUARTERLY REPORTS

ADVERTISING EXPENDITURE
ESTIMATES

FOOD AND DRUGSTORE
SYNDICATED
PANEL AUDITS OF
INVENTORY AND SALES

PERIODIC CONSUMER
SURVEYS (Awareness,
Attitude, Usage)

DAILY, WEEKLY, OR MONTHLY REPORTS

SPECIAL STORE AUDITS

SALES ACCOUNTING REPORTS

WAREHOUSE WITHDRAWAL
REPORTS

CONSUMER PANEL REPORTS

SALES CALL REPORTS

COLLECTION, ANALYSIS, INTERPRETATION, CATALOGING

REPORTED OUT →

IN STORAGE, ON CALL

REPORTED OUT

MARKETING INTELLIGENCE LIBRARY OF PRIMARY AND SECONDARY DATA

IRREGULARLY ISSUED REPORTS

ADVERTISING QUALITY

PRODUCT QUALITY

BASIC CONSUMER
WANTS AND NEEDS

BASES FOR
SEGMENTATION

CONSUMER AND MARKET
REACTIONS TO SPECIAL
STIMULI (e.g., Promotions,
Products, Packages,
Advertising)

MONTHLY, BIMONTHLY, OR QUARTERLY REPORTS

CONSUMER
Awareness, Attitudes,
Purchase, and Use

FACTORY
Sales and Inventory

WHOLESALE
Withdrawal Rates

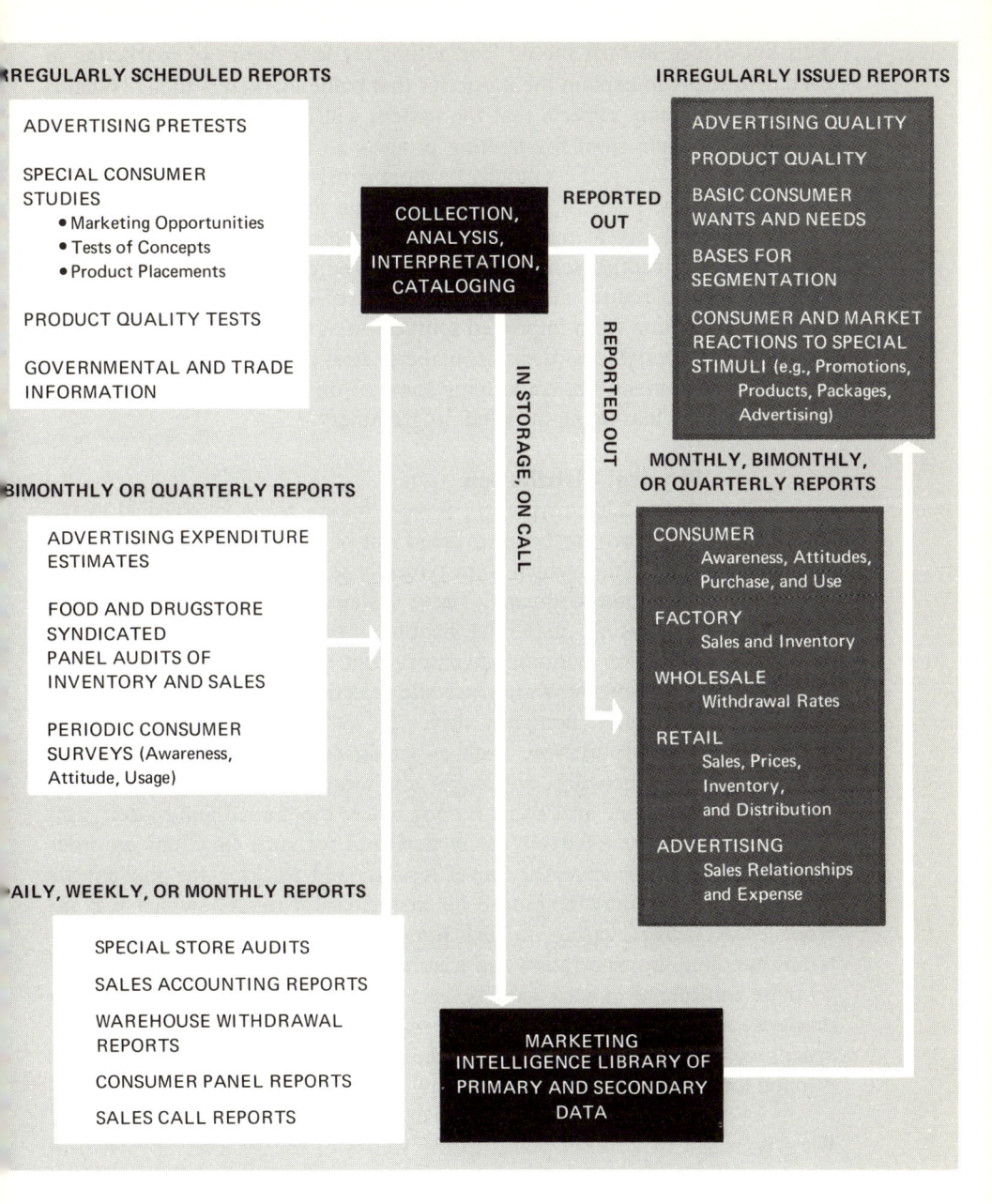

RETAIL
Sales, Prices,
Inventory,
and Distribution

ADVERTISING
Sales Relationships
and Expense

Exhibit III. **Mead Johnson's Marketing Intelligence System**

Benefits Realized. Mead Johnson's marketing intelligence system has been helpful to management in a number of ways. In addition to giving executive early warning of new trends and problems, and valuable insights into future conditions, it is leading to a systematic *body* of knowledge about company markets rather than to isolated scraps of information.

Systems Approach to Marketing

This knowledge in turn should lead ultimately to a theory of marketing in each field that will explain the mysteries that baffle marketers today. What is more, the company expects that the system will help to free its marketing intelligence people from fire-fighting projects so that they can concentrate on long-term factors and eventually be more consistently creative.

Despite these gains, it is important to note that Mead Johnson feels it has a long road still to travel. More work is needed in linking individual data banks. Conceptual schemes must be proved out in practice; ways must still be found to reduce an awesome volume of data, swelled periodically by new information from improved sources, so as to make intelligence more immediately accessible to decision makers. And perhaps the biggest problem of the movement, one underlying some of the others, is the difficulty in finding qualified marketing-oriented programmers.

Physical Distribution

A veritable revolution is now taking place in physical distribution. Total systems are being evolved out of the former hodgepodge of separate responsibilities, which were typically scattered among different departments of the same company. These systems include traffic and transportation, warehousing, materials handling, protective packaging, order processing, production planning, inventory control, customer service, market forecasting, and plant and warehouse site selection. Motivating this revolution are the computer, company drives to reduce distribution costs, and innovations in transportation, such as jet air freight, container ships, the interstate highway network, and larger and more versatile freight cars.

Distribution is one area of marketing where the "bread-and-butter" uses of the computer are relatively easily deployed for such functions as order processing, real-time inventory level reports, and tracking the movements of goods. Further into the future lie mathematical models which will include every factor bearing on distribution. Not only will packaging, materials handling, transportation and warehouse, order processing, and related costs be considered in such models; also included will be sales forecasts by product, production rates by factory, warehouse locations and capacities, speeds of different carriers, etc. In short, a complete picture will be developed for management.

Program in Action. The experiences of the Norge Division of Borg-Warner Corporation point up the values of the systems approach in physical distribution. The firm was confronted externally with complaints from its dealers and distributors, who were trying to cope with swollen inventories and the pressures of "loading deals." Internally, because coordination of effort between the six departments involved in distribution was at a minimum, distribution costs and accounts receivable were mounting persistently.

To grapple with this situation, Norge undertook a comprehensive analysis of its distribution system. Out of this grew a new philosophy. A company executive has described the philosophy to me as follows:

> An effective system of physical distribution cannot begin at the end of the production line. It must also apply at the very beginning of the production process—at the planning, scheduling, and forecasting stages. Logistics, in short, is part of a larger marketing system, not just an evaluation of freight rates. We must worry not only about finished refrigerators, but also about the motors coming from another manufacturer, and even about where the copper that goes into those motors will come from. We must be concerned with *total flow*.

To implement this philosophy, the appliance manufacturer took the following steps:

(1) It reorganized the forecasting, production scheduling, warehousing, order processing, and shipping functions into *one* department headed by a director of physical distribution.

(2) The management information system was improved with the help of EDP equipment tied into the communications network. This step made it possible to process and report data more speedily on orders received, inventory levels, and the actual movement of goods.

(3) Management used a combination of computer and manual techniques to weigh trade-offs among increased costs of multiple warehousing, reduced long-haul freight and local drayage costs, reduced inventory pipeline, and the sales value of an improved "total" product offering. Also assessed were trade-offs between shorter production runs and higher inventory levels, thereby challenging the traditional "wisdom" of production-oriented managers that the longer the run, the better.

(4) The company is setting up new regional warehouses.

As a result of these moves, Norge has been able to lower inventories throughout its sales channels and to reduce accounts receivable. These gains have led, in turn, to a reduction of the company's overall investment and a concomitant increase in profitability.

It is essential to note that even though Norge has used operations research as part of its systems approach, many aspects of the program are qualitative. Thus far, the company has found that the development of an all-encompassing model is not warranted because of (a) the time and cost involved, (b) the probability that the situation will change before the model is completed, (c) a concern that such a model would be so complex as to be unworkable, and (d) the difficulty of testing many of the assumptions used. In addition, management has not tried to quantify the impact of its actions on distributor and retailer attitudes and behavior, possible competitive countermoves, and numerous other factors contributing to results.

Toward Total Integration

The integration of systems developed for product management, product innovation, marketing intelligence, physical distribution, and the other functions or "subsystems" embraced by the term *marketing* creates a total marketing system. Thus, marketing plans composed according to a step-by-step outline, ranging from enunciation of objectives and implementational steps to audit and adjustment to environmental changes, constitute a complete application of systems theory. Further, as the various subsystems of the overall system are linked quantitatively, so that the effect of modifications in one element can be detected in other elements, and as the influences of competitive moves on each element are analyzed numerically, then the total scheme becomes truly sophisticated.

PLUSES AND MINUSES

Two elements underlie the use and benefits of systems theory —order and knowledge. The first is a homely virtue, the second a lofty goal. Marketing is obviously not alone among all human pursuits in needing them; but, compared with its business neighbors, production and finance, marketing's need is acute indeed. The application of the systems concept can bring considerable advantages. It offers:

A methodical problem-solving orientation—with a broader frame of reference so that all aspects of a problem are examined.

Coordinated deployment of all appropriate tools of marketing.

Greater efficiency and economy of marketing operations.

Quicker recognition of impending problems, made possible by better understanding of the complex interplay of many trends and forces.

A stimulus to innovation.

A means of quantitatively verifying results.

These functional benefits in turn yield rich rewards in the marketplace. The most important gains are:

A deeper penetration of existing markets—As an illustration, the Advanced Data Division of Litton Industries has become a leader in the automatic revenue control business by designing systems meshing together "hardware" and "software."

A broadening of markets—For example, the tourist industry has attracted millions of additional travelers by creating packaged tours that are really product-service systems. These systems are far more convenient and economical than anything the consumer could assemble himself.

An extension of product lines—Systems management makes it more feasible to seek out compatibilties among independently developed systems. Evidence of this idea is the work of automatic control system specialists since the early 1950's.[5] Now similar signs are apparent in marketing. For example, Acme Visible Records is currently dovetailing the design and sale of its record-keeping systems with data-processing machines and forms.

---

[5] See *Automatic and Manual Control: Papers Contributed to the Conference at Cranford, 1951,* edited by A. Tustin (London, Butterworth's Scientific Publications, 1952).

A lessening of competition or a strengthened capacity to cope with competition—The systems approach tends to make a company's product line more unique and attractive. Carborundum's innovation in metal-removal systems is a perfect illustration of this.

Problems in Practice

Having just enumerated in glowing terms the benefits of the systems approach, realism demands that I give "equal time" to the awesome difficulties its utilization presents. There is no better evidence of this than the gulf between the elegant and sophisticated models with which recent marketing literature abounds and the actual number of situations in which those models really work. For the truth of the matter is that we are still in the foothills of this development, despite the advances of a few leaders. Let us consider some of the obstacles.

Time and Manpower Costs. First of all, the systems approach requires considerable time to implement; it took one company over a year to portray its physical distribution system in a mathematical model before it could even begin to solve its problems. RCA's Electronic Data Processing Division reports models taking three to five years to build, after which holes in the data network have to be filled and the model tested against history. Add to this the need for manpower of exceptional intellectual ability, conceptual skills, and specialized education—manpower that is in exceedingly short supply. Because the problems are complex and involve all elements of the business, one man alone cannot solve them. He lacks the knowledge, tools, and controls. And so many people must be involved. It follows that the activation of systems theory can be very costly.

Absence of "Canned" Solutions. Unlike other business functions where standardized approaches to problem solving are available, systems must be tailored to the individual situation of each firm. Even the same problem in different companies in the same industry will frequently lead to different solutions because of the impact of other inputs, unique perceptions of the environment, and varying corporate missions. These factors, too, compound time and expense demands.

"Net Uncertainties." Even after exhaustive analysis, full optimization of a total problem cannot be obtained. Some uncertainty will always remain and must be dealt with on the basis of judgment and experience.

Lack of Hard Data. In the world of engineering, the systems evolved to date have consisted all or mostly of machines. Systems engineers have been wise enough to avoid the irrationalities of man until they master control of machines. Marketing model-builders, however, have not been able to choose, for the distributor, salesman, customer, and competitor are central to marketing. We must, therefore, incorporate not only quantitative measures of the dimensions of things and processes (e.g., market potential, media outlays, and shipping rates), but also psychological measures of comprehension, attitudes, motivations, intentions, needs—yes, even psychological measures of physical behavior. What is needed is a marriage of the physical and behavioral sciences—and we are about as advanced in this blending of disciplines as astronomy was in the Middle Ages.

Consider the advertising media fields as an instance of the problem:

A number of advertising agencies have evolved linear programming or simulation techniques to assess alternate media schedules. One of the key sets of data used covers the probabilities of exposure to all or part of the audience of a TV program, magazine, or radio station. But what is exposure, and how do you measure it? What is optimum frequency of exposure, and how do you measure it? How does advertising prevail on the predispositions and perceptions of a potential customer? Is it better to judge advertising effects on the basis of exposure opportunity, "impact" (whatever that is), messages retained, message comprehension, or attitude shifts or uptrends in purchase intentions? We do not have these answers yet.

Even assuming precise knowledge of market dimensions, product performance, competitive standing, weights of marketing pressure exerted by direct selling, advertising and promotion, and so on, most marketers do not yet know, except in isolated cases, how one force will affect another. For instance, how does a company "image" affect the setting in which its salesmen work? How does a company's reputation for service affect customer buying behavior?

Nature of Marketing Men. Man is an actor on this stage in another role. A good many marketing executives, in the deepest recesses of their psyches, are artists, not analysts. For them, marketing is an art form, and, in my opinion, they really do not want it to be any other way. Their temperament is antipathetic to system, order, knowledge. They enjoy flying by the seat of their pants—though you will never get them to admit it. They revel in chaos, abhor facts, and fear research. They hate to be trammeled by written plans. And they love to spend, but are loath to assess the results of their spending.

Obviously, such men cannot be sold readily on the value and practicality of the systems approach! It takes time, experience, and many facts to influence their thinking.

Surmounting the Barriers

All is not gloom, however. The barriers described are being overcome in various ways. While operations research techniques have not yet made much headway in evolving total marketing systems and in areas where man is emotionally engaged, their accomplishments in solving inventory control problems, in sales analysis, in site selection, and in other areas have made many businessmen more sympathetic and open-minded to them.

Also, mathematical models—even the ones that do not work well yet—serve to bolster comprehension of the need for system as well as to clarify the intricacies among subsystems. Many models are in this sense learning models; they teach us how to ask more insightful questions. Moreover, they pinpoint data gaps and invite a more systematized method for reaching judgments where complete information does not exist. Because the computer abhors vague generalities, it forces managers to analyze their roles, objectives, and criteria more concretely. Paradoxically, it demands more, not less, of its human masters.

Of course, resistance to mathematical models by no means makes resistance to the systems approach necessary. There are many cases where no need may ever arise to use mathematics or computers. For the essence of the systems approach is not its techniques, but the enumeration of options and their implications. A simple checklist may be the only tool needed. I would even argue that some hard thinking in a quiet room may be enough. This being the case, the whole trend to more analysis and logic in management thinking, as reflected in business periodicals, business schools, and the practices of many companies, will work in favor of the development of the systems approach.

It is important to note at this juncture that not all marketers need the systems approach in its formal, elaborate sense. The success of some companies is rooted in other than marketing talents; their expertise may lie in finance, technology, administration, or even in personnel—as in the case of holding companies having an almost uncanny ability to hire brilliant operating managers and the self-control to leave them alone. In addition, a very simple marketing operation—for example, a company marketing one product through one distribution channel—may have no use for the systems concept.

APPLYING THE APPROACH

Not illogically, there is a system for applying the systems approach. It may be outlined as a sequence of steps:

1. *Define the problem and clarify objectives.* Care must be exercised not to accept the view of the propounder of the problem lest the analyst be defeated at the outset.

2. *Test the definition of the problem.* Expand its parameters to the limit. For example, to solve physical distribution problems it is necessary to study the marketplace (customer preferences, usage rates, market size, and so forth), as well as the production process (which plants produce which items most efficiently, what the interplant movements of raw materials are, and so forth). Delineate the extremes of these factors, their changeability, and the limitations on management's ability to work with them.

3. *Build a model.* Portray all factors graphically, indicating logical and chronological sequences—the dynamic flow of information, decisions, and events. "Closed circuits" should be used where there is information feedback or go, no-go and recycle signals (see Exhibit II).

(*continued on page 90*)

WHAT IS THE SYSTEMS APPROACH?

There seems to be agreement that the systems approach sprang to life as a semantically identifiable term sometime during World War II. It was associated with the problem of how to bomb targets deep in Germany more effectively from British bases, with the Manhattan Project, and with studies of optimum search patterns for destroyers to use in locating U-boats during the Battle of the North Atlantic.[1] Subsequently, it was utilized in the defeat of the Berlin blockade. It has reached its present culmination in the success of great military systems such as Polaris and Minuteman.

Not surprisingly, the parallels between military and marketing strategies being what they are, the definition of the systems approach propounded by The RAND Corporation for the U.S. Air Force is perfectly apt for marketers:

> An inquiry to aid a decision-maker choose a course of action by systematically investigating his proper objectives, comparing quantitatively where possible the costs, effectiveness, and risks associated with the alternative policies or strategies for achieving them, and *formulating additional alternatives if those examined are found wanting*.[2]

The systems approach is thus an orderly, "architectural" discipline for dealing with complex problems of choice under uncertainty.

Typically, in such problems, multiple and possibly conflicting objectives exist. The task of the systems analyst is to specify a closed operating network in which the components will work together so as to yield the optimum balance of economy, efficiency, and risk minimization. Put more broadly, the systems approach attempts to apply the "scientific method" to complex marketing problems studied *as a whole*; it seeks to discipline marketing.

---

[1] See Glen McDaniel, "The Meaning of The Systems Movement to the Acceleration and Direction of the American Economy," in *Proceedings of the 1964 Systems Engineering Conference* (New York, Clapp & Poliak, Inc., 1964), p. 1; see also E. S. Quade, editor, *Analysis for Military Decisions* (Santa Monica, California, The RAND Corporation, 1964), p. 6.

[2] Quade, *op. cit.,* p. 4.

But disciplining marketing is no easy matter. Marketing must be perceived as a *process* rather than as a series of isolated, discrete actions; competitors must be viewed as components of each marketer's own system. The process must also be comprehended as involving a flow and counterflow of information and behavior between marketers and customers. Some years ago, Marion Harper, Jr., now chairman of The Interpublic Group of Companies, Inc., referred to the flow of information in marketing communications as the cycle of "listen (i.e., marketing research), publish (messages, media), listen (more marketing research), revise, publish, listen. . . ." More recently, Raymond A. Bauer referred to the "transactional" nature of communications as a factor in the motivations, frames of reference, needs, and so forth of recipients of messages. The desires of the communicator alone are but part of the picture.[3]

Pushing this new awareness of the intricacies of marketing communications still further, Theodore Levitt identified the interactions between five different forces—source effect (i.e., the reputation or credibility of the sponsor of the message), sleeper effect (the declining influence of source credibility with the passage of time), message effect (the character and quality of the message), communicator effect (the impact of the transmitter —e.g., a salesman), and audience effect (the competence and responsibility of the audience).[4] Casting a still broader net are efforts to model the entire purchasing process, and perhaps the ultimate application of the systems concept is attempts to make mathematical models of the entire marketing process.

Mounting recognition of the almost countless elements involved in marketing and of the mind-boggling complexity of their interactions is a wholesome (though painful) experience. Nevertheless, I believe we must not ignore other ramifications of the systems approach which are qualitative in nature. For the world of marketing offers a vast panorama of non- or part-mathematical systems and opportunities to apply systems thinking. We must not become so bedazzled by the brouhaha of the operations research experts as to lose sight of the larger picture.

---

[3] "Communications as a Transaction," *Public Opinion Quarterly*, Spring 1963, p. 83.

[4] See Theodore Levitt, *Industrial Purchasing Behavior* (Boston, Division of Research, Harvard Business School, 1965), p. 25ff.

4. *Set concrete objectives.* For example, if a firm wants to make daily deliveries to every customer, prohibitive as the cost may be, manipulation of the model will yield one set of answers. But if the desire is to optimize service at lowest cost, then another set of answers will be needed. The more crisply and precisely targets are stated, the more specific the results will be.

5. *Develop alternative solutions.* It is crucial to be as open-minded as possible at this stage. The analyst must seek to expand the list of options rather than merely assess those given to him, then reduce the list to a smaller number of practical or relevant ones.

6. *Set up criteria or tests of relative value.*

7. *Quantify some or all of the factors or "variables."* The extent to which this is done depends, of course, on management's inclinations and the "state of the art."

8. *Manipulate the model.* That is, weigh the costs, effectiveness, profitability, and risks of each alternative.

9. *Interpret the results, and choose one or more courses of action.*

10. *Verify the results.* Do they make sense when viewed against the world as executives know it? Can their validity be tested by experiments and investigations?

Forethought and Perspective

Successful systems do not blossom overnight. From primitive beginnings, they evolve over a period of time as managers and systems specialists learn to understand each other better, and learn how to structure problems and how to push out the frontiers of the "universe" with which they are dealing. Companies must be prepared to invest time, money, and energy in making systems management feasible. This entails a solid foundation of historical data even before the conceptual framework for the system can be constructed. Accordingly, considerable time should be invested at the outset in *thinking* about the problem, its appropriate scope, options, and criteria of choice before plunging into analysis.

Not only technicians, but most of us have a way of falling in love with techniques. We hail each one that comes along—*deus ex machina*. Historically, commercial research has wallowed in several such passions (e.g., probability sampling, motivation research, and semantic scaling), and now operations research appears to be doing the same thing. Significantly, each technique has come, in the fullness of time, to take its place as one, but only one, instrument in the research tool chest. We must therefore have a broad and dispassionate perspective on the systems approach at this juncture. We must recognize that the computer does not possess greater magical properties than the abacus. It, too, is a tool, albeit a brilliant one.

Put another way, executives must continue to exercise their judgment and experience. Systems analysis is no substitute for common sense. The computer must adapt itself to their styles, personalities, and modes of problem solving. It is an aid to management, not a surrogate. Businessman may be slow, but the good ones are bright; the electronic monster, by contrast, is a speedy idiot. It demands great acuity of wit from its human managers lest they be deluged in an avalanche of useless paper. (The story is told of a sales manager who had just found out about the impressive capabilities of his company's computer and called for a detailed sales analysis of all products. The report was duly prepared and wheeled into his office on a dolly.)

Systems users must be prepared to revise continually. There are two reasons for this. First, the boundaries of systems keep changing; constraints are modified; competition makes fresh incursions; variables, being what they are, vary, and new ones crop up. Second, the analytical process is iterative. Usually, one "pass" at problem formulation and searches for solutions will not suffice, and it will be necessary to "recycle" as early hypotheses are challenged and new, more fruitful insights are stimulated by the inquiry. Moreover, it is impossible to select objectives without knowledge of their effects and costs. That knowledge can come only from analysis, and it frequently requires review and revision.

Despite all the efforts at quantification, systems analysis is still largely an art. It relies frequently on inputs based on human judgment; even when the inputs are numerical, they are determined, at least in part, by judgment. Similarly, the outputs must pass through the sieve of human interpretation. Hence, there is a positive correlation between the pay-off from a system and the managerial level involved in its design. The higher the level, the more rewarding the results.

Finally, let me observe that marketing people merit their own access to computers as well as programmers who understand marketing. Left in the hands of accountants, the timing, content, and format of output are often out of phase with marketing needs.

CONCLUSION

Nearly 800 years ago a monk wrote the following about St. Godric, a merchant later turned hermit:

> He laboured not only as a merchant but also as a shipman . . . to Denmark, Flanders, and Scotland; in which lands he found certain rare, and therefore more precious, wares, which he carried to other parts wherein he knew them to be least familiar, and coveted by the inhabitants beyond the price of gold itself, wherefore he exchanged these wares for others coveted by men of other lands. . . .[6]

How St. Godric "knew" about his markets we are not told, marketing having been in a primitive state in 1170. How some of us marketers today "know" is, in my opinion, sometimes no less mysterious than it was eight

---

[6] *Life of St. Godric*, by Reginald, a monk of Durham, c. 1170.

centuries ago. But we are trying to change that, and I will hazard the not very venturesome forecast that the era of "by guess and by gosh" marketing is drawing to a close. One evidence of this trend is marketers' intensified search for knowledge that will improve their command over their destinies. This search is being spurred on by a number of powerful developments. To describe them briefly:

The growing complexity of technology and the accelerating pace of technological innovation.

The advent of the computer, inspiring and making possible analysis of the relationships between systems components.

The intensification of competition, lent impetus by the extraordinary velocity of new product development and the tendency of diversification to thrust everybody into everybody else's business.

The preference of buyers for purchasing from as few sources as possible, thereby avoiding the problems of assembling bits and pieces themselves and achieving greater reliability, economy, and administrative convenience. (Mrs. Jones would rather buy a complete vacuum cleaner from one source than the housing from one manufacturer, the hose from another, and the attachments from still another. And industrial buyers are not much different from Mrs. Jones. They would rather buy an automated machine tool from one manufacturer than design and assemble the components themselves. Not to be overlooked, in this connection, is the tremendous influence of the U.S. government in buying systems for its military and aerospace programs.)

The further development and application of the systems approach to marketing represents, in my judgment, the leading edge in both marketing theory and practice. At the moment, we are still much closer to St. Godric than to the millenium, and the road will be rocky and tortuous. But if we are ever to convert marketing into a more scientific pursuit, this is the road we must travel. The systems concept can teach us how our businesses really behave in the marketing arena, thereby extending managerial leverage and control. It can help us to confront more intelligently the awesome complexity of marketing, to deal with the hazards and opportunities of technological change, and to cope with the intensification of competition. And in the process, the concept will help us to feed the hungry maws of our expensive computers with more satisfying fare.

D The Systems Concept in Information Management

7 Communications and Systems Concepts*

RICHARD A. JOHNSON
FREMONT E. KAST
JAMES E. ROSENZWEIG

An understanding of the role of communication is vital to the development of information-decision systems which, in turn, provide the proper flow of information among decision points in business organizations.

Communication plays an integral role in implementing the managerial functions of planning, organizing, and controlling. It is a key component which allows organizations to function as open systems, including some degree of feedback control. It involves information flow, a vital element in managerial decision making. Much attention has been focused on person-to-person, individual-to-group, group-to-individual, and group-to-group communication. In short, the term means many things to many people.

While there are many avenues which could be explored under the heading "communication," our concern in this selection will be the broad (or macro) aspects of communication in business and industry. We shall investigate communication systems (or, as we prefer, systems of information flow) in organizations. Also, we shall discuss the integration of the communication system and decision making via an information-decision system. The following topics will be covered:

Terminology
Communication Systems
Communication Problems
Communication and Organization
Communication, Organization, and Decision Making
Information-decision Systems

*Adapted from **The Theory and Management of Systems** (New York: McGraw-Hill, 1967), pp. 92–110. Used by permission of McGraw-Hill Book Company.

TERMINOLOGY

It will be helpful to examine the terminology surrounding the communication process. The purpose will not be to develop a composite definition. Rather, it will be to place the various terms in proper perspective and provide a basis for subsequent discussion. Numerous definitions (or connotations) of the term *communication* have been set forth according to the purpose of various writers or researchers. For example:

> *Communication* comes from the Latin *communis,* common. When we communicate we are trying to establish a "commonness" with someone. That is, we are trying to share information, an idea, or an attitude. . . . The essence of communication is getting the receiver and the sender "tuned" together for a particular message.[1]

An Air Force pamphlet states:

> In its broadest sense the term "communication" refers to the whole process of man's life in relation to the group. It covers a vast and varied field of human action. All the basic social institutions—numbers, language, music, graphic art, science, religion, government—have the function of creating a community of thought, feeling, or action among people. The word "communication" is therefore merely one way of designating the subject matter of education. Language, however, is the chief means of communication.[2]

Communication is intercourse by words, letters, or similar means, and it involves interchange of thoughts or opinions. It also presents the concept of communication systems, for example, telephone, telegraph, or television. Communication implies information; the terms are part of the same family.

Information

In the broadest sense information has been defined as "that which is communicated." Another common definition of information is a "patterned relationship between events." It adds to knowledge or intelligence. Information is evaluated in terms of its pertinence for decision making. Facts, numbers, and data are processed to provide meaningful information—an increment of knowledge. For example, miscellaneous accounting data provide information when arrayed in balance sheets and income statements. Ratio analysis and graphic displays of pertinent relationships provide even more meaningful information.

---

[1] Wilbur Schramm, *The Process and Effects of Mass Communication,* University of Illinois Press, Urbana, Ill., 1954, p. 3.

[2] *Communications Techniques,* Air University, USAF Extension Course Institute, 1954, p. 3.

But if the problem is one of evaluating the effectiveness of a new advertising campaign, traditional accounting data, however elaborately processed, may be meaningless. Thus what constitutes "information" depends on the problem at hand and the decision maker's frame of reference.

The numbers 422434 can be processed to read 42-24-34 and the result is probably of more interest to males than females. The phrase "74 with one out of bounds" would mean more to a golfer than a nongolfer and its impact would depend on the source. For Arnold Palmer it would depict a bad day; for any of the authors it would suggest cheating, an inordinate amount of luck, or a nine-hole course.

Information can be conveyed in many ways, both formally and informally. Periodic reports with a standard format provide formal feedback on the operating system. The "grapevine" illustrates how informal interpersonal relationships provide channels of communication.

Information is the substance of communication systems. In its various forms—electronic impulses, written or spoken words, informal or formal reports—information provides a basic ingredient for decision making. The concept of information for decision making will be developed in more detail later in this chapter.

Information Theory

Information theory, or the mathematical theory of communications, has been described as a powerful tool for studying various systems. The foundations of information theory are generally attributed to Claude Shannon.[3]

By invoking certain basic assumptions (ignoring semantics or meaning), a simplified set of mathematical relationships was developed which is useful primarily in the technical aspects of information transmission.

Information theory is used as a tool in determining the rate at which information can be transmitted under certain specified circumstances. Some of the factors affecting transmission might be the nature of the signal source, whether the signal is discrete or continuous; the nature of the channel and, in particular, its capacity for transmitting information; the nature of the noise, if any, which disturbs the transmission; and the fidelity criterion by which the adequacy of the transmission is judged.[4]

Information theory in the sense employed by Shannon, Weaver, and others has a much narrower meaning than might be connoted by the term. For example, if we assume that a *theory* (according to the dictionary definition) is a body of theorems presenting a clear, rounded, and systematic view of a subject, and further, if we assume that information is "that which

---

[3] Claude Shannon and Warren Weaver, *The Mathematical Theory of Communication,* University of Illinois Press, Urbana, Ill., 1949.

[4] Harry H. Goode and Robert E. Machol, *System Engineering,* McGraw-Hill Book Company, New York, 1957, p. 428.

is communicated," then *information theory* would necessarily be an extremely broad subject. Although a wide range of applications is claimed for information theory, most of these are in the technical aspects of transmission. Some of the subdisciplines are filtering theory, detection theory, and the analysis of signal statistics. Information theory is cited as an integral part of such areas as the theory of communication, the theory of automata, the theory of automatic control systems, the analysis of languages, and informational aspects of physics. There are fields where information theory is cited as operative and unifying, e.g., thermodynamics, statistical mechanics, photography, language, models, gambling, cryptology, pattern recognition, and computer technology.

One author divides information theory into three principal areas: communication systems, mathematical theory (a branch of probability theory and statistics), and various considerations of entropy and uncertainty applied to physical and biological systems. He goes on to say:

> The one thing information theory does not pertain to is "information"! The sense in which the term is used in the theory is quite arbitrary in that it has almost no relation to the term as popularly understood.[5]

For our purpose the concept of communication systems or information flow must be broader than that represented by information theory in its technical sense. Therefore we shall try to avoid the terminology used in information theory, or at least broaden the connotation as needed.

Information Technology

Another concept that has developed in the general area of communication is information technology. Technology is defined as applied industrial science or as systematic knowledge of the industrial arts. When applied to the broad connotation of information—that which is communicated—information technology would seem to cover a wide spectrum. An even broader connotation for this phrase is indicated by several authors. For example, Whisler and Shultz state:

> Within the last decade we have seen rapid and extensive progress in the application of quantitative techniques to the analysis of management problems. Three areas of activity are involved: (1) the use of mathematical and statistical methods, with or without the aid of electronic computers; (2) the use of computers for mass integrated data processing; and (3) the direct application of computers to decision-making through simulation techniques. These areas are clearly interdependent, although the nature and

---

[5] Robert C. Hopkins, "Possible Applications of Information Theory to Management Control," *IRE Transactions on Engineering Management,* March, 1961, p. 41.

the degree of interdependence are still undergoing exploration. We will lump these areas together here under the heading "information technology."[6]

Without question, problems of information flow or communication are of vital concern in each of these three areas. If management decision making is viewed as the focal point in the application of quantitative techniques of analysis, then information flow becomes an integral part of the total system. However, many additional factors are involved in the question of management decision making; therefore the use of the phrase "information technology" to encompass the entire field is misleading.

Systems of Information Flow

Information flow is one of the several integral systems in a business or industrial organization. And the systems concept is the over-all framework within which communication or information flow logically fits. Furthermore, we visualize the systems concept as a vital aspect of the entire managerial process, including planning, organizing, and controlling. Communication systems, or systems of information flow, will be presented as the vehicle through which the key management functions can be integrated and administered.

COMMUNICATIONS SYSTEMS

In their early writings on information theory Shannon and Weaver presented a basic symbolic representation of a communication system as shown in Figure 1. This basic model has been adapted by other writers since that time by changing some of the terminology or by making the model more elaborate. In all cases there is an information source which provides the raw material for a message which is to be transmitted to a destination. The general model includes a transmitter and a receiver, with the receiver connected directly to the destination. Also involved is the concept of a noise source which theoretically interferes (to some degree) with information flow between the transmitter and receiver. With a larger system, noise or interference obviously could come at numerous junctures within the subsystems. Regardless of the size or sophistication of the system, communication always requires three basic elements—the source, the message, and the destination. Noise transmission and reception are elements which also can be considered in the basic model. Yet these items can take on so many forms that it is useful to think of an even more abstract model of source, message, and destination. Some writers substitute the words *encoder* and *decoder* for *transmitter* and *receiver* in order to depict a more general process.

---

[6] George P. Shultz and Thomas L. Whisler (eds.), *Management Organization and the Computer*, The Free Press of Glencoe, New York, 1960, p. 3.

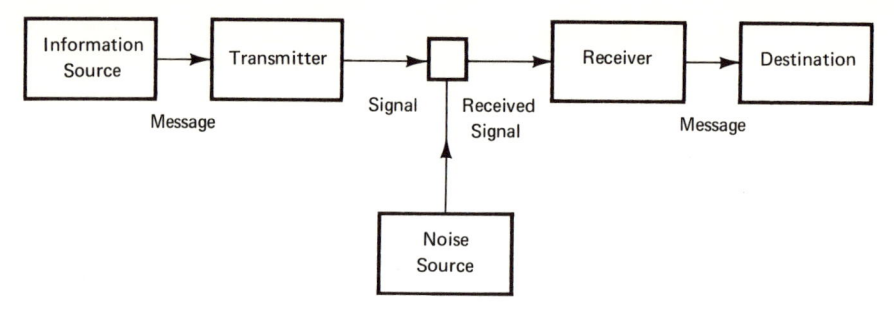

```
Information                                          
 Source    →  Transmitter  →  □  →    Receiver   →  Destination
                           Signal  Received
            Message                Signal          Message
                              ↑
                            Noise
                            Source
```

Source: Claude E. Shannon and Warren Weaver,
The Mathematical Theory of Communication,
University of Illinois Press, Urbana, Ill., 1949, p. 98.

Figure 1. **Symbolic Representation of a Communication System**

Examples of communication systems can be abstracted in terms of the model shown in Figure 1. The usefulness of such an approach is explained by Schramm as follows:

> Now it is perfectly possible by looking at those diagrams to predict how such a system will work. For one thing, such a system can be no stronger than its weakest link. In engineering terms, there may be filtering or distortion at any stage. In human terms, if the source does not have adequate or clear information; if the message is not encoded fully, accurately, effectively in transmittable signs; if these are not transmitted fast enough and accurately enough, despite interference and competition, to the desired receiver; if the message is not decoded in a pattern that corresponds to the encoding; and finally, if the destination is unable to handle the decoded message so as to produce the desired response—then, obviously, the system is working at less than top efficiency. When we realize that *all* these steps must be accomplished with relatively high efficiency if any communication is to be successful, the everyday act of explaining something to a stranger or writing a letter, seems a minor miracle.[7]

By checking day-to-day experiences in either face-to-face or organizational communication it is easy to find instances where *all* the steps indicated above are not in effect, and hence where a communication system is not working optimally. Visualizing the complexities involved in modern organizations, ideal conditions cannot be expected for all communication processes. However, such conditions can provide goals which can be used as a frame of reference in designing and implementing systems of information flow.

[7] Schramm, *op. cit.,* pp. 4–5.

Communication Apparatus

Three types of communication have been set forth which involve human beings: (1) intrapersonal, (2) interpersonal, and (3) mass communication. In addition, there are examples of man-machine or even machine-machine communication systems. Ruesch and Bateson describe the communication apparatus of man as follows:

> (a) His sense organs, the receivers
> (b) His effector organs, the senders
> (c) His communication center, the place or origin and destination of all messages
> (d) The remaining parts of the body, the shelter of the communication machinery [8]

This model can be integrated with the general symbolic representation of a communication system by physically locating information source and destination in contiguous positions. Furthermore, phase d of the above listing could be broadened to include organizations and institutions of varying size and complexity, or it could involve an entire society in the case of mass communication. Thus the various types of communication can be depicted by the basic model set forth above.

Man uses his communication system:

> (a) To receive and transmit messages and retain information
> (b) To perform operations with the existing information for the purpose of deriving new conclusions which were not directly perceived and for reconstructing past and anticipating future events
> (c) To initiate and modify physiological processes within his body
> (d) To influence and direct other people and external events.[9]

Human beings are involved in communication systems of various sizes and degrees of complexity. They are involved in their intrapersonal communication system, which is a part of their own physiological and mental processes. They are involved in interpersonal systems when communicating to one or more people. In the area of mass communication the individual can participate to varying degrees, depending on the particular issues and his involvement.

The same hierarchy can be established for one machine communicating with itself in the sense of automation or feedback control; a machine controlling a group of machines (numerical-control applications); or more complex man-machine systems of communication and control. In all cases,

---

[8] Jurgen Ruesch and Gregory Bateson, *Communication,* W. W. Norton & Co., New York, 1951, pp. 16–17.

[9] *Ibid.,* pp. 17–18.

the concept of systems being developed as over-all frameworks for subsystems can apply. All the various levels and types of communication indicated can be analyzed or developed in their own context, and yet each must be considered in terms of its relationship to a whole. Thus over-all systems concepts should be recognized when analyzing communication in general, and the same principles apply when considering detailed aspects of systems or subsystems.

COMMUNICATION PROBLEMS

Breakdowns in interpersonal relationships and organizational behavior often are attributed to faulty communication. While separation of specific causal factors is difficult to practice, it is useful to categorize problems for analysis. For example, Shannon and Weaver identfy three levels of communication problems:

> Level A. How accurately can the symbols of communication be transmitted? (The technical problem.)
> Level B. How precisely do the transmitted symbols convey the desired meaning? (The semantic problem.)
> Level C. How effectively does the perceived meaning effect the conduct in the desired way? (The effectiveness problem.)[10]

Guetzkow develops two foci of attention, "communications as message *flows* and communications as message *contents*."[11] These two schemata can be integrated if "message flows" refers to technical and structural problems of accurate transmission and if "message contents" refers to semantic problems. The effectiveness of communications depends on performance in both categories.

The narrow applicability of information theory (to technical aspects of transmission) was mentioned previously in the discussion of terminology. Progress in technology makes it feasible to consider problems at other levels. Semantics and effectiveness certainly would be affected if technical aspects could not be solved. Communication systems should consider the mechanical and structural aspects of accurately transmitting symbols. In human interpersonal relationships, however, other communications problems seem paramount.

The question of semantics in communication is one which has received considerable attention from researchers and writers,[12] since variation in word connotation can alter significantly the meaning of a message.

In communication systems the goal is *understanding*—getting the sender and receiver "tuned" together for a particular message. Although repetition

---

[10] Shannon and Weaver, *op. cit.*, p. 96.

[11] Harold Guetzkow, "Communication in Organizations," in James G. March (ed.), *Handbook of Organizations,* Rand McNally & Co., Chicago, 1965, p. 534.

[12] S. I. Hayakawa, *Language in Thought and Action,* Harcourt, Brace & Co., Inc., New York, 1949.

(redundancy) can be helpful, there is no direct correlation between the amount of communication or information transmission and the degree of understanding. Several basic problems are apparent according to Guetzkow.

> When the symbols fail to carry the full contents of the messages, their semantic properties are transformed as they are handled within a communication flow—either by omission of aspects of the contents, or by the introduction of distortions.[13]

Some of the sender's meaning is lost in the process of encoding and transmitting a message. A memo may not reflect accurately the manager's feeling about a situation. Direct conversation with his staff may help clarify the issue, but even in this case his tone of voice or facial expression can alter the message significantly. The use of graphic display adds another dimension—"a picture is worth a thousand words."

Another basic problem in achieving understanding in communication systems is that of decoding. Even if a message were coded and transmitted accurately, it is unlikely that it would be decoded in the same way by everyone receiving it. People read, see, and hear what they want to read, see, and hear. Memos, statistics, and diagrams are interpreted in terms of value systems which are as unique to individuals as fingerprints. A person's perception or "image" of the environment depends on his sum total of past experience; messages are distorted as receivers "read in" meanings not intended by the sender. A report from headquarters to several branches might be interpreted several ways with each receiver quite satisfied that he "got *the* message." Zalkind and Costello summarize their findings on the problem of managerial perception as follows:

> Without vigilance to perceive accurately and to minimize as far as possible the subjective approach in perceiving others, effective administration is handicapped. . . . Research would not support the conclusion that perceptual distortions will not occur simply because the administrator says he will try to be objective. The administrator or manager will have to work hard to avoid seeing only what he mants to see and to guard against fitting everything into what he is set to see.[14]

Understanding is facilitated if there are means and time for feedback and verification. If the issue can be "talked out" there is a chance that people can emphasize and understand. However, time pressure works against this process. If information flows on complex issues must be accelerated, the probability of complete understanding decreases. Distance and medium of communication also affect the process significantly.

---

[13] Guetzkow, *op. cit.*, p. 551.

[14] Sheldon S. Zalkind and Timothy W. Costello, "Perception: Some Recent Research and Implications for Administration," *Administrative Science Quarterly*, September, 1962, p. 235.

Understanding on the part of organization members is critical in implementing plans appropriately, and it is central to the control function as well. For example, the central theme in the whole field of cybernetics is that of communication and control.

> In giving the definition of Cybernetics in the original book, I class communication and control together. Why did I do this? When I communicate with another person, I impart a message to him, and when he communicates back with me he returns a related message which contains information primarily accessible to him and not to me. When I control the actions of another person, I communicate a message to him, and although this message is in the imperative mood, the technique of communication does not differ from that of a message of fact. Furthermore, if my control is to be effective I must take cognizance of any messages from him which may indicate that the order is understood and has been obeyed.[15]

In this sense, unless there is effective control the communication process has not been complete.

While several large problem areas in the general theory of communication systems are evident, communication is a vital and necessary element in everyday existence. We are concerned primarily with its role in group activity; therefore, let us consider the relationship between communication systems and organizations.

Communication and Organization

Communication has been receiving more and more attention in organizational contexts. Management has long been concerned with "getting its message across" to the workers, that is, communicating downward throughout the organization. In terms of the problem areas cited previously, management often is concerned with its lack of effectiveness in the communication process and may not be entirely familiar with the semantic problems involved. In other cases, administrators are concerned with upward communications, that is, soliciting the attitudes and feelings of the lower echelons and encouraging their transmission upward through the hierarchical structure. In addition, management is interested in communicating its message outward to other institutions in the form of public-relations efforts directed at customers, stockholders, and the general public. Emphasis is being focused on "tuning" all parts of the system to the same frequency.

Organization structure is definitely tied to communication systems. The relationship is apparent when formal structures, channels, and media are involved; for informal alignments and irregular information flow the relationship is not as evident. Communication does not necessarily follow stated

---

[15] Norbert Wiener, *The Human Use of Human Beings,* Houghton Mifflin Company, Boston, 1954, p. 16.

organizational arrangements, or vice versa. Numerous overlaps and gaps are evident in most organizations, phenomena which cause problems. Deutsch explains these relationships in the following manner:

> Communication and control are the decisive processes in organizations. Communication is what makes organizations cohere; control is what regulates their behavior. If we can map the pathways by which communication is communicated between different parts of an organization and by which it is applied to the behavior of the organization in relation to the outside world, we will have gone far toward understanding that organization. . . .
>
> Generally speaking, the communications approach suggests lines of attack in the study of organizations. First, instead of concentrating on the ostensible purpose of the organization, it will concentrate on two questions: how are the formal and informal communication channels of the organization connected, and how are they maintained?[16]

These suggestions for research indicate that organization structures might follow the development of communication systems rather than vice versa. For many organizations, communication systems have been designed to follow organizational lines without recognition of the fact that this may not provide for optimal flows of information for decision making. This concept of organizing and communicating for decision making will be explored in more detail in the next section.

Some of the problems in communication systems for decision making have resulted from changes in organizational relationships in recent years. Companies have been faced with dynamic world conditions, rapidly changing technology, changing markets, and other similar phenomena which have required adaptation on their part. Such have been made, but without recognition, in many cases, of the impact of the organizational changes on communication systems. Thus much information that was appropriate under older arrangements now has become obsolete. Furthermore, additional types of information are urgently needed in order to plan and control current operations. According to Daniel:

> Unfortunately, management often loses sight of the seemingly obvious and simple relationship between organization structure and information needs. Companies very seldom follow up on reorganizations with penetrating reappraisals of their information systems, and managers given new responsibilities and decision-making authority often do not receive all the information they require.[17]

---

[16] Karl W. Deutsch, "On Communication Models in the Social Sciences," *Public Opinion Quarterly,* Fall, 1952, pp. 367–368.

[17] D. Ronald Daniel, "Management Information Crisis," *Harvard Business Review,* September–October, 1961, pp. 112–113.

Granting that organization structure and communication systems are inextricably intertwined, there remains the problem of which comes first. Although this problem does not seem important from the standpoint of research or analysis, it becomes increasingly significant as one attempts to design either an organization or a communication system. This question will be considered in more detail in Chapter 13, Systems Design* (implementing the systems concept). At this point, however, it will be helpful to bring the subject of decision making into the discussion.

COMMUNICATION, ORGANIZATION, AND DECISION MAKING

In this section several points of view will be presented concerning the interrelationships of these three topics. There are scholars and writers who view organization as the fundamental element for consideration; others who look upon decision making as the key activity to analyze; and still others who would point to the communication system as the underlying framework. We hold no brief for any particular point of view; rather, we are interested in integrating the various ideas by means of the concept of information-decision systems.

Pfiffner and Sherwood describe the relationship between decision making and communication systems as follows:

> The relationship between the communications system and decision-making is extremely important. If decision-making and communication processes are not identical, they are so interdependent they become inseparable in practice. As a result all studies of communication inevitably involve decision-making.[18]

As indicated in Chapter 3,* there have been several relatively distinct approaches to the study of organizations: (1) the traditional view, characterized by emphasis on some logical arrangement for dividing the work, hierarchical structure, and specialization; (2) the human relations view, developing the concept of cooperative relationships, participation, and informal organization; (3) the professional view, stressing the role of knowledge, creativity, and innovation; (4) the decision-making view, focusing on the study of an organization as a decision-making units; and (5) the systems view, the integration of subsystems into an operational whole. The decision-making system (or organization) includes information, objectives, strategies, alternatives, probabilities, and consequences. The function of the organization is to facilitate the flow of information and the making of appropriate decisions. In this view, the communication system appears paramount, with organization structured around it as a frame of reference. In

---

* Chapters 3 and 13 are not included in this book—Editors.

[18] John M. Pfiffner and Frank P. Sherwood, *Administrative Organization,* Prentice-Hall, Inc., Englewood Cliffs, N. J., 1960, p. 308.

turn, the communication system is considered primarily as a supplier of information for decisions. More and more attention has been devoted to organizations as decision-making units. In a pioneering work in this area Simon states:

> The anatomy of the organization is to be found in the distribution and allocation of decision-making functions. The physiology of the organization is to be found in the processes whereby the organization influences the decisions of each of its members—supplying these decisions with their premises.[19]

If organizations are complex networks of decision processes, there must be decision points throughout, ranging from individuals at the lowest operating levels to policy-making groups at the top. The primary aspect of the physiology of the organization is the communication system, which supplies premises for decisions at various points in the organization; that is, each decision point can be considered an information-processing unit with input, processing, and output. Such an arrangement fits the formal, symbolic representation of the communication system shown in Figure 1. Thus the decision process can be considered an extension of the communication process; it can be a relatively simple intrapersonal communication or decision system or range through interpersonal communication or decision systems of varying size and complexity. This connection between decisions and communications is stressed by Dorsey as follows:

> Thus decision may be conceived of as a communication process, or a series of interrelated communication events. A decision occurs upon the receipt of some kind of communication, it consists of a complicated process of combining communications from various sources, and it results in the transmission of further communication.[20]

This analogy to the intrapersonal communication or decision process can be expanded to the interpersonal decision-making situation.

A manager decides issues based on the current information received in conjunction with previously developed strategies, procedures, or rules. Depending on the level in the organization and/or the type of decision (programmed or unprogrammed), the decision maker has several alternatives. If the matter is fairly commonplace and routine, he can dismiss it quickly, particularly if there are rules or procedures covering the situation. If the matter at issue is more complex, more of an unprogrammed nature, the decision maker may require additional inputs and may request some consultation on the part of subordinates, superiors, or peers. In any case, the

---

[19] Herbert A. Simon, *Administrative Behavior,* The Macmillan Company, New York, 1959, p. 220.
[20] John T. Dorsey, Jr., "A Communication Model for Administration," *Administrative Science Quarterly,* December, 1957, p. 309.

communication process is obviously important and the flow of proper information to the decision points throughout the organization appears vital. If administration or management were thought of primarily as decision making and if the decision process were considered as essentially a communication process, including a network of communication systems, then administration or management could be viewed as a communication process. According to Dorsey:

> Structurally, administration can be viewed as a configuration of communication patterns relating individuals and collectivities of varying sizes, shapes, and degree of cohesion and stability. Dynamically, administration appears as a patterned swirl and flow of communications, many of them channeled through transactional "circuits" between persons and persons, persons and groups, and groups and other groups.[21]

For our purposes, concepts of communication patterns and flows are particularly important. The patterns relate communication to organization, and the flow concept relates to decision making. Thus the several concepts —communications, organization, and decision making—are inexorably interwoven.

INFORMATION-DECISION SYSTEMS

The concept of information flow is central to the development of systems concepts and communication. Since a system by definition requires interrelationship among parts to constitute a composite whole, a system of information flow would necessarily provide information throughout various subsystems and would entail some feedback mechanism in order to represent a closed-loop system.

A simplified system is represented by Figure 2, a skeletal model of an organization showing the basic flow of information necessary for objective accomplishment. Management considers internal capabilities in light of environmental information in the process of establishing goals and objectives. Premises with regard to governmental relations, political conditions, the competitive situation, customer needs and desires, and many other factors, evolve over a period of time and form a frame of reference for management plans. Plans for repetitive and nonrepetitive activities are transmitted to the operating system and to storage in the control system for later comparison with operating results. Detailed orders, instructions, and specifications flow to the operating system.

Feedback is obtained on the output of the system in terms of factors such as quality, quantity, and cost. The operating system is monitored in order to maintain process control and input inspection provides feedback at the earliest stage in the operating system. Information flow is an integral

[21] *Ibid.*, p. 310.

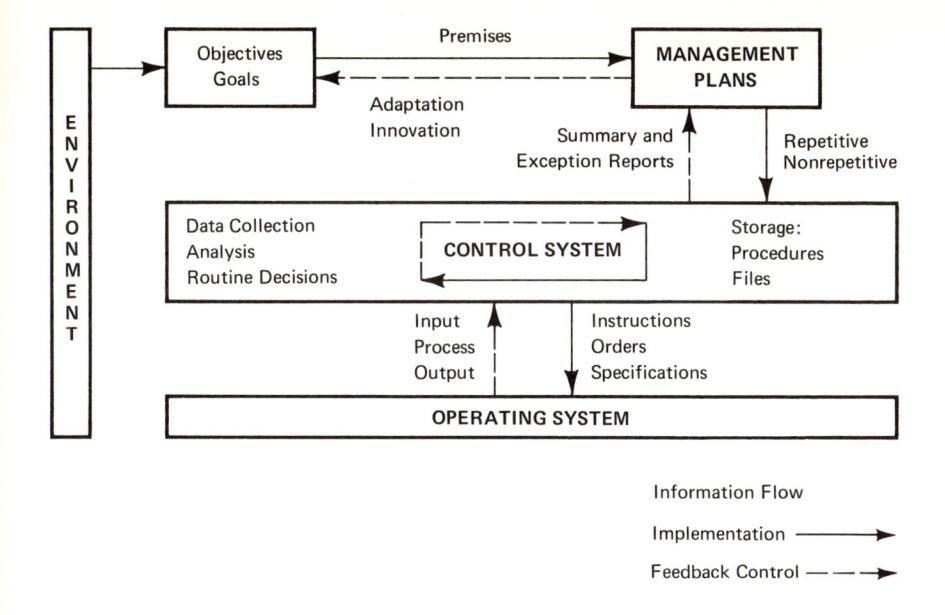

Figure 2. **Information Flows in a Business Organization**

part of the control system because it provides the means of comparing results with plans. Feedback data from various phases of the operating system are collected and analyzed. The analysis consists in processing data, developing information, and comparing the results with plans. Decisions also are made within the control system itself because routine adjustments can be preprogrammed in the set of procedures or instructions. Within the control system itself there is a flow of information to implement changes to the program based on feedback from the operating system. Thus, procedures are changed and files updated simultaneously with routine decision making and adjustments to the operating system.

Summary and exception reports are generated by the control system and become a part of higher level control in terms of adaptation or innovation of goals and objectives. Subsequent planning activity reflects such feedback and the entire process is repeated. Over time, an organization "learns" through the process of planning, implementation, and feedback.[22] Approaches to decision making and the propensity to select certain ends and means change as organizational value systems evolve. This basic or simplified model of information flow can be applied to any organization; it shows the necessary flow of information regardless of the sophistication of the machinery and equipment involved.

The term *information-decision system* is used to emphasize the fact that information developed should be requested in light of the decisions to be

---

[22] Richard M. Cyert and James G. March, *A Behavioral Theory of the Firm*, Prentice-Hall, Inc., Englewood Cliffs, N. J., 1963, p. 123.

made throughout the organization. Thus an information-decision system should be designed as a communication process relating the necessary inputs to the stored information and the desired decisional outputs. It is likely that decisions at a given stage in the organization represent output from one communication process and information for a subsequent decision at the same level, a lower level, or a higher level. The over-all information flow must be regarded as a system with many interdependent elements and subsystems.

Information-decision systems should be considered in conjunction with the fundamental managerial functions: planning, organizing, and controlling. If organization is to implement planning and control, if organization is tied to communication, and if communication is represented by an information-decision system, then the key to success in planning and controlling any operation lies in the information-decision system. Its importance cannot be overemphasized.

In his discussion of the management information crisis caused by too rapid organizational change, Daniel states:

> The key to the development of a dynamic and usable system of management information is to move beyond the limits of classical accounting reports and to conceive of information as it relates to two vital elements of the management process—planning and control. . . . We hear more and more these days about new techniques for inventory cost, and other types of control, but information systems for business planning still represent a relatively unexplored horizon.[23]

He goes on to describe several kinds of information required for planning: environmental information, competitive information, and internal information. While most companies have some systematic approach to development of internal information for planning purposes, few have formal systems for developing information concerning competitors' plans, programs, and past performance. Nor do they deal in a systematitc fashion with the social, political, and economic environment of the industry or industries within which they operate. Formal recognition of the decisions which must be made at various points and of the type of information required to do an optimal job in that decision process should point the way toward development of information flows which will be helpful.

Differences in the type of information needed for planning, on the one hand, and control, on the other, should be recognized. The contrast can be seen in terms of the following attributes of information:

> 1. *Coverage*—good planning information is not compartmentalized by functions. Indeed, it seeks to transcend the divisions that

[23] Daniel, *op. cit.,* p. 113.

exist in a company and to provide the basis on which *integrated* plans can be made. In contrast, control information hews closely to organizational lines so that it can be used to measure performance and help in holding specific managers more accountable.

2. *Length of time*—planning information covers fairly long periods of time—months and years rather than days and weeks—and deals with trends. Thus, although it should be regularly prepared, it is not developed as frequently as control information.

3. *Degree of detail*—excessive detail is the quicksand of intelligent planning. Unlike control, where precision and minute care do have a place, planning (and particularly long-range planning) focuses on the major outlines of the situation ahead.

4. *Orientation*—planning information should provide insights into the future. Control information shows past results and the reasons for them.[24]

This emphasis on the differences between information appropriate for planning purposes and that appropriate for control purposes indicates the importance of carefully designing information-decision systems. Blind adherence to organizational patterns for the flow of information often will hamper the development of an optimal system. Particularly where there have been organizational adjustments and there is a mixture of functional organization and program or product organization, the development of an information-decision system becomes critical. Key decision points must be identified and the concept of flows of material and information must be kept paramount when designing over-all systems of information flow. In such systems, the planning function can be carried out with the necessary information and premises, the organization can be adjusted to reflect the decision-making activities involved, and control information can be readily developed along appropriate lines.

SUMMARY

Throughout history the transmission of information has been a key to progress. Efficient communication is important in all fields of human endeavor. However, as society has become more complex, as technology has increased at an accelerating rate, and in spite of improvements in communication media, it is becoming more and more difficult to communicate effectively. The growth of organizations and increased specialization and functionalization have developed barriers to communication in many spheres of activity. Scientists and researchers find it more and more difficult to communicate on a broad scope. Managers of business and industrial organizations find that communication and understanding are increasing problems in their day-to-day operations.

On the other hand, technical breakthroughs in data-processing equipment have provided an opportunity for development of integrated systems

[24] *Ibid.*, pp. 117–118.

of information flow. In spite of this opportunity, however, few organizations have really capitalized on it. In order to do so, management must be cognizant of the role of communication in the primary managerial activities: planning, organizing, and controlling.

Information-decision systems can be developed which provide the proper flow of information among decision points in the organization. The organization then can be structured around such systems of information flow. Both formal and informal communication must be recognized. Management might well analyze informal communication patterns in some detail because the information-decision system may follow "natural" patterns or systems, even though they are not recognized in the formal organization structure. Once the over-all information-decision system has been established, the functions of planning and control are greatly facilitated.

Systems concepts are vital to the establishment of communication or information flow. Over-all systems are comprised of subsystems of communication processes; these are represented as flows of information through a decision process. A hierarchy of such processes can be established and fitted to the framework of an integrated, information-decision system.

8 Information Flows and the Coordination of Business Functions*

DAVID BENDEL HERTZ

The author identifies eight major decision areas in a firm which have significant revenue and cost effects. Unless these decisions are coordinated, and future consequences estimated, the firms may fail. Coordination of the streams of information that flow between functional centers will assist management in the integration of the decisions.

Even in the smallest of businesses, the interrelationship of functional activities must be recognized if the business is to survive and prosper. In a small business, a single executive makes the day-to-day decisions and develops the longer range ideas and plans which will spell the success or failure of the business over the years. In doing so, he can often

---

*From Wroe Alderson and Stanley J. Shapiro (eds.), **Marketing And The Computer** (Englewood Cliffs: Prentice-Hall, Inc., 1963), pp. 80–95. Used by permission of Prentice-Hall, Inc.

keep in mind such factors as production schedules, customer requirements, prices, legal problems, banking relationships, inventories, and competitive activity. The possibility of maintaining a clear view of all these factors rapidly diminishes with increasing size. Indeed, it is sometimes surprising that business ventures have sufficient stamina to withstand the difficulties which automatically stem from lack of coordination, conflicting policies, and the pursuit of contradictory goals by different functional areas. Often the sales department places maximum emphasis upon price and ability to deliver on demand in its selling efforts, while the production activity is stressing quality and custom performance. Conversely, the sales department stresses production according to customer needs, while manufacturing is developing mass production machinery, long production runs and high inventory. Such conflicts are an obvious result of differing *short run* objectives within the various functional areas of a business. In the small business, the top executive often combines many of the functions in his own person. He keeps within his own mind the information storage, the estimates of joint consequences, and the formulas for compromise which make coordinated decisions possible. If his information, estimates or formulas are faulty, then the probability that his business will be a success is correspondingly reduced.

What holds for the small business man is true with even more force for the large business—with one mitigating circumstance. The large business often has a greater lease on life through the possession of greater resources and can live through more mistakes of miscoordination than can the small. In a sense, the consequences of such mistakes take longer to manifest themselves. On the other hand, if enough of them are made—whether in information storage and transmission, in the estimating of the consequences of decisions, or in the formulas for compromise—the large business will be as badly off as the small, and with much more unfortunate effects upon the whole economic community.

No one would deny that marketing decisions are part of the crucial apparatus of running a successful business. Prices, number and kind of products, customer services, advertising and promotion—decisions in each of these areas will affect the long term market position and health of the business. The sales and marketing executives see themselves primarily as facing the customer directly and as determining the share of market and volume of business done in each product through the stimulation of customer demand. It should also be clear that they are helping to determine production schedules, inventories, cash in the bank *and* profits. In fact, subtle and unrecognized as the influence may be, these other areas have influence on the share of market the sales executives are able to obtain, on the prices they set, and on the profit the company earns. In dealing with marketing decisions, one courts disaster if he ignores requirements of coordination with other functions. Modern methods of analysis and the advent of computers have made the competitive potential and the competitive requirement of coordination necessary for long run survival.

COST AND REVENUES—THE CONSEQUENCES OF DECISION MAKING

The development of information in a form which will allow for estimating future consequences of decisions is crucial to modern management. What is the character of these estimates? As far as the executive is concerned, they must tell him what costs he may expect to incur and what revenues he may expect to receive as a result of the particular decision. In essence, he would like to know the immediate and long term effect on profits of a decision to establish a certain price, to hire a certain number of new salesmen, to open a new warehouse, to drop a line of products, and so on. It is not enough, however, to know only the narrow consequences of the decision. The lowering of the price on product A may be estimated to yield a given increase in sales volume for A along with a certain amount of additional profits on that product. If there are other related products involved, it will also be necessary (for "good" decision making) to know what will be the effect of the new price on *their* sales and profits. One must know whether additional inventories of A will have to be carried, the cost consequences thereof, and the effect of the additional demand for A on the production schedules for other products.

As far as decision making is concerned, the business man keeps records of past activities in order to improve the accuracy with which he can estimate the future consequences of his actions. Therefore, the way in which he has collected and maintained information in the past will influence his ability to make "good" decisions in the future. One of the most significant results of the installation of analytical methods and computers may be the effects on data processing for decision making. The information storage, handling, and transmittal systems within an organization are completely revamped, and the computer automatically changes the way decisions *can* be made. In contrast, if the *proper* information required for "good" decision making is already being collected, stored, and transmitted to the right people, the decision making process will be subject to little or no instantaneous improvement.

As a rule, the business man is engaged in a series of relatively continuous decision making processes. Year in and year out, he will ordinarily make decisions on a regular and periodic basis about inventories. He will also decide on the size of the labor force, on specific production schedules, on advertising budgets, on promotions and many other matters. From time to time, he will make what may be called "one-shot" decisions. Such decisions might be to build a new plant, to acquire another business, to add a product line, to change the organization structure, or to liquidate the business. Although there is no hard and fast rule in assigning decisions to either the continuous or the sporadic category, most businesses usually have to make both kinds of decisions. Important differences exist in the processes involved in determining the alternatives, in estimating the long run consequences, and in working out what appears to be the best course of action in the two cases.

In the first instance, where the decisions are continuous and are made on a regular basis, emphasis must be placed on the collection, storage and analysis of past information to give a clue as to the consequences of changing the decision process. When a decision to be made is of a type which has not been made in the past and which is not likely to be made again for some time in the future (for example, the building of the first central warehousing facility for a business operation), the consequences of various specific decisions can be estimated in detail but nothing is known for sure of the consequences of employing alternate methods of making such decisions. So-called "simulation" techniques have been devised to get around the difficulty of few decisions and long time periods for viewing their consequences. In essence, these kinds of decisions change the basic design characteristics of the business. The continuous decisions, on the other hand, adjust the operating characteristics for greater or lesser efficiency on a day to day, week to week, or month to month basis.

Thus, we must subject the *methods* whereby we make decisions to analysis and scrutiny. In fact, one of the greatest advantages associated with approaches making use of the newly available computational tools is their capability for using changes in methodology and examining quickly the consequences of such changes. In the installation of an inventory control system, it is possible to examine the changed level of inventory, the relative change in customer service, and the number of production orders or purchase orders placed within comparatively short periods of time after a new decision process is first used. Note that it is not the decisions themselves which are critical to the future health of the business, but rather the decision making methods. Perhaps the best analogy to use is that of a poker game. The rules of poker are relatively simple, and virtually anyone can play. However, even following the rules, one can make decisions as to betting, taking cards, etc. in many different ways. One player may make all his decisions strictly on the basis of hunch without any knowledge of the relationship of one kind of hand to another in terms of the odds on getting such a hand. Another player may know the odds involved and use them in addition to his psychological judgments in making decisions. Although the first player might from time to time be lucky and win in some games, it appears obvious that a superior decision making process on the part of the second player would usually win out. The same thing holds true in the competitive business world. Each of the actions taken by business will have some smaller or larger effect on the outside world and will affect virtually all the internal activities as well. If we know enough about these effects, we can establish the best decision making processes to give us the best chance of "winning" (although there is no guarantee that we would achieve the "optimum" results).

This type of knowledge has another very important result. When decisions of the one-shot variety are made, as noted previously, they involve changing the design characteristics of the business operation. In any process, it is much more likely that one will be able to estimate the consequences of design changes if one knows the present operating characteristics in the greatest possible detail. It is exactly this kind of knowledge that provides for the best simulation of future activities under the new procedures. Therefore, the internal application of continuous improved decision making methods will have far reaching results with respect to the ability to make better long run, one-shot decisions.

No matter how large, bureaucratic, or impersonal an organization becomes, the decisions described above hinge upon and are reflected in the behavior of individuals. This is plainly seen in the small business where an executive maintains intimate contact with all the functions the business fulfills. Although the location of decision making authority in the large business is not as clear, the need for coordination of the behavior of those working in different functional areas becomes even clearer. Also, the method of coordination establishes the pattern for future decision making and problem solving in the organization.

The best way to assure gradual deterioration of competitive posture and erosion of the ability to meet the requirements of the future is to attempt to maintain the same behavioral attitude towards problems and toward decision making as has existed in the past. It is only with the introduction of new methods and new ways of facing the unknown future that the business can be assured of decision making strength. The introduction of analytical and quantitative methodology, the use of computers, and the development of the necessary interconnections between the functional operations of a business enables us to meet today's problems and today's competition. More important, it prepares the foundations for problem solving in the longer range future. A number of streams of information which flow between functional centers must be carefully coordinated if the value of these devices is to be fully realized.

COORDINATION—MAJOR INFORMATION FLOWS

Long Range Forecasting

There is a thread of information which runs throughout a business, generally from the top down, which concerns the views of the business's decision makers concerning a long range future. There is no way to avoid having such an attitude and most of the "single shot" decisions are made in terms of some sort of a long range forecast. This forecast may well be simply that the businessman has no way of foretelling what will happen, and, therefore, assumes he knows absolutely nothing about the long range future. This is certainly a valid approach and will lead to very specific consequences in decision making. Another approach often used is to assume that the long range future will be very much like the present or the immediate past. Or, if trends are involved, one may assume that the trends will continue as they have for some specific past period. All of these are perfectly legitimate ways of laying out the future so as to be able to make

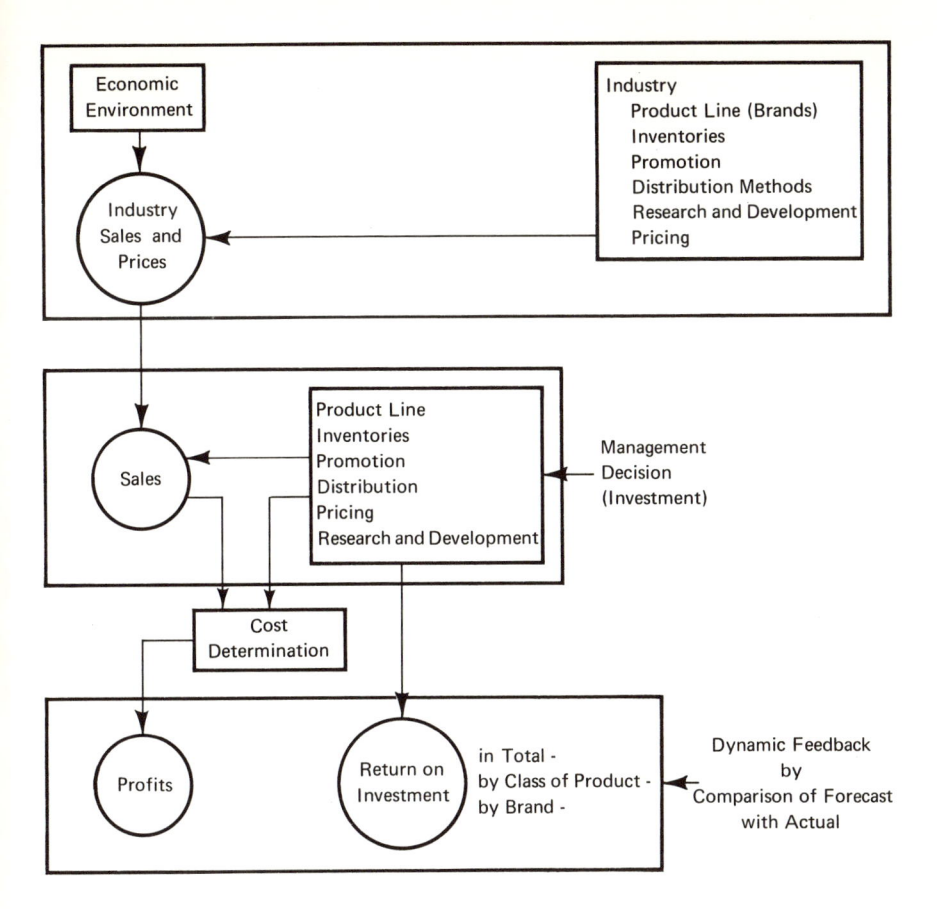

Figure 1. **Coordination of Business Functions.**

decisions today. The important thing to recognize in terms of the institution of new devices and new methods of decision making in a business is that each functional area must periodically make decisions on the basis of a long term view. If one department of a business makes decisions on the assumption that the long term future is a blank, and another department assumes that the future will be precisely like the present, the resulting decisions are likely to conflict and perhaps even to nullify each other as far as profitable results are concerned. The information which the business uses in forecasting the long range future must be coordinated and the specific forecasts of the outlook dovetailed sufficiently so that joint effective decision making is possible.

Active long range forecasting is certainly a requirement of modern competitive business. In this connection, one must not be misled by the term "forecasting." Forecasts which are a single estimate of some future state of economic affairs are almost certain to be incorrect. If such an estimate turns out to be correct, this is probably a coincidence. There are several reasons why forecasts will inevitably be incorrect. These include the inherent errors in the data which are used to make them up and, perhaps more importantly, the fact that they are estimates of conditions which exist in an "organized complex" of activities in which one action brings an (unknown) counteraction. These socio-economic systems of organized complexity have stability and predictability in many senses, but not in the same way that physical systems ordinarily do. It is exactly the characteristics of stability which the proper long range forecasting information flows attempt to describe. These stability characteristics should be described in terms of probabilities that a given estimate of a future state of affairs is likely to be wrong. With probability forecasting, a businessman is enabled to take current action with specific knowledge of risks defined through consideration of alternative forecasts.

Short Range Forecasting

Long range forecasting provides the setting within which the various functional activities of a business are carried out. Short range forecasting triggers specific day-to-day and continuous action on the part of the components of such an organization. As with long range forecasting, a specific prediction as to the likely state of affairs tomorrow, next week, or next month will determine the kinds of decisions that are made in many areas of a company's activity. For example, a prediction that next week will be a period of intense sales demand may lead to many specific decisions, such as increasing inventories, increasing labor force, adding work shifts, and expediting purchase orders. Obviously, if the production department is acting on the basis of one short range forecast and the sales department on the basis of another, wires will almost surely get crossed and the ultimate profit of the firm will be reduced.

The same set of events, however, can be forecast in different ways with differing values for various specific uses in the firm. For example, sales may be forecast at one level for inventory purposes and another for promotional purposes. Both these forecasts may be entirely correct for the uses to which they are put. One may state that sales will be no less than such and such a value with a specific probability, while the other may state that sales will be no greater than some amount, again with some specified probability. Both forecasts are of the same set of events, but they differ in actual values and, of course, in use. For given kinds of decision making, it is likely that there will be kinds of forecasts which are particularly efficient. What appears necessary is not a single forecast nor the same forecast being used throughout the enterprise, but rather the coordination of the function of forecasting and the flow of information relating to forecasts throughout the firm.

Cost Information

The objective to be attained by using computers in marketing is improved decision making through the ability to tap, to analyze, and to apply in better ways crucial information about the firm. No information could be more important than that pertaining to costs. In some sense, there is no decision, marketing or otherwise, which does not hinge on a knowledge of costs. Yet, many management information systems do not normally develop those cost data which are necessary for good decisions. For example, in knowing costs in a coordinated way throughout the functional and operating divisions of a business, one virtually has already made a series of important decisions. Profit performance by product line, by product line and geographic markets, by sales territory, by type of outlet, among others, can only be determined by a knowledge of costs. Decisions relative to such things as customer service, new product introduction, and promotional campaigns are shaped by the kind of cost information available to marketing, engineering, and production personnel. Such information is thus one of the key kinds of knowledge which enables a business to operate in a coordinated fashion, provided that the various functional areas have carefully defined and measured their costs. In many areas, profitable decision making requires detailed and clear understanding of the opportunity costs available not only on a departmental or divisional basis, but to the entire business.

Allocating Resources

If a business is to be operated in a coordinated fashion, the manner of allocating specific resources to specific tasks must be developed with considerable care. If the same resource (say, a machine) is assigned to several tasks at once through lack of coordination, then confusion, lost production and probably higher costs will ensue. However, many more subtle problems than this exist in the area of resource allocation. Proper information systems must be developed to ensure balanced use of resources, and to prevent production bottlenecks, stock-outs in inventory, low turnover rates, and poor utilization. Coordination of production facilities with a marketing plan is possible only when careful consideration has been given to the balancing problem. For example, one can consider current and future customer demands by product and by geographic location in the light of alternate production sources. Utilizing knowledge of costs, fixed facility costs are determined for each production plan, and through the use of various decision making models, variable costs can be minimized within each fixed cost program. Very often, under such coordinating procedures, one can find considerable areas for saving in variable costs. Alternately, with possibly small increases in variable costs, large reductions in fixed costs are possible. If such information is made available to all segments of the firm, the organization will acquire new knowledge with respect to the real meaning of the resources at its disposal and gradually begin to be able to plan the use of those resources in more and more profitable ways. Thus, one more important thread of information which is required for the coordinating process is for each major decision making center to know how each resource is to be employed.

Activity Sequencing

In addition to knowing how the various resources are to be used, the order in which things are done must also be known. Furthermore, there are many activities in which order cannot be changed if an operation is to be successful. For example, if we are considering a special promotion which requires new packaging, the promotion cannot be effective if the new packages and the product in those packages are not ready before an advertising campaign is launched. As a rule, specific information is required at specific times by specific individuals in carrying out tasks similar to these. It is also very helpful in coordinating business functions to lay out critical paths for information flows and events which are associated with such regularly occurring events as the implementation of major advertising campaigns, the preparation of catalogues, the introduction of new products, and the phasing out of old products. Much of this can be done with the help of computers. More importantly, much of it must be done in order to prepare the way for the use of computers. The more the decision makers in the various departments of a business know about who is going to do what at what time and how much it is going to cost, the more closely coordinated will the functions of that business be.

Acquiring Resources

If we have developed the flow of forecast information about the longer range and shorter range future, if we know a good deal about the costs of alternative actions, if we understand the role of each piece of equipment and of each person, we will have advanced a long way down the road to having a coordinated operation. The culmination of such a coordinated plan is rather clear knowledge of the resources needed in the future and the time they will be needed. Thus, the next and perhaps inevitable step in the information flows which tie a business together is that relating to the acquisition of resources. Resources may be materials, equipment, personnel, money, marketing and advertising devices, media, and ideas. Resources generally cost money and are usually intended to serve a specific purpose. Unwanted resources; resources which are acquired before they are needed, thereby typing up the firm's energy and capital; resources which do not perform as they were originally intended: all serve to drain away potential profits. Therefore, we must coordinate the acquisition of resources within the framework of the needs of the firm and its ability to utilize and pay for the items involved.

Performance Evaluation

All of the information streams mentioned above combine to provide business management with an ability to examine the "possible." More specifically what we have been talking about are methods of examining or looking at the consequences of alternate ways of operating or making decisions within a business enterprise. Given this ability, we can proceed to determine not only what the business ought to do, but whether what it has done comes close to achieving what it could have done. In this way, we can evaluate the performance of the various functional activities of the business, of the various individuals, and of the business as a whole. It is possible to put together the information available from forecasting, cost determination, resource allocation, activity sequencing, and resource acquisition into a comprehensive picture that will tell us which departments have done as well or better than seemed feasible, which divisions and individuals have improved performance or have shown themselves unable to operate as satisfactorily as they ought, and which products have performed in accordance with expectations and possibilities. Given such evaluations, business management can operate so as to change in the future what is "possible" and therefore what is likely to happen.

COORDINATION—DECISION AREAS

The ultimate reason for coordinating business functions is to make decisions in every area which will help the firm toward greater profits, rather than hinder it by conflicting with decisions or activities in some other part of the operation. The flows of information affecting such decisions cut across departmental lines and serve as the net which keeps the various functions from operating independently. Indeed, it is because functional areas cannot operate as profitably independently as they can in a single enterprise that we have the modern business entity. To summarize these thoughts on the need for and ways of coordinating business functions we shall examine some specific decision areas briefly and discuss the pervasive effects of decisions made in them.

In order to provide for adequate coordination of the functions of a business in making decisions, one must first understand the fundamental questions which these decisions raise. Then, it will be possible to collect quantitative data and qualitative information, and to choose the type of analyses required to determine the ramifications throughout the firm of alternative courses of action. It will be essential to review constantly the results of coordinated plans of action, once these are implemented. This requires the measurement of significant relationships between the goals of the firm and its economic and technological characteristics. The remainder of this book will outline types of models and specific approaches to many of the problems we are discussing. The cases included will indicate many of the detailed implications of specific decision procedures. These initial remarks are intended to raise a series of questions in order to emphasize not only the desirability, but the essentiality of coordination. As analysis, improved information systems, and decision procedures are gradually implemented in the firm, one's ability to determine the relationships among the objectives which are considered significant will improve continually.

Let us list the major decision areas and indicate how decisions in each of these areas raise questions with respect to all the others.

MAJOR DECISION AREAS
1. Promotion and advertising
2. Production and production scheduling
3. Distribution and customer service
4. Products, lines and plans
5. Pricing
6. Investment in new plant and equipment
7. Investment in acquisitions
8. Research in new products and new marketing concepts

As we noted earlier, each major decision area involves revenue and cost effects which must be spelled out in detail. Answers to decision making questions cannot properly be determined in one area independently of the others. Forecasting, for example, must provide a sound basis for an understanding of the likely position of markets and products in the future. It, in turn, will include and be based on much market research from beginning to end. We shall outline the basic questions which confront the particular function and indicate subsidiary questions which must be answered to give an aggressive and profitable result. We shall also mention some quantitative data which are relevant to the particular decision making activity, although this procedure is not intended to be comprehensive.

Promotion and Advertising

The basic question with respect to promotion and advertising concerns the total size of the promotional and advertising budget and the means by which it should be distributed among products, among brands, by media, by regional markets, and by types of activity. To answer this question, we need to know the relationship between the firm's total promotion and its sales in the various industries in which it may be a factor. Further, we must know the share of advertising and the share of sales by type of product for the industry and within the enterprise, as well as sales and promotional shares by individual products within the company. These questions are simply the starting point for a coordinated attack on this particular problem.

In addition, it is necessary that we understand the manufacturing and distribution cost effects of any changes in sales induced by a particular promotion. We must take into account the fact that increased sales and production of different products in different areas may influence costs in many different ways. From a strategic point of view, we need to understand the feedback effects of the company's promotional policies relative to the industry's response to these policies. We all know that the successful innovator is often emulated (with greater or lesser success) by others in a particular industry. This is true whether the actions originally taken pertain to advertising, promotion, pricing, product development, or plant expansion. Thus, an intensified advertising program is likely to induce competitors to follow suit. What are the effects of such advertising programs on the firm's sales, once other firms in the industry have reacted with programs of their own? From an economic point of view, we would like to have the promotional resources expended in such a way that the last dollar spent on each activity is equally profitable. Thus, the success of the overall program will depend on the media used, and the skill in which advertising is employed in developing specific marketing strategies and in estimating or forecasting their relative net profit contributions. The need for coordinated information in problems such as these cannot be overestimated. The basic problem as it affects decision makers is often misunderstood and the use of computers to aid decision making is only in its infancy. It is the objective of the cases and models described in this book to lay out tasks for future improvements.

Production and Production Scheduling

In terms of production and production scheduling, the basic questions here relate to how much of each type of product should be produced, where it should be produced, and when. The adjustment of production to forecasts and actual orders is, of course, related to promotional decisions and pricing policy. Among the significant questions is the effect on our costs and thereby on net profits of changing product mix at a particular plant or location. The kind of data that is necessary to provide genuine answers to these questions is a forecast of sales by type of product for at least each year for several years ahead. Part of this forecast certainly involves estimates of realized prices in the future for each of the product categories. We need to determine the direct or marginal costs for each of the major products and to have some reasonable understanding of the problem of joint costs where we manufacture more than one product in a plant. Programming models are of considerable assistance in reaching answers to these questions.

Distribution and Customer Scheduling

Closely related to the production and production scheduling problem is that of inventory distribution and customer service. We need to determine where and in what quantities we wish to stock each of our products and the types of service we are prepared to offer and stand behind for our customers. If we choose to offer 24 hour service, this will be a major factor in inventory determination and our net profit picture. We also need to determine what we plan to do when actual inventory departs from our expected or intended stocks. Where should the adjustments in production and stocks be made and how may these adjustments be facilitated by decisions in the area of promotion and pricing policies?

The distribution system of the company will have a geographical structure and a hierarchical structure. Decisions to change either of these will influence investments, in the case of warehouses or local distribution points, or promotional activities, in the case of determinations as to the channels to be employed and the services offered. A number of related questions will be constantly under investigation. Given the regional demand patterns for various products, where should warehouses, facilities, and distributorships be located? What is the best size of these operations? How large a territory should they serve? Should the company directly control distributorships, at least those serving larger markets? If not, what margin allowed distributors produces the greatest net profit for the company? A large amount of coordinated data is essential to a proper set of answers to these questions. We need to know carrying costs at each distribution level, throughout costs, transportation costs in and out of distribution points, distributors' and retailers' margins by products and by market areas, and the ultimate cost of customer service. None of these costs should be considered fixed and immutable. This is an important aspect to the dynamic operation of a modern business. It is, in fact, because we can change costs or ultimate sales that we make changes in our business's operating characteristics. Therefore, when the problems mentioned above come under consideration, attention should be given to possibilities of making changes which will affect costs and thereby net profitability.

Products and Product Lines

Most firms neglect the problem of deciding on adequate and proper variety. The question here is: what is the optimal number of different brands, packages, or other types of variety we can offer to the consumer? This is related to a number of other questions which must be specifically answered, such as how products should be categorized and how these categories should be broken down. This problem of categorization is of extreme importance to advertising and promotional policies and raises an immediate subsidiary question. What is the relative importance of the physiological bases (such as taste, shape, and feel) and the psychological bases (which may be largely shaped by advertising and promotion) to product preference? There are many situations in which advertising's pull is far more important than any degree of physical differentiation that might exist. Promotional activity is required if only to inform the public of some slight differentiation of the product on which the psychological preference may be based. The relative merits of increased advertising on existing products versus the introduction of products that are new in either a physiological or psychological sense needs to be carefully assessed. Intertwined with this problem and the area of pricing, the question of the number of brands required to reach markets composed of consumers of different income levels is almost certain to arise in the consumer products industry. In the capital goods area, the question of relative price-quality considerations is of equal importance.

Pricing

We have already mentioned the effect of price levels on the results of decisions in other areas. Briefly, the significant pricing question involves the appropriate level and structure of prices for the various categories of products and, possibly, of brands within these products. It is necessary to know how price concessions can be used to introduce or to reinforce products in the market. We have already mentioned the possible use of price adjustments to bring inventories into balance with demand—some imbalance must occur from time to time despite the very best forecasting estimates. Although price concessions are not the only means of rationalizing inventories, they certainly can be considered as an alternative. Immediately on serious consideration of price decisions, questions arise as to how changes in the level of prices will affect demand for the specific product changed and for all other products. It is also necessary to relate the promotional effects to the prices consumers are welling to pay. Our data requirements for doing an adequate job in the area of pricing include price and consumption data for all the company's products with due allowance being made for whatever geographic price structures exist. As far as possible, comparable data for competitors' products should also be obtained.

Investment Decisions

The analysis required to answer questions as to investment in current products, new products, or in the acquisition of new businesses, clearly necessitates adequate answers to all the other questions previously raised. Among other things, we need to answer the questions of when, where, and how capacity for old or new products should be expanded or contracted. Such questions are an outgrowth of questions in production, pricing, sales and other decision areas. In the ordinary day to day situation, plant capacities are more or less fixed. To answer questions as to what future capacity should be, we develop programs for altering this capacity in a simulated way and determine the expected profits from various programs of plant expansion or contraction. This hypothetical plant may involve new plant or equipment or the acquisition of existing firms, along with new products to be added to the line. Products outside of the firm's experience, of course, require detailed and separate study and not a mere extension of questions raised in the production and inventory areas. In research and development decision making, we are concerned with the question of the addition of new products, the modification of existing products, and the elimination of undesirable products. Decisions in these areas require a clear understanding of market position, costs, and net profitability.

The profitable ordering of practical economic decisions in the business world requires a careful coordination of all elements of the business operation. The increasing interdependence and complexity of marketing decisions leaves the era of the "independent" brilliant salesman behind. The use of increased knowledge of the effect of business decisions in one area on activities in another, and the development of computer programs which will boil large masses of data down to understandable and realistic terms present an opportunity in marketing as well as a challenge to management. It will not be easy to meet this challenge, since new habits will have to be learned and many experiments undertaken to determine ways of operating in a changed environment. But competition will force on all business an increasing rational usage of the tools which are now at hand.

Figure 1 (see page 115) summarizes the requirements for continuing coordination in managerial decision making. From an overall forecast by industry, we move to share of markets where management decides how and when to make its investment in resources and production and promotion, and thence to the ultimate net result which is a return on the stockholder's investment. Ours is not necessarily an easy world for those who manage and make decisions. The marketing executive must recognize that all the things which happen in a business affect the marketing function and that his decisions, in turn, affect the remainder of the company. The manager must also recognize that there are no fixed and final answers. Continual change in the economic environment and in the dynamic organization within a business must lead to adaptive decision making on virtually a day to day basis.

PART THREE

The Role of Information in Marketing Planning

The compelling force underlying the need for marketing planning is the tremendously accelerating rate of social and economic change occurring in the world today. As a result, the risks associated with business decisions also are increasing in number and magnitude. Companies are diversifying and their organizational structures are becoming so complex that management coordination is becoming a monumental task. Yet, according to Stern, "the marketing concept demands integration of effort in order to maximize profits. Thus the two factors of organization complexity and market orientation reinforce the essentiality of the same function—marketing planning."[1]

A plan is a statement of the goals sought and the means expected to achieve them. More specifically . . . "it (planning) is the continuous process of making *present entrepreneurial* decisions systematically and with the best possible knowledge of their futurity, organizing systematically *the efforts* needed to carry out these decisions and measuring the results of these decisions against the expectations through an organized systematic feed-back".[2]

---

[1] Mark E. Stern, **Marketing Planning,** New York: McGraw-Hill, 1966, p. 1.
[2] Peter F. Drucker, "Long Range Planning: Challenge to Management Science," **Management Science,** Vol. 5, No. 3, April 1959, p. 239.

Planning, in other words, includes all "entrepreneurial and technical activities and processes involved in setting forth those company goals and departmental objectives, assessing market opportunities, generating possible strategies through which to achieve the objectives, designing detailed marketing programs, integrating the individual programs into a marketing plan, and adjusting the plan to changes in the environment."[3]

In order to provide a sound basis for effective marketing planning, it is imperative that managers have an understanding of consumer wants and needs and the environmental factors which affect them, plus a realistic appraisal of the firm's resources as compared with those of competitors. Based on knowledge of these factors, marketing executives must make decisions involving choice among risky alternative courses of action. Planning for such decisions warrants the continuous collection and analysis of pertinent information. This processed information, sometimes called marketing intelligence, is used to make decisions regarding product-planning, pricing, promotion, and physical distribution.

The current question facing us is whether today's information systems, our traditional marketing research departments, are adequate to supply the information and analysis needed by marketing and other company executives to respond rapidly and optimally to changing opportunities and challenges. The answer given by most contemporary writers is that they are not. In an earlier article, Kotler stresses that "the marketing research department generally lacks—both in spirit and form—a conception of itself as the total information arm of the modern marketing executive."[4]

Considering the very close interrelationship between planning and information, it is imperative that we become more systematic in our approach to both. Far too often, planning has been described as an art, and thus has not been given enough analysis and thought. In today's complex competitive environment, however, management is now placing greater emphasis on planning and is constantly seeking more efficient ways of programming the firm's activities over time. Thus, the development of mathematical decision-making models, the emphasis on the creation of organized information systems, and the availability of high-speed computers have had, and will continue to have, a decided impact on planning.

---

[3] Stern, op. cit., p. ix.

[4] Philip Kotler, "A Design for the Firm's Marketing Nerve Center," **Business Horizons,** Fall, 1966, p. 64.

A   Nature of the Marketing Planning Process

The Role of Planning in Marketing*   9

WENDELL R. SMITH

The hard core of the "marketing concept" is the effective and scientific use of marketing planning which, in turn, has emerged as the logical out-growth of the acceptance of marketing research and development.

Perhaps the most important innovation being discussed in management meetings and conferences these days is the marketing management concept, sometimes referred to simply as the marketing concept. Marketing people, both teachers and businessmen, are simultaneously pleased and puzzled by this development. They are pleased that at long last the necessity for a more professional approach to marketing management and general management is gaining recognition. They are puzzled by the relatively sudden, almost explosive, rate of acceptance of a philosophy neither new nor revolutionary to thoughtful students of marketing theory and practice.

Some of the more meticulous professionals in marketing are also disturbed by an apparent lack of precision in many of the statements being made about this marketing concept—disturbed by the fact that its many proponents are not in agreement as to just what the concept means and implies.

At present, the so-called marketing concept appears to be an umbrella term used to describe one, several, or even all of the following developments in the basic components of effective marketing operations:

1. A marked increase in the degree of market orientation of top management thinking. Specifically, marketing considerations are increasingly coming to provide the framework within which other factors such as engineering, finance, and manufacturing are positioned and analyzed.

---

*Reprinted from **Business Horizons,** national quarterly publication of the Graduate School of Business, Indiana University, Vol. 2 (Fall, 1959), pp. 53–57.

2. An increased recognition of the importance of planning marketing activities in a systematic way and using marketing plans as the springboard for over-all plans and budgets.

3. The emergence of the notion that innovations in marketing (new outlets, channels, and so on) are just as revitalizing as new products.

4. A trend toward positioning marketing executives in the organization structure in ways compatible with effective market orientation and planning.

Probably the last trend provides the most readily observable evidence that something new has been added. The appointment of directors of marketing or vice-presidents for marketing who, in addition to the usual "downstream" responsibility for determination of the marketing mix and directing marketing action, are also responsible "upstream" as members of the general management team shows that the marketing concept is more than just a currently popular expression. However, important as organizational recognition of the marketing concept may be, the success of the concept in increasing marketing productivity will depend largely on the second component—scientific marketing planning.

MARKETING PLANNING

Planning in marketing, in its broadest terms, may be thought of as the exercise of analysis and foresight to increase the effectiveness of marketing activities. Planning, therefore, is necessarily concerned with (1) the goals or objectives that the firm seeks to attain; (2) the operating system through which the firm is attempting to achieve these goals; (3) the quantity and quality of effort needed for their achievement; and (4) the firm's capacity for generating this effort.

This is not to say that, prior to the emergence and recognition of the marketing concept, marketing operations were necessarily fortuitous and unplanned. Perhaps the crucial point is that developments in the economy, and in society generally, have operated so as to stimulate the emergence of planning as a conscious or explicit function. Among these developments are (1) the increasing complexity of products, services, and marketing operations and the environment in which they exist; (2) acceptance of the expectation of change—substantial change—as part of the "normal" operating environment; and (3) our ability, through research, to identify and control certain factors (images) in the marketing situation.

The recent period of business recession revealed the need for planning in some companies where that need had previously been concealed by the rapid growth caused by great technological advances or other external factors. In other instances, the recession caused planning to be eliminated or put on the shelf. Because management identified the concept narrowly, planning was regarded as a tool of growth rather than as a rational means of achieving the most profitable adjustment to current and future market conditions, regardless of the stage of the business cycle.

MARKETING STRATEGY

Much has been said and written about the sequence of steps involved in the development of sound marketing plans. The first step is usually identified as the determination of the goals or objectives that are to be accomplished by the marketing action being planned. This is true only to the extent that the firm has the results of a careful review of its present position as a foundation upon which to determine realistic goals and feasible objectives. If the firm is not fully aware of the characteristics of its current position in the market, such preplanning analysis must precede the process of goal definition. Hence, determination of goals and objectives may turn out to be the second step in planning instead of the first. While it is often true that the mere identification and statement of goals and objectives puts the firm well on its way toward their achievement, it is likewise true that those experienced in the planning of marketing activities tend to approach this step cautiously. Alternative sets of goals and objectives are regarded somewhat in the light of hypotheses to be tested, and the selection of the appropriate alternative becomes an important product of the planning operation itself. The feasibility of a goal can be evaluated only by review of the action plan necessary for its achievement. Therefore, in practice, the initial stages of the planning process may merge with the final steps in research and development until the criteria of feasibility have been satisfied. At this exploratory, perhaps experimental, stage in the planning process, strategy considerations become paramount as a true prelude to the development of the action plan that will finally emerge, complete with timetables, budgets, campaigns, and schedules for personnel deployment.

There are many ways in which the nature of marketing strategy can be described. Regardless of definition, however, marketing strategy is primarily concerned with the creative elements of a goal-directed marketing plan. It describes, in general terms, the basic elements of the way in which the firm plans to get from where it is to where it wants to be. Marketing strategy then becomes the central theme that integrates and co-ordinates the many and diverse components of effort to be stipulated in a marketing plan.

PLANNING OBJECTIVES

It is worthy of note that the product line of today's marketing planners is exceedingly broad. At any given time, a firm can have one big plan or many little plans. Plans may emerge routinely, almost unnoticed, as the first stage of budgeting activities; or their development may represent a special, sometimes herculean, effort that has been triggered by anticipation of change in the firm's marketing situation. However, the great majority of firms find that their planning activities result largely from the desire to develop rational programs to achieve one or more of several objectives. These objectives may be grouped into two basic categories; the distinction between the categories depends on time considerations.

The first group is comprised of objectives giving rise to recurrent and continuous planning associated with appropriate procedures for control and evaluation. These objectives are:

1. Enabling the firm to maximize profits for a stated operating period by increasing sales or margins and/or by reducing marketing costs. This is the classical economic motivation that accounts for recurrent and regular attention to the planning function.

2. Gaining or maintaining a desired share of the market. This is an objective that has emerged concurrently with the rise of imperfect and monopolistic competition.

The second category is made up of objectives giving rise to special (*ad hoc*) planning. Such objectives include:

1. Bringing about a change that will influence the performance of marketing functions by means such as:
   a. Improving the layout of a store or warehouse
   b. Accomplishing a more appropriate geographic allocation of sales effort
   c. Installing a more smoothly operating marketing organization structure

2. Preparing for the future by developing a program that will be activated when and if a specific contingency arises, such as:
   a. The lapse of a patent or franchise
   b. Movement of competition in a particular direction
   c. Release of a new product for marketing
   d. A substantial change in the economic environment

3. Preparing for a major change in the direction or in the scope of the firm's activities, such as would result from major construction, acquisition, merger, or entering a new channel of distribution.

Implicit in all of these planning objectives is acceptance of the idea that "flying by the seat of the pants" is definitely impractical and that there are still enough unanticipated hazards to make the future exciting even though full advantage is taken of all of the aids to planning that contemporary marketing research techniques can provide.

DEVELOPING STRATEGIES

While, in my opinion, marketing strategies are inherently creative, this does not mean that the process of their generation depends on the availability of an inspired genius. As a matter of fact, an orderly method for developing strategic concepts is one of the most basic aspects of the modern approach to marketing. In general, marketing strategies evolve from study of the firm itself, from study and analysis of competition, and from study of the market.

As was pointed out earlier, the generation of marketing strategies essentially begins with a careful review of the present position of the firm in relation to competition and in relation to the markets that it serves. Such analysis reveals rather quickly whether or not the strategy should be essentially defensive—that is, designed to compensate for and to correct weaknesses in the present operation—or offensive, in the sense of leading to plans designed to capitalize fully on the relative strengths or advantages that the firm enjoys. A defensive strategy might be one designed to eliminate a relative weakness, hence to increase profits, thereby increasing the profitability of an existing volume of sales. On the other hand, an offensive strategy would be oriented toward increasing profits by pumping additional products through an existing marketing mechanism, hence producing disproportionately small increases in total marketing costs. While strategies may vary in terms of the degree of rationality that they represent, they necessarily provide the creative sense of direction essential to planning.

As contemporary economists have so eloquently pointed out, many marketing strategies are developed with primary reference to the present and prospective future behavior of competition. Again, strategy may be essentially defensive insofar as it may be influenced by present or expected future competitive threats; or it may be offensively directed at points at which competition is or is expected to become vulnerable. Whether stated or not, such elements are probably implicit in most strategic concepts.

From my point of view, the most important and fundamental marketing strategies are those directly related to the accomplishment of goals or objectives defined in terms of the market. Solid marketing research is the stuff out of which such strategies can be built.

Much time could be spent in elaboration of the almost unlimited list of market-based strategies that could be developed and adopted as guides to the planning of marketing activities. Obviously, strategies generated from market study must be feasible from the point of view of the characteristics of the firm and competition. Let us look at two examples of the ways in which market data may suggest an orderly method or approach to strategy generation.

In the first place, analysis of trends in demand for present products or services is fundamental. An unfavorable trend in demand suggests a choice between strategies designed to reverse the trend or to accept and adjust to the development. Similarly, a favorable trend suggests a choice of strategies concerned with how the firm can profit most from this happy state of affairs without overextending itself or producing imbalance in its situation.

Second, analysis of market structure will reveal whether or not the market is homogeneous, a situation in which the requirements of consumers or users are very much the same; or heterogeneous, a situation in which individual requirements vary and hence would be imperfectly satisfied by a limited offering to the market. In the first case, the situation of homogeneity, one would logically follow a strategy designed to bring about the convergence of individual market demands on a single or limited offering to the market. This is usually accomplished by product differentiation, achieved through advertising and promotion. On the other hand, if the market is heterogeneous, it may be better to accept divergent demand as a market characteristic and to adjust product lines and marketing strategy accordingly. Such a strategy has been referred to as a strategy of market segmentation, which consists essentially of approaching a heterogeneous market as if it were a group of smaller homogeneous markets (market segments) with differing product needs and preferences.

This strategy also often involves substantial use of advertising and promotion, but the objective becomes that of informing the market segments of the availability of goods or services produced or presented as meeting their needs with greater precision. Whereas a strategy of product differentiation may be classified as essentially a promotional strategy or approach to marketing designed to produce the convergence of demand compatible with mass production, market segmentation is essentially a merchandising strategy. It subordinates the desirability of production economies to the desirability of simplifying the demand manipulation component of the marketing process.

CONCLUSION

To sum up, I have tried to suggest, first, that the hard core of the so-called marketing concept that is attracting so much attention today is effective and scientific use of market planning. Second, the first, and perhaps crucial, phase of the planning process—the prelude—is the generation of marketing strategies or strategic concepts to provide the essential linkage between where you are and where you want to be by guiding the specifics of the planning operation in the appropriate direction. Finally, this creative component of planning—marketing strategy—is developed by study of the firm, competition, and the market. Strategy provides the vehicle for plans to enable the firm to move toward realization of its market opportunity in ways that are feasible, because they have been designed only after full consideration of the firm's strengths and weaknesses and the competition it must face.

This, then, is the new marketing that is emerging—emerging as the logical outgrowth of the acceptance of marketing research and development as the partner of the technical research and development that is the pride and not (we hope) the despair of our times.

The Application of Operating Control Systems to Marketing* 10

CARLOS R. VEST

The general management problem of how to consider a major functional unit of an organization is explored by using the "black box" systems approach where marketing is considered a system and is examined from the point of view of the relationship between marketing inputs, outputs, feedback, control, and "the marketing process itself."

INTRODUCTION

It is proposed that the process of marketing can be accurately described by considering the marketing process as an administrative system.

The term "system" is a broad concept. As with most complex concepts, the definition of "system" can be accomplished by describing the process as it is seen from several different organizational levels, or from several points of view within the same organizational level.

In this paper, both points of view will be considered. The term "system" has been defined by Johnson as "an organized or complex whole; an assemblage or combination of things or parts forming a complex or unitary whole."[1] This follows closely the dictionary definition which defines a system as "an assemblage of objects united by some form of regular interaction or interdependence," "a complete exhibition of essential principles or facts, arranged in a rational dependence or connection," and "a complex of ideas, principles, etc., forming a coherent whole."[2] All these definitions will apply in this paper where an administrative system will be considered as a way of analyzing the total marketing process so that all of the business fundamentals and their relationships are considered during the on-going administrative process.

Optner has considered systems to be of two types, "structured" and "incompletely structured."[3] Structured systems are those physical systems

---

*Reprinted from John S. Wright and Jac L. Goldstucker (eds.), **New Ideas for Successful Marketing** (Chicago: American Marketing Association, June 1966), pp. 94–110.

[1] Richard D. Johnson, Kast, Fremont and Rosenzweig, *The Theory and Management of Systems* (New York, N. Y.: McGraw-Hill Book Co., Inc., 1963), p. 4.

[2] Webster, p. 863.

[3] Stanford L. Optner, *Systems Analysis for Business Management* (Englewood Cliffs, New Jersey: Prentice-Hall, 1960), p. 8.

which are constructed of electrical and mechanical parts and designed to operate in highly predictable ways. Incompletely structured systems are those systems in which a human is part of the processing unit.

When a human becomes part of the system, the processing functions are more loosely executed than when a machine is used, as in the structured system. Since there is no model which describes every human action, there is no way of knowing how each phase of the system process will be implemented. It can be predicated with confidence, however, that it will lack the machine-like efficiency, reliability and accuracy of the structured system. Administrative systems of industrial and business enterprises fall into the incompletely structured category.

A convenient way to analyze a system will be borrowed from the way in which a computer is organized. A module will be considered and used to describe the attributes of both complicated high level systems and simple basic subsystems. This module concept will make no exception as to the type of data being processed or the type of processor being utilized. However, it will provide a way of looking at the fundamental functional relationships which exist in any on-going administrative process. The module concept has also been described as the "black-box" method of system analysis.[4] The concept is actually borrowed from electrical engineering where the system is considered to be contained within physical or administrative boundaries which can be easily specified. However, the processes that take place within the boundaries are not directly observable and must be deduced from observed responses (outputs) when known inputs are injected.

In this sense the "black-box" model contains three properties: the input terminals, the output terminals, and the box itself (or the processor). A fourth property has been developed by Wiener in his discourse on cybernetics where he has indicated that all systems, physical and non-physical, are both information systems and feedback systems.[5] Taking this into account, therefore, the module must have a self-organizing or self-regulating ability to be considered as an on-going system process. This property is usually referred to as "feedback."

A certain amount of system performance must also be attributed to the system environment, both internal and external. This environmental function acts as a control on the system process and must be considered in any systems analysis.

The systems module may be illustrated as in Figure I, and will have a total of five properties: an input function, an output function, a processor, a control function, and a feedback loop. The input function will provide a

---

[4] *Ibid.*, p. 3.

[5] Harry H. Goode and Robert E. Machol, *Systems Engineering* (New York., N. Y.: McGraw-Hill Book Co., Inc., 1957), p. 393.

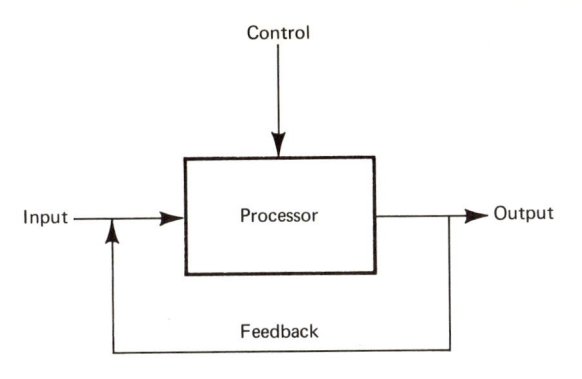

Figure I: **Generalized Systems Module**

means of getting into the system and to the processor in order for the administrative process to begin. The output function will provide a means of getting out of the system after the administrative process has been completed. The processor function will provide a means of performing the administrative process. The control function will provide a means of monitoring the processor so as to insure operation according to the administrative environment in which it is located. The feedback function will provide a means of monitoring the output and delivering the results of the administrative process back into the system. This will insure a more nearly correct output during future operations.

MARKETING AS A SYSTEM

The concept of the systems module will be used in this paper to describe the marketing system.

Output

When analyzing the marketing process as a system, the first function to be considered is the output since this establishes the purpose for the system. A marketing system has several outputs, the most obvious of which is sales. As a result of this selling activity, the marketing system becomes the official company interface point with the customer and potential customer groups. It also becomes, therefore, the primary source of the information that the company requires in order to be effective in the customer environment. This information requirement, then, adds two additional outputs to the marketing system: first, to supply the operational information to management, and second, to supply technical information to that part of the company responsible for the technical decisions on which the company products are based.

Input

To achieve the outputs discussed above requires that the correct inputs be made available to the processor. The one input the marketing system must have in order for the system to produce a sale is a saleable product. This saleable product can be simply an idea. The idea can come from any source such as internal engineering investigations, or it can result directly from actions initiated by a customer or even a competitor. Another source, of course, is the modification or extension of existing products which the company has developed previously. Again, this idea can come from within the company or from other sources.

A most important input to the marketing system is information. Its availability, accuracy and timeliness is the core of the systems marketing operation. For the system performance to approach its optimum value, a complete knowledge of the desired market must be obtained. This requires information on all customers and potential customers as well as information on all competition and potential competition. Information on the customer is required at all levels, including the past activity in the market area of interest and future plans of action insofar as it is possible to obtain them. Finally, in the case of industrial marketing, the customer's corporate objectives must be fully understood in order to take maximum advantage of their expressed purpose in being in existence.

Another input of vital importance to the marketing system is information on competition. Competition is an essential element of all markets under the free-enterprise system, but good information will allow a more realistic evaluation of its expected impact.

The final input to be considered is information on the company's internal capability. The loss or gain of key individuals or capability can make the difference between profit and loss, other things being equal. Therefore, marketing must always be aware of the status and capability of the company as a whole.

Processor

Since marketing is the administrative system under consideration, the processor of the module is marketing. In all cases of systems analysis, the system under study is, by definition, the processor. The processor element of the system under study must be deduced by observing the system output when known inputs have been injected. The input and output factors discussed above suggest the possibility of the existence of a number of subfunction or subsystems within this system processor unit.

A planning function is suggested. It is proposed that all planning starts with research in some kind of a market intelligence function. In this system "Marketing Intelligence" is the function which determines who and where the customer is; what he needs, wants, and will buy; where and how he will buy; and how much he will pay.

Included in the marketing intelligence activity is the company's general management plan for the overall company as well as facts, ideas, and support from other parts of the company including manufacturing, finance, legal, and the various employee and public relations functions.

The market intelligence activity, then, should be the basis for a master marketing plan specifying the type of business in which the company should be engaged and including broadly its product line. The various elements of all markets must be identified with respect to location, size, and sales potential.

The plans resulting from the market intelligence activity must be used for some purpose. This suggests a "market development" function where specific product plans and programs can be developed for specific product models. Time schedules, product size, capacity, range, style and appearance information must be co-ordinated and furnished to the company engineering function in order that the product engineering cycle can begin. At this point prices, terms and conditions can be considered.

Another implied function within the processor is that of "sales." Selling is an action process that consists of: (1) establishing contact with the market, (2) arousing interest in the company products, (3) creating a preference, (4) submitting a product, (5) negotiating a transfer of title, and (6) keeping the customer sold.[6] It is suggested that these are three separate major marketing steps or functions controlled by a master sales plan. Items (1) through (3) are primarily an "advertising and promotion" process; items (4) and (5) consist of a personal "selling" process; and item (6) is a multifunctional "post-sales" activity.

These major functions or subsystems in the processor activity are required to accomplish the marketing system process and will be considered as separate items in this paper. The actual subsystem interconnections will not be postulated. It is obvious that they are not simple series or parallel networks but are instead complex series-parallel arrangements with interlocking feedback loops.

Control

All administrative systems must operate in an ambient environment that limits or controls their activity. The marketing system is no exception and must consider both internal and external controls. Externally, the normal laws of commerce limit what can and cannot be done in the marketing of products of any type. Controls can be considered internal to the system when they monitor the way in which operations are to be conducted. The basic posture of the company's long-range objectives and intentions as set forth by top management will be translated into various plans and policies that tend to control all phases of the company, including marketing.

---

[6] Fredrich R. Messner, *Industrial Advertising* (New York: McGraw-Hill Book Co., Inc., 1963), p. 5.

Feedback

Finally, the system must provide a means for correcting future operations based on the reaction of those who have received the initial outputs.

THE MARKET INTELLIGENCE SUBSYSTEM

Subsystem Input

Subsystem input can be considered the procurement of information believed to be pertinent in the intelligence process. This is a dynamic, interacting process. There is no clear-cut starting or stopping point. However, for the purposes of analysis it can be assumed that the first general step is the procurement of data or so-called raw intelligence. These data will include a multitude of items. They will be in varying stages of completeness and will have assorted degrees of relevance to the current problems faced by marketing and company management.

There are many sources of intelligence data, both internal and external to the marketing system and the company organization. However, it should be noted that the intelligence subsystem will soon become useless if the raw data are gathered at random. Those who collect, evaluate, and produce marketing intelligence information must be acutely aware of the important unanswered questions in the minds of the management decision makers. Intelligence, like knowledge, knows no boundaries either as to substance or source; and the procurement of data to be fed into the intelligence subsystem is a vital management function of all the various marketing and technical functions of the company.

Subsystem Output

Subsystem output is the result of sifting, sorting and judging the credibility of collected information, drawing pertinent inferences from its analysis, and interpreting such inferences in keeping with the requirements of product development, sales, administration, advertising and promotion, management, and other areas of marketing and engineering. Not all or even most of the data processed by the marketing intelligence subsystem is of the type immediately sought by decision makers. However, an efficient intelligence subsystem will attempt to anticipate the needs of management and produce considerable information that is to be stored as insurance against future requirements.

The output function also includes the act of disseminating or communicating the intelligence findings to appropriate management decision makers or to those responsible for implementing management decisions. A most essential and crucial step in the intelligence process is the dissemination of the final product, for intelligence, by definition, is foreknowledge. It is information which should be known in advance of action.

Subsystem Processor

Since a marketing intelligence subsystem is the administrative subsystem under consideration, the processor of the systems module will be intelligence. In all cases of systems analysis, the system under study will be the processor.

Subsystem Feedback

This is the act of communicating the reaction of the user of the product back to the subsystem input and making appropriate corrections. The intelligence process should not be considered as routine steps in a well-defined procedure. Instead, a high degree of "feedback" and interrelationships between the elements of intelligence knowledge and other subsystems in the marketing process must be maintained. In order to be effective, the collector of raw data needs guidance from management as well as from all users of the intelligence product. Communications must be maintained between all elements of the subsystem and those functions using the subsystem output so that the collector and collator have some idea what the company and marketing management need to know. Management, in turn, must be supplied with enough basic information so that they recognize that certain elements in the picture are missing.

In a strict sense, evaluation of intelligence takes place at the point of collection and continues during the subsystem process. Considerable responsibility for evaluation and analysis, however, must be considered as part of the feedback process. Feedback occurs only after information has been gathered, indexed, reduced into manageable form and presented to a user. This is the point in the process which is one of the most critical phases in the processing cycle. The collector then has access to the source, the completed intelligence product based on previous inputs, and the current requirements of the user. The result is an efficient collection based on this knowledge. The requirement is eventually satisfied by the process of iteration.

Subsystem Control

Subsystem control in the intelligence subsystem consists of those environmental factors which affect system operation. Included in this category are company policies, company directives, government laws and regulations, company financial conditions, and ethics.

THE MARKET DEVELOPMENT SUBSYSTEM

Subsystem Input

Product Idea Data. Product ideas come from a multitude of sources. These should be evaluated to determine if they are worthy of the investment of time and money by the company. Since the market development subsystem is the company focal point for the consideration of new products, this will be a primary input to the system.

Customer Requirements and Habits Data. Data concerning customers' "needs and habits" are required. This is available from a number of sources, the primary one being the marketing intelligence subsystem. The customer viewpoint is desirable not only when the introduction of new

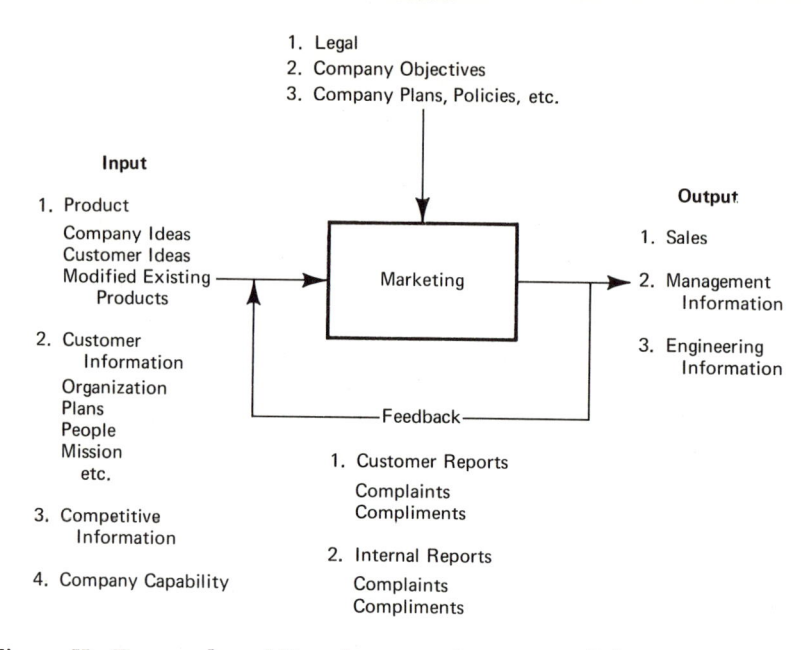

```
                          Control
                        1. Legal
                        2. Company Objectives
                        3. Company Plans, Policies, etc.
                                │
                                ▼
   Input                                              Output
   1. Product                                         1. Sales
      Company Ideas                ┌───────────┐
      Customer Ideas               │           │      2. Management
      Modified Existing  ────────▶ │ Marketing │ ───▶    Information
      Products                     │           │
                                   └───────────┘      3. Engineering
   2. Customer         ▲                                 Information
      Information      │
      Organization     │
      Plans            └──── Feedback ────┐
      People
      Mission                 1. Customer Reports
      etc.                       Complaints
                                 Compliments
   3. Competitive
      Information          2. Internal Reports
                              Complaints
   4. Company Capability       Compliments
```

Figure II: **Research and Development System Module**

products is contemplated but also as a gauge of the necessity for either redesigning or eliminating established products.

Competitive Product Data. In appraising current competitive products and products lines, it is vital to have all of the characteristics which are truly significant from the point of view of customers, prospective customers, and lost customers. Price, operating cost, engineering design, state-of-the-art, ease of maintenance, appearance, shape, size and weight, and other factors are often of basic importance.

Specification Data. Functional product specifications, as dictated by the customer, are quite different from those generated later by company technical personnel. The product purchaser may state his requirements in technical terms or in terms indicating functional needs, both of which must be translated into engineering specifications.

Management Data. Unless management objectives are clearly stated, known to be timely, and worthy of consideration, a certain amount of market development effort is likely to be misdirected and wasted.[7]

Subsystem Output

Product Scope Recommendations. Problems of product scope arise frequently and from many directions. A loss of sales volume, unused

---

[7] Gerald A. Busch, "Prudent Manager Forecasting," *Harvard Business Review*, Vol. 39, No. 3 (May–June 1961), p. 118.

production facilities, the success of competitors with new products, requests for special products from customers, unexpected results of technical research efforts, the opportunity to purchase product ideas of going concerns, a feeling of vulnerability because of a narrow product line, and the likelihood of product development or improvement by competing concerns may all be reflected in the company's product scope. The basic idea behind product scope recommendations is that reasoning can be applied to the choice of products for development. The implication is that products should not be grouped haphazardly and that there is a better way to proceed toward a grouping of products which is rational and directional in view of overall company objectives.

Product Specifications. While knowledge of customers' requirements has a variety of marketing and management uses, nowhere is it more important than in dictating product specifications. No vendor of goods can afford to forget that the specifications of those goods should ultimately be market or customer oriented. The product must be developed so that it will satisfy and sell readily to potential customers having been built to their requirements. This frequently means that the technical functions must be educated to realize that the customers' ideas rather than their own must dictate product characteristics.[8]

Competitive Product Appraisal. This is the determination of the standing of the company, product and the complete product line in relation to competing products and lines as viewed through the eyes of customers and prospects.

Customer Requirements and Habits Information. Finally, a vital output of the subsystem is an analysis of customers' and potential customers' requirements and habits as projected into the future.

Subsystem Processor

Since a Market Development Subsystem is the administrative subsystem under consideration, the processor of the systems module will be market development.

Subsystem Feedback

The market development subsystem must work closely with the engineering functions of the company, as well as with others in the technical and non-technical areas of the organization. This work does not stop with the output of information and the presentation of recommendation. It must be focused on getting decisions made and clearly defining the courses of action through the mechanism of management and engineering feedback.[9]

---

[8] American Management Association, *Organizing the Product Planning Function*, p. 65.

[9] American Management Association, *Organizing the Product Planning Function*, p. 16.

The engineer today can create almost any product if he is provided with definitive customer requirements. But customer requirements are constantly changing. The subsystem feedback loop will provide these requirements based on a solid foundation of facts as revealed by the customer reaction to products and suggested products of the entire marketing system.

Subsystem Control

Subsystem control in the Market Development Subsystem consists of those environmental factors which affect system operation. It is suggested that the following include the more important of these factors:[10] (1) financial strength, (2) physical plant, (3) location, (4) patent position, (5) customer acceptance, (6) specialized experience, (7) personnel, and (8) management.

THE ADVERTISING AND PROMOTION SUBSYSTEM

Subsystem Input

Sales and Management Data. Sales and management objectives are primary inputs to the subsystem. Each business has its own major objectives peculiar to the current conditions under which it operates. Since one of the main purposes of advertising and promotion is to assist in making sales, it is of primary importance that the subsystem be provided with the specific sales objectives that the promotion is to support. Once this is accomplished, the subsystem can then acquire and process the necessary data to support these objectives.

Engineering and Development Data. It is essential that the subsystem output be based on accurate technical facts. The major source of these facts are the company designers, engineers, researchers and other technically trained people.

Marketing Intelligence Data. Before the subsystem begins to produce an output which will satisfy specific sales objectives, there are a number of units required from the Marketing Intelligence Subsystem. These include where prospective buyer and company organizations are located, who within these companies has buying influence, and why they are or are not buying particular products.

Subsystem Output

Subsystem output is the result of processing technical inputs with management and sales objectives to produce an optimum advertising and promotion product. The primary outputs are as follows: (1) trade publications space, (2) general publications space, (3) direct mail (geographically), (4) direct mail (national), (5) catalogs and sales literature, (6) educational booklets, (7) publicity and public relations, (8) internal sales promotion, and (9) trade show activity.

---

[10] Charles H. Kline, "The Strategy of Product Policy," *Harvard Business Review*, Vol. 33, No. 4 (July–August 1955), p. 92.

Subsystem Processor

Since advertising and promotion is the administrative subsystem under consideration, the processor of the systems module will be advertising and promotion. The actual processing techniques will not be explored since this is considered beyond the scope of this paper.

Subsystem Feedback

This is the act of communicating the reaction of the user of the advertised and promoted product back to the subsystem input and making appropriate corrections. Measurement of advertising and promotion results can be made to seem overly simple. Other than subjective opinions, the only true measure is the number of actual sales which the advertising and promotion produce or help to produce. One approach to quantitative measurement is by tabulating inquiries using keyed returns from particular advertisements. While it has value, it also has limitations.

The effect of advertising and promotion is a pyramidal one. It may be that the effort is preparing a prospect over a period of several years to become a customer. Then, suddenly the prospect makes an inquiry on a particular promotion effort. The mistaken conclusion is that the one advertisement really got results when as a matter of fact, the integrated product finally exceeded the minimum threshold of the prospect.

Subsystem Control

Subsystem control in the advertising and promotion subsystem consists of those environmental factors which affect system operation. Included in this category are company policies, company directives, government laws and regulations, company financial conditions, and ethics.

THE SALES SUBSYSTEM

Subsystem Input

Management Data. Management objectives are primary inputs to the subsystem. Each business has its own major objectives which are peculiar to the current conditions under which it operates. These will be interpreted and processed to obtain realistic sales objectives.

Technical Product Data. Tangible and concrete data on the existing company products, research and development capabilities, processes, and service potential are basic inputs to the subsystem. Technical properties of competitive products should be considered at this point in the process.

Customer Problem Data. The problem facing customers in marketing their own products should be an input to the sales subsystem.

Customer Intelligence. The sales subsystem must have intimate knowledge of the company's customers. The customer buying practices, including the various levels of approval required for any given type of negotiation, must be understood. When dealing with government agencies, the normal method of funding is an important consideration.

Sales and Contract Awards. The sales which are made and the contracts which are awarded as the result of successful marketing efforts become a part of the marketing system at this point.

Subsystem Output

Internal Coordination. The sales subsystem cannot do all the selling for the company. It should, however, be the coordination of specific sales information with engineering, manufacturing, contracting, finance, other marketing subsystems, and other company functions. All of these groups must be aware of the market potential in any given endeavor, and they must understand the marketing problems the company faces in its struggle for a successful order. Each function should understand that they are part of the company sales team with an important role in helping to obtain new business.

External Coordination. The subsystem also has an output which works directly with the customer in satisfying his requirements.

Sales Philosophy. Another very important output of the subsystem is the company selling philosophy. This philosophy is an important input to several of the other marketing subsystems who in turn base their activities on its content. It is based on management objectives and policies of the company as a whole.

Customer Relations. With regard to the psychology of selling, this means that the salesman must be a competent public relations man and a good service engineer. He usually performs these functions in advance of the company's actual felt need.

Sales Plans. Probably the most important output of the subsystem is the company sales plan. This is the document that implements the internal coordination described above and describes how the subsystem plans to integrate the company activity to obtain a sale or a contract award for a specific business opportunity.

Subsystem Processor

Since sales is the administrative subsystem under consideration, the processor of the systems module will be sales. In all cases of system analysis, the system under study will be the processor.[11]

Subsystem Feedback

The activity of the sales subsystem is a much more dynamic process than the other marketing subsystems. It is, therefore, necessary that frequent reports on the status of sales and proposals be prepared for management information. The frequent review and analysis of all outstanding business opportunities solves another equally important problem, that of providing much of the data required for the short-range projection of the

---

[11] Optner, *op. cit.*, p. 12.

company's business opportunities. When such data are combined with data from other areas of the business, they provide the necessary basis for forecasting company operation for several years in advance.

Subsystem Control

Subsystem control in the sales subsystem consists of those environmental factors which affect system operation. The subsystem is, of course, subjected to the same internal environment that have been described for the other marketing subsystems. Externally, however, the environment is a very severe one with respect to the many legal aspects of selling to all the laws of commerce imposed on any selling organization.

THE POST SALES SUBSYSTEM

Subsystem Input

Technical Data. Technical surveys for the purpose of product service consists of analyzing the service needs of customers and adopting the product to those needs. These technical surveys should begin with the original product engineering effort and continue throughout the product cycle.

Management Data. The product service function requires management policy inputs as there will always be some documentary exchange between the customer and the product service function. The subsystem must include, as a part of its process, the management position on service and its relation to the general marketing program.

Customer Data. Inputs from the customer are necessary in order that realistic plans on product service can be formulated. Information on type of installation, use, location and environment are necessary in order that a service program can be determined. This data when processed with the company technical data will result in a product service program which will be realistic to both the company and the customer.

Subsystem Output

Product Installation. Product installation as an output varies in its importance according to the type of product. Some products do not need to be installed in the ordinary sense, although the product must always be integrated into the customer's environment in some manner.

Product Demonstration. The manufacturer must educate his customer on how to use the product he has developed. In new technical areas and with highly complicated products which are difficult to operate, or have a wide variety of applications, product demonstration as an output is most important.

Technical Maintenance. After the product has been delivered to the customer and he has been educated to its operation and use, the company still has an obligation to provide technical maintenance. Some products, of course, require very little technical maintenance while others require constant service during their useful life, which may be many decades. To meet the marketing and company objectives it is obvious that product service is a significant subsystem output to the manufacturer and the customer.

Subsystem Processor

Since the post sales subsystem is the administrative subsystem under consideration, the processor of the systems module will be post-sales. In all cases of systems analysis, the system under study will be the processor.[12]

Subsystem Feedback

The product service function is in a most favorable position to provide the company the product information uncovered during the service process. This information is then transmitted to the Marketing Development Subsystem and the Sales Subsystem for the purpose of better adopting or furnishing additional products to meet the customer needs. Thus, the marketing system is a continuous, cyclical process, reaching through consumption as a way of determining that utility is actually realized by the customer and that products are adjusted to the customer needs.

Subsystem Control

Subsystem control in the post-sales subsystem consists of those environmental factors which affect systems operations. The subsystem is, of course, subjected to the same internal environments that have been described for the other marketing subsystems. Externally, the product service function must also operate in an environment of legal control. In a free enterprise economy the limits to which a company must extend product service is determined largely by the customer. If the customer is willing to pay for more service, the company will usually provide it. Nevertheless, society has provided some legal requirements primarily to protect the public from negligence and unscrupulous practices. Many of these requirements pertinent to the product service of manufacturers are found in the Uniform Sales Laws and the law of Tort.

Bibliography

Books

Goode, Harry H., and Machol, Robert E. *Systems Engineering.* New York: McGraw-Hill Book Co., Inc., 1957.

Johnson, Richard D., Kast, Fremont E., and Rosenzweig. *The Theory and Management of Systems.* New York: McGraw-Hill Book Co., Inc., 1963.

Messner, Fredrich R. *Industrial Advertising.* New York: McGraw-Hill Book Co., Inc., 1963.

---

[12] Optner, *op. cit.,* p. 12.

Optner, Stanford L., *Systems Analysis for Business Management.* Englewood Cliffs, N. J., 1960.

Periodicals

Busch, Gerald A. "Prudent-Manager Forecasting," *Harvard Business Review* (May–June, 1961), Vol. 39, No. 3, pp. 57–64.
Felton, Arthur P. "Conditions of Marketing Leadership," *Harvard Business Review* (March–April, 1956), Vol. 34, No. 2.
Kline, Charles H. "The Strategy of Product Policy," *Harvard Business Review* (July–August, 1955), Vol. 33, No. 4.

Reports

American Management Association. *Organizing the Product Planning Function.* American Management Association Research Study No. 59. New York: American Management Association, 1963.

B Information in the Marketing Plan: The Traditional Research Approach

11 The Role of Research in Marketing Management*

HARRY V. ROBERTS

The very real contributions research can make to marketing decision making are cited, but the author also warns that "research is often aimless fact gathering that fails to provide help in making decisions except by accident."

Expansion of marketing research reflects a growing belief that the methods of science are useful in solving the problems of business management. Effective application of marketing research, however, is neither easy nor automatic; and some have even contended that on balance actual applications have been more ineffective than effective.[1] This paper represents an attempt to formulate a framework for analysis of conditions under which marketing research can be expected to be effective and to make incidental suggestions for increasing effectiveness. This framework is founded on *a priori* reasoning and impressionistic evidence; its presentation here is drastically condensed; but it may nonetheless be suggestive both to those who apply research and to those who are intrigued by research for its own sake.

DECISION MAKING

Marketing management can be viewed simply as the continuing attempt to recognize and solve specific marketing problems. A *problem* exists when an objective is desired and there is uncertainty as to how it can best be achieved. A *decision* is the selection of some course of action (or inaction) to attain the objective. There are three imperatives in the process of decision making: (1) possible actions must be recognized; (2) the results

---

*Reprinted from the **Journal of Marketing,** national quarterly publication of the American Marketing Association, Vol. 22 (July, 1957), pp. 21–32.

[1] For example, see John E. Jueck, "Marketing Research—Milestone or Millstone?," *The Journal of Marketing,* April 1953, pp. 381–387.

of different actions must be predicted; and (3) the order of preference of these predicted results must be assessed. Research is potentially useful for at least the first two of these.

RESEARCH AND INTUITION

"Research" can be contrasted with "intuition" (or "judgment" or "common sense") in the decision-making process.

Research is any relatively systematic, formal, conscious procedure for evolving and testing hypotheses about reality or, in more modern terms, for making decisions. The words "systematic," "formal," and "conscious" differentiate "research" from "intuition." The distinction between research and intuition is not a sharp one, especially since intuition is an essential ingredient of good research, but the major differences of emphasis are these:

(1) While both research and intuition are ultimately oriented toward predictions, intuition is oriented toward narrow and immediate predictions rather than general hypotheses fruitful of many specific predictions.

(2) Intuition is learned, if at all, by experience and demonstration rather than by formal study.

(3) Intuition is seldom subject to logical scrutiny or formal empirical testing.

(4) Research uses such technical tools as mathematics, logic, experimental methods, and statistical inference.

Since research is intuition plus science, it is easy to assume that research can improve upon intuition in the social sciences and business management as well. There is, however, reason to be skeptical of this assumption. A distinguished economist has said,

> We seem to be forced to the conclusion, not that prediction and control are impossible in the field of human phenomena, but that the formal methods of science are of very limited application. Common sense does predict and control, and can be trained to predict and control better; but that does not prove that science can predict and control better than common sense. And it seems very doubtful whether in the majority of social problems the application of logical methods and canons will give as good results as the informal, intuitive process of judgment which, when refined and developed, becomes art.[2]

In order to formulate useful generalizations about the role of research in marketing, two closely related issues must be considered: (1) potential

---

[2] Frank H. Knight, *The Ethics of Competition and Other Essays* (London: George Allen and Unwin, Ltd., 1936), pp. 132–133. See also pp. 116–117 and 119.

contributions of research to marketing problems and (2) identification of characteristics of marketing problems that make these problems more or less accessible to attack by research.

POTENTIAL CONTRIBUTIONS OF RESEARCH

There are four major kinds of contributions that research can make toward decision making in marketing: (1) systematic description and classification of marketing "facts" as exemplified by the censuses of population and distribution or the data of the Audit Bureau of Circulation; (2) substantive hypotheses that can be used to make predictions; (3) logical and mathematical tools for classifying relevant variables, exploring the logical relationships among hypotheses, and deriving the predictions implied by hypotheses; and (4) the inferential tools of statistics.

Systematic Description and Classification of "Facts"

It is easy to forget and hard to evaluate precisely the contribution of a wealth of descriptive materials to marketing management in America, and indeed these materials are often not even thought of as "marketing research" because of their descriptive rather than analytic orientation. Yet, a little reflection on the pervasive use in marketing, for example, of census materials suggests their indispensable role.

Substantive Hypotheses

In physics the body of substantive hypotheses is large, relatively well articulated by logical connections between individual hypotheses, and well verified by actual testing of the accuracy of predictions derived from hypotheses. In short, one may speak meaningfully of "physical *theory*." By contrast, the so-called "social" or "behavioral" sciences, which have the greatest potential relevance to marketing, *consist largely of apparently unrelated empirical observations with relatively little theory to articulate these observations*. These disciplines rarely contain hypotheses of direct usefulness in solving the specific problems which arise in marketing. Moreover, most current marketing research is *ad hoc* empirical work with little substantive carry-over from one study to another. The so-called "principles" in textbooks rarely yield concrete predictions as to the effect of proposed marketing actions. For example, "principles" of copywriting and advertising format are often listed, but advertising men frequently disagree on the choice of the most effective advertisement.[3]

The main theoretical instrument for potential guidance in marketing is the axiom of rational behavior, which has been applied mainly in eco-

---

[3] Most textbook principles are really proverbs; for each "principle" there is an equally plausible "principle" stating the opposite. See Herbert A. Simon, *Administrative Behavior* (New York: The Macmillan Company, 1948), pp. 20ff.

nomics.[4] Supply and demand theory based on the rationality postulates has some relevance for marketing problems. For example, even without precise quantitative estimates of elasticities of demand for automobiles, this theory will predict the effect of setting the retail list price of cars below the competitive price on (a) the distribution of income between dealers and manufacturers, (b) the rate of production of automobiles, and (c) the rate of sale to consumers of "optional" accessories.[5]

Even though there are few predictive hypotheses in the social sciences, these sciences may often be useful in marketing by suggesting what to look for as opposed to predicting what will be found. Thus, a psychologist might be able to suggest possible advertising appeals that would not occur to a copywriter who lacked a formal background in psychology, even though psychological theory probably could not predict the most effective from a given list of appeals.

Logical and Mathematical Tools

Logical and mathematical tools are essentially languages for the analysis of problems. The concepts of supply and demand schedule, for example, would facilitate the analysis of economic—and some marketing—problems even if they had no predictive value at all. Pure formal logic may also be helpful. For example, there is one advertising "principle" that the advertising message should reach as wide an audience as possible and another that frequent repetitions of the advertising message are desirable. Logic suggests immediately that either "principle" by itself is inadequate and that the real problem is to find some optimal combination of wide coverage and intensive repetition. Similar examples are easy to find; in all of them, logic serves to formulate the real issues and avoid futile talking.

In recent years many new mathematical tools have been made available for possible use in making marketing decisions. For example, various mathematical models have been proposed for problems of strategy, programming, learning, inventory decisions, mass and small group communication, economic forecasting, queuing, capital budgeting, diversification of risk, and so on. Actual applications have undoubtedly lagged behind advance publicity, but enough has been done to suggest exciting developments to come.

Statistical Inference

Statistical inference is potentially useful in marketing as a tool for securing and interpreting empirical observations so that a "rational"

---

[4] Kenneth J. Arrow, "Mathematical Models in the Social Science," *Cowles Commission Papers, New Series, No. 48* (Chicago: Cowles Commission for Research in Economics, 1952), p. 137.

[5] Milton Friedman, "Notes on Lectures in Price Theory" (unpublished manuscript based on notes prepared by David I. Fand and Warren J. Gustus, The University of Chicago Press, 1951), pp. 15–16.

decision can be made in the face of uncertainty. In *experimental* applications, managerial actions are actually tried out with the aim of discovering the responses to these actions. All other applications are *nonexperimental* or *"observational."*

> Evidence cast up by experience is abundant and frequently as conclusive as that from contrived experiments. . . . But such evidence is far more difficult to interpret. It is frequently complex and always indirect and incomplete . . . its interpretation generally requires subtle analysis and involved chains of reasoning, which seldom carry real conviction. . . .[6]

Experimental methods, by contrast, yield evidence free of such difficulties of interpretation so long as: (1) The underlying conditions of the past persist into the future. (2) The experiment is run sufficiently long that responses to experimental stimuli will have time to manifest themselves. (3) The population being studied can be broken down into smaller units (families, stores, sales territories, etc.) for which the experimental stimuli can be measured and for which responses to the stimuli are not "contagious." (4) The experimentor is able to apply or withhold, as *he* chooses, experimental stimuli from any particular unit of the population he is studying. (5) Neither the stimulus nor the response is changed by the fact that an experiment is being conducted. (6) The sample size is large enough to measure important responses to experimental stimuli against the background of uncontrolled sources of variation.

The key to modern statistical design of experiments is withholding experimental stimuli *at random*. To the extent that randomization and the other conditions above are met, the responses actually observed will reflect the "true" effects of the stimuli plus random or chance variation. Statistical procedures then need cope only with the interpretation of chance variation. Observational methods must cope both with chance variation and possible systematic error, and systematic error eludes rigorous statistical treatment. For example, one can compare purchases of an advertiser's product between readers and nonreaders of a recent advertisement and try to make statistical allowance for the fact that readers are potentially different from nonreaders in many respects other than the simple fact of seeing or not seeing the advertisement; but after all such allowances, there is no guarantee that systematic differences do not persist. For example, a statistician might make statistical adjustments for factors such as economic status, education, sex, age, etc., that might distinguish readers from nonreaders of the advertisement and then find that the adjusted purchase rate of the product is still higher among readers than nonreaders. *Even if* the statistical adjustments have succeeded in making the two groups comparable in respect to *all*

---

[6] Milton Friedman, *Essays in Positive Economics* (Chicago: The University of Chicago Press, 1953), pp. 10–11.

variables associated with the tendency to respond to the advertisement's message—and there is never any guarantee in observational studies that this has in fact been achieved—it still may be true that those people who buy the product are more likely to notice and read the advertisement or at least to remember, or say that they remember, having read it.

These fundamental limitations of observational techniques notwithstanding, marketing research has already drawn heavily on them and will do so increasingly in the future. The development of sound methods of sampling of human populations is recent, and advances are still being made. Much of current marketing research has been made possible by this development of sampling theory and practice. Similarly, the development of psychological scaling and factor analysis—which may be viewed as statistical tools—has had a noticeable influence on current practice. Moreover, there are many potentially valuable statistical tools that have not yet been widely applied in marketing research, and others will undoubtedly be developed.

CHARACTERISTICS OF MARKETING PROBLEMS THAT INFLUENCE ATTAINMENT OF AN ECONOMICAL SOLUTION BY RESEARCH

Every marketing problem is different, but certain criteria determine the compatibility of particular problems and methods of research. In the simplest type of problem situation, the proposed actions are given. The response to the actions must be predicted and a decision made in the light of the desired objectives. General economic conditions, actions of competitors, and other actions of the firm are assumed to continue unchanged. Later these assumptions will be relaxed. In each of the criteria listed below, the phrase "other things being equal" should be considered implicit.

The more rapid the response to marketing actions, the easier the problems for research. Often the quality characteristics of manufactured products can be measured only after a long time. Thus, the resistance to weathering of different paints could be tested by (1) actual weathering over five years or (2) accelerated testing in a laboratory. It is well known in product research that accelerated testing is capricious and often perverse.[7] In marketing the shortcomings of accelerated testing are at least as serious but less likely to be discovered, especially for institutional and "indirect-action" advertising and promotion. By contrast, direct-action selling effort such as local and mail-order advertising—for which accelerated testing is unnecessary—has been researched widely with obvious success.[8] In addition to the rapidity of response to direct-action selling effort, there is often a second

---

[7] Eugene W. Pike, "Testing Components for High-Reliability Systems" (unpublished paper given at the National Meeting on Airborne Electronics of the Institute of Radio Engineers, Dayton, Ohio, May 13, 1953).

[8] For a typical example, see *Printer's Ink,* July 11, 1952, pp. 35 and 110.

explanation for success of research: responses are often readily *traceable*. Hence we set down:

The easier it is to trace response to marketing actions, the easier the problem for research. Responses to sales effort are frequently difficult to trace, partly because the many forms of selling effort that impinge on the ultimate consumer are often closely interrelated and many of them are designed to work indirectly. For example, an argument frequently advanced for the use of national advertising to *consumers* is that *dealers* are favorably motivated thereby. Further, consumer buying decisions may be interdependent because of "conspicuous consumption," "word-of-mouth," or "opinion leadership." There are tools for coping with the problem of traceability. Selling stimuli often can be traced to relatively small geographic areas or relatively short time periods. If the buying decisions of consumers are interdependent, the contagion of purchase may be less important between small geographic areas than between individual consumers.

When measurement of the desired responses to marketing actions is impossible or uneconomic, the problem will be easier to the extent that satisfactory substitute responses can be found. If response to sales stimuli takes too long to manifest itself or is difficult to trace, a substitute response highly correlated with buying responses can be sought. Copy tests, consumer jury ratings, preference studies, and many techniques of questionnaire design and psychological measurement are based upon substitute responses.

In deciding on the validity of proposed substitute responses, there are three closely related approaches: (1) to verify by research that the substitute response is closely correlated with the response of ultimate interest for a class of problems similar to the one being studied, (2) to draw on general theoretical knowledge, and (3) to draw on experience and intuition.

It is hard to find validations of substitute responses in product research. In marketing, there are relatively few documented examples with details of the process of validation. Most of these examples fail to show significant differences for the sales responses but show significant differences for the corresponding substitute responses, usually preference measurements.[9] Here is the dilemma. Should one use preference measurements that show significant differences in response to different selling stimuli but for which results are not related in any known way with sales measurements? Preference measurements may be correlated with sales responses and are perhaps more sensitive. Seymour Banks has suggested that:

---

[9] See, for example: James H. Lorie and Harry V. Roberts, *Basic Methods of Marketing Research* (New York: McGraw-Hill Book Company, Inc., 1951), pp. 209–211; Seymour Banks, "The Measurement of the Effect of a New Packaging Material upon Preference and Sales," *The Journal of Business,* April 1950, pp. 79ff.; and G. Maxwell Ule, unpublished doctoral dissertation in progress, The University of Chicago, School of Business.

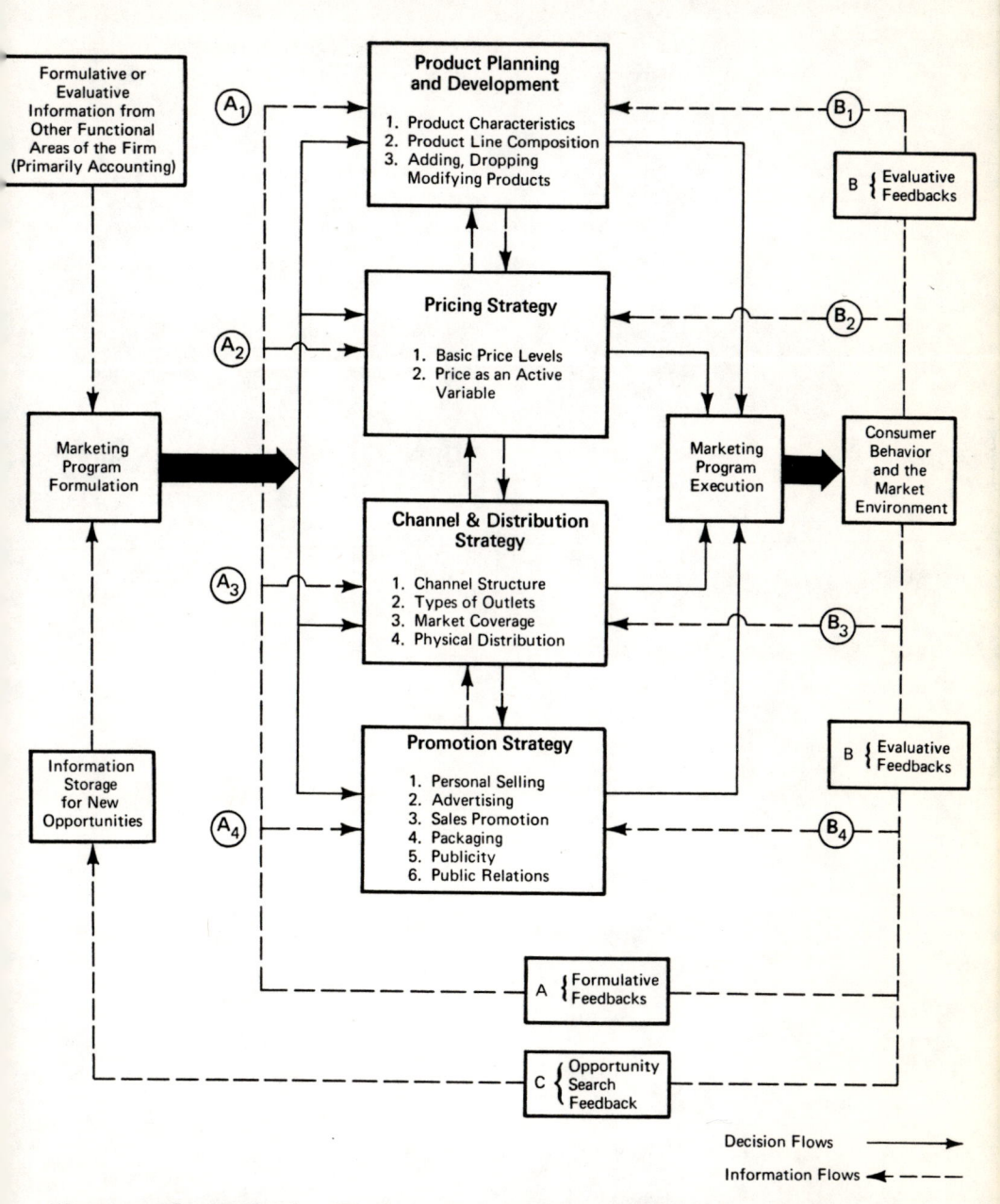

Figure 1. **The Marketing Management Process and Information Flow**

> . . . a preferent test can select the best of a series of proposed alternatives, but it cannot tell how much effect the use of this best alternative will have upon sales.[10]

But Banks has also published an excellent counterexample to this speculation.[11] George Brown has suggested in informal discussions that the "chain of causation" from selling stimulus to buying response might be divided into stages: opportunity for exposure to selling effort (for example, read the magazine in which an advertisement appears); actual exposure to selling effort (for example, read the actual advertisement); acquisition of information about or confidence in the product; formation of the intention to buy; and actual purchase. Measurements can be made at any stage of this chain. One might speculate that measurements would be more valid the closer they are to actual purchase, but this is at best only a plausible speculation. In the absence of evidence, speculation is unavoidable; but the search for validation of substitute responses should continue.

To the extent that experimentation is economically feasible, the problem is easier to solve by research. Properly designed experiments are free of many of the limitations of observational studies. Businessmen generally are often better situated to conduct sound experiments than is commonly believed. Actions taken as a result of business decisions represent direct intervention of a kind that is usually impossible in the social sciences. Both "test-tube" experiments as a prelude to final marketing decision and continuing experiments thereafter are often possible and entail little added cost, especially when marketing policies can be introduced piecemeal geographically.

Randomized experimentation is impossible only for "all-or-none" decisions. Major plant construction and advertising in national media are examples. John Jeuck listed major marketing innovations made without research and concluded, ". . . the really significant marketing achievements, the big chance . . . is dependent primarily on imagination and on the skills of management."[12]

Even when randomization through space is precluded, randomization *over time* may be feasible if the full response to selling stimuli—such as special promotions undertaken intermittently at randomly chosen time periods—is rapid and if the statistical behavior of sales in the absence of experimentation is well understood.[13] Unfortunately, the full response may

---

[10] Seymour Banks, *ibid.,* p. 80.

[11] Seymour Banks, "The Prediction of Dress Purchases for a Mail-Order House," *The Journal of Business,* January 1950, pp. 48–57.

[12] John J. Jeuck, "Marketing Research Today: A Minority Report," *School of Business Publications I,* The University of Chicago, undated, p. 10.

[13] See R. L. Anderson, "Recent Advances in Finding Best Operating Conditions," *Journal of American Statistical Association,* vol. 48, no. 264 (1953), pp. 789–798.

not be manifest sufficiently rapidly. Thus the initial effect of premium offers may be a very substantial increase in the rate of sales followed by a decrease if the premium mainly affects timing of purchases rather than their total amount.

Finally, experimentation may be undesirable if the stimulus or its response is seriously modified by the fact that an experiment is being run.

The success of research in problems that cannot be economically attacked experimentally depends on the adequacy of observational methods. Evaluation of adequacy of observational methods is also frustrated by the absence of evidence, but plausible guides can be offered.

The more adequate the theoretical knowledge, the more adequate are observational methods based on this knowledge. When theoretical knowledge is very good, satisfactory predictions can be made on the basis of existing theory without further recourse to observational study. Bridge building and other feats of engineering construction illustrate this point. More frequently, theory is simply an invaluable aid in the design and interpretation of research, whether observational or experimental. But while experimentation can reach valid results in problems for which theoretical knowledge is wholly or partly lacking, observational studies are seriously weakened when theory is sparse. There is relatively little marketing theory, and intuition must often guide the use of observational techniques. The distinction between "research" and "intuition" therefore becomes very blurred, as in certain areas of medical research in which valid experiments are difficult and theoretical knowledge is meager. In both marketing and medicine, the questions which cannot be subjected to valid experimentation are frequently resolved by the intuition of the practitioner.

Observational techniques may be more adequate to the extent that statistical allowance has been made for disturbing variables that may obscure the relationship being studied. By statistical allowance is meant crossclassification, standardized averages, multiple regression, and related techniques. These techniques are often used in observational studies to answer the question, "what would have happened if certain disturbing variables had not varied?" It seems always prudent to attempt to answer this question within the resources available for research. Except in experimental studies, of course, there is no guarantee that the answers are satisfactory within the usual allowance for chance error.[14]

There are a few special devices, not as widely used as they might be, that may enhance the effectiveness of observational methods in marketing research. (1) Aggregate data can be divided into components, as when sales are studied by territories or families. "Sales analysis," which seems to have lost favor by comparison with survey methods, illustrates the approach. (2) Rates of change through time can be studied instead of absolute levels. While this "before-after" approach is common in sales tests,

---

[14] See, for example, W. Allen Wallis and Harry V. Roberts, *Statistics: A New Approach* (Glencoe, Illinois: The Free Press, 1956), ch. 9.

its use in observational studies is rare, perhaps because of the current emphasis on single surveys. (3) Insightful comparisons can be made such as comparisons of product awareness of advertised and competitive brands during a special campaign or Alfred Politz's comparison of attitudes toward car acceleration with strength of accelerator spring.[15] (4) Different observational methods may be used to attack a single research problem. The degree of convergence of their results may indicate the confidence to be accorded the results of any one of the approaches.

To the extent that changes in present conditions may have to be allowed for, the problem is more difficult for research. Two cases need to be considered: (1) changes that would have occurred anyway; and (2) changes that are, at least in part, responses to the decision in the particular problem.

Changes that would have occurred anyway. The best-known examples are shifts in general business conditions or in demand conditions confronting a whole industry. General economic conditions have such relevance to marketing (and other) problems of the firm that economic and sales forecasting is of great importance. A treatment of the usefulness of research in economic forecasting is beyond our present scope.[16]

As to the modifications of marketing decisions that should be made in the light of predicted changes in economic conditions, economic theory is relatively useful. For example, there is considerable evidence on the difference in response of prices and outputs of durable and nondurable goods or of retail and wholesale prices to changes in economic conditions.

Changes in part influenced by the decision under consideration. The classic illustration analyzed by economic theorists is the situation of duopoly or other small-number competitive situations. The analogue in marketing is easy to find. Suppose, for example, that a company were able by experimental methods to estimate the productivity of its advertising expenditures and that a leading competitor had maintained his advertising unchanged during the period of the experiment. As a result of the experiment, the company might sharply increase its advertising expenditures, making the tacit assumption that the competitor would make no change. The competitor—observing this increase—might increase its advertising, possibly "cancelling out" the effectiveness of the first company's added expenditure and leaving

---

[15] Alfred Politz, "Science and Truth in Marketing Research," *Harvard Business Review,* January–February 1957, pp. 121–122.

[16] See, for example: Harry V. Roberts, "A Method of Improving Sales Forecasts," *Proceedings of Golden Triangle Conference of the American Marketing Association,* 1956 (American Marketing Association, Inc., 1956), pp. 97–102; Robert Ferber, "Sales Forecasting by Correlation Methods," *The Journal of Marketing,* January 1954, pp. 219–232; James H. Lorie, "Operations Research and Short-Run Sales Forecasting" (paper delivered before the Second Annual Meeting of the Operations Research Society of America, May 21–22, 1954); Irving Schweiger, "The Contribution of Consumer Anticipations in Forecasting Consumer Demand," in National Bureau of Economic Research, *Short-Term Economic Forecasting,* Studies in Income and Wealth, vol. 17 (Princeton: Princeton University Press, 1955).

both companies in their original sales position vis-à-vis one another. The experiment would have been entirely adequate for determining what would have happened in the absence of a response by the competitor, but it could lead to a bad decision in the absence of a prediction as to what the competitor would do; how soon he would do it; and what effect, if any, his response would have on the rate of sales of the first company. Competitive responses and interactions also raise serious problems in the interpretation of observational data.

The guessing of competitive reactions may be an art highly dependent on intuition and experience, with formal research perhaps serving chiefly to supply salient background facts. Psychology and social-psychology do not appear to offer useful predictions. Even if the competitive responses could be predicted, their effect on sales could be estimated at best by observational methods.

Finally, the task of research is easier for problems that can be studied and solved independently of other problems because indirect effects do not then have to be considered. One of the key tasks of management—and research—is the fragmentation of the complex of problems facing a company into smaller problems that can be considered relatively independently of other problems.

THE EFFECTIVENESS OF RESEARCH IN THE DISCOVERY OF POSSIBLE NEW ALTERNATIVES FOR ACTION

An essential part of problem solving is the discovery of alternative possibilities for action besides those initially considered or—in alternative terminology—the "identification of problems." This is closely analogous to "formulation of hypotheses" where words like "accident" and "inspiration" readily come to mind. In the context of marketing, John E. Jeuck has said:

> . . . It seems likely that research can do very little in a positive or creative way to lead to those new possibilities that are the essence of creative market development and exploitation. That is simply to say, I suppose, that marketing success depends more upon the imaginative and aggressive personality who may in the process of development make many errors than it does upon the careful collation of facts and the cautious investigation of alternatives that are the hallmark of research operations.
>
> In that connection, one must be impressed with how unlikely it would have been for Sears, Roebuck ever to have made a really strong start if Richard Sears had had a clear view of what is usually uncovered in the consumer survey. One wonders how many other companies would have never been started if they had relied upon the typical consumer survey to guide them in their selection of products and policies. . . .[17]

[17] Jeuck, *op. cit.*, p. 7.

To the extent that Jeuck's comments represent more than a criticism of the frequent use of more or less stereotyped methods in marketing research, they are seriously misleading. Research is probably more effective in unearthing new possibilities for action than in predicting the response to existing ones.[18] Research focuses attention on possible actions that probably would not have been recognized in the absence of research. The new ideas that turn up as an unexpected by-product of research are frequently more valuable than the objectives originally sought. The very discipline of objective recording of data forces people to look at things they would never have looked at otherwise and to question assumptions that would not otherwise have been challenged: research can be a protection against complacency and a stimulus to imagination.

Quality control illustrates a new method of research aimed primarily at the discovery of new possibilities for action.[19] The basic idea is that a repetitive process such as a manufacturing or marketing operation is measured at periodic intervals, often by sampling methods. Statistical procedures —"control charts"—have been devised in order to detect systematic changes of the process. The detection of such changes provides a warning that the process should be immediately investigated to see what has happened and to discover "assignable causes." By discovering the "assignable cause," management can either remove a source of trouble or retain and possibly apply more widely an improvement that otherwise might have been lost. Quality control methods, then, suggest looking for trouble and therefore opportunity at times and places where the search is likely to be rewarded.

"RESEARCH" VERSUS "INTUITION"

Many problems in business are and should be attacked without the benefit of formal methods of research—especially relatively minor and nonrecurrent problems and those that require very quick decisions. Research would then cost more than its benefits. But though intuition sometimes yields a snap decision without any reflection, it may also involve soul searching and interminable committee meetings, both of which are expensive in terms of executive time.

---

[18] The impressions reported here are based on fairly extensive examination of applications of research in several areas of management. Many of these applications —about 300—were made by students in the 9th, 10th, and 12th Groups of the Executive Program of the University of Chicago who were given the assignment of applying statistical methods to problems in their own companies. See Harry V. Roberts, "Statistics in Middle Management," *Management Science,* vol. 1, nos. 3–4 (1955), pp. 224–232.

[19] The "classic" in this field is Walter A. Shewhart, *Economic Control of Quality of Manufactured Product* (New York: D. Van Nostrand Company, Inc., 1931). A recent text is Eugene L. Grant, *Statistical Quality Control,* revised edition (New York: McGraw-Hill Book Company, Inc., 1952).

If the criteria for the applicability of research enumerated above are examined carefully, four seem just as applicable to intuition or informal decision making as to formal methods of research: (1) the more rapid the response to actions, (2) the more easily responses can be traced, (3) the more adequate the substitute responses that can be found, and (4) the fewer the changes in existing conditions that need to be taken into account, the easier is the problem for *either* research or intuition. The criteria that appear to discriminate between research and intuition are the economic feasibility of experimentation and, failing experimentation, the availability of adequate observational tools.

RESEARCH AND THE EXECUTIVE

Many "practical issues" limit the use of research in marketing.

Some managerial problems are really ethical or value problems rather than factual ones. For example, there might be a problem of deciding whether or not to market and promote a cold remedy in the face of good evidence that the remedy had no measurable impact on colds. For such value choices, research or any rational decision-making process is clearly irrelevant. But genuine value problems in marketing probably occur less frequently than generally believed.

"Science" and "research" are very often used as weapons rather than as tools for the analysis of problems. Often research serves to postpone the need for a decision to change policy, to "prove" points, to win arguments, and even to persuade people to buy the product. When research is used predominantly for persuasion, it is almost always used more or less dishonestly. The most subtle form of dishonesty and perhaps the most prevalent is the presentation of only part of the evidence and the suppression of the rest. Such dishonesty is often undetected but nonetheless futile simply because it is a weapon open to all parties. The prevalence of obvious disagreements between experts tends to reduce the layman's respect for research, and the suppression of unfavorable information is likely to become habitual.

Even when intentions are laudable, research is often aimless fact gathering that fails to provide help in making decisions except by accident. Some executives ignore research findings that are inconsistent with conclusions they have already reached; in the name of "evidence," some research men try to persuade executives to make decisions unsupported by the actual research. Perhaps the most revealing symptom of the practical difficulty of using research well is the frequent failure to define adequately the objectives of research. This failure probably stems from a lack of understanding as to what a full statement of objectives really involves and how much hard thinking it demands. Careful formulation of objectives need not and should not preclude the search for the unexpected "by-products" that are often so useful, nor does it preclude the collection of certain basic information—such as the rate of retail sales of one's product—in advance of current problems. But it is only too easy to lapse into the relatively mechanical assembly of information and quietly wander off into irrelevancy so that even useful information may not be properly understood by management even after sustained and aggressive attempts by research men to "sell" their product.

The failure to specify objectives adequately stems in part from human failings but also from the common tendency to regard marketing research as something essentially different from management or as a field for experts who supply the information needed for decisions to executives who then use intuitive judgment in arriving at the final decision. While there are potential advantages to be gained from specialization of functions, the intimate relationship between "research" and "intuition" together with the fact that the final decision rests with management puts on management the primary responsibility of using research well.

Marketing research is only one of the many fields of business in which experts in research aid executives. The executive's task is to use and evaluate the work of the expert without fully understanding the expert's discipline. The dependence on experts, of course, is not unique to business; the most unnerving example for many people is their own dependence on doctors. The executive's dependence on experts has also been recognized and sometimes deplored. The time, ability, and effort required to attain reasonable competence in any field of science ordinarily limits researchers themselves to relatively narrow specialization. Yet, the executive must make good use of the advice of many experts. To say that this task is extremely difficult is only to say that rational or even partly rational decisions are hard to make.

Perhaps the most important potential contribution of "research" in marketing comes from the relatively objective viewpoint that research encourages even among those who do not directly execute it. (The increasing orientation of management toward the "consumer point of view" is probably traceable to marketing research.) One cannot help being impressed by the frequency with which data contradict strongly held beliefs or suggest completely new alternatives for action. However difficult it may be to acquire the needed objectivity, the acquisition is probably not much more difficult for executives than for technically trained research people. In those areas of research where scientific experimentation is seldom used, of which marketing research is one, there are few occasions on which the research man is really "proved wrong," and it is being proved wrong rather than technical training *per se* that probably makes for genuine objectivity. Unfortunately, observational data usually can be interpreted in many plausible ways and frequently fail to convince either research men or executives that their previously held views were wrong.

One can be proved wrong also in the realm of logic, and the importance of sound logic in decision making should not be overlooked. Commonplace examples of importance are easy to find in practice: the assumption that the demand curve is infinitely inelastic for small price rises though not for large ones and the use of full costs rather than marginal costs in making decisions on output. While some errors of logic are extremely subtle and hard to detect, it would not seem unreasonable to expect that executives might learn to avoid the obvious ones. Mistakes of empirical inference also probably turn more frequently on elementary errors than on subtle ones.[20]

Two prerequisites to more effective use of marketing research by executives can be embraced under "objectivity" and some understanding of basic tools of research—particularly logic, economics, and statistics. The fundamental key, however, is the executive's understanding that research, like management itself, must be evaluated ultimately by predictive tests. The single most useful step in fitting research into marketing management would be greater recognition of the fact that the essence of research is neither surveys nor samples but the evolution and testing of hypotheses about marketing by testing the predictions to which they lead.

There is, of course, much more to management than research. There are difficulties in applying research with which we have not attempted to deal, particularly the extent to which the scientific approach to management might dull intuition or lead to overintellectualization that could easily paralyze decisive action. Again, an executive who knows a certain venture to be a long shot may not try nearly so hard to make it succeed as if he believes, erroneously, that it is very likely to be successful. There is little which can be said about these things except to venture the opinion that they are probably overrated in importance. For each man who succeeds in apparently irrational ventures or whose intuition seems to surpasss rational calculations, there are many for whom irrationality is the prime cause of failure.

12 Phasing Research Into the Marketing Plan*

LEE ADLER

Marketing research, as generally applied today, is out of step with other marketing activities, particularly marketing planning. Marketing research must break away from its emphasis on narrow investigations of limited usefulness and contribute to the accumulation of information needed for making long-range decisions.

---

[20] See Wallis and Roberts, *op. cit.*, ch. 3.

*Reprinted from **Harvard Business Review,** Vol. 38, No. 3 (May–June, 1960), pp. 113–122.

Because of its preoccupation with gathering unrelated facts, the pressures of day-to-day business, and other unfortunate tendencies, marketing research today tends to be out of phase with other marketing operations.

The key to a larger and more important role for research is a systematic effort to design individual studies so that they not only contribute useful knowledge for short-term marketing needs but also help in the development of a long-range departmental program.

In making research planning effective, it is important to set up the work so that a series of studies can "feed in" to the needs of the marketing department as a whole.

Firms that have successfully used research planning have discovered in it a variety of important advantages, ranging from more sophistication and economy in the design of studies to better anticipation of marketing problems.

In the past few years there has been much talk about the creation of a unified concept of marketing research that would make it possible for researchers to grapple with marketing problems as seen by top management. Unfortunately, to date, this idea has remained talk more often than it has become action. As a consequence, marketing research is not helping to solve management's problems as it might.

If research executives want to assume more responsible positions in the corporate structure, they will have to find ways of increasing the contribution of their groups to the successful implementation of the marketing concept. By "marketing concept" I refer, of course, to the idea of customer rather than factory orientation, and to the idea of making integrated use of all the tools of marketing.

OBSTACLES TO PROGRESS

Success for the research executive is not likely to come easily. He inherits a legacy of practical difficulties. In company after company a gap exists between marketing research needs and fulfillment. Breakdowns of communication occur between researchers and marketing management. And many researchers' studies—prettily bound and lavishly illustrated with charts—gather dust.

Why? One reason looms large. The problems that marketing management must deal with are broad-scale and complex. But the problems that are defined for investigation by researchers are so delimited that the findings made either deal with too small a piece of the total problem or cannot be easily related to other aspects of the total problem. They lose their link with reality as the top marketing executive sees it.

What accounts for marketing research being out of phase with marketing in so many firms? There are, I believe, five principal reasons:

(1) *Preoccupation with the gathering of unrelated facts*—On the whole, American marketing researchers are busy collectors of isolated bits

and pieces of information, but they pay scant attention to constructing bodies of knowledge. In part, this tendency derives from the history of research in the United States. Still in its formative years—50 years old altogether—the marketing research function has enjoyed substantial growth only since World War II. As a result, expectations from research have been modest. Many a corporate executive, if he authorizes research at all, has not looked for—and still does not look for—more than a mechanical assemblage of "facts" which he may or may not apply to the problem at hand. Accompanying this limited role for research have been limited budgets, staff, and time for doing a job thoroughly.

It is not surprising, then, that it is only accident when several studies in a field can be related to each other so that the whole is greater than the sum of the parts, or even as great as the sum of the parts.

(2) *Pressures of day-to-day business*—The competitive pressures of American business result in a demand for concentration on urgent, immediate problems to the exclusion of the more leisurely contemplation of broad problems. Of course, it is understandable that *some* short-range assignments of applied research cannot be readily integrated into any larger scheme. But to the extent that today's frantic drive to solve short-range problems deflects attention from the more fundamental and thornier problems of the long term, the urgencies of the market place do disservice to broader scale research.

This failing is not entirely the responsibility of researchers themselves. If pressing problems need solution, they must be solved, whether or not they contribute to a system of hypotheses for longer range study.

(3) *Insistence on rigorous methodology*—Robert K. Merton has noted that "the American [researcher] raises aloft the standards of affirming adequacy of empirical data at any price, even at the price of surrendering the problem which first led to the inquiry."[1]

A case in point is the work of David Riesman. His studies have appeared to many to offer significantly new ways of looking at the American way of life, with important consequences for marketing management in his analysis of our consumption-oriented economy.[2] Yet the ardent defenders of rigorous methodology have criticized Riesman for his relaxed, impressionistic approach to his studies. The trouble is that the socio-psychological well-springs of our culture do not readily lend themselves to multiple correlation analysis. How can Riesman possibly cite levels of significance in his discussion of the "other-directed" personality?

Our culture is so complex and the forces prevailing on American consumers so numerous and subtle that a technician has trouble getting at them.

---

[1] *Social Theory and Social Structure* (Glencoe, Illinois: The Free Press, 1949), pp. 205–206.

[2] See *The Lonely Crowd* (New Haven: Yale University Press, 1950); and *Faces in the Crowd* (New Haven: Yale University Press, 1950).

By contrast, an approach which permits a freer play to imagination and a broader sweep to an investigation than statistical designs will allow stands a better chance of showing a more complete view of our society.

(4) *Tendency to specialize*—Applied research also mirrors the specialization of knowledge and function that characterizes American civilization. To a certain extent, the researcher and his work exemplify the popular observation that excesses of specialization result in "knowing more and more about less and less."

(5) *Recurring love affairs with new techniques*—In a curious way, the very advances made in marketing research contribute to the trend toward specialization by leading to a preoccupation with technique instead of content.

For example, during the past decade more and more behavioral scientists have joined the ranks of business researchers. And these men have had a healthy effect in broadening the horizons of applied research; they have made available entirely new dimensions and tools for solving problems. But instead of these welcome additions to the armory of researchers being integrated into a battery of weapons designed to combat problems in their totality, they have helped fragment research even more. The spotlight has played around on the methods, leaving the problems themselves partly in the dark.

Again, the injustice of pointing accusing fingers only at the researchers must be emphasized. As marketing management has become increasingly enamored of the new disciplines, it has created a demand for applied sociological and psychological research. And in research, too, the customer is always right.

Take motivation research. From being virtually unknown in the 1940's, the technique blossomed into the research giant of the late 1950's. Rightfully, the behavioral scientists insisted on documenting William I. Thomas' observation that if men define situations as real, they are real in their consequences.[3] So the psychologists proceeded to demonstrate that products have not only rational meaning and serve utilitarian purposes for consumers, but also have symbolic and emotional meanings. Then, not so long ago, when there was great fascination with the discovery that men unconsciously regarded their cars as surrogates for the mistresses they enjoy in their fantasy lives, it was almost forgotten in Detroit that a more basic *raison d'être* for the automobile is to get people from one place to another at fairly reasonable cost. The stage was set for sexless and inexpensive foreign cars to have a field day.

The foregoing is, of course, oversimplified, and it is not intended as an attack on motivation research, already much maligned. I simply want to stress that new methods have succeeded too well in making American researchers and their clients technique-oriented instead of problem-oriented.

---

[3] William I. Thomas and Florian Znaniechi, *The Polish Peasant in Europe and America* (New York: Alfred A. Knopf, Inc., 1927).

A few years ago, probability samples were all the rage. Today is it fashionable to use the semantic differential technique. Preoccupation with any one method hurts marketing.

MEETING THE CHALLENGE

All this puts the research director in a tough spot. If, bowing to the needs and pressures just outlined, he designs and carries out studies dealing with very narrow problem areas, his findings will not fully meet the needs of marketing management. But if he goes to the other extreme and examines general, abstract questions, his data may have no validity at all for a particular firm in a particular situation. Somehow he must define his problems concretely enough to be manageable.

Is there a way out of this dilemma? I believe that there is. It seems to me that the solution lies in the formulation of an *over-all, long-range research program for each firm and for each market*. This program would be used to guide the design of individual studies so that they not only contribute knowledge for the short term but also contribute to the evolution of a unified body of information needed to implement the marketing concept over the long term.

There is a common expression among advertising men about the need to "see the big picture." What they mean by this expression is, of course, the importance of having a framework of knowledge about their clients' problems, including every step involved in getting the product from the factory into happy and repeated use by the consumer. Having this framework, they can then relate individual bits and pieces of information to the whole. Short-range problems are seen for what they are. The day-to-day concerns of advertising the product do not become confused with the total problem of marketing it.

What the alert advertising man does more or less impressionistically (or through disciplined intuition) when he looks at "the big picture" provides the key to the kind of research approach that is needed. Essentially, this approach calls for the prior or simultaneous formulation of long-range marketing objectives and the spelling out of the plans, policies, and programs calculated to reach those objectives through the use of the appropriate marketing tools. Describing these goals and plans in detail inevitably exposes the need for certain data which, in turn, leads to a listing of research projects over the same term as the marketing plan. It also suggests a priority order for their completion.

Here, in outline form, are the major steps that some progressive companies are taking in building long-range research programs which develop concurrently with, which parallel, which inform and are informed by the master long-term marketing plan:

1. Decide on long-term marketing objectives.
2. Enumerate in detail the policies, plans, and programs needed to attain the objectives.

3. Identify roadblocks barring progress toward goals and specify the areas where further information is necessary.
4. Define what and how the marketing research function can contribute to information gathering and problem solving.
5. Obtain the agreement of all members of the marketing team to objectives, plans, and programs.
6. Set up a priority order and timetable for the research projects.
7. Allocate the necessary budget, personnel, and facilities for implementing the program.

DEVELOPING THE PROGRAM

Defining a company's long-range goals is a painful, soul-searching process. But, as we have all learned by now, these goals should be as concrete as possible; this helps both in setting up plans and in assessing performance after the programs go into effect. Obvious as this seems, it is surprising how many companies continue to define an objective as "to boost sales" when more down-to-earth statements of sales targets are needed, such as:

Increase unit sales.
Sell the whole line, not items.
Improve share of market.
Concentrate on key accounts.
Introduce new products successfully.
Gain greater immediate profitability.
Open new territories.

Such objectives, alone or in combination, are specific enough to help in the choice of tactics to implement the master marketing plan. In the assignment of sensible goals, research can help by turning up data on such questions as:

What share of market is rightfully ours?
What payout period on investment should we strive for?
Are we going after the best markets?
Should we be in this business in the first place?

For example, the marketing plan of a producer in the transportation field was predicated for many years on the oversimplified sales goal of selling as much of its service as possible. This firm believed that all men were potential customers. Hence, the only criterion available to it for the proper use of such tools as advertising copy and media selection was that of reaching adult males. Later, marketing research showed that there was an enormous concentration of potential customers among businessmen who traveled considerably. The sales goal was then defined more specifically so as to concentrate marketing efforts on this crucial market segment. As a result, it was possible to reach the market more effectively and economically.

Team Activity

Effective long-range planning is necessarily a team activity. In addition to the immediate members of the marketing team, headed up by the marketing vice president or his equivalent, many companies have found it wise to have production, finance, and control men participate sufficiently so that (1) they understand and accept the marketing targets established and (2) the marketing goals harmonize with the over-all corporate objectives. In a framework of this kind the researcher can contribute more than he himself is able to see. The value of his data is not limited to what he can infer from it.

The responsibility of marketing to develop such a role for research is exemplified by Westinghouse Electric Corporation's philosophy:

"The entire organization (research, engineering, production, and marketing) must work together to determine what the customer wants, how best to produce it, how to motivate its sales, and how to deliver it."[4] To achieve this over-all goal, each division of the Westinghouse organization is bound into the over-all plan and its contributions clearly delineated. Simultaneously, marketing and product research are specified at each phase of the cycle leading from initial customer indications of what they want to their ultimately being sold what they want. Each individual research study is coordinated with the other elements of the program and becomes a part of the whole structure of marketing knowledge.

PROBLEMS & SOLUTIONS

To understand the planning approach better, let us turn now to some concrete problems. These will help to show the kinds of alternatives that confront managers wishing to make research an integral part of marketing, and the kinds of decisions that contribute to progress.

Media Selection

A good type of problem to begin with is media selection because, for many firms, it is a vital part of the larger problem of developing a unified marketing strategy. Moreover, not only do considerations of product, budget, market position, marketing objectives, and creative strategy affect media choice, but it is also influenced by numerous psychological and personal factors, by the diverse selling activities of media themselves, and by the various individuals in companies and advertising agencies who participate in buying space and time. EXHIBIT I represents an attempt to portray these relationships schematically. Now here, briefly, is an illustrative case history:

---

[4] James Jewell, vice president of marketing, Westinghouse Electric Corporation, in an address before the Marketing Committee of the National Association of Manufacturers, Spring, 1958.

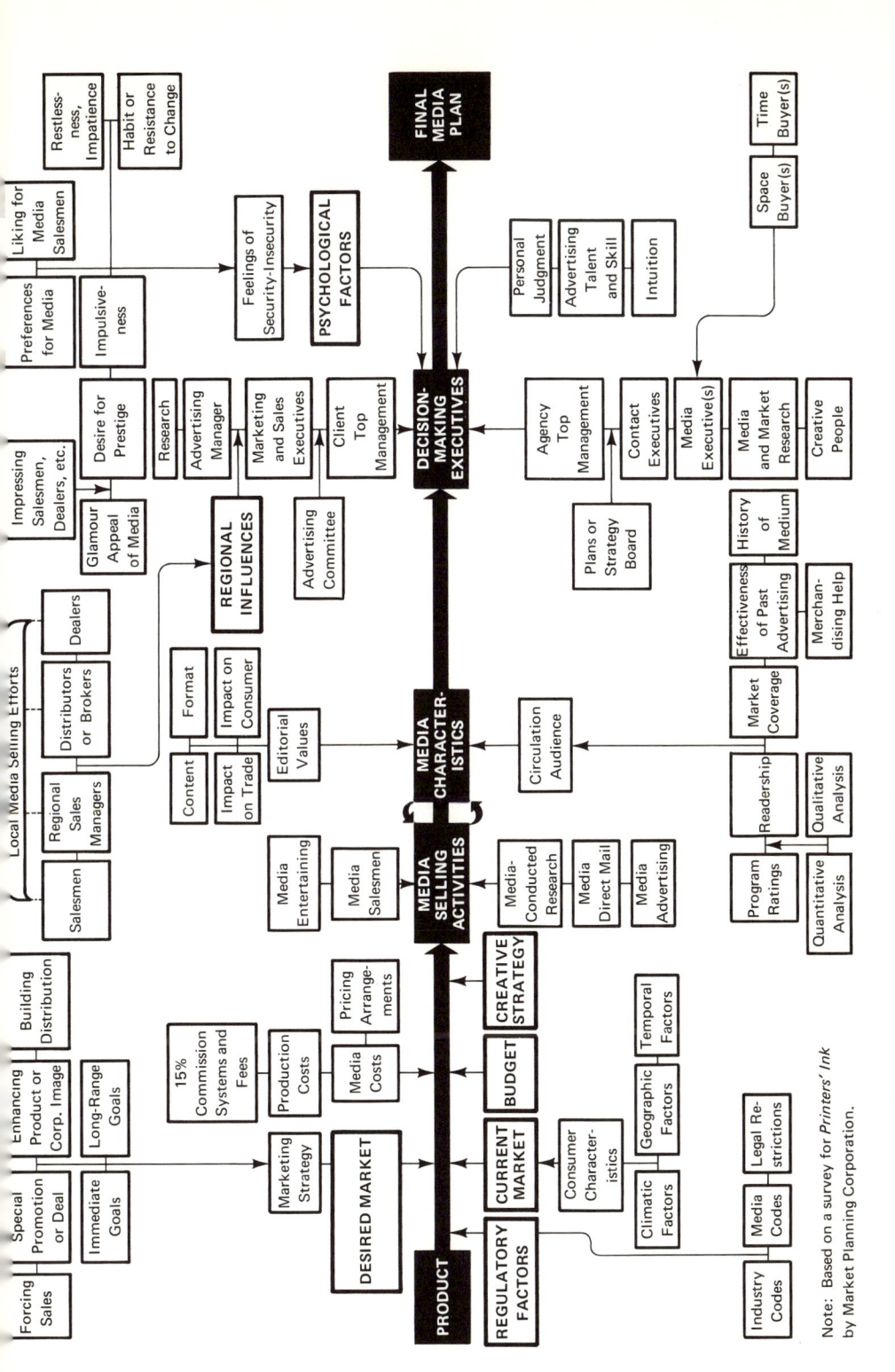

Exhibit I. **Factors and People Influencing Media Selection**

In 1958 the Market Planning Corporation (now Marplan) was commissioned by *Printers' Ink* to assess the forces which affect media selection and to show how advertisers' decisions in this area are reached. One of the alternatives considered by the research team assigned to conceptualizing the problem was to isolate one or two crucial variables and intensively analyze their influence on media selection. Here are three examples of what might have been done:

(1) It would have been legitimate for a researcher to design a study to explore the awareness of and attitudes toward media's own marketing activities (advertising, direct mail, research, personal selling, and so on) on the part of advertisers and advertising agency executives.

(2) It would have been equally proper for a researcher to design a study to investigate the range and differential roles of personnel at advertising agencies and their clients in selecting media.

(3) A technique-oriented motivation researcher might have concerned himself with the unconscious reasons affecting the selection of some media and not others, the correlation between certain personality types and choice of certain media, and the influence of prestige, habit, and other emotion-laden factors.

Another approach would have been to design research which would come to grips with *all* phases of the problem. It was foreseen that a narrowly designed project would preclude obtaining sufficient information by which to judge the relative importance of the factors analyzed compared with others known to exist but not investigated. However, this alternative presented the difficulty of sorting out numerous factors and, in all likelihood, the disadvantage of being unable to make precise statements about the findings.

At first, therefore, the research team appeared to have a choice between dealing with a small problem with a high degree of scientific rigor or dealing with a large problem with only moderate scientific rigor.

It was then recognized that the advantages of the two research philosophies might be well mated in the form of a plan which would allow enough breadth for rich hypothesis formulation, on the one hand, and means for quantifying some of the findings, on the other hand.

The techniques chosen reflected this hybridization approach, too. For instance, the major instrument of research was that of the "depth" interview, using the "probes" of the psychological researcher to dig deeper after the respondent had exhausted his spontaneous comments, but the interviews were sufficiently structured by question guides to follow a broad outline and thus allow for systematic analysis.

As a result, it was possible to reach conclusions that would not have emerged from a one-dimensional study of one aspect of the problem. If, for example, the study had been more narrowly conceived and been an analysis of reactions to the various tools used by media men to sell space and time, it would have yielded data on how to strengthen media's selling approach—useful but of tactical value only. As it was, the broader approach covered the roles of various executives in decision making, and this produced data of a more basic nature, with more implications for management. Among other things, it was learned that a far greater number of men exercise some influence than had been hitherto suspected, ranging from the lowliest media clerk at the agency up to the chairman of the board of the client firm. This suggested the need for media to reach *every* decision-influencer, not just the media buyer, the account executive, or the advertising manager.

"Feed-In" Process

To make planning effective, it is important to conceive of and set up programs so that a series of research studies can feed into the picture.

In the case just described, for instance, the first research project was followed up by a second designed to probe even more deeply into the factors affecting the selection of major media classes: newspapers, radio, magazines, television, and the business press. Still other studies were projected to evaluate the problems of more specific media groups, such as station representative firms and news magazines. In other words, the over-all, long-range plan was being used to guide the development of individual studies so that they would not only contribute knowledge needed for immediate decisions but would also be helpful in constructing a theory of media marketing that would be useful for the long term.

There is no one rule for systematizing this "feeding-in" process. To a considerable degree it depends on the nature of the problem. For example:

In the case of a firm planning a new product, the research process might last at least several years and go from initial consumer research through product testing, analysis of the most suitable channels of distribution, test marketing, and then repeat consumer research to check on product satisfaction and use—with each study being atomistic in design and yet contributing to the over-all picture.

By contrast, in the study of media selection just described, "feed in" occurred in two ways: (a) the first study was broad-gauge enough so that its separate parts contributed importantly to the desired whole, while (b) later studies were planned to add more brush strokes to the picture.

A New Product

Let us turn now to a more detailed problem in new product marketing. The case I shall describe here concerns a leading manufacturer of consumer durables. Since the innovation represented a radical departure from the proven product in its field, the company felt the need for considerable research. As Exhibit II shows, the research followed a logical sequence (dates and some of the details of the plan have been disguised):

Phase I. As soon as the technical feasibility of making the new item was determined, but before the company had committed any significant funds to

		1957	1958	1959	1960	1961	1962

PRODUCT RESEARCH

1. Laboratory Testing
2. Consumer Usage Test
3. Consumer Attitude Survey
4. Consumer Market Study

SALES PROMOTION RESEARCH

5. Product Name Test
6. Product Package Test
7. Evaluation of Merchandising Materials

DISTRIBUTION AND SALES RESEARCH

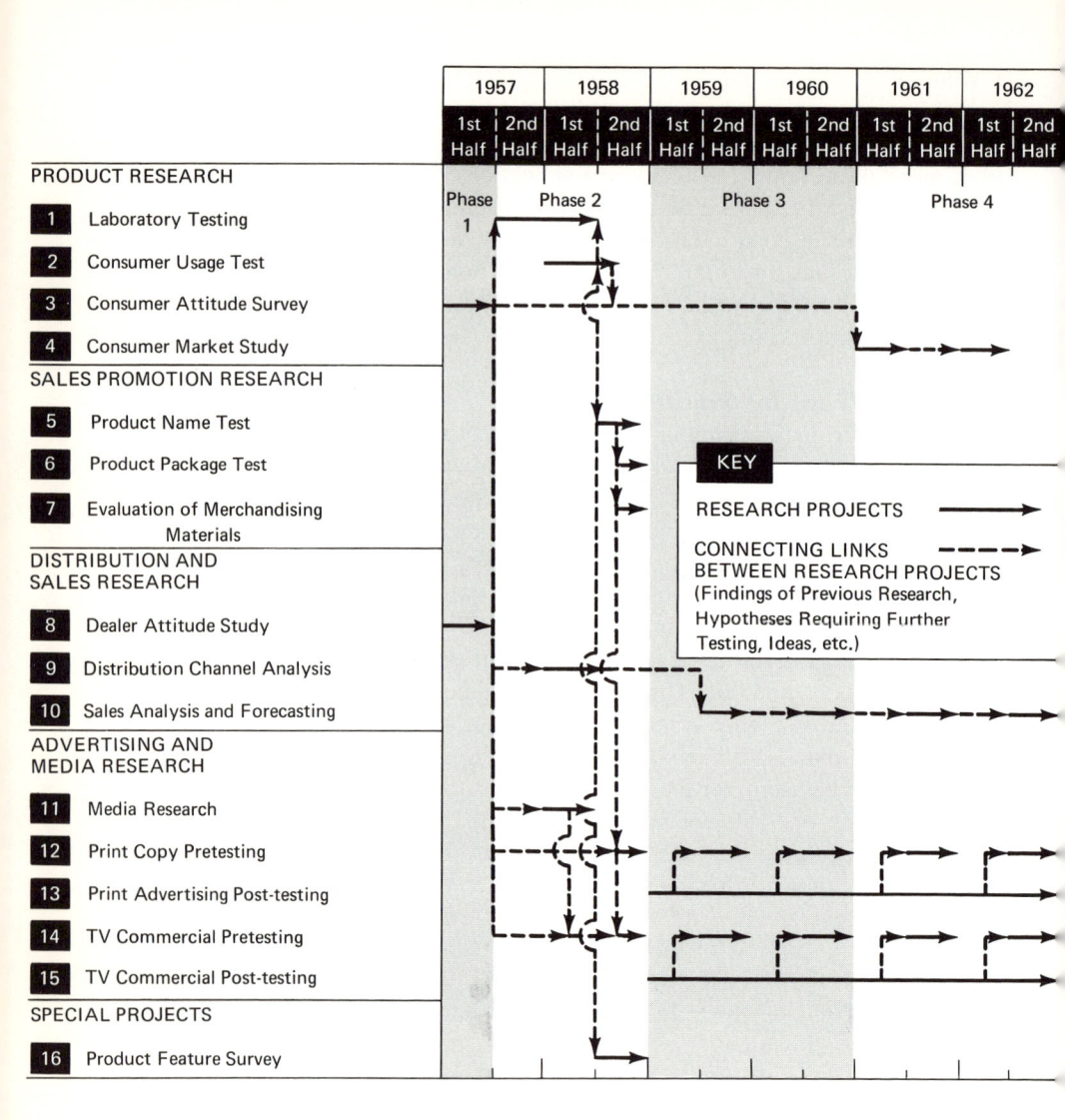

8. Dealer Attitude Study
9. Distribution Channel Analysis
10. Sales Analysis and Forecasting

ADVERTISING AND MEDIA RESEARCH

11. Media Research
12. Print Copy Pretesting
13. Print Advertising Post-testing
14. TV Commercial Pretesting
15. TV Commercial Post-testing

SPECIAL PROJECTS

16. Product Feature Survey

KEY
RESEARCH PROJECTS ───▶
CONNECTING LINKS ----▶
BETWEEN RESEARCH PROJECTS
(Findings of Previous Research, Hypotheses Requiring Further Testing, Ideas, etc.)

Exhibit II. **Six-Year Marketing Research Plan for a New Consumer Product** (Market Introduction—Spring 1959)

the idea, consumer and dealer attitudes were sought. Was there enough dissatisfaction with the current product to create a solid foundation for marketing a new one? Would dealers carry and support such a product? What ideas did consumers and dealers have that might improve on the proposition?

Phase II. The response to these questions being encouraging, the company authorized product development and laboratory tests. The latter were conducted both by company personnel and, later on, by an outside testing firm.

With product development proceeding favorably, research went into high gear early in 1958. The marketing research director designed a consumer usage test to measure product performance under normal conditions. As soon as findings became available from this research to serve as guidance, a test was conducted to select the name that would best convey a favorable image of the product. Next several package designs and dealer sales promotion and merchandising materials were prepared and tested. Each research project was feeding into the succeeding one as the marketing mix for the new product took shape.

In the meantime, the consumer survey had pointed up a possible problem involving one product feature. The problem was referred back to product development and testing; a modification in the design was made, and a special consumer test was conducted to check the acceptability of the revised feature to consumers. The funds for this research were drawn from a reserve set aside at the initation of the whole plan for unforeseen problems.

During Phase II the marketing research department also analyzed its dealer organization to help sales management choose the broad classifications of dealers and also the individual dealers particularly well qualified to get the product off to a good start. This step was especially important since there were not enough units produced initially to supply all retailers. As the exhibit indictes, the earlier dealer attitude study was useful in selecting trade channels.

Media research was also undertaken to answer the questions: (1) which media classes to use and (2) which specific media to use. As soon as it was decided that consumer magazines and spot television would be the principal media, the agency began to prepare advertising. The consumer surveys were used extensively in determining creative strategy. Ads and commercials were then pretested to ensure that the most effective appeals possible would be used.

Phase III. During this stage, the company instituted what were to become *continuous* research projects. These projects included pretesting new printed and broadcast advertising, as well as tests of advertising after it had appeared, using regular rating services for this latter work. The exhibit indicates that the findings from "post-testing" were used to improve the ads subsequently designed and pretested.

Simultaneously, the company began a program of *continuing* sales analysis, which included breakdowns of sales by categories of retail trade, salesmen, price lines, geographic areas, and so on. This activity was designed to lead to annual sales forecasts that could be used to formulate more accurate production and marketing plans. Territorial sales analysis is also being used to assess salesmen's performance and to set up area potentials, sales quotas, and a sales incentive program.

Phase IV. The company is now in this phase. A large-scale consumer survey is planned for two years after market introduction. Management expects that by this time there should be sufficiently broad distribution and consumer experience with the new product to make such a study informative and practicable from a cost standpoint.

For succeeding years, the firm's marketing research director has recommended repeating from five to ten of the key questions of the large-scale consumer study, either in a mail survey among members of a consumer panel or as part of another national study. The purpose of this continuing research is to trace trends in product penetration and acceptance at low cost.

IN RETROSPECT

Marketing research planning—particularly the long-range variety—is not easy, and the approaches to it contain various pitfalls. But five important advantages of planning show that it is worthwhile to cope with the problems and circumvent the pitfalls.

1. *Those firms which have most successfully used this kind of planning have discovered that it not only helps to pinpoint areas of needed research but contributes to far more sophisticated research.* For instance:

In 1957 a major oil company defined its marketing objectives for the following decade with a view to maximizing its share of the market in each of the states it served. In detailing its plan, it was recognized that more knowledge would be necessary in numerous areas. (There were wide variations in marketing opportunities and in the company's status in each state, which complicated the planning picture considerably.)

Accordingly, demographic and automobile ownership and expenditure trends in each state were studied; trends in public and private transportation and highway growth were considered. Many other questions were examined —for example, the pricing structure of the industry; practices in service station ownership, operation, and personnel; changes in consumer shopping habits; the rising influence of private brands; and pertinent developments in such other fields as highway retailing.

In effect, a study of nearly every factor that conditioned the firm's marketing effort was built into the over-all research program. This resulted in more useful findings than could have been obtained by "bits and pieces" studies of the diverse facets of petroleum marketing.

2. *Another common benefit is a multidimensional quality to the research.* It may have breadth; that is, it may cover different sectors of the marketing front. It may also have *depth;* that is, more than one type of research may be used in a sector over a period of time. Thus:

In the case of a whiskey brand, motivation research was utilized to explore attitudes toward the product. This qualitative study furnished insights of considerable value in planning the creative strategy for the promotion of the brand. Subsequently, it became important to determine exactly how widespread these consumer attitudes were, both geographically and among socio-economic groups. Accordingly, the attitudinal data were quantified through the use of a structured questionnaire and a large nationwide probability sample.

Market analysis, employing secondary data from trade and government sources, then documented the size, character, and potential of given markets, while a briefer study among liquor retailers identified their reactions to the brand.

Strengthening the multidimensional character of this research was the use of parallel questions to cement the separate studies together. Thus, in the consumer studies respondents were queried about a unique product characteristic. The counterpart of this question was then put to dealers. By relating the findings from both surveys, important conclusions were reached leading to better promotion.

Thus, it was learned that retailers had not been sufficiently motivated (in terms of higher markup, local advertising, special merchandising aids, and so forth) to learn the whiskey's unusual sales appeal, let alone use it to push the brand to their customers. It was thus logical to recommend stronger preselling to consumers coupled with a promotional "deal" for retailers which made it worthwhile for them to stress the brand's unique sales story.

All in all, the sum of this research in terms of value was greater than the mere addition of its parts.

3. *Long-range research planning is economical.* By taking inventory of research needs, it is occasionally possible to combine what would otherwise be two studies into one, with consequent savings. An industrial goods manufacturer achieved such an economy in this way:

His sales department was concerned about negative attitudes on the part of the firm's wholesalers toward a new functional discount policy. The sales manager was interested in having research conducted on this matter. In the meantime, the head of the public relations department was evolving a new campaign and required knowledge of wholesalers' attitudes in the industry. As a result of joint planning, these respective needs were made known, and the research manager was able to map out one trade survey to fill both needs.

Economy also results from the fact that research is permitted a more logical and useful sequence of development.

4. *Planning tends to assure greater application of research to marketing problems.* Fewer reports wind up gathering dust. The reason is plain: by building research into the plan, making it an integral part of marketing activity, and obtaining greater acceptance for it by members of the marketing team, it can be brought to bear on problems far more effectively. Also, of course, a project is likely to be more useful if it has its birth in marketing problems or information deficiencies. Technique is not confounded with problem solving, and research becomes more sensitive to the needs of management.

5. *More marketing problems are anticipated.* This means that research can be provided in sufficient time to eliminate some of the "fire-fighting" that characterizes the operations of so many companies.

Pitfalls to Avoid

As with any other relatively new procedure, there are "bugs" in long-range research planning which need to be eliminated. The hard lessons from experience of companies in the vanguard of planning can be summarized briefly like this:

(1) Do not leave the planning to the director of marketing research alone. He is only one of the marketing team; the procedure requires a joint effort to be successful. The research director's contribution during the planning stage is:

> To help isolate problems amenable to research and delineate fuzzy information areas.
> To outline the scope and method of research which will prove most effective.
> To indicate the contribution research is expected to make.
> To furnish time, cost, and personnel estimates to help in setting up timetables, budgets, and staff requirements.

(2) Do not attempt to incorporate too much detail into the plan, particularly for any period more than a year away. The usual consequence is to become bogged down in details that lead to frustrations, delays, and, at worst, abandoned plans.

(3) Modify the plan as often as market and other conditions dictate. The very life and value of a program stem from its flexibility and responsiveness to the market place. A static plan soon becomes a worthless plan.

(4) Formalize the plan by committing it to paper and distributing copies to all of the individuals involved in its development and use. Although this may sound a bit naive, it is amazing how many hours are spent in meetings creating a long-range plan without an official record being compiled of the decisions reached. It is also valuable to have responsible officials initial the document. Psychologically, it builds up their stake in the plan's soundness and success.

(5) See that there are sufficient funds, personnel, and facilities for the marketing research department to carry on the bigger job called for by thinking ahead.

CONCLUSION

To serve management better, marketing research must become broader gauge. It must escape its preoccupation with narrow investigations of limited utility. It is true that broad definitions of problems often make for unmanageable research projects, but this is not a major obstacle. The solution suggested is to devise long-range research plans so that they will guide the design of individual studies. Research can then furnish data needed for today's decisions *and* contribute to the accumulation of information needed for making long-range decisions.

To begin, marketing management must be able to define its long-range goals and details the action programs necessary to attain those goals. This detailing of plans inevitably highlights problems and information gaps. Marketing research should then be called on to map out long-range plans to solve the problems and fill the information gaps. A timetable should be agreed on, and the plan implemented with the help of the necessary budget aid, personnel, and facilities.

Operating executives in marketing are not the only ones to gain from planning. Research practitioners themselves stand to benefit considerably. We are all familiar with such epithets for researchers as "residents of ivory towers," "the slide rule brigade," and so on. The images thus created, right or wrong, have helped relegate the research function to a position of limited stature. The planning concept, with its emphasis on what research can do for departmental operations, can help to change all this.

It can be reasonably anticipated that the hunger for certainty in marketing operations will result not only in more calls for helpful facts but in increasing demands for measures of marketing effectiveness. The opportunity for research executives is exciting. To the extent that they are able to see a marketing problem in its totality, they will be seeing it as top marketing executives do. By thus being alert to general management needs, they will have won half the battle for greater recognition and acceptance.

C   The Modern Information Explosion

13   Will Managers Be Overwhelmed by the Information Explosion?*

HOWELL M. ESTES

We are in danger of "'drowning" in information, but the author feels that a "goal orientation" approach will enable us to control, manage, and use the information.

Someone—I think he was from the RAND Corporation—has said that often a good question is more important than a good answer.

That man understood that the best answer in the world, in too many cases, may have no relation whatever to the question that should have been asked. But the right question focuses attention squarely where it belongs. This idea harks back at least as far as Socrates, who taught by asking the proper questions in a logical sequence. Today, most of us recognize that classic problem-solving starts with the essential step of identifying the problem.

One pointed question that has come down through the centuries is from the poet Juvenal. "Who," he asked, "is going to guard the guards themselves?"

My primary question today is in a similar vein, namely: "Who is going to manage management information?" This, to me, qualifies as a good question, in fact one of the vital questions of our time.

To assure you that I am necessarily sensitive to the problems of management in general, and particularly to those of management information, let me briefly state the three guises in which I appear before you. These are: (1) military commander; (2) a government manager; and (3) a man with a business to run.

First, I am the Commander of the Military Airlift Command, a major command of the United States Air Force. Our principal mission is to provide strategic, combat and specialized airlift services for all Department of Defense elements and some other agencies of the Federal Government—up

---

*Reprinted from **Armed Forces Management**, Vol. 13, No. 3 (December, 1966), pp. 75–84.

to and including the President. Our Command—MAC—is also responsible for such other missions as Aerospace Rescue and Recovery; Air Weather; Aerospace Audio-Visual services, including combat photo documentation; aerial photo mapping, geodesy and gravimetry; and finally Aeromedical Evacuation, both intertheater and domestic. These Technical Services, as we call them, are also performed for other agencies besides the Air Force.

Secondly, MAC is the Operating Agency through which the Secretary of the Air Force discharges his responsibility as DOD Single Manager for Airlift Services. As Executive Director of that agency, I am, therefore, a government manager in a somewhat broader context than the usual military commander.

Thirdly, what we call "common user airlift," including purchase of $550 million civil contract airlift, is financed under an Air Force Industrial Fund; thus, a portion of my fiscal responsibility is more commercially oriented than is the case with most military commanders. Which is why I say that I have a business to run.

The responsibilities outlined in that little thumbnail sketch help me to remain a very industrious student of management and of management information.

But that is only the beginning. In writing, at least, MAC has had these diverse responsibilities for many years. And it has been partially financed under the industrial funding concept since 1958.

That today's pressures for vast improvements in management of the Military Airlift Command differ from those of past years is the result of the revolution we are experiencing in airlift—a revolution compounded of changes in national military policy; of such products of advancement in the aeronautical arts and sciences as today's C-141 and tomorrow's giant C-5; and of the revisions these two factors are in process of effecting in our operating concepts and methods.

The important point is that the potential offered by this revolution will never be realized without a wholly new approach to management and to the management information that each management level will require. The tremendous productivity, flexibility and responsiveness of these new aircraft will demand that our thinking processes and our management reactions be as radical as the C-141 and C-5 themselves.

Now there is an interesting coincidence concerning the C-141 and C-5 which dramatizes one of our dominant problems. The C-141 has a maximum structural payload capacity of about 35 tons. Keep that figure—35 tons—in mind for a moment. In the competition for the development and production of the C-5, five contractors participated: three for the airframe and two for the engine.

In reply to the Air Force Request for Proposal, the five competitors sent in an aggregate of 240,000 pages—not counting any copies. That's at least a 40-foot bookshelf containing 480 500-page volumes. Since 30 copies of each proposal were required, the total weight of the paper submitted was 35 tons—the maximum payload of today's C-141!

It took more than 400 Air Force experts five months to read and evaluate that mass of data. This, to me, hardly represents progress in the management of management information. One reason is that we didn't know exactly what questions to ask—so we asked far too many in our RFP. After that exercise, we asked ourselves some very pertinent questions. Weren't we, for example, asking for too much detail on matters which should properly be the concern of the contractors?

Why did we need 7,000 pages of cost data when this was a price competition and the contract was fixed-price-incentive? And weren't we asking for detailed design, rather than simply specifying performance requirements —and letting each contractor achieve them in his own way?

True, these questions were asked after the 35-ton fact. But they were asked and they are good questions, which should help us to manage management information far better next time we go out with an RFP.

I think we also have to acknowledge that all questions about management information are somewhat after the fact. We are already well into the age of information systems, quasi-systems, pseudo-systems, unrelated masses of computer hardware, and far too many types and classes of software. But our management of information has by no means improved to the same extent as the systems have multiplied.

So the question—how to manage management information—must be asked. And we must have at least a reasonable set of possible answers very soon, before we are all engulfed, inundated and strangled in an unremitting flood of information—too much to even be able to determine how much of it we could very well have done without.

In this, perhaps, our main hope may be illustrated by the story of the layman who witnessed the dedication of the 200-inch telescope at Mount Palomar in 1948. He sidled up to the Chief Astronomer and said:

"Modern astronomy sure makes man seem insignificant, doesn't it?"

"Yes," the scientist replied, "but don't you see—man is the astronomer."

However, if we are drowning in information, it is a flood of our own making—and, therefore, our own creature to control, manage and use for our own purposes. The word "purposes" hints at one solution for control— goal orientation—and I will address the significance of goals to management information a little later on.

First, I would like to outline what I see as some of the basic problems; then, after a few words on goals, I will suggest what would seem to be the framework for at least one approach to the answer.

The first problem, rather than being peculiar to management alone, is universal—the very fact of the Information Explosion. In science alone, the growth of knowledge has been astronomical. Da Vinci could say, in the 15th century, that he was familiar with the entire body of scientific literature existing at that time. Even as late as the 19th century, Gauss had a full grasp of every branch of mahematics.

Today, no scientist can hope to keep abreast of even a small percentage of the work published in his own sub-subbranch of his particular discipline. In fact, it has been estimated that it is cheaper to re-do a technical project—if the cost is less than $100,000—than to go through the process of trying to learn if someone has already solved the problem. Thus, the overall volume of information is so great, and access to it so limited, that it is sometimes too difficult or too expensive to search out the precise bit that would be helpful.

The second problem arises from the rapid growth and the increasing complexity of the areas which have to be managed. The order of magnitude of effort that I mentioned we must expend in preparing to manage the revolution in airlift is only a single example. Everyone in commerce, industry, engineering, science, the professions and government feels the force with which the growth curves are pulling apart. The thing we have to manage are growing geometrically, while our knowledge of how to manage seems to increase only arithmetically at best. Thus, there is more to manage, and more information to manage it with—but, by some new form of math, "more plus more" seems to add up to less in the way of control.

Third is the constantly increasing speed with which decisions must be made. Instant communications over more and more channels; speed of travel and distribution; and the rapidity with which information is generated—all allow less and less time for reflection and deliberation. A transatlantic cable contains 75,000 tons of copper wire—while Telstar handles more channels of communication more effectively with less than a ton of materials. But there has been no matching order of improvement in man's ability to absorb all these additional inputs and come up with an instant output—a decision.

Fourth, the common information needs of managers have not really been clearly identified. There has been more emphasis on how information should be presented than on what information is required to begin with. This, too, is related to the question of goals—which, as they set the limits of a playing field, can also delimit and contain the profusion of information, and determine what is "out of bounds."

Fifth, there is a great need for a vertical information structure supported by a common data base. Decision is essentially the apex of a pyramid built on a broad substructure of alerting, exploring, and analyzing. Each level of the structure must have access to a common base of information—or data bank, if you will. To whatever extent a general purpose digital computer can quickly and accurately mechanize a great portion of the fundamental processes, to that same extent will the manager be able to make better and more timely decisions.

But if the computer has in a sense solved some portion of this fifth problem—or any of the others—it has also spawned a sixth and perhaps most critical problem.

An old Danish proverb says that prediction is difficult, particularly when it pertains to the future. Thus, when the primitive ENIAC computer was built in 1946, the fact that the thing worked seemed to be a sufficient end unto itself. The mathematicians and engineers at once saw a means of solving what had once been impossibly long equations. But how many saw what ENIAC really was—the rudimentary beginning of a potential revolution in the Information Sciences?

The first automobiles were called "horseless carriages"—and that is precisely what they looked like, designed for tradition rather than function. In the same way, the first computers were seen as faster calculating machines or more copious filing systems. And so today, 20 years after ENIAC, we are, in effect, using third-generation computers for bookeeping and filing.

So the essence of the sixth problem is this: We are doing with our electronic brains what the neurophysiologists tell us we do with our brains—utilizing them at a small percentage of their actual capacity. We look at a machine that can carry out fantastically rapid arithmetical and logical operations—and fail to see its full potential as an ingenious tool that can and must be usefully integrated into a full-spectrum management information system.

The seventh and final problem on my list—which is undoubtedly related to each of the other six—is the basic question of goals for management information. Dr. Alain Enthoven, Assistant Secretary of Defense for Systems Analysis, has said this:

> . . . the systems analysis approach bears no essential relationship to computers at all . . . This shouldn't be surprising, because the really difficult and important part of doing a good analysis is not the computation; it is formulating and defining the problem, clarifying the obectives, and determining which assumptions ought to be considered.

Although he was speaking specifically to systems analysis, I would think the Secretary's statement bears with equal validity upon the entire problem of management information systems. What he was addressing particularly was the necessity for setting goals.

I must admit that in this matter of setting goals, the higher level manager has a unique and difficult problem. As Professor Peter Drucker has expressed it:

> A balance between the measurable and non-measurable is a central and constant problem of management. In many ways it is the problem of management and the true decision area.
>
> Measurements which do not spell out the assumptions in respect to the non-measurable actually misinform. Yet the more we can quantify the truly measurable areas, the greater the temptation to put all our emphasis on these—the greater, therefore, the danger that what looks like better measurement and control will actually mean less 'control,' if not an organization out of control altogether.

Professor Drucker has an excellent point. It is my own opinion that while our measurement methodology should take his point into account, the goals we establish must be in some way measurable or else they are not true goals. Short of this, there is no way for us to know whether we have attained our goals or not—or to determine how far short we may have fallen—or to decide how to close the gap between what we meant to achieve and what we did accomplish.

For a simple analogy, we might think of servomechanisms—machines for which man sets a goal and which then tend to regulate themselves in achieving and holding that goal with a fair amount of stability. Take, for example a furnace theromstat and an aircraft autopilot.

In the one case, man sets the thermostat for a desired temperature and after that his house should remain within tolerable limits of that temperature. In the latter case, the human pilot feeds a desired set of directions into the automatic pilot, and the autopilot will then maintain the aircraft satisfactorily close to those parameters.

However, with the thermostat, you don't say to the gadget on the wall, "I'd like to remain warm and comfortable, so take care of it." What you do is set the pointer to a specific degree of temperature—65° or 68° or whatever you choose.

By the same token, you don't tell the autopilot that you'd like to get to Milwaukee in the least time at a safe altitude. Instead you see the controls for a specific compass heading, altitude and attitude—and the machine will keep you a few degrees to either side of these figures until either the gyros have drifted too much or you crank in a new set of numerical instructions.

In either case, the goals must be specified in definite quantitative terms or there is no way for the mechanism to know what you desire from it. The same is true of organizational goals.

But there is one fundamental difference. When the house gets warmer or colder than the selected temperature, the control mechanism opens or closes the circuit that turns the furnace off or on. When the autopilot senses that external forces are pushing the aircraft off the preselected path, it actuates servomotors to move the control surfaces and correct the discrepancy. Man, having once set the initial conditions, is out of the loop—and we have a closed-loop feedback system.

In an organization, on the other hand, the loop is open—with only the manager to complete the feedback circuit. The mechanism is not self-regulating. When goals are not being achieved, the manager must know it—he must know why—and he must know what corrective action to take. For all of these, he needs information.

In setting goals, then, we determine which things spell the difference between success and failure. Having done that, we have decided which things require the closest attention of management.

Thus, management information which does not relate to purpose—usually expressed in goals—has little significance. So we might say that goals express purpose in terms of what or how much we expect to achieve in a given period of time.

Expressing goals quantitatively provides a language for relating actual results to these projected goals. So we need information for—at the very minimum—these three purposes: (1 setting goals; (2) scheduling events to achieve these goals; and (3) measuring results against the goals. Then, if there is any divergence between achievements and goals, the manager needs further information to determine the reasons. He can then take corrective action, either to improve performance or, if necessary, to recast his goals in a more realistic mold.

Thus, an organization is designed for a specific purpose or set of purposes—and managed in such a way as to achieve those purposes. To know what the purposes are; to know whether they are attainable; to organize for their attainment; to know whether they remain valid in the dynamism of changing situations; to know whether they are being achieved; and—above all—to know why or why not: for these management objectives we must have information.

Most of all, however, we need very good information on how much of what kind of information our particular purposes really demand. All of this means to me that we must have a manager of management information.

Classically, the functions of management encompass: (1) planning; (2) organizing; (3) directing; (4) coordinating; and (5) controlling. A case can be made for the thesis that each of the first four functions must be carried out with control in mind. But control is not an end in itself, nor can it be performed in a vacuum.

That, again, is why it is so essential to establish goals, because only in reference to goals does control have any meaning—or any possibility of being achieved. For purposes of this discussion, we might assess planning and controlling as two of the more important functions of management. For simplicity's sake, let us define planning as the setting of goals, and controlling as the means of achieving them.

Planning, therefore, must anticipate that control is a categorical necessity. Any type of planning which does not look ahead to control is unrealistic. It would then seem to follow that, in planning, it is essential to identify the information that will be required for control. Further, it would appear that the information so identified, if it is to be managed, must itself be planned, directed, and controlled.

Planning, in this case, includes identifying the information requirements of each echelon of management, and developing uniform methods of responding to these needs. It covers the necessary research, analysis, design, and development of the management information system.

In the area of directing, the objective is to put the system to work. This means the assignment of information responsibilities at all levels, and—of the utmost importance—the developing of attitudes among the functional staff through which it can grasp a corporate picture of what is going on.

In control, finally, the prime objective is a system for measuring the effectiveness of the management information system itself. From this point, as with any control mechanism, there is a feedback path right back to planning.

In many corporate organizations, the data base serving the entire corporate body tends too often to be compartmentalized. Each functional manager, in effect, draws from his parochial hoard of information. He then further filters, isolates, and manipulates the data before presenting it to the corporate manager in the guise of useful information. Thus, we can visualize the corporate manager as being surrounded by his functional managers —each talking to him, in effect, in a different language.

As compared to this situation, what we need and fortunately have in some cases is more along these lines: it begins with a single data base for the entire corporate body. Each of the functional managers draws, as required, from this bank. Of necessity, each will perform certain operations on the data before passing it up. Here it is useful to think of a little quasi-algorithm, which goes: Data + Analysis = Information; Information + Judgment = Decision.

The first equation means that the functional manager analyzes portions of the common data base in the light of his own department's functions, knowledge, and goals. But he must also be aware of the relationship of his information to that of all the other functional managers—and of its impact upon corporate goals.

This awareness—this substitution of a corporate overview for a parochial purview—is the province and purpose of the Management Information Manager. It is one of his functions to see that Managers A, B, C, D, and E, and so forth, all draw from the common data base. He then monitors all upward reporting to assume that the data which has been analyzed into information is related—in a common language and with a common purpose— to all other information from the other functional managers.

A hypothetical and perhaps slightly exaggerated example will demonstrate the system in action. Let us consider Managers A, D, and E—who are responsible for, respectively, Personnel Procurement and Training; Procurement; and Research and Development.

Assume that this organization is procuring a major new weapon system. Manager D, in charge of procurement, reports that this process is on schedule, and he anticipates no major problems. A, who has to procure and train the people to operate and maintain the system, is likewise on target and sees no trouble ahead.

Manager E, the R&D man, is developing a training device which A will have to use to train his people in the system D is procuring. E reports that his entire program is going well.

And it is—from his point of view. The training device is far behind schedule, but it only represents, say, .1% of E's total program. So, not relating this small proportion of deviation to the profound impact it will have on the scheduled operation of the entire weapon system, he does not report trouble. He does not see the trouble.

The information manager, however, in monitoring the entire program and in typing all the information together, would have seen the warning signs long enough in advance to forestall a major corporate problem. One of the most useful devices at his command in this area is "logic diagramming," of which the well-known PERT network is one example.

In my own headquarters, the Director of Management Analysis functions as the Management Information Manager. As a derivative of his activity in this role, he and his staff also: act as an educator in management techniques; serve as a helper and consultant in analyses conducted within other staff agencies; and above all operate as a catalyst for speeding up within the staff the process of analytical improvement.

These functions and duties are, of course, delegated. The responsibility itself cannot be delegated—in the last analysis, the burden resides with the top manager. In my own case, I am taking every means I can devise to do three basic things: (1) to promote the growth of a genuine analytical capability at all levels of management throughout the command; (2) to achieve a fundamental, command-wide understanding of the tremendous necessity for that kind of capability; and (3) to develop an efficient, modernized information system which will make the previous two possible.

This is easily said, but by no means automatically done in my own organization or in any other. Like aeronautics and airlift themselves, management is undergoing a revolution, which is being vastly accelerated by electronics. And every revolution has to overcome an amount of inertia before it becomes self-sustaining. Max Planck, who himself helped to revolutionize physics, put it this way:

> A new truth does not triumph by convincing its opponents and making them see the light, but rather because its opponents eventually die, and a generation grows up that is familiar with it.

So there is great hope in the new generation of management that is growing up cheek by jowl with electronic computers. But we cannot wait for them to take over, or we will have long since been drowned in the flood of information.

I would like to conclude, then, by recalling what Norbert Wiener said when someone asserted that man could always pull the plug on the machine before the machine could control man. With a machine doing millions and billions of calculations a second, Dr. Wiener replied, the man will have been overwhelmed and bypassed long before he can ever know it is time to cut off the power.

Information, including management information, is growing by the microsecond and even the nanosecond. We cannot turn off the flow. We had therefore better learn to control it—and we are already running late.

Information Becomes a Hot Item* 14

This article is a summary description of the many service companies that are in the business of providing information to clients. It also describes the growth of the field and draws conclusions about the future of the "information firms."

The businessman in need of information—from basic economic statistics and stock prices to legal precedents and consumer credit ratings—now has almost as many choices of how to obtain it as a housewife has in a supermarket.

Of course, business has always had access to paid information. Companies such as Dun & Bradstreet and Standard & Poor's in credit and financial matters, F. W. Dodge Co. in construction statistics, and A. C. Neilsen in market research, built their businesses by selling information.

Now these old-line information suppliers are being joined by a diversity of new sources, including computer makers, economists, consultants in engineering and programming, market research outfits, Western Union, and other communications companies. And there's a flurry of mergers, acquisitions and joint operations as the computer specialists try to tie in with existing data banks and information services.

I. SPREAD OF COMPUTERS

The combination of the computer's ability to digest, store, and spew out mountains of data, plus communications hookups and smart marketing is making information a new business. "The inquiry industry represents a fantastic market," says Robert A. Leonard, general manager of International Telephone & Telegraph Corp.'s Data Services operation. ITT already has a data bank for economic forecasting and maintains one on world trade statistics for the United Nations.

At Bunker-Ramo Corp., already in the financial data services business with stock prices, Vice-President Luther A. Harr, Jr., says "the field is going to explode." The company is testing an information retrieval system for the National Aeronautics & Space Administration.

And McGraw-Hill, Inc., with long established information services under its tent, is selling new computer-produced construction market data through the F. W. Dodge Co., and plans to handle on-line, time-shared

---
*Reprinted from **Business Week,** May 14, 1966, pp. 164–166. Used by permission of McGraw-Hill Publications Inc.

corporate financial data through the Compustat computer of Standard & Poor's, now a McGraw-Hill subsidiary.

Better Service

Users still get thick wads of computer-printed reports from most services. But now they are more comprehensive, more accurate, and better suited for business use. Some services provide data in tape or card form that's more economical for users who generally put it through their own company's computer. And a handful of services deliver the information by Teletype or desk-top display tubes that look like TV sets.

International Business Machines Corp. moves into the field this week through a new Information Marketing Group whose first service will be special industrial market product reports. IBM will assemble special studies designed to give producers of industrial materials and supplies reports on their customers, share of market, potential sales volume and the like on specific products. Further ventures in the field may include direct-to-the-user services with keyboard or data display terminals.

IBM's Entry

The service is based on the license it got last November to sell Dun & Bradstreet's file of corporate information on some 390,000 U.S. businesses, representing 95% of all manufacturing companies. This data bank is combined by computer with customers' sales and an economic model of production and use of industrial goods called the "input-output" series. This series is derived from the Commerce Dept.'s Office of Business Economics data. Previously these data were used only for broad national planning, not for specific business sales problems.

It works this way. Buyers of the service give IBM their lists of customers for specific products, sales or unit volume, and sales territories. The computer searches through the D&B company data bank and the input-output data and breaks out the company's market potential and actual market share by purchasing industry, plant size, territory, and other precise categories. This detail is much finer than any other such breakdown available, says IBM. Data are figured to full four-digit Standard Industrial Classifications categories, thus providing sufficient precision to pinpoint "fabricated rubber products" rather than a broader "rubber goods" category.

Initially, IBM will offer eight sales categories in the rubber and plastics industry, but products sold by some 250 industries will eventually be included in the service.

"It's the merging of two data banks with the computer," explains L. E. Donegan, Jr., manager of the group. "It's a new business for us, and the first of other services that will follow in the future," he adds.

II. A GROWING FIELD

So far, IBM's move is the biggest in what has been largely a specialist's field. Small outfits already have specialized data banks; some even deliver the data direct to the consumer via a computer terminal in his office. Next month, for example, Dr. Kenneth S. Kretschmer and Howard A. Engelsen, economists and computer specialists, will provide the first dail-in data bank for economic analysis and forecasting. Some 2,000 different economic series will be stored in a computer at Carnegie Institute of Technology in Pittsburgh, on tap by Teletype.

On Wall Street, Robert Zipf and Harris Hyman have been offering information on municipal bonds since last fall. Their remote access data bank and calculation service is called Munitype. The computer and magnetic drum memory stores bond data and schedules and prepares the interest rate bids.

A competitor, Ultronics Systems, the stock price data service, also has a bond data bank service called FACTS, and a computer data bank, Recallit, where users can set up a private data library for such things as charge accounts and credit checking. The Ultronics stock quotation service, a data bank in itself, feeds closing stock prices to the Compustat operation of Standard & Poor's.

Compustat, in turn, keeps computer tape records of 1,000 companies' stock prices, sales, earnings, dividends, capital investment—a total of 60 items. Subscribers get updated magnetic tapes for their own computers or printouts that they can use for security analysis, trust portfolio work, and other industry comparison studies. Already some 50 subscribers—mostly banks and brokers—use Compustat's tape service, says President H. Russell Morrison, but the value of the data will be greatly increased when it is stored in S&P's new Control Data 3300 computers that will ultimately handle 50 to 100 inquiries. S&P will offer remote inquiry devices such as TV-like screens to display stock charts.

The Mellon National Bank of Pittsburgh already gets direct service from Bunker Ramo's Teleregister stock system. Closing prices are sent by high speed data lines from New York into Mellon's computer. Portfolio studies for the bank's investment department are then prepared overnight by the computer, enabling officers to review holdings the next day.

New Uses

Even law texts, including case precedents and statute law, will be available in law offices in a joint operation of Western Union Telegraph Co. and Legal Research Service, Inc. WU will supply a big computer for storage, and provide a Telex teleprinter in law offices or libraries.

Some types of information are too voluminous for data transmission, too costly to deliver by wire, or not needed so quickly; computer print-outs are fine for these. D&B files, for example, fit this category, as do the construction project reports collected by McGraw-Hill's F. W. Dodge Co. But the computer can sift such masses of data for new, salable information such as the special Management Control Service that F. W. Dodge salesmen are offering to building material and equipment manufacturers and others selling in the construction industry.

The service covers the major sales opportunities for the construction industry, the 21,000 or so projects and buildings a year valued at $500,000 or more each. According to Richard B. Miller, Dodge vice-president, the computer can sort out on a custom basis such facts as type of building or engineering project, highways or bridges, location, value, number of stories, and square footage. Name and location of owner, architect, and consulting engineers are also available.

Miller says the information can be used at all levels of marketing management from over-all planning and evaluation down to supervising field sales forces. Since Dodge reports cover nearly 100% of big projects except in a couple Western areas, the data are much more comprehensive than any other means of sales forecasting or management control of sales and market share.

Big supermarket chains have found they have a gold mine in their own computer inventory control systems. The data can be used to show how well grocery and household products are selling—and in turn, the data can be sold to big soap and package goods manufacturers. Now some half dozen information services are vying to sign up the supermarket chains for access to their data [*Business Week* Mar. 5'66, p. 83].

III. THE OUTLOOK

Some companies selling information by computer are still wondering what fees to charge for data. IBM's new service is priced at between $3,500 and $10,000 per report, a figure that marketing manager Lester M. Gottlieb feels is far less than the cost of accumulating conventional data.

Another question is how information-based companies and computer-based outfits are going to link up for new services. Already there have been a handful of mergers and acquisitions as market data firms were snapped up by the computer programming and service outfits such as CEIR, Computer Sciences Corp., and Computer Applications.

Costly Ventures

ITT's Leonard is of the opinion that "dissemination of information in the future won't be limited to publishing companies." Perhaps the biggest reason is that large sums, two or more times the basic cost of the computer, must be spent for programming and preparation of the data bank. These costs can be recovered only if the service is successful over the years. So far, companies with knowhow in computers have taken the risk.

"The computer information service fits our skill mix," says Donegan of IBM. "We have a large number of the critical skills available to prepare and sell this information. We look on ourselves as developers and final salesmen rather than the reservoir of information."

At McGraw-Hill, Executive Vice-President Robert E. Slaughter gives another view: "The dominant factor in the whole picture is the data factor, and the determination of markets and the ability to serve them profitably."

Slaughter says many computerized services are technically possible but too costly to draw many customers. "We are investigating major new areas of services including electronic means of distributing information on a real time basis." But he adds that when studies now under way in the F. W. Dodge and Sweets Catalog divisions reach the market, it will likely be in conjunction with "an outside supplier of computers and communications."

15 The Thrust of Information Technology on Management*

OLIVER W. TUTHILL

The author believes that the most significant message for managers concerning the impact of information technology upon our society is not that it provides new methods for managing, but that our enterprises are undergoing vast and radical change.

Today management is confronted by the explosive development of business data systems with resultant prolific and complex problems; but they portend an era of unparalleled progress in management efficiency, in productivity gains, in over-all economic growth, and—as an end result—in the general welfare of mankind.

To survive and thrive in this competitive era, management must master and make *full* use of the new information technology. That term, as I use it, means the marriage of computer science to the communications art; and all the varied techniques of information control, storage, retrieval, and transmission which are evolving from that wedlock. Even now this relatively young science, or art, is having a profound effect on our life and times, due to developments in factory automation, in data processing and communications, and in computer design.

The most significant message for managers concerning the impact of information technology upon our society is *not* that it provides new methods for managing, but that our enterprises are undergoing vast and radical change.

CHANGE CHALLENGES

But the initiative still belongs to management. Management can adapt to this change and flourish on the new facts of business life. Our situation is something like that of the old cavalry sergeant who was demonstrating the use of a saber to new recruits:

*Reprinted from **Financial Executive,** January, 1966, pp. 18–27.

"Can anyone tell me," he asked, "why the saber is curved from point to hilt?"

One recruit—probably an MIT grad—thoughtfully answered that he suspected the blade was curved to concentrate the striking force on a relatively small area.

To which the sergeant replied—rather colorfully—that only a raw recruit in the army would be stupid enough to try to sound intelligent.

"Remember this," he barked, "in case you're ever asked again. *The saber is curved so it will fit the scabbard!*"

And this is the essence of management's problem in adapting to the demands of modern business. Managers must fit into a scabbard that is changing shape, and they must bend or break—or design a new scabbard!

INFORMATION TECHNOLOGY TOUCHES EVERYONE

Only a handful of years have passed since computer science hammered its first crack in the structure of the business world. That crack —which began at the base of the organizational structure as firms started using computers to automate various clerical and production routines—now has spider-webbed the entire edifice.

No person, no company, no country can be either immune or aloof to the impact of information technology on human society. In America we have an edge—but no corner—on this new technology. More and more it will bring increasing competitive pressure from all parts of the world. We have no monopoly on education or technical know-how. Our major advantage lies in our diverse resources for education and research; and staying out in front demands that such leadership continue, under the stimulus of both private and public policy.

The invention of the steam engine by James Watt triggered a revolution that gave us mass production and a series of continuing social changes which have altered the life of everyone. During the two centuries since steam was first put to work, technology has developed at a tempo which permitted management to adjust—in its own good time—to slowly changing economic and social conditions as they occurred.

FASTER PACE OF PROGRESS

Information technology today—spawned by the union of computers and communications—is creating every bit as great a revolution as that started by Watt. And the tempo of change has accelerated. It is rushing headlong at management, giving precious little time to adjust. The hazards of coping with change are greater as the margin for error narrows. Management is driving a faster car today, and reaction time must shorten.

It is primarily this fantastic *rate of change* which sets current technological progress apart from the old industrial revolution and its conflict between *laissez-faire* business and the general welfare of society. Today the pressures of competition or political concern for the public interest will force laggard managers into line or into limbo if they put off learning how to grow with the changing environment. In short, a more sophisticated management is essential as the momentum of socio-economic change continues to increase.

That is why my observations will focus on what information technology means to managers. But before I wade into *that* pool, I might mention briefly some of the factors involved in the rising rate of change—in addition to information technology. All of these factors are so interrelated with the advance of scientific research that they are fundamentally managerial in nature.

FACTORS PUSHING RATE OF CHANGE

Our bulging population, with 250 million in sight for America at the end of this century, is stimulating the economy even as it tends to overload the declining market for low-skilled labor. And with the population boom comes a corresponding increase in innovation, in the quantity and level of imaginative thought being applied to the myriad problems of sprawling cities, food production, and education.

Mass education is both a factor in some of the problems posed and the ultimate solution of others. It is, in fact, the final answer to the social burden of change in the years ahead. Better education will be a requisite for almost any occupation as emphasis shifts from manual skills to the ability to absorb, organize, and interpret information. At the same time, mass education refines desires, expands markets, and, in itself, contributes to social change.

Our generally more highly educated population is mobile. It has wheels, it travels, it communicates. And it reflects changes in the social mix which urgently affect business planning. For instance:

There is a tremendous and continuing increase in the over-all standard of living. The middle class continues to spread, as wealth is created and redistributed, with a resulting demand for more and better goods and services.

There is a marked increase in the number of old people and young people. Because of these growing extremes in our population, products are being redesigned and new industries created.

Suburbia, sired by the automobile, has in turn created the shopping center and the supermarket, requiring revolutionary methods of product distribution.

The increase in leisure time has given birth to new industries and revitalized old ones. And culture follows where education and leisure lead. Today we spend more money on classical records than on baseball, our national sport. (I suspect that TV also has had a hand in this statistical rebalancing of interests!)

SOCIAL CHANGE AFFECTS BUSINESS

These changes indicate the plasticity of modern society and how extensively it is being reshaped by some of the major forces working within it. Managers must recognize and understand the influence of the same forces—and the changes they create—on the future of their businesses.

Even though we are all aware of the human impact of such social changes, it is useful to note several of the ideas about these changes which are floating in the public mind. These ideas, whether they are true or not, will have real influence on policy, because people act on belief and opinion.

Automation of factory operations is substantially reducing the number of people employed in production. The hard fact of automation is that it now requires only 9 per cent of our total population to produce all the food and manufactured goods we use. While this does not take into account all of the "backup" people involved—the white collar workers, distribution people, and retail employees—it nevertheless is a significantly small number of people *directly* engaged in farming and factory work. Some economists estimate that 20 years from now, only *two per cent* of our total population will work in direct production of food and goods.

NEED FOR RETRAINING

The decreased need for people in production jobs will have a major impact on the goals and scope of union activity—and bring increased pressure for government controls on the rate of change to automation. The fade-out of traditional job fields will stimulate pressure on business, unions, and government to re-educate and find new jobs for people displaced.

Re-education and re-employment are always considered serious problems by many influential people. Some estimate that each week 30,000 or more workers in the United States lose or change their jobs because of the advance of automation. There are other thousands who, except for automation, would have been hired for such jobs. This has been called the "silent firings." On the other side of the automation coin, we find that many thousands of new jobs—in fact, new industries—are being created by the computer. Also, automation—by permitting a reduction in the real price of products—increases demand, thus generating countless jobs in sales, distribution, and service.

The shortened work week appears to many to be a solution. In fact, we may someday find that man's central activity is related to his leisure rather than to income-producing work. In turn, this trend should further accelerate recreational and service activities as well as make a decided impact on how and where we live.

INTERNATIONAL GROWTH OF BUSINESS

World-wide corporations should accordingly grow in number and size. With necessary information readily at management fingertips, it will be possible to take the pulse of diverse and critical business activities, no matter where in the world they may be. This growth of multi-national business, coupled with the ability of computers to translate from one tongue to another, will contribute to a further breakdown in language barriers. And such widespread expansion of business activities beyond national borders should exert stronger pressure for the growth of larger political combinations.

Competition should intensify as wider use of information technology emphasizes the human differential in company capabilities. This stiffening competition is certain to bring an even greater surge in business research and development aimed at better service, improved quality, and lower costs. The intensified international nature of business competition also will impose a mandate on government to help maintain America's position through research in human and technical problem areas.

The growing emphasis on science and research, and the increasing expansion of leisure activities, imply that greatest vocational opportunity will come in professional and service areas. Specialized education—often at remarkably high levels—will be required for many important jobs, and men of truly outstanding capability will be sought after more than ever.

MANAGING IN THE MIDST OF CHANGE

That is a brief look at some of the ideas springing from information technology, as it and other factors in the spectrum of social change color our managerial outlook. Let's concentrate our attention on specific challenges which the new science throws down to us.

Back in the 1950s, with business booming, the Bell System decided to computerize high-volume repetitive clerical jobs, believing that this would provide an effective solution to the massive paperwork problem. Today, some ten years later, most routine clerical activities in the telephone business have been mechanized to some degree.

Yet it has been found that clerical jobs—not including telephone operators—have *grown* from a level of 90,000 a decade ago to about 115,000 today. Without mechanization, our clerical force requirement would be a factor severely limiting progress.

These past ten years of experience with data-processing systems have been educational for us. And I believe the lessons hold true outside the telephone business.

First—substitution of computers for clerical effort has *not* caused wholesale job displacement, although mechanization has slowed down the rate of expansion in clerical positions. Obviously, a major factor in this experience has been the healthy condition of the general economy, permitting steady growth in our business.

Second—we must develop an organized discipline of business information systems to replace the piecemeal approach that now prevails. The big benefit will come when we learn to use computers for their unique ability to give management meaningful information, when and where it is needed.

Third—the magnitude of problems posed by the introduction of sophisticated computer techniques is only now beginning to be recognized by our managers. A piecemeal approach merely involves the application of computers to automate clerical jobs, as has been done in many other businesses. For instance, the automation of billing procedures is often simply an elaboration of the way the job was done without buttons to push. This is a far cry from the provision of a complete information system.

MANAGERS ARE FLOODED WITH DATA

The information which pours onto management desks has been compared to a daily newspaper printed without headlines, capital letters, or spacing between lines and words—in effect, an incomprehensible *mess* and not a message! The vital views may be there, but it lies buried almost beyond human retrieval.

All effective action in business is based on pertinent, *timely* information. Computers, linked with networks of information retrieval devices, have almost unlimited capacity to record, store, and move information. In the future—one might even say from *now* on—the effective interplay of people, information and machines will be an important factor in determining whether management succeeds or fails, whether a business prospers or perishes.

But management—at the highest levels—has tended to be slow in coming to grips with the full implications of information technology. Despite a demonstrated willingness to buy the necessary machinery, management often seems reluctant to devote its personal interest and talent to an area where the stakes are potentially so great.

Too often management's attitude toward the new science seems like that of an amnesia victim trying to piece together his missing personality from the contents of his wallet; there's a lot of poking around and head-shaking at the odd bits of information, but little recognition.

CHANGE AND THE ORGANIZATION

A natural sense of insecurity keeps us from facing up to this new and unfamiliar development. It is so fraught with significance that we instinctively try to dodge the destiny of radical change which it implies. After all, as Professor Tom Whisler at the University of Chicago has said:

"Organizations are methods which men have arrived at to maintain the *status quo*."

And that observation elaborates the idea discussed by William McNeill, chairman of the History Department of the University of Chicago—that the fundamental nature of man has not changed very much through all the centuries. Our increasing store of knowledge usually tends to complicate and strengthen the defenses against danger which threatens the tribal compound. Maintaining the pleasant present environment can require a lot of energy!

What we really want, when we must face change, may be called *"a new idea that has stood the test of time."* And that kind is a little hard to come by! Management is always torn by opposing tensions: the "survival pull" of holding on to gains already made, and the "growth pull" of being creative and innovative in building enterprises.

CREATIVITY VERSUS CONFORMITY

If organization structure and routines are very rigid—and they can be, when management fails to readjust rapidly to changing conditions—then creative intellect in the lower echelons may be a handicap to efficient operations. When "don't question the rules" performance is demanded, a bright man will only foul it up.

How can we consciously set up an organization to produce the kind of innovation needed under the demands of drastic environmental change? How can we regroup people to make a more rational response to the new conditions of business life?

We must relinquish a certain amount of order in an organization if we want to provide a creative atmosphere, just as top-flight advertising agencies give up formality and order to stimulate their creative people.

Fortunately, successful management has had long experience in resolving the paradoxical tensions which strain any organization. The answer, of course, lies in *careful planning to meet external change by producing internal change.* In order to discipline the use of computer technology in handling information flow, top management must first of all set up a planning structure and environment to analyze company operations and objectives. Ideally, such a planning group should embody all the virtues of disciplined thoroughness and creative brilliance, with intelligent control, support, and direction coming from the top of the organization.

A HARD LOOK AT BASIC AIMS

This analyzing requirement is the greatest initial impact of computer science on business. It forces managers to rethink their basic business goals, to restudy their own aims and responsibilities. It forces original thinking, and questioning of traditional patterns of operation. Such demands on management cannot be delegated.

Automation in any phase of a business is a critical area where managers cannot shirk the job of managing. Instead of acting on this crucial fact, management can become so intimidated by the complexity of its new hardware that it allows technicians not only to operate the gadgetry, but actually to make decisions about its purpose and use!

The problem-solvers, the new professionals who are charged with the care and feeding of computers, can too easily become top management's *alter ego* in reality if management does not fulfill its planning responsibility.

MANAGERS MUST MANAGE

The basic problems of information systems are: defining objectives, markets, methods, organization, attitudes. They demand *managerial* skill, imagination, and experience—rather than that of the technical experts whose responsibility it is to implement decisions, not to make them. Symphony orchestras, staffed by virtuosi, still need conductors!

Because information technology widens the horizons perceptibly for almost any company, a broad view of basic business aims will be best for the long pull. For instance, the motion picture industry proclaims that it is in the *entertainment* business. I am in the *communications* business. This is not just a matter of semantics but of basic philosophy. Economic history is littered with the wreckage of firms which took too narrow a view of their business.

Let me make a few more suggestions about management's initial planning responsibilities, prior to installation of information systems. Computers are important because they make it possible, for the first time, to organize many kinds of business operations into systems, and to control these systems far more precisely than ever before. But these new control techniques place extraordinary demands on people at all levels in an organization.

EXPANDING OPPORTUNITIES

At the bottom of the company hierarchy, people fear—and face—the risks of possible job displacement, of learning new skills, of breaking up comfortable routines.

The same is true higher up in the organization structure; and the higher the fears go, the more influence and effect people will have in resisting changes which top management has decided must be the means to long-term goals of the organization.

These changes are much more far-reaching than simply another step in the familiar routine of industrial progress. Because of this, any kind of automation program must include provision to cushion the shock of change on employees. When we disrupt routines which have become habits, people whose lives are shaped to those habits will be squeezed through a psychological wringer. This wringer can be very painful to the human beings in any organization if management fails to plan to alleviate it. The first step—and perhaps the most important—is to give employees the *full story* of what will happen to them and their jobs to the extent that it is known.

They also need to know what specialized training and retraining will be necessary. They must be encouraged to adjust to change and make a place for themselves in the new order of business life. Certainly there is no lack of opportunity. For example, capable computer programmers are now in very short supply. Some 40,000 are employed in the entire United States. It's estimated that 200,000 will be needed by 1970.

But this area of retraining involves specifics with which most managers are already familiar in automating clerical routines.

INFORMATION FOR CONTROL AND PLANNING

Intelligent planning will generally reveal two basic streams of information flowing through an organization. The first may be called *control* information, because it fulfills most of the decision-making needs of middle and lower management. It is usually historical in nature and deals with money, material, people, and their performance. Segments of this *control* information flow were among the first candidates for computer applications, but on a piece-part basis. Combining all elements in this flow into a total computer and communications system will produce either one or a series of *operating control information systems*. This provides a constant check on day-to-day results in a business.

The second information stream may be called *planning* information. This is the strategic information about critical business problems, and it flows at higher levels in the organization. It is the crucial stuff—sometimes intuitive and vague—out of which executive decisions often are carved.

Let us consider first the *operating* information system. It is the usual starting point in business data automation, and some of its effects on the organization can be severe.

MANAGEMENT BY EXCEPTION

Installation of operating information systems with feedback techniques will introduce the principle of *management by exception*—that is, directing management attention only to performance which is off-target according to established criteria. This principle is clearly stated in Exodus XVIII as proposed by Jethro to Moses, ". . . every great matter they shall bring to you but any small mattter they shall decide themselves."

With exception reporting, the volume of data flowing to operating managers will be greatly reduced because on-target performance can proceed without help. This principle will thus relieve middle and lower management of much data gathering and evaluation. Computers also will take over a considerable amount of the scheduling of manpower and allocation of resources, which now requires much of operating management's time and judgment. One major result is a flattening of the decision-making process—while at the same time managers are freed to do creative work.

At Illinois Bell computer logic has been applied to scheduling and allocation problems in the area of billing. Our system uses critical path analysis to determine the best scheduling of personnel and machines for maximum efficiency on our many overlapping, repetitive monthly work operations. Critical path analysis means determining those operations which can be completed with time to spare, and those which have no slack time at all. The latter are "critical" operations, around which the rest of the job is built. Without computers, because of the tremendous number of computations required, it is not feasible to use this operations research technique. One great benefit of this system is that the manager is now freed to handle truly *managerial* problems, those which require his highest skills.

He can spend more time on the complex questions involving organization philosophy, planning, personnel evaluation, and other management areas where his human abilities are paramount. But this is not to say that he will be eager for the change.

REACTION TO CHANGE

David G. Scott, president of the Continental Assurance Company, recently expressed some very pertinent thoughts on freeing of managers from the clerical work they are often required to do:

> Much of the manager's time is now spent in comfortable routines which are basically unproductive, but since they are part of the landscape with which he has been long familiar, he will hesitate to eliminate them. To do so would be to abandon the easy part of his job. It is going to take a lot of convicing to compel acceptance of the thought that much of what the manager has been doing can be done as well by a machine. Much of the information that flows over the manager's desk reaches him only because he is expected to sort the useful items out of the mass. Many of his decisions, which seem to be the result of judgment and thought, are really automatic!

Mr. Scott's comments point up the kind of management resistance to change which will be a phenomenon of our growing switch to modern techniques in management, and which managers must be ready to meet.

A NEED FOR REAPPRAISAL

For twenty-five years or so, companies have steadily decentralized, and the reason is clear. As they grew more complex or diversified, direct control by one man or a small headquarters group was no longer possible. Decentralization progressed as companies expanded, because the science of gathering and passing on information was not far enough advanced.

But times have most certainly changed. Now the problem is not how to *get* information to the top in a hurry, but how to keep *useless* information from hampering top management in its job. And, along with that problem, there is the question of how management is to decide on the exception information it needs to act effectively.

The result, as John Diebold states in his book, *Beyond Automation,* is that management has a capacity never known before in large organizations to centralize certain decision functions. The advances made in communications between machines as well as people now permit direct, cheap, and instant flow and feedback of information between any geographic points.

Whereas the organizational decision once fell automatically on decentralization, it now could as easily fall on centralization.

This also means that traditional concepts of departmental responsibility will change. The new technology provides ways to build information systems which transcend the need for a compartmentalized structure based on functional specializations. Organization shifts are bound to occur as businesses turn to new concepts of functional *integration* in place of the old "pigeonhole" approach. A new breed of multi-functional managers must be found for business—whether from the ranks through retraining or from the raw as young trainees.

THE FUTURE MANAGER

Certainly emphasis will be placed upon expertise in sophisticated management techniques and on the development of professional attitudes toward the job of managing. In a sense, these "managers of the future" will be management scientists, oriented to the systems approach which deliberately *expands* a business problem until all the significant, interacting components of it can be appraised as a system. This is quite different from much of current management practice which tries to reduce a complex problem to its known critical factors, in order to get it to manageable proportions. Applying computers to management problems requires that we accumulate and program complete information on the whole spectrum of company operations where this is pertinent.

The new management scientists may tend to be less company-oriented, from a loyalty standpoint, than our present-day managers. They may reflect the attitude which a professor in the Graduate School at the University of Chicago reports observing in his students. He calls them "more skilled and more insolent." They will surely be more impersonal in their future relationship with employers, and quite probably more independent. Regardless of this attitude, a much tighter discipline in the years ahead is certain to descend on every business organization in the wake of computerization of information channels.

CRUCIAL ROLE OF PLANNING

Let me return to *planning* systems, which involve the data we need to make the more crucial, long-range decisions in our businesses.

Knowledge—provided it is timely and to the point—offers power and control. A manager can quickly suit his actions to his aims when he knows what is going on in his business almost as soon as events occur. But he must also understand—with comparable speed—what is happening in the market place in order to make really sound decisions.

Traditionally, much of the information at the top manager's disposal has been too inaccurate, incomplete and untimely for fully organized and analytical reasoning. Partly because of this, he has needed a high talent for intuitive judgment—for assaying variables and unknowns by rules of thumb, shrewd guesses, and sensitive mental antennae. Working with the computer both enables and forces him to think more explicitly and analytically.

USING THE COMPUTER CREATIVELY

The top man can now control his business and assess its environment with incomparable effectiveness, in two ways. First, he will have relevant facts as they arise; and he will get those facts promptly and abundantly enough to control the circumstances they describe while those circumstances are still developing.

But ample supply of timely facts alone will not suffice. Unless the executive understands how they are related to each other—and particularly how the relationships may be changing—he will find little value in the variety or timeliness of the information. He will know very little more than he does now about the interplay of variables.

He must therefore rely on the machine in another way. Through creative use of information processing, he can employ one or more of the management science techniques—such as critical path analysis, simulation, or game theory—to help him understand the changing relationships of business variables.

Simulation, which is the technique of imitating potential experience by hypothesizing model business situations on the computer, holds great promise for clearing away much of the uncertainty an executive faces. Many ill-defined problems can be converted into well-structured and soluble ones. The machine's unmatched capacity to compare facts lets it choose from limitless alternatives, to assess consequences and provide probable conclusions based on the logic furnished by managers beforehand.

Let me warn, however, that while use of the computer techniques may diminish the mechanical chores of decision making, it does not eliminate any of the inherent risks. It merely defines—more clearly and explicitly than ever before possible—the risks and penalties associated with each choice.

DECISION MAKING STILL TOUGH

As Gilbert Burck suggests in his book, *The Computer Age,* management *planning systems* based on information technology will make the job of the top manager at once easier and harder. He will be faced with less uncertainty in the sense that he will know more about what is going on that affects his business. But he will have to think harder and more precisely to make good use of his knowledge. He will gain extra time to practice creative interrogation and long-range strategy, but the actual process will not be any easier than it is now. In the end, the top manager will be more analytical in his judgments, but his intuition will be more valuable than ever.

In summary, let me briefly restate some of the major effects information systems are likely to have on business organizations.

> The hierarchy of management will flatten, and much stratification will disappear. In effect, this will streamline and lighten the organization.

> A concomitant of this change is that the decision area is broadened as top management moves closer to its field operations. Managers in the fielyd, conversely, will be much closer to the top.

> Departmental boundaries will be arranged as emphasis shifts to functional integration rather than the separation necessary under present decentralized organization.

Discipline will be tightened as operating methods and results come under the almost instantaneous observation of top management. This makes it imperative that human as well as economic rules are applied in judging performance.

Traditional managerial career lines will change to fit the new pattern of the organization, and managers must master new skills to succeed.

Finally, the ability of computers to sort out options, test profit potentials, and evaluate alternate approaches means that information needed in decision making should appear *where* and *when* needed. Competition will intensify because the size and complexity of an organization will no longer be an excuse for clumsiness in getting vital information to the point of decision.

MEETING THE CHALLENGE

Management cannot neglect the implications or challenge of such change. We are moving into the midst of it, and we are—to some extent—managers of it. The Bell System has taken a step toward preparing its top managers for the challenges ahead by setting up a seminar on information technology and its effects. Each week, using the facilities of our data communications school in Cooperstown, New York, we blanket small groups of top Bell System executives with the best and most up-to-date briefing possible in five days.

I am convinced that the new awareness this kind of exposure to information technology produces is going to brighten the future of my own organization. I hope that my remarks have stimulated your own sensitivity to the new problems we all face as business managers.

Bibliography

1. Burlingame, John F. "Information Technology and Decentralization," *Harvard Business Review*, November–December, 1961.
2. Churchman, C. West, Russell L. Ackoff, and E. Leonard Arnoff, *Introduction to Operations Research*, John Wiley and Sons, 1957.
3. Diebold, J., "What's Ahead in Information Technology," *Harvard Business Review*, September, 1965.
4. Evans, Marshall K., and Lou R. Hague, "Master Plan for Information Systems," *Harvard Business Review*, January–February, 1962.
5. Gallagher, James D., *Management Information Systems and the Computer*, American Management Association, Inc., 1961.
6. Green, J. C., "Information Explosion, Real or Imaginary," *Science*, May, 1964.
7. Haller, G. L., "Information Revolution," *Science Digest*, May, 1964.

8. Hattery, Lowell H., and Edward M. McCormick (eds.), *Information Retrieval Management,* American Data Processing, Inc., 1962.
9. Hockman, John, "Specification for an Integrated Management Information System," *Systems and Procedures Journal,* January–February, 1963.
10. Limberg, Herman, "Blueprint for a Management Information System," *Data Processing for Management,* March, 1964.
11. McDonough, Adrian M., and Leonard J. Garrett, *Management Systems, Working Concepts and Practices,* Richard D. Irwin, Inc., 1965.
12. Optner, Stanford L., *Systems Analysis for Business and Industrial Problem Solving,* Prentice-Hall, Inc., 1965.
13. Reitzfeld, Milton, "Effective Reports: The Poor Man's Management Information System," *Records Management Journal,* Winter, 1964.
14. Stoller, David S., and Richard L. Van Horn, *Design of a Management Information System,* The RAND Corporation, P-1362, 1958.
15. Tou, J. T., "Information Systems: Learning, Adaptation and Control; Report of Computer and Information Science Symposium," *Science,* September, 1963.
16. Wooster, H., "Post-Mortems Can Be Fun; the Cost Analysis of Information Systems," *Library Journal,* July, 1965.

16 Marketing Intelligence Systems: A DEW Line for Marketing Men*

Just as our Distant Early Warning radar network can cue us to enemy actions, so this new technique can give managers marketing information on which to act, in time to act. Companies now using it say it is competitively invaluable. It is not yet widespread, but the need for it is becoming apparent.

Marketing intelligence may seem like a fancy name for marketing research.

It isn't.

Marketing research usually focuses on a specific problem or project. A marketing research department might seek to discover why the competition has a larger share of the market in certain regions, or it might test consumer reactions to a certain proposed product. Whatever the activity, marketing research projects tend to have a definite beginning, middle and end.

*Reprinted by permission from **Business Management,** January, 1966, pp. 32ff Copyright 1966 by Management Magazines, Inc.

A marketing intelligence system, on the other hand, does not focus on specific problems. Rather, it is a thermostat that monitors the market place continuously so the company can adjust its actions from day to day or month to month. A sound marketing intelligence system should prevent real problems from arising.

The first such system made its appearance at the Mead Johnson division of Edward Dalton Co., Evansville, Ind., in 1961. Its creator, Dr. Robert J. Williams, explains its usefulness this way:

"The difference between marketing research and marketing intelligence is like the difference between a flash bulb and a candle. Let's say you are dancing in the dark. Every 90 seconds you're allowed to set off a flash bulb. You can use those brief intervals of intense light to chart a course, but remember everybody else is moving, too. Hopefully, they'll accommodate themselves roughly to your predictions. You may get bumped and you may stumble every so often, but you can dance along.

"On the other hand, you can light a candle. It doesn't yield as much light, but it's a steady light. You are continually aware of the movements of other bodies. You can adjust your own course to the courses of the others. The intelligence system is a kind of candle. It's no great flash on the immediate state of things, but it provides continuous light as situations shift and change."

THE IDEA IS TAKING OFF

There are several indications that this idea is spreading, and spreading fast.

Back in 1960, Marion Harper, Jr., president and chairman of the board of the Interpublic Group of Companies, New York, delivered the 16th Charles Coolidge Parlin Memorial Lecture. In it, he proposed that companies establish a new management post—Director of Intelligence Services. He complained that there was (in 1960) no university curriculum in which such a man could be trained. So, at the conclusion of his talk, Harper pledged $50,000 on behalf of his company to establish at one university a program of studies leading to a graduate degree in research.

Today, there are at least two other such programs. In 1961, the Wharton School of Finance and Commerce at the University of Pennsylvania undertook the investigation of a curriculum revision to include courses in gathering useful market intelligence. And in the fall of 1964, the Harvard Graduate School of Business Administration established a Marketing Research and Information Systems course. Its introductory case study was the marketing intelligence system that Robert Williams established at Mead Johnson.

Williams' title at Mead Johnson was indicative of an early awareness of the need for this new function, à la Harper's proposal. Williams came into the firm as director of marketing intelligence. (He has since moved, in mid-1965, to Dow Chemical Co., Midland, Mich., where he is manager of consumer products marketing, marketing research department.) Just six weeks ago, *Advertising Age,* a trade paper, carried this item: "Robert Riordan has resigned from D. P. Brother & Co. to become director of marketing information of Falstaff Brewing Co., St. Louis, a new post."

Other signs of the marketing intelligence idea on the move:

In late 1964, an extensive study of 1,000 of the nation's largest corporations, conducted by Edward L. Brink of the Wharton School, turned up 80 companies that had established some kind of formal marketing information system. A healthy number of other companies in the study indicated plans to activate such systems. Just five weeks ago, the top management of one of the nation's most successful food processing firms had placed before it a lengthy proposal for the establishment of a marketing intelligence department.

HOW DOES A MARKETING INTELLIGENCE SYSTEM WORK?

According to Williams: "The marketing intelligence department at Mead Johnson was presumed to report with great reliability whether there was a tiger loose in the streets. Having reported that there was, it was up to the brand managers—who actually had the profit responsibility—to decide whether they were going to run and hide, or stand and fight, or just pretend the tiger wasn't there and hope they'd be overlooked." The point is that firing-line managers must be given the facts on which to act, in time to act.

Setting up a marketing intelligence system to spot the tigers before they spot you isn't an esoteric or mysterious art. It doesn't depend on cultivating sources of information not now readily available, nor on increasing the types of information that are available, nor even on the computers that make information available faster (although really sophisticated systems need a computer to sift through masses of data very quickly and report out relevant information). The system does depend, however, on coordinating and integrating the information system with the day-to-day operation of the business.

What kind of information should be sought?

"That which provides the marketing executive with continuous surveillance of his markets, and which is directly related to the actions he can take," says Williams. "As a starting point in designing the information system, one might study the decisions that are available to the men the system is to serve. Consider, for example, the actions that might be taken by the brand manager responsible for marketing a small-ticket consumer item:

"He can set the price of the product, and vary it from time to time through discounts and deals.

"He can change the performance characteristics and functions of the product within narrow limits by ordering changes in formulation, manufacturing processes or packaging.

"He can regulate the total advertising pressure and media mix.

"He can alter copy themes, style and appeals within the advertising.

"He can offer guarantees and vary their terms.

"He can take a number of merchandising and promotional actions, such as couponing, sampling, in-store demonstrating, contests, etc.

"He can offer sales incentives and bonuses, either to the salesmen he controls or to the retailers who handle his product.

"He can vary trade terms, offer quantity discounts, provide advertising and display allowances and so forth.

"Obviously," says Williams, "one doesn't expect a brand manager to take these actions in serial order, or at random or just to keep busy. Ideally, they are taken as responses to a certain market situation."

Therefore, to ascertain the information necessary to enable this man to act, determine the market situation that would call for any of the above actions. For example, what market conditions would make it worthwhile to give away free samples? Similar questions could be asked about all the other possible actions.

When you've defined the market conditions that might trigger any of the marketing actions listed, you can then specify the kinds of market data that will identify these conditions.

It isn't necessary, however, to record the cues for every possible marketing action. "Usually, the number of different kinds of data required is not large," Williams says. "A relatively small number of observations of the market place will describe market situations of considerable variety and complexity."

Naturally, the relevant information is not the same for every type of business. But let's continue with the brand manager of the small-ticket consumer products. He would probably find these measures sufficient to describe all of the market variations on which he could take action:

Measures of retail activity. Total consumer spending for all brands in his product class as well as spending for each individual major brand; distribution of each brand in the retail outlets; retail prices; inventories.

Observations of consumer reaction. Total number of consumers in the market; proportion aware of each major brand; proportion using each major brand; consumer perception of the benefits of each major brand; circumstances controlling use of product and important factors in brand selection.

Information about trade activities. Deals and promotions; new product introductions; point-of-purchase materials, packaging changes; consumer promotions.

Media usage. Expenditures and copy changes for each major brand in the product class.

There are no unusual types of information here. Information in the first group comes from typical store audits. The simplest kind of consumer interviews produce information for the second group. Salesmen can easily collect and report information for the third group and advertising audits deliver information for the fourth group.

"Rumors, or information gained from commercial spying or from *sub rosa* or accidental sources, cannot be integrated into a marketing intelligence system," says Williams. "By its very nature, such information is collected unsystematically and is not always dependable. The strength of a marketing information system is that it is based on information from dependable sources that is reported at planned intervals." That's the only way changes and trends can be identified. And a change in the market situation is what should trigger marketing action.

At the same time external information is being gathered, so should internal information be collected to dovetail with what comes in from the field.

For example, it can be important to compare factory sales with retail sales. Suppose one subtracts the dollar value (at factory prices) of retail purchase from the dollar value of factory sales for the same month. If the difference is positive, this indicates that you are selling to retail outlets faster than consumers are buying the products. The appropriate corrective action falls to the advertising department; it must find ways to accelerate consumer purchases. If the difference is negative, then consumers are buying your goods faster than factory sales are replacing them. So, the sales staff must concentrate on boosting factory sales. If the difference is zero, or near zero, then product flow can be considered smooth, and the only remaining concern is whether or not volume is satisfactory.

Also, the amount of inventories in your distribution channels (whether too much or too little) along with information about consumer purchase rates, provides a basis for precise short-term forecasts of factory sales.

The essence of a marketing intelligence system is to produce exception reports—reports that indicate deviations from the prevailing market conditions. Computers are almost certainly called for, because of their ability to scan masses of data and deliver only the exceptions to the norm in a relatively short amount of time. When raw market data is fed into the computer on a weekly or monthly basis, the company can be fairly certain of not being caught flat-footed by a major unforeseen shift in the market situation.

LONG-RANGE IMPORTANCE

However good it may be, a marketing intelligence system is simply supposed to provide a company with a quick reflex. The company is able to make intelligent short-term moves to enable it to keep up with—or ahead of—the competition.

What about the kind of marketing research that looks beyond the horizon? This, too, is growing in importance.

Walter Talley, director of marketing for Southwestern Engineering Corp., Los Angeles, stresses the importance of what he calls marketing research and development. In an article published in *Business Horizons,* he states: "Obviously, the introduction of new ways of selling products has been going on since the beginning of time. What is new is the effort to systematize this process and to convert this type of marketing creativity from a sporadic and personal act of spontaneous generation to an organized activity that will ensure—as far as this is possible—that the business will have a reasonably steady supply of new marketing approaches . . . This is why an increasing number of companies are organizing under a variety of different names, what amounts to the function of marketing research and development."

Are these long-range research activities inconsistent with a marketing intelligence system that is geared to produce information for short-term action?

"Not at all," says Robert Williams. "By establishing a computerized system whereby you learn about problems before they become real disasters, you free your market research people for the more important job of investigating the social and economic factors that will affect your company in the next five to 10 years. This is where the real breakthroughs come. But you won't reap them if your marketing research people are constantly involved in crisis projects designed to correct negative developments. When your marketing researchers aren't always putting out fires, that's when they can be figuring ways to abolish fires altogether."

Information Systems in Marketing* 17

BELDEN MENKUS

It is wrong for the purchasing agent to turn his back on the operations of the supplier. The agent should know as much about his supplier's activity as he knows about the mechanics of his own firm.

Essentially, marketing is a communicative phenomenon; its needs and problems are those of information manipulation. Yet the lack of adequate information handling techniques in the marketing function demonstrates the failure of systems men to deal more than superficially with the "total" corporate enterprise.

Within a relative handful of years the concepts and methods of integrated information handling have completely altered our essential approach to management. Yet the vital marketing function has been relatively untouched by the transformation. In no other area of business operations have the techniques of information systems been less used. In no other area of business do they have greater unrealized potential.

*Reprinted from **Systems & Procedures Journal,** July–August, 1963, pp. 10–14.

Information systemizing has immediate application to such fundamental areas of marketing as product line development, pricing structure, distribution operation, sales force management, advertising, and sales forecasting. Systematic information manipulation can help marketers find the answers to such basic questions as: What level of advertising expenditure is realistic in a specific product market situation? Is it preferable to work through a distributor or to sell direct in a given sales situation? What is a valid measure of the salesman's use of his time? What are reliable, yet universal, measures of advertising effectiveness?

WHAT ARE THE MARKETING FUNDAMENTALS?

Essentially marketing is a communicative phenomenon. Its needs and problems are those of information manipulation—gathering, evaluating and using data. Marketing fundamentals embrace five interrelated functions in a broad operative process:

First—product design—translating the idea into a marketable item.

Second—manufacturing—translating production drawings into a deliberable product.

Third—advertising and sales—translating the customer's desire into a verified order.

Fourth—physical distribution—translating the customer order into promptly delivered goods.

Fifth—billing and collection—translating the customer order into cash in hand.

So long as a marketing organization (or any other organization, for that matter) functions properly there is a firmly established pattern of information flow within its component parts.

It is best to distinguish between information *pattern* and information *system*. Information *pattern* is the actual manner in which information moves through the organization. In theory, this flow may be compressed formally into rigid, slow-moving, organizational channels of communication. More likely in practice it breaks out of these channels and moves rapidly and somewhat erratically through informal, personal contacts.

Information *system* is an attempt to discipline and to refine the already existing information pattern. The basic objectives of this effort are to assure that all essential information is made available, and that effective and efficient use is made of all available information.

In the corporate marketing information situation we are dealing with more than a simple buyer and seller relationship. The marketer is at the center of a dynamic complex of communicative relationships. These intricate interrelationships defy simple meaningful reduction to a mere handful of multi-column statistical reports.

At one and the same time the marketer is involved in a continuing information pattern that touches his supplier, producer, sales organization, competitor, and the community at large, as well as his ultimate consumer.

Each marketer, is intrinsically, a part of the larger community, without regard to the nature or extent of either his competition or his customers; but those points of the basic marketing information pattern that touch the community and the competitor are beyond the scope of this presentation. The first relationship involves the interchange of information inherent in the community's role in our free economy as both regulator and promoter of the marketer's basic activities. The latter relationship involves the fascinating area of corporate information security, a discipline of growing importance and increasing sophistication.

We concern ourselves, then, with those segments of the marketing information pattern that touch the supplier, the producer, the sales organization, and the ultimate consumer.

The manufacturing operation is subordinated to the overall marketing objective. Manufacturing is not an end in itself. It functions only to provide the raw material for the marketing operation. In other words: The organization does not exist merely to produce. It exists, instead, to market what it produces.

The supplier has a vital stake in the total marketing enterprise. His position is one of a partner. He should be vitally involved in product design, production continuity, and all of the other dynamic factors in the marketing process to which he is functionally related.

STANDARD SPECIFICATIONS NEEDED

Organizationally, the purchasing function is the point at which contact is made with the supplier. It demands articulate, highly competent professionals who know the supplier's specialty as well as he does. This is not the place to put men who have failed to produce satisfactorily elsewhere in the organization.

WHAT COMMUNICATION FAILURES CAN DO

Ideally, the purchasing function should maintain a continuing, realistic, and effective relationship with the supplier. Too often, however, purchases are made on price comparisons alone, without regard to optimum quality or to ultimate supplier resources. Or, delivery schedules are developed arbitrarily without regard to the best use of supplier capabilities. In some instances, due to a total lack of genuine communication, the supplier does not really know or understand what the marketer wants or needs.

The classic example of the basic marketing information problem is the predictament faced by the maker of a certain brand of packaged laundry bleach. The powdered chemical is packed in an envelope of soft, clear plastic. The product package is designed to dissolve completely when dropped into the hot water in the washing machine. This permits the bleach powder to mix quickly and directly with the wash water. A simple process, but the situation becomes complicated when the company finds a new source for the plastic envelope. Top management is still congratulating itself for finding a cheaper envelope when the complaints start to come in from customers. Briefly, the new envelope is a crucial several millimeters thicker, and is of a different chemical composition than the envelope used when the product package was developed. The results: Packages totally refuse to dissolve in wash water, sealing their contents inside. Or, the packages do not fully dissolve, leaving damaging blobs of plastic on clothing or in the machine itself.

There's an immediate moral to be drawn here—accountants, budgeteers, and other economic theorists notwithstanding—the cheapest product is not always the best buy. Cost considerations must be balanced by those of quality and suitability.

There's also another simple point to be taken: the availability of information and the correct use of it could have prevented this corporate error. And we'll return to this example later on.

The first step in improving information flow with suppliers lies in transforming the procurement function from passive to active. It is all too common for purchasing men to know nothing of their suppliers and their problems. It is not rare to find men in responsible procurement positions who have never been inside the plants of the suppliers with whom they deal. The answer probably lies in converting the basic function into one of liaison and expediting.

We must revise the recently developed interrelated ideas of value analysis and quality control. Rather than remaining static means of evaluating intrinsic product worth and supplier performance, these functions must become vehicles for coordinating product needs and delivered value. The twin restraints and disciplines of value analysis and quality control will not achieve full effectiveness until they become the basis for a genuine interchange of information between marketer and supplier.

In moving from ordinary hunch and intuition buying to intelligent purchasing we must come to regular reliance on standard specifications for routine procurement. A computerized system for product ordering and related inventory control will remain two-dimentional unless it is related to the specifications involved in the procurement process. A system for reducing product wants to written specifications is a commonly overlooked normal outgrowth of a program for written administrative directives—whether they are known as procedures or anything else.

The distinctions between supplier and producer dissolve when product manufacture is contracted out to a supplier facility. The basic information pattern problem for both marketer and producer is ending the isolation of production functions from the basic marketing process. As already noted, the interrelated disciplines of value analysis and quality control will achieve maximum effectiveness in the manufacturing process when they become the media for a dynamic information interchange. Organizationally, the manufacturing function must be tied to sales operations. Conceptually, it must be made customer conscious. To begin with, the basic objectives of manufacturing must become product quality and craftsmanship. In our obsession with cost-conscious efficiency we have produced the desired statistics, but have lost all concern for the real value of what we have produced.

In addition, the manufacturing function must receive information "feed back" from both the sales operation and the customer. Product orientation of the sales force must be a continuing responsibility of the manufacturing function. As our technology becomes increasingly more complicated the order will more often go to the man who better understands application of his product—including the special features and the limitations. Essential information interchange will not take place when sales management acts to separate sales and manufacturing—as when field men or distributors are brought in for extended sales conference periods that carefully exclude all contact with production people.

Development of equipment descriptions and instructions must not be left to the fanciful devices of advertising people. A comprehensive and accurate presentation must not be set aside for one that is visually appealing and nothing else.

Periodic product revision must be built into the continuing manufacturing process. Applied creative effort and validation of ideas are inherent in the initial product design activity. They must be repeated. Product revision must be manufacturing's continuing corrective to customer reaction, both negative and positive.

To return to our example of the envelope for the bleach packets: Information flowing from customers directly or through the sales force should have alerted manufacturing to the inadequate performance of the plastic envelopes. It remains a paradox of modern marketing: Decision-makers will spend vast amounts to communicate with their customers. Yet, they will purposely make it difficult if not impossible for their customers to communicate with them.

INFORMATION NEEDS ARE THREE-FOLD

It should be noted here that in dealing with these areas of information flow we are dealing with both long range and short range immediate problems. In theory they can be separated. In the dynamic situation of actual operations these considerations are intermingled. A constant corrective action is possible only where information flows freely and continuously through the marketing information complex. And we are dealing with quality as well as quantity. Thus, it will not always be possible in the commonplace, straight, statistical table to analyze the significance of:

Buying pattern differences among customer classes in one market area and in all market areas.
Order volume differences in product lines among customer classes in a given market area and in all market areas.
Product item turnover differences in a single market area and all market areas in terms of damage and obsolescence.

In areas such as these mere numbers and statistical relationships are not necessarily indicative of anything significant.

Information needs of the sales organization are themselves three-fold in nature. These categories are not mutually exclusive but somewhat overlapping. The communicative relationship involves the advertising, distributor, and sales representative activities. Primarily, each must act as the intermediary in customer communication with the marketer. In addition, each needs a new appreciation of the quality of the information with which he is dealing. This demands accuracy, integrity (which is not necessarily the same thing as accuracy), and a respect for the native intelligence of the customer.

In general this means that you can not lie to all of the people all of the time—without being discovered. Failure to recognize this has meant for at least one manufacturer the gradual loss of business in all product areas and the abandonment of several in which he had traditionally operated. Specifically this means that you cannot continue to tell people that delivery can be made in two weeks from the factory when it has never been made in under six months, or that the equipment can be operated by anyone when it takes a graduate engineer to do the job.

All three information areas—advertising, distributor, and sales representative—must be kept aware of price changes, product revisions and similar activities "back at the ranch." All are as much partners in the basic marketing operation as is the supplier.

Information interchange between the marketer and all three should determine the basic customer contact priority, and the relative importance of each item in each product line. Thus, you must deal with such questions (sometimes on a seasonal or market cycle repetitive basis) as "Is there a secondary market?" Thus, in this instance, one might need to ask more specifically:

> Can an item being sold now to commercial decorators for painting work also be sold through hardware and garden supply outlets to the home handyman?
> Can this be done in all market areas or in just selected ones?
> Can this be done seasonably, or is it possible to market the item in this fashion throughout the year?

Customer preferences and similar factors are in constant change. Thus, both the answers and the questions must undergo continuing revision based upon the dynamic information interchange we have already mentioned. For one further example, grocery merchandisers have failed to make their distribution along the lines of regional preferences sufficiently flexible to react to the increased mobility of our population beyond regional boundaries.

NO PLACE FOR "BUG LETTERS"

Finally, we come to the marketer's direct communicative relationship with his customers. As we have noted before, marketers need to rediscover accuracy, integrity, and respect for the native intelligence of the customer. The marketer needs to realize that his communication with the customer is a two-way proposition. The customer needs to know that he is important to the marketer.

Thus, suppose the dealer fails to honor the marketer's product warranty, and the customer writes the marketer about it. The customer shouldn't get a "bug letter" telling him a sad story about the problems of competitive pressures in that particular industry.

The customer must always know that his problems and his complaints are important. The writer knows of one small firm that is gradually gaining control of its segment of the office equipment market from a number of massive corporations which have competing product lines. The secret: Management of that smaller firm gives personal attention to every letter of complaint—or suggestion—that comes in. And, each one of these letters is circulated among the production and sales segments of the organization, for each must react in detail to the basic idea in the letter, no matter how odd or off-beat it may be.

To return again to our powdered bleach marketer. In line with the firm's traditional manner of doing things, complaining customers received vague form replies to their letters. These complaints were round-filed (in effect), and not shared with the sales and production people. Nothing was done until a major distributor went to the top man in the concern at the time falling sales in that product line became obvious.

But, to compound the basic error, the company refused to inform either its sales force or its customers of the problems. Thus, sales of this product line continued to drop. And the company failed to make realistic use of its production lot control system by calling in the defective products. Thus, quantities of this merchandise continued to reach customers long after the basic production error had been corrected.

THE CLASSIC FAILURE

The marketer's communicative relationship with his customer must be *comprehensive, meaningful* and *clear.*

> Comprehensive means that he tells the essential story about the product. Too often the customer reads a lengthy, elaborate, and colorfully illustrated pamphlet designed to introduce a product to him, but he is unable to find out its cost, size, speed, and other vital facts.
>
> Meaningful means that he uses significant terms to tell his story. For instance, a marketer won't impress a young mother by telling her that his product won't need servicing for three years. He will impress her by telling her that the same product won't need servicing until her two-year-old child is ready for kindergarten. The harried young mother doubts her youngster ever will make it to kindergarten.
>
> Clear means that he uses short, colorful, and almost obvious words to tell his story. For just one instance, it is far better to say that a product will last and last instead of referring to its reliability.

In concluding this discussion we face the impact of all of these matters upon men working with systems in general and management information systems in particular. The information needs of marketers demonstrate the almost classic failure of systems men to deal more than superficially with the functioning organization. And these needs demonstrate that in the present state of development of the management information art it is deceptive to speak of a "total" system.

PART FOUR

The Emergence of Marketing Information Systems

Previous sections have described the need for a more carefully integrated and directed flow of marketing information. Yet, as Cox and Good point out in this section, few companies are very far along in taking advantage of an approach that has great potential and where the technical aspects are no long an obstacle.[1] This is in spite of the fact that the marketing men of many corporations are generally highly enthusiastic about the promise of computer-based information systems. There are several reasons for this delay. One is the problem of the design of the information system itself. The system must be related to the organization of the firm. In many cases, the problem of a suitable organizational framework has never been satisfactorily resolved. Large scale multi-functional information systems highlight basic organization problems.

Secondly, just as there is no one proper organizational structure for all firms, there is no single, precise description of the proper information system for all firms because there does not exist a generalized information system. The marketing information system must be both conceived and managed as an entity.[2]

[1] Donald F. Cox, and Robert E. Good, "How to Build a Marketing Information System," **Harvard Business Review,** Vol. 45, No. 3 (May–June, 1967), p. 145.
[2] Kenneth P. Uhl, "Better Management of Market Information," **Business Horizons,** Spring, 1966, pp. 75–82.

A third problem is caused by the fact that the information system is formulated in response to what each participating executive feels he needs. Regretfully, few executives have developed fully articulated and dependable models of buyer behavior.[3] Yet these beliefs and opinions will determine the nature of the information gathered and the basic form of the system.

In spite of the above, it is possible to become acquainted with some guidelines to follow in studying systems that are in operation, and in making decisions about the form of a proposed system. The first group of readings in this section deals with the design of systems, the next describes the implementation of systems, the third group is devoted specifically to some of the problems that have emerged as a result of attempts to adopt the systemic approach, and the final group summarizes the state of the art.

It would be a mistake for the reader to assume that the slow pace of actual implementation and use of MIS will continue. Each of the readings, even the ones that highlight the problems that have appeared when management applied this new approach, contains suggestions for the avoidance of these problems in future applications. The readings identify factors to consider in designing and implementing systems and guidelines to follow. Some articles are at the conceptual level, others deal with specific applications. Taken as a whole, they support the belief of the editors that the marketing information systems approach will provide not only the basis for greater efficiency in marketing management but will provide the buyer with a much higher degree of satisfaction than previously.

---

[3] John A. Howard, "Organization Structure and Its Underlying Theory of Buyer Behavior," John S. Wright and Jac L. Goldstucker, editors, **New Ideas for Successful Marketing** (Chicago: American Marketing Association, 1966), pp. 87–93.

A The Design of Information Systems

Better Management of Market Information* — 18

KENNETH P. UHL

Information, to be useful in making decisions, must be available and used in a systematic fashion, both of which are difficult conditions with today's typical organization structure. As we improve information systems, many new organizational forms will be implemented which will take their shapes based on market needs and problems, not on informational restraints.

Many executives have been dismayed to discover that corporate excellence in production and finance alone has not led to success. Excellence in marketing is also needed. As a result, the marketing function has been elevated to the vice-presidential level, and many firms have begun to orient their activities to their customers' needs. It has been hoped that this increased emphasis on marketing, popularly called the marketing concept, would promote the needed marketing excellence—but all too frequently it has not. Instead, marketing problems have continued to grow larger and become more difficult.

Attempts at solutions have been many, and successes have been few. A common response has been to restructure marketing organizations. Older and simpler line-and-staff structures have been strengthened with more staff specialization and changes in titles and authority bases. Multiproduct firms have created merchandising offices and have experimented with brand managers or product managers. Multimarket firms have experimented with varying degrees of geographical decentralization and have installed various territorial marketing managers who have been charged with profit responsibility.

---

*Reprinted from **Business Horizons**, national quarterly publication of the Graduate School of Business, Indiana University, Vol. 9, No. 1 (Spring, 1966), pp. 75–82.

But success has been spotty, at best, and improvement is still needed. This author's contention is that the handling of marketing information must be better managed—and the focus is on how to do it.

To begin, extensive rethinking is required about both the use and the management of marketing information in the firm. In terms of use, management must insist on planning, organizing, directing, and controlling the marketing function through information as a replacement for "management" by intuition. This means that necessary information must be both available and used.

In terms of management, the old separate segments of intradepartmental information programs are largely unmanageable as composite programs. Instead, new facilities and new organizational structures must be envisioned and installed. The need for such correction has been overwhelmingly obvious to executives who have gained control over production, finance, and other areas through the development and use of information programs.

Similar, if not greater, gain can be accomplished in marketing. Enough has been learned by some firms to indicate that marketing fat can be converted to muscle through the development and use of adequate marketing information programs. The need for marketing information improvements is obvious; the emphasis here will be on plans and programs to bring about such improvements.

MARKETING INFORMATION ENTITY

The basic structural weakness in virtually every ill-informed firm has been the absence of one entity for processing marketing information. Such firms have been typified by the presence of uncoordinated bits and pieces of the information function scattered here and there. Marketing information as an activity has seemed to be everywhere; it has belonged to no one and has received little development and use by these firms. As a result, they do not consider marketing information an activity that is manageable or even worthy of management. The marketing concept has not been developed sufficiently to make management see the need for composite marketing information systems.

A fundamental requisite for better managed marketing is that the scattered information activities be both perceived and managed as an entity. That is, these activity components must be (1) identified throughout the organization, (2) thought of as being parts of a whole, and (3) managed as an information unit.

These components, furthermore, must be managed through a single, separate, and centralized office. One director must be responsible for the entire marketing information program in all of its scattered locations. Through such an arrangement all marketing information activities can be managed as a system—a system which by its very nature must circulate and function internally and wherever the firm wishes to market its offerings.

There is no single precise description of the activities, responsibilities, and authorities of marketing information offices, nor is there one organizational arrangement that is patently superior to all others. Some broad guidelines, however, can be applied to a multitude of specific situations.

ESTABLISHING AN INFORMATION OFFICE

The office of marketing information must assume broad and pervasive responsibilities. Specifically, it must be responsible as consultant, coordinator, and controller for each of the basic marketing information components—searching/securing, analyzing, transmitting, storing, and using. Some difficulties do result, particularly because of the traditional treatment of the marketing information function.

The last component, the *using* function, is the most demanding and the least aided by recent technological advances in information handling. Basically, to manage the using function, the director's office must know who needs what information, when, and why. Knowing "why" is essential if the office is to serve as both manager and consultant. The office must make known to users the firm's information resources, including their costs;[1] it must be able to evaluate information requirements and requests and to moderate and temper those which appear unreasonable. To do this the office must have the capacity to discern which offices should have what information. It must also be able to consult with using units relative to what information they should be using and how they should use it. In other words, to information users, the office should be synonymous with both marketing information and its effective use. The director serves as a consultant to the organization, though, like the company attorney, he has the obligation to be authoritarian when more than advice is needed. Finally, the using component dominates and dictates to the information system. The system exists solely to facilitate better management—better management through more and better information availability and use.

The components of *searching/securing, transmitting, analyzing,* and *storing* must be completely under the guidance of the marketing information office. These four components, while different in form, are similar in how they should be managed. The overall task of the office is to see that each component is present in correct capacity, properly allocated in the organization, and performed with necessary efficiency—all relative to the needs of the using units. In other words, the office must see that there is not too little or too much searching/securing, transmitting, analyzing, and/or storing capacity relative to the using needs of the organization, and that

---

[1] Some of the problems of cost and benefit estimating are discussed in R. S. Alexander, "Let's Have a Marketing Research Done," *Journal of Business,* Seton Hall University (December, 1963); David W. Ewing (ed.), *Effective Marketing Action* (New York: Harper and Bros., 1958), pp. 219–223; and Wroe Alderson and Paul Green, *Planning and Problem Solving in Marketing* (Homewood, Ill.: Richard D. Irwin, Inc., 1964).

capacity is properly allocated and efficient. Continuing audits of the information components relative to users' information requirements provide the information office with the guidance it needs for the management of the marketing information function.

This is not to suggest that all four of these activities should be performed by the information office. Clearly, it would be a most unusual organization and situation in which these four components could be centralized within an information office or any other single office. Their management must be centralized, but the actual operations are likely to be located in many different departments. Each activity should be located where it can be performed most efficiently, relative to the needs of the using units.

Some of the activities must be largely centralized in the information office, while others can be performed far more efficiently in a number of locations. For example, at a minimum, the information office must serve as a central information index and know rather precisely what information is available and where. In this case, information may be stored in various locations throughout the firm. However, random access memory storage units, computers, and electronic transmission facilities have opened up new possibilities for massive centralization of information storage.[2]

About the same statements can be made about information analysis. Simple analysis encourages performance in securing and using units. However, more complex, more difficult, or more burdensome numerical problems suggest the advantages of centralized analysis and use of specialists and computer facilities. Also, more complex non-numerical analysis calls for use of specialists. A case in point is the type of analysis and synthesis performed by brand managers in developing advertising proposals. And a not-to-be-forgotten objective of the information manager is to get each necessary information component performed efficiently. This goal requires, among other things, seeing that each is performed by the correct unit.

The searching/securing and transmitting components must be carefully controlled because of their diverse and widespread nature. Gerald Albaum, an information research expert at the University of Arizona, has clarified the diverse nature of information by classifying it into two categories: planned and unsolicited.[3] The planned type can be assigned to various offices based on source contracts and searching/securing capacity. Where these do not permit use of noninformation offices, these supply components can be assigned to the marketing information office. For example, a sales

---

[2] While numerous articles and books are available, a single publication containing views of both academicians and businessmen is: George P. Shultz and Thomas L. Whisler (ed.), *Management Organization and the Computer* (Chicago: The Free Press of Glencoe, Illinois, 1960).

[3] Gerald Albaum, "The Hidden Crisis in Information Transmission," *Pittsburgh Business Review* (July, 1963), p. 1.

group may have both the capacity and the source contacts to actively search/secure and transmit information on competitive pricing patterns. In contrast, the same sales group would not have the capacity to search/secure customer segment profiles or to gauge product images. These tasks, therefore, would normally accrue to a special marketing information group.

Unsolicited (that is, incidental) information, in contrast to planned information, cannot be anticipated relative to specific kind, source, timing, or availability. For example, a competitive firm may be planning to lower the price on its entire product line by 20 per cent. Receipt of this information prior to initiation of the action certainly would be useful, but is not normally available. Much marketing information cannot be anticipated.

Searching/securing and transmitting incidental information calls for (1) information sensitivity by all members of the organization, (2) transmission channels direct enough that small scattered facets have a chance for meaning and survival by reaching a central assembly point while they are still alive, and (3) in general, an organizational environment that encourages incidental information sensitivity, receptiveness, and transmission. Their eyes, ears, and other senses of the organization obviously cannot be centralized. But to create the necessary environment and facilities requires centralized management of the information function.

It has been shown that a single, separate marketing information office must exist to make one person responsible for all marketing information within the company. And because both the information-using units and the supplying components are scattered, the emphasis of information management must be on coordination and consultation, but with the element of control vested in the office. The office must oversee the entire area of marketing information. The director must be concerned with company-wide management of all of the marketing information components. Parts of these components may be largely centralized and therefore under the immediate control of the information director. Others, because of their locations, must be managed somewhat less directly through numerous overlays. In this latter and more difficult control situation, the success of the information office will be largely dependent on its ability to gain recognition as the marketing information specialist.

ADAPTING THE ORGANIZATION

Information requirements and environments of firms are somewhat diverse; no one information system or information organizational structure is able to fit the needs of all. Development of detailed and specific organizational frameworks for information offices is beyond the scope of this article, but some observations can be made about the placement of the office in the organization.

First of all, the major purpose of the organizational structure is to provide a framework that will facilitate efficient management of the firm's information function. And this problem concerns not only the marketing director and his staff, but all top corporation policy makers. Because the information function must undergo sweeping changes, extensive and penetrating rethinking is called for about frameworks that will encourage development and use of information for marketing control. This focus must not be exclusively on the marketing area, for solutions may require company-wide attention.

Three possible locations for the marketing information office merit serious consideration. Two of these, the marketing research office and the merchandising office, are within the marketing division. The third location is outside marketing in a company-wide information office. The most favorable location is determined largely by (1) the prevailing information climate (that is, the extent of development and the use and respect for marketing information) and (2) the existing marketing organizational structure. These influences will become more explicit as the location alternatives are explored.

Marketing Research Office

The first and the most obvious location to consider as headquarters for the marketing information function is the existing company-wide marketing research office. After all, its manager typically reports directly to the marketing vice-president, and the sole concern of such an office is with marketing information. In addition, there may be no other recognized marketing information specialist. However, these points require further examination because they hold the basic insights as to the information climate in a firm.

The company-wide research office appears, on many organizational charts, to be on a common plane with the advertising and selling functions. In practice, however, it may be deeply shrouded in the marketing organization with few people, little funds, and even less influence. In such situations, the office is probably concerned with but a small portion of the total marketing information needs of the organization. In fact, it probably is limited to problem-focused research—and only problems it can manage.[4] Also, the advertising and sales groups in such situations dominate and provide most of what little information they believe they need—and the marketing research office, if not held in contempt, is suspect, and perhaps rightly so. When this situation prevails, the company-wide marketing research office cannot be changed to the far broader marketing information office. At best, under proper nurturing, it might become a useful part of it.

On the other hand, the marketing research office may regularly provide continuing information for control and planning through sales or distribution cost analysis or both, measures of market opportunity and sales fore-

---

[4] This point is well expressed by Lee Adler in "Phasing Research Into the Marketing Plan," *Harvard Business Review* (May–June, 1960), p. 113: "But the problems that are defined for investigation by researchers are so delimited that the findings made either deal with too small a piece of the total problem or cannot be easily related to other aspects of the total problem."

casts, as well as special fire-fighting help. In such cases it probably is a respected and helpful ally to the advertising and sales groups, and it may be perceived by the organization as being on at least equal footing with these groups. Unfortunately for marketing research, this sort of pattern is uncommon. In firms where this favorable kind of situation prevails, however, the company-wide marketing research office can be a good base for the company-wide marketing information office.

As such, the office remains an integral but expanded part of the marketing structure and reports to and draws its authority directly from the marketing vice-president. This arrangement does not gain formal company-wide integration of *all* information activities. However, such a favorable organizational orientation can foster informal and, perhaps, sufficient common and integrated use of information facilities and information.

Merchandising Office

The other existing location within the marketing area that can contain the orientation and capacity to develop into the marketing information office is the company-wide merchanding office. This office is normally responsible for the coordination and control of the activities of product or brand managers. These have been successful where they have been able to remedy otherwise inept marketing information programs; this they have done by determining marketing information needs, fulfilling the recognized needs, and using the marketing information in planning activities. The managers have had to become information scavengers. In light of their planning needs, they have scrambled among the existing structures and functions seeking and assembling advice and information. In brief, they have pulled the scattered information function together in behalf of each product.[5] (Their achievement of this function has been somewhat inadvertent, in that primary emphasis has been on preparation of merchandising and advertising plans and proposals.)

This shows that the successful merchandising office has had considerable exposure and experience in management of marketing information activities. For this reason firms with successful brand and product management structures can transform the merchandising office into the even broader information office. Such an information office continues to report directly to and draw its authority from the marketing vice-president. However, it is broadened to include such activities as marketing research and continuous information flows.

---

[5] For more extensive views of brand and product manager activities see Gordon H. Evans, *The Product Manager's Job,* AMA Research Study 69 (New York: American Management Association, 1964); B. Charles Ames, "Payoff from Product Management," *Harvard Business Review* (November–December, 1963, p. 142; and Harold Sekiguchi, "The Product Manager Concept and Its Role in Product Administration," unpublished Ph.D. dissertation, University Library, University of Iowa, 1964.

Not all firms containing a merchandising office should try to convert it into their marketing information office. There are two obvious blocks. *First,* many merchandising offices and their activities are too overlayed with existing structures and activities. As a result, conflicts, duplications, and ambiguities could persist and lessen the effectiveness and efficiency of the office as well as of the entire marketing organization. *Second,* the major emphasis may have been on preparation of plans and proposals—not on information as such. In such cases, the office has too little information know-how to be able to serve as the base for the company-wide marketing information office.

In such situations, the merchandising office must be carefully examined as to its functions and capacity relative to the firm's proposed marketing information system. The needed activities must be moved into an information office and the old merchandising office removed from the structure.

Outside the Marketing Structure

In many firms the marketing area does not provide a suitable climate for the development or use of a marketing information office. In such firms marketing and its management simply are not far enough removed from the old sales management concepts. That is, they are not sufficiently information-oriented. This may not be obvious; organizational charts and titles may give little hint of the condition which may be marked by the following characteristics. Marketing has been granted vice-presidential status, the accompanying responsibilities of forecasting, budgeting, and planning have been grudgingly accepted and poorly performed. In addition, broad marketing research has been discouraged, and new attempts at managing marketing information consistently fail. In such cases only rudimentary marketing information is available—and the marketing managers are largely to blame. Because of their lack of ability or unwillingness to investigate new methods, managers have continued to try to guide the marketing division by instinct, intuition, or formula, even when the firm's size and pressure of competition have called for use of new tools and information. In such an environment, marketing information does not serve as a management aid.

Top management should listen no longer to excuses for this shoddy style of "management." In these situations, where intuition has run wild, appropriate marketing information programs cannot be developed solely within and by the old line sales and marketing types. Top management must cause marketing information offices to be both *developed* and effectively *used.*

A primary purpose of placing the marketing information office outside of a marketing division is to get it into a more favorable climate. The office, therefore, must be in an environment that encourages marketing information development and use; conducive to this goal is a location with other information activities. It is also true that the office must work through and have a close relationship with marketing operating units. It must have the proper base of authority, but even more important, marketing units must perceive the arrangement as being reasonable and proper. This situation is facilitated by the creation of a company-wide information office containing not just marketing information, but also information relative to production, finance, and other areas.

Central Information Office

To this point, poor information climates have been considered as the impetus for establishment of separate, central, company-wide information offices. In addition, however, such an arrangement offers inherent advantages that should be considered by managers whose firms already enjoy favorable information climates. Basically, the central information office offers (1) opportunities for increased efficiency, (2) greater perspective, and (3) more effective use of information—all of which contribute to better management.

Brief elaboration may provide more meaningful insight. Such a company-wide information office, reporting directly to the president, on a vice-presidential level at least, gives increased and dramatic sanction to the information function, its operation, and information use. In addition, it raises the authority base, which, while hardly replacing the need for diplomacy, aids it and improves information management.

Such an office provides greatly improved information perspective that is required to see all facets and to detect and eliminate duplication and misallocations of information components. Also, the director, with more perspective than would be possible were the office located in the marketing structure, can be a better judge of information needs, among nonmarketing units in particular. In general, increased perspective facilitates fulfillment of the responsibilities of the office.

Finally, centralization of information *management* facilitates centralization of appropriate facets of information components, which leads to increased opportunity for specialization, and increases the ability and the capacity of the information function. Basically, computer, storage, transmitter, and human facilities and know-how become more jointly available to the marketing task, as well as to all others. No one activity is isolated, but instead, advances in one, more readily become available to others through this closer integration. For example, cost accountants cannot remain concerned only with production, and computers cannot be purchased solely for financial and production needs. Both machines and men can be selected primarily because of their abilities to render the largest information payoffs; this is the purpose of company-wide information offices.

The fundamental requisite for better managed marketing is that the marketing information function be both perceived and managed as an entity. In terms of the information components, there must be a single, separate, and centralized management of the marketing information program. That is, the entire program—all of its components, all of its facets, all of its scattered locations—must be the responsibility of one director. His responsibilities must be broad and pervasive, for this control situation is not an ordinary one. The information director must be responsible as consultant, coordinator, and controller of each of the information components. Some of these components may be largely centralized and consequently under the direct control of the director. Others must be managed somewhat less directly through numerous overlays. In this latter and more difficult control situation, the office must gain recognition as the ultimate source of information know-how.

Three locations can be considered for the information office. Firms with strong, well-received, well-respected company-wide marketing research offices may be able to broaden them into marketing information offices. Another suitable location is the merchandising office. This office will have the best chance for success where it has had considerable exposure and experience in management of information activities. Finally, in some firms the information office simply cannot be located in the marketing structure because the prevailing information climate is just too suppressive. In such situations creation of company-wide information offices, including the marketing information office, seems to be the best way to cope with a very difficult, but all too common problem. And even firms with favorable information climates may be better able to develop and use information systems that are managed from company-wide information offices.

In the past few years much has been written about the impact that computers and other improved information handling facilities will have on organizational structures and on management. Some have viewed the advances and concluded that they will result in massive centralization with almost no middle management, while others have said that the advances will encourage the use of more decentralized forms of organization.[6]

A relevant focal point that has been implicit in this study is that the new technology—particularly information analysis, storage, and transmission—will be an immense aid to information management and, in turn, to information use. Random access memory storage units and computers and accompanying accessories and know-how will both permit and encourage (if not dictate) increased recognition of information systems, per se, as well as increase centralization of information functions. But clearly, total centralization of the system would be most unusual because of the nature of its basic components. Finally, neither massive organizational centralization nor decentralization is likely to be dictated by (1) increased use of the new technology, (2) management of the information system as an entity, or (3) increased centralization of the information system. Instead, improved information systems will facilitate many organizational forms—forms that will

---

[6] For example see Edward McCreary, "Countertrend to Decentralization: Top Management Tightens Controls," *Dun's Review and Modern Industry* (July, 1959), pp. 32–34; and Harold F. Smiddy, "Managerial Decision-Making," *Advanced Management* (November, 1958), p. 10.

take their shapes based on market needs and problems, not on information restraints.

Top management's success in remedying its marketing malady through a central information office depends largely on the extent to which it is able to:

1. Locate and develop the marketing information office outside the influence of the old line marketing group.
2. Locate within the office as much of the marketing planning and control activity as is necessary to ensure effective use of the office
3. Restrict information duplication and back-up activities in the marketing division once they are assigned to the information office (that is, allow marketing management no alternative information aid).
4. Establish a company-wide information office and structure to contain the marketing information office.

Marketing Intelligence for Top Management*

WILLIAM T. KELLEY

Today's top executives typically are "snowed under" by the deluge of information crossing their desks. It is imperative, therefore, that companies organize the flow of this information so that decision makers can use it more efficiently and effectively.

Since 1961, when the author first proposed the term "Marketing Intelligence" in connection with a curriculum revision at his university, several American firms have set up information services departments; and others are considering the step.

Yet many executives are quite unaware of the rapid developments taking place at this new frontier of management; or, if aware, they have not developed information about it. It is hoped that the present article will serve to orient and inform management about a functional area that promises to move rapidly within the next few years.

Historically, the problem of the businessman has not been how to deal with a superabundance of information. Rather, it has been how to "wrangle" a bare minimum of data sufficient to make reasonably good decisions. To a large extent marketing research came to be recognized as an important staff

---

*Reprinted from the **Journal of Marketing,** national quarterly publication of the American Marketing Association, Vol. 29 (October, 1965), pp. 19–24.

function in the 1930s and 1940s because it could partially alleviate this informational scarcity, albeit at rather high costs.

Today, by contrast, the business executive often feels "snowed under" by the deluge of facts, figures, surveys, censuses, articles, and so on that pile up on his desk. To make matters worse, his own organization is busy generating such a plethora of operating facts, figures, reports, staff studies, and the like that he finds it virtually impossible to read, let alone digest, them. Yet he is always haunted by the feeling that he has overlooked some important report or study that might make a vital difference to the welfare of his firm.

Recognition of a problem, as is true in the diagnosis of a disease, is the first step toward its solution. So, let us provide a setting for the problem before we discuss what to do about it.

CLASSIFICATION OF INFORMATION FLOWS

First off, it may be well to review a bit of communication thory. Two major kinds of information flows may be distinguished: external and internal. An *external-information flow* is the dissemination of meaningful symbols from the business organization to the external environment, or from the surrounding environment to the organization. *Internal-information flows* are those that flow within the organization.

External Information

First, one may designate whether the external flow proceeds from the company toward the market, or from the market toward the firm. The former will be termed "outward" and latter "inward."

Outward flows are generally organized in respect to kinds of mass communication media employed, and degree of control that the firm exercises over the communication media. Thus, there is advertising (nonpersonal flow of communication), and selling (person-to-person channels), in which the content flowing through the media is strictly controlled by the company. Public relations involve nonpersonal and personal communication media in which the content is not well-controlled but depends on an external "relay source" (for example, editor) to interpret and pass along the firm's message (for example, press release).

The *inward flows* involve two major categories of information: market information and economic information.

Market information may be compared with tactical military intelligence; it evaluates shorter-run tendencies in the immediate marketing environment, with special reference to market factors affecting the company's product(s) or service(s). One kind of flow is market news: information gathered from published sources (secondary information)—the government, commercial reporting services, business press, business research bureaus, and so on. The other entails the setting up of channels and gathering primary information under the auspices of the firm, employing marketing research techniques. The gathering of primary data may be compared with custom tailoring of men's suits, whereas secondary data may be compared with ready-to-wear garments, available to all in standardized sizes and colors.

Economic research is the gathering of strategic information, that is, that of longer-run significance to the company. It collects data on the macro-economic environment (consumer income trends, gross national product, production, employment, international accounts, etc.) that are useful to the company in expanding its time horizon to enable it to engage in longer-range planning.

A large business firm should centralize information collection and storage at some central point where it will be readily available to all other parts of the firm. Past as well as present statistics, reports, general studies, and special studies ought to be deposited and carefully cataloged and cross-referenced for future retrieval and consultation. This library facility could well have much of the data on computer tapes and punch cards, as well as in the more conventional form of books, monographs, and bound reports.

Internal Information

Internal information is that which flows within the company. It takes four directions: downward; upward; and horizontal, both back and forth.

The flow of communication *downward* is supposed to follow formal organization channels, as exemplified by the typical company organization chart. The pyramidal form of organization is the most common—the flow of orders and directives goes from the chief executive through a hierarchy of executives, finally reaching the worker "on the firing line."

Then there is supposed to be an *upward* feedback loop, a flow of information upward which apprises the executive as to what is going on. How well are the plans and orders being carried out? How much did we make? Sell? At what costs? How is our morale? These questions, and many others, give rise to a need for arranging the upward flow of administrative data-accounting, financial, sales, advertising, and production data generated within the company which enable the management to appraise the effectiveness of the firm's performance and its deployment of resources (that is, input-output relationships).

Another type of *upward* flow is found in the informal feedback loops. The formal feedback loops (administrative data) are carefully described and stereotyped (accounting reports, sales reports, etc.). Informal feedback relates to assessment of intangible factors in the organization. Because it is intangible, it is too often neglected by the organization. Yet such information is important for management to have, as it deals with vital matters such as employee morale, employee attitudes toward their work, the company, bosses, work associates, etc.

Collecting internal information of this sort is difficult; and there are substantial barriers to upward communication in any organization. Nevertheless, research methods such as attitude surveys, group discussions, and suggestion systems are frequently employed to construct informal upward feedback loops. A certain amount of useful intelligence may also be gathered from listening in on the informal employee communication channels, often termed "the grapevine."

Horizontal flows of information take place when people on the same level communicate with one another. *Formal communication* involves information flows between officials who are *supposed* to communicate, according to the company organization chart—for example, the vice president for marketing confers with the vice president for manufacturing regarding sales plans.

Informal channels relate to communication among people of similar rank who do not necessarily have to communicate—for example, informal meeting between advertising director and treasurer who have been personal friends of long standing.

The content of formal, horizontal communication is not difficult to acquire, since written records or tapes are generally left—such as minutes of meetings, conference reports, and memoranda. But seldom is a record left of informal communication. Yet a study of such communication may reveal "power constellations" within the firm quite at variance with formally designated relationships. Any complete intelligence service function should appraise *all* informal channels—both horizontal and vertical—and secure content for analysis where possible.

INTELLIGENCE PRODUCTION

As we aggregate all of these information sources and focus them at one point in the organization, a tremendous deluge of information is bound to be encountered. What is to be done with all of it?

Here one may fruitfully borrow from techniques developed by military intelligence agencies. A staff must be set up to arrange channels, and gather information from all collecting points; economic research, marketing research, market news, administrative data, and internal information. It is then verified and validated—an evaluation of the probable reliability of the data is made. Tests are brought to bear—source reliability in the past, internal consistency, consistency among different sources, investigation of research methodology employed in the study, and the like. After validation, it is filtered or "boiled down" into its essentials.

The objective is not to filter out bits of information that will make some difference, but to eliminate irrelevant or unimportant material. The information is shortened up, sharpened up, and interpreted. It is then analyzed in relation to significance for different divisions or departments. Then the reports are prepared and distributed to those departments that should be interested in the particular matter.

In some cases there may be followups to make sure (1) that those vitally concerned have in fact received the data, and (2) that they understand the report.

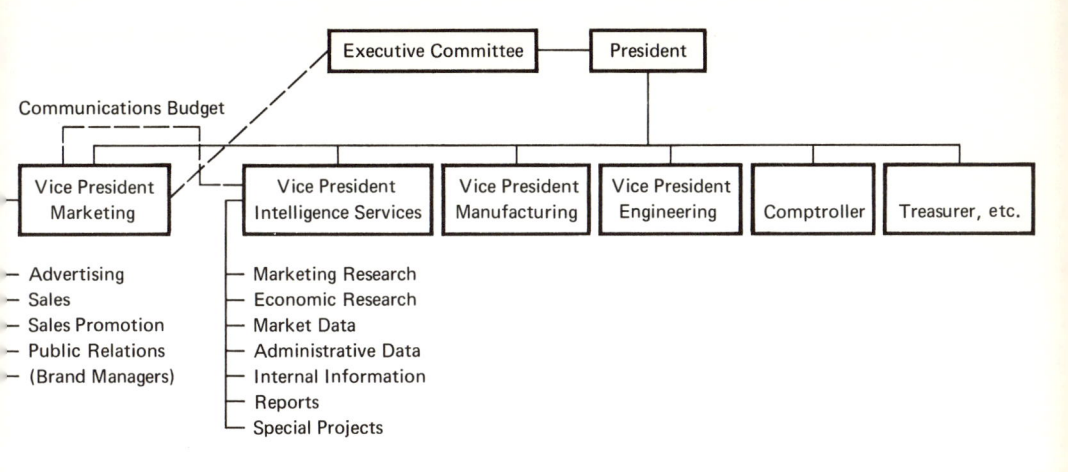

Figure 1. **Organization of the Intelligence-Services Division**

PLAN OF ORGANIZATION

An organization chart of the intelligence-services division is shown in Figure 1. Divisional status is assigned to the service. The director should have vice-presidential rank, and he should be on a par with the other important second-echelon executives. He should report directly to the president or chief executive of the company so that reliable, first-hand information may flow to that official. If the intelligence officer were to report through an intermediary (relay), some vital information would be "lost" to the president or, worse, distorted.

The Vice President, Intelligence Services, has six departments reporting to him: marketing research, economic research, market data, administrative data, internal information, and reports. The library could be made a separate department (the seventh), or could be put under market data.

In addition, a Special Projects Department might be added. This would undertake special research, involving covert sources of information, both internal and external.

Modification for Decentralization

The organization pattern discussed would be modified somewhat for the decentralized company. In this case each subsidiary or semi-autonomous department would have its own intelligence-services division reporting to the subsidiary's president or general manager. It would handle information of particular interest to the subsidiary. Great care would be required to avoid unnecessary duplication of information collection and storage between the subsidiary and the parent company. This could be controlled by careful demarcation of specific areas of responsibility for information kinds or classes between the two organizations.

Carefully specified communication channels and procedures would need to be laid down, so that the subsidiary routinely furnishes the parent with all major reports. Likewise, the parent company must be sure that the subsidiary routinely gets all major information, and also minor intelligence of special interest to the subsidiary in question. The intelligence resources of the parent would be much broadened by having subsidiary intelligence units on which to draw, and vice versa.

Such cross-communication should help to alleviate a difficulty so often encountered in decentralized organizations, "the right hand not knowing what the left hand is doing." It would enrich the formalized reporting and informal contacts through mutual executive visits that now so typically serve to keep both parties (parent and subsidiary) informed on a somewhat catch-as-catch-can basis.

Budgetary Control

As suggested by Marion Harper, Jr., the Intelligence-Services Division should be coordinated with the marketing or promotion division by means of a communications budget.[1] Each division would independently prepare its budget estimates; and these would be combined into one overall communications budget.

There are several advantages to this procedure: better control of communication; better central planning for future communication efforts; and better balance between inward and outward communication flows.

As to the latter point, the pitting of promotional expenditures against intelligence-service proposals would help to "sell" the later to top management, since the ratio of expenditures between promotion and intelligence would be so much in favor of promotion. By so doing, the Vice President of Intelligence Services would have to demonstrate how the dollars for which he was applying would bring more fruitful results than the same funds *added to* the promotion budget. In other words, desirable competition between the two functions would be introduced.

In connection with budgeting, little is presently known about the proper decision rules for intelligence services. For every department, obviously there is a point at which the marginal cost of an additional unit of information to the company is just equal to the marginal utility (enhanced tactical or strategic power on the market, more efficient operations internally leading to cost reduction, etc.) derived from it.

This kind of analysis would be desirable for the Vice President of Intelligence Services to utilize in his budgetary justification. At present methods of measuring and calculating this are unavailable.

RATIONALE FOR INTELLIGENCE SERVICES

As Marion Harper, Jr., further pointed out in his Parlin Memorial Lecture, there are a number of substantial benefits to be expected from the establishment of such a centralized service.[2]

---

[1] Marion Harper, Jr., "The Marketing Communication Budget," *Printer's Ink*, Vol. 267 (June 25, 1959), pp. 86–94.

[2] Marion Harper, Jr., "A New Profession to Aid Marketing Management," *Journal of Marketing*, Vol. 25 (January, 1961), pp. 1–6, at pp. 1–2.

1. Expansion of Time Horizons

As he aptly put it: "To manage a business well is to manage its future; and to manage the future is to manage information."[3]

Forecasting the future is an inevitable function of management. In proportion as the future horizon is moved out and the accuracy of prediction is improved, in the same proportion will the survival and growth probabilities of the firm be enhanced. Good forecasting requires vast amounts of the highest-quality data, for many variables must be taken into consideration. The systematic collection and evaluation of such data at one place in the company will greatly improve both the quantity and quality of forecasting data available to the planning officials of the firm.

No one can completey eliminate risk from human decisions, because no one can ever expect to have *complete* facts about any marketing situation, even possessed of a good intelligence-services division. In other words, the term "informed decision" is a relative one. But a poker player who by keen observation can assess the other hands and predict the next play has a much better probability of winning than one who depends mainly on other factors.

2. Better Machinery for Gathering Information

Decision-making is becoming an increasingly complex process, with a multiplication of both knowns and unknowns. And information-gathering becomes more crucial, since there are ever more unknowns coming into the decision-making matrix, and since the influence and direction of these unknowns must be evaluated. This puts a great strain on information-gathering resources in the modern business firm, a need to which the firm must be responsive.

3. Better Production of Finished Intelligence

Present times have been called the "Age of Information Revolution." The supply of data has been increasing in the past decade, probably at a rate of geometric progression. Literally billions of facts and figures are generated by the federal government alone each year. Add to that the great proliferation of vast electronic computers, each capable of storing and using millions of facts, and we may feel threatened by a mass of data that, due to sheer size alone, seems as if one day it will overwhelm us.

Certainly busy executives in a large corporation need an intermediary —a filtering device—that will receive, handle, evaluate, "boil down," and direct into proper company communication channels those data, and those data only, that are both reliable and necessary.

Otherwise, valuable executive time will be wasted in search for the nuggets among the vast lode pile of undigested and unrelated facts. And

---

[3] Same reference as footnote 2, at p. 1.

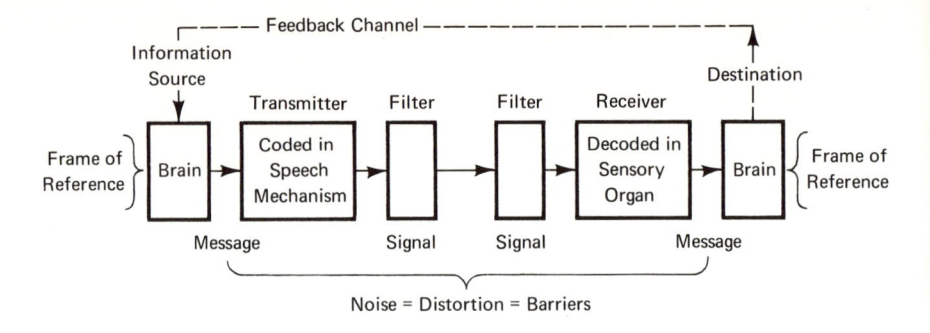

```
┌───── Feedback Channel ──────────────────┐
│                                          ↑
Information                          Destination
Source                                    │
         Transmitter   Filter   Filter   Receiver
         ┌─────────┐  ┌─────┐ ┌─────┐  ┌─────────┐
Frame of │ Coded in│  │     │ │     │  │Decoded in│         Frame of
Reference│  Brain  │→ │Speech│→│     │→│     │→ │ Sensory │→ Brain   Reference
         │Mechanism│  │     │ │     │  │  Organ  │
         └─────────┘  └─────┘ └─────┘  └─────────┘
           Message     Signal  Signal     Message
                    Noise = Distortion = Barriers
```

Figure 2. **Distortion of information**

not enough nuggets are likely to be extracted to make well-supported decisions. Setting up a machinery to convert the vast flows of raw statistical materials and facts into a finished product represents at least a partial solution to the problem of "breeding" uncontrolled data.

4. Reduced Confusion of Top Policy-makers

As information multiplies, management needs protection from the specialist.[4] The data-generating people tend to be specialists; and they may tend not to "see the forest for the trees." Thus, quite unwittingly they may distort the information they feed top management.

The Vice President of Intelligence Services should be a generalist. Inddeed, his position at the apex of all communication flows will inevitably give him the "overall picture," the knowledge of all (not just some) of the implications of the information that he manages. Therefore, he will be able better to draw up specifications of the kinds of information most useful for top-policy formulation and decision-making.

5. Prevention of Distortion of Information

Many observers have noted that distortion occurs in a message when it passes through too many relay points or brains. The process may be diagrammed as in Figure 2.[5]

The first distortion occurs at the left of the diagram, when the perception of facts is made. The facts are filtered through the psychological frame of reference of the source. They are interpreted according to built-in biases, prejudices, blind spots, etc., that exist in his brain.

The communicator then codes the information into symbols or langauge. This causes further distortion and loss of meaning, since he can never express through language precisely what he has in mind and wants to convey.

---

[4] Same reference as footnote 3, at pp. 3–4.
[5] William W. Maier, *Upward Communication and Suggestion Systems* (Berkeley: University of California, 1962); p. 36.

Indeed, the less concrete and the more abstract his communication is, the more approximate and fuzzy it tends to become.

When the message is transmitted, two more filters are met, occasioned by "noise" in the system and imperfect sending and receiving devices (speech organs and aural receptors). Typically, 30% of the message is lost due to the two signal filters.[6]

Then the message is received, perceived, and fitted into the destination's frame of reference (that contains biases, prejudices, and blind spots). All this results in a highly imperfect and distorted transmission of the message when just two relay points are involved.

Imagine what happens when five or six relay points are concerned in the transmission of the information, a by-no-means uncommon situation (for example, worker tells foreman, foreman tells superintendent, superintendent tells plant manager, plant manager tells executive vice president, executive vice-president tells president).

In practice, most of the information received by top management has been put through multiple relay points, multiple filters, and multiple frames of reference. The result must be a picture of reality that is highly abstracted and highly distorted.

Moreover, the information will probably be biased in a given constant direction by folkways, mores, group ways of seeing things introduced by the history, traditions, and interests of the company. This results in everybody in the firm tending to look at things the same way. It creates great, shared blind spots among the top executives and planners which may well destroy the ability of the firm to react to market changes in time and to take effective action. This, of course, jeopardizes the longer-term survival of the company.

Another biasing factor in upward communication is the fact that the subordinate tells the "boss" things the subordinate knows the boss wants to hear. The "underling" learns that it is not always expedient to convey unfavorable or discouraging facts. And the subordinate, due to *his* conditioning, may well ignore the disturbing information that *he* receives, suppress it, and not consciously even have it to transmit.

This biasing and suppression of information might be reduced by opening a direct, reliable communication channel to the top executive group via the head of intelligence services. A good intelligence officer is trained to recognize and evaluate bias and distortion. If he is secure in his job, he is not likely to suppress unfavorable information or concoct spurious favorable information.

6. New and Better Sources of Information

As an expert in communications, the Vice President of Intelligence Services would find ways of getting better and more reliable data, due

---

[6] Claude E. Shannon and Warren Weaver, *The Mathematical Theory of Communication* (Urbana: University of Illinois Press, 1949), p. 96.

to his knowledge of sources and his ability to evaluate them. He has the overall picture of what is going on, and could best assay where there are needs for information and what to do to develop the data needed.

7. Creative Intelligence Functions

Actually intelligence services work on a "jigsaw-puzzle" basis —they painstakingly gather little bits and pieces of information, fit facts, relate them until the grand design emerges. One military-intelligence expert says that 90% of the information gathered by military intelligence is overt, and only 10 covert.[7]

Obviously if the pieces of information are scattered all over an organization, no one can do this fitting together. By centralizing the function, the Director can perceive the whole pattern and can report his findings to top management. Incidentally, a great deal of industrial espionage might be eliminated by a central intelligence function; after all, overt information that is cheaper, easier to obtain, and carries no unfavorable ethical connotations might tend to be substituted for covert information collection.

IMPLICATIONS

Better evaluated, more reliable, and concise information should afford the basis on which better decisions and policies could be formulated by top management. The cost of providing for this type of organization should be more than offset by the more efficient tactical reactions of the firm to the ever-changing marketing conditions.

20 Information Flow and Decentralized Decision-Making in Marketing*

GERALD ALBAUM

Many companies are, and have been, aware of the importance of information in making sound marketing decisions. Yet when a company evaluates its own methods for handling information flows, it may find that it is not using effectively even the marketing information it already has.

---

[7] Ladislas Farago, *War of Wits: The Anatomy of Espionage and Intelligence* (New York: Funk & Wagnalls Co., 1954), p. 53.

*Reprinted from **California Management Review**, Vol. IX, No. 4 (Summer, 1967), pp. 59–70.

The author gratefully acknowledges the comments and suggestions made on earlier drafts of this article by Professors Edwin Filippo and Thomas Petit of the University of Arizona and Professor Philip Kotler of Northwestern University.

The view that a business firm is an operating or functioning, integrated whole—or total—system is rapidly gaining acceptance in many companies as a top management operating philosophy. One of the many subsystems that leads to an effectively operating total business system is the flow of information and analysis to facilitate decisions, whether such decisions are for purposes of prediction (planning and development), control, or problem solving. When viewed as the conversion of information into action through the decision-making process (as controlled by various policy directives), it is obvious that management success depends to a great extent on the availability and timely use of information at all organizational levels.[1] The flow of information makes the entire organization an effective, integrated whole. Information as used here is not restricted to the types produced by the accounting system, but includes all the data and intelligence needed by the decision makers.

The information subsystem of a total business system is made up of a number of different specific information systems.[2] Many business firms consider *marketing information* to be one of the most important specific systems. Certainly, without adequate, accurate, and timely information, marketing managers cannot accomplish the major task facing them—determining, implementing, and controlling what has come to be known as an "optimal" marketing mix. This means that, unless the information subsystem is effectively integrated into marketing strategy, a company cannot hope to fully achieve the goals it has set for itself.

This article will present a model, showing how a business firm—especially a large multiproduct company that has decentralized its operations and decision making—might organize its marketing information system so as to effectively integrate marketing information into marketing strategy. Although somewhat abstract and theoretical in nature, the model can serve as a foundation upon which a company can base the structure of its own specific marketing information system.

Integration of Information

Have business firms effectively integrated the information subsystem into marketing strategy? In other words, is the marketing information system functioning so that business managers are getting the information needed to manage the marketing mix in the most effective way? The answer to this question is both yes and no—*the integration has been only partially effected.*

Today, a major informational problem faces many business firms, and these companies are either underestimating its significance or are unaware

---

[1] Charles R. Klasson and Kenneth W. Olm, "Managerial Implications of Integrated Business Operations," *California Management Review*, VIII:1 (Fall 1965), 25.

[2] See John Dearden, "How to Organize Information Systems," *Harvard Business Review*, XLIII:2 (March–April 1965), 69–71.

that it even exists. The problem is that in most firms, especially large, decentralized, multiproduct companies, management is not using all the marketing information that exists and is available within the total organization. Thus, management has not learned to use effectively the marketing information it already has, and the flow of information within the organization is not entirely free. Somewhere along the communication channel, much information gets misplaced, lost, delayed, or distorted. The result is that some information never reaches decision makers who could put it to good use, reaches them too late to be useful, or arrives in a form that makes it useless. This situation can be described as one in which there exists a type of organizational or internal slack—"individual energies potentially utilizable for the achievement of organizational goals are permitted to be diverted."[3] Such a situation is especially serious in the case of horizontal communications between the various operating or decision units in a decentralized company.[4]

Cases where managers are "ignoring" this problem are not hard to find. Many marketing executives have told me that their company has no information problem at all or that they feel they have other problems which are of more concern to them.

AN EXAMPLE

For example, one manager feels that his company has more pressing problems than worrying about whether or not information is flowing. He believes that what information is needed can be easily obtained. A vice-president of a radio and television manufacturer recognizes that the over-all problem of cross-flow of information exists in his company. However, not much is being done to correct the situation, as it is felt that this problem is of lesser significance than others that the company has to cope with. The philosophy of a large soap and dentifrice producer is that no problem exists with respect to the horizontal flow of information within his company; if the users of information are not getting the information they need, then they are not doing their jobs.

Not all companies have ignored this problem. For instance, about three years ago, the president of a leading business firm established a task force to study the structuring and organizing of business information systems work in the company, broadly from the over-all company standpoint and also within its many decentralized units. Since this company's approach to

---

[3] R. M. Cyert, E. A. Feigenbaum, and J. G. March, "Models in a Behavioral Theory of the Firm," *Behavioral Science*, IV:2 (April 1962), 82.

[4] The results of an experimental study that supports this contention are presented in my "Horizontal Information Flow: An Exploratory Study," *Journal of the Academy of Management*, VII:1 (March 1964), 21-33.

information systems work is from an over-all business standpoint, it involves an optimum integration of information work into its various functions. Regarding marketing information, it is the personal observation of one executive of the firm that, in general, the marketing function within the various operating units is somewhat less advanced in the area of information handling, etc., than are other activities of the company such as engineering, manufacturing, and finance. The outcome of the task force's study is not yet known.

TYPES OF INFORMATION

Types of Marketing Information

Not all types of marketing information fail to be transmitted between the operating or decision units of a decentralized business firm. Certainly, when a manager in one operating unit requests certain information from other units, it will probably be supplied—if the potential user knows where to request it and if it is available. Furthermore, if necessary, such information can be supplied regularly once it is known that a need for this information exists. This type of marketing information can be called *planned information,* because its receipt by a manager is anticipated and its collection obtained through some type of planned "research" effort, involving systematic data gathering. Thus, planned information is received by a decision maker because he has asked for it.

But planned marketing information is only one type of marketing information received by a manager. On occasion, a manager of a operating unit will receive information unexpectedly from other operating units in his company. This type of marketing information can be called unsolicited information in that it is information which may, in fact, exist within and is obtainable from within the company, but which potential users do not know is available unless they happen to chance upon it. A manager is dependent upon others in his organization as suppliers and transmitters of this type of information.

UNSOLICITED FLOW

For example, in an electrical manufacturing company decentralized along product lines, a salesman of circuit breakers was told by a customer that a foreign producer had announced the development of a new gas which reportedly had great potential in place of air in air-blast circuit breakers and could have applications in certain types of widgets (manufactured by another operating unit). If this information is transmitted to the widget unit by this salesman or his manager; it is unsolicited information to the manager who receives it.

Unsolicited information will tend to flow freely to the extent that the possessors of such information know who are the potential users—although

Information Flow and Decentralized Decision-Making

a time lag may be involved—unless, of course, the person who has the information does not think it important enough to be transmitted or there are personal reasons for not forwarding the information. In such an unstructured information transmission process, a specific item of information may pass through a number of relay points in its movement from initial sender to ultimate recipient, and each of these points acts as a filter. Possible undesirable results of filtering information are blockaded information flow or the injection of bias or distortion. The greater the number of relay points through which an item of information must pass, the greater is the likelihood that it may get lost, be held back, or become distorted.

In addition to classifying information according to the degree of effort put forth by the potential user to obtain information (which has just been done), information can be viewed on the basis of the marketing forces that influence and reflect an operating or decision unit's behavior.[5] On this basis, information may be either *external* or *internal,* depending upon whether it is about phenomena or forces that exist or operate *outside* or *inside* an operating unit. For example, information about customers, suppliers, or competitors of an operating unit or information concerning another operating unit's behavior would be external information, while information about an operating unit's product, advertising, or cost structure is internal information.

Information Sources

There are a number of possible sources that can be tapped for marketing information. An operating unit may obtain information from these various sources directly or indirectly. Thus, at one time, a source may provide an operating unit with information directly, and, at another time, this same source may be the generator, but not the provider, of information. In the second situation, some other source is the one from which the operating unit actually gets the information.

Sources of marketing information may also be classified as external or internal. External sources are those generators or providers of information located outside an operating unit, and include customers, dealers, suppliers, competitors, government agencies, and *other operating units in the company.* Internal sources include departments or individuals located within an operating unit, such as the accounting department or the research and development department, and the field sales force.

---

[5] This discussion is in terms of operating units rather than the company as a whole because in a highly decentralized company the operating units generally will be profit responsibility centers. In this type of a situation each profit center is a quasi-autonomous company. Obviously what is said about operating units applies equally to the company as a whole.

Effective Transmission

The extent to which marketing information is effectively transmitted horizontally in a decentralized company depends upon:

The ability of managers to specify their needs.

The degree of knowledge potential users and possessors of information have regarding each other.

The degree of knowledge potential possessors of information have regarding the needs of potential users.

The type and length of communication system set up to facilitate the movement of information.

A whole host of human factors that can be called "organizational climate."

Available evidence and casual observation suggests that, in many decentralized companies, potential senders and users of marketing information know relatively little about each other. Furthermore, communication channels in such companies, if formalized, tend to be long and complex, and appear to be structured to facilitate only the movement of planned information. No formal provisions are usually made for handling unsolicited information, particularly that which is generated from or provided by external sources.

NO SIMPLE ANSWER

Organizing an Information System

How can a company's marketing information system be organized to facilitate the intracompany flow of all marketing information? There is no simple answer to this question, since the organization appropriate for a specific company depends upon the degree to which marketing information already flows within the company and upon the amount and nature of the resources its management will commit to developing and implementing the system. To organize a marketing information system so that it is effectively integrated into marketing strategy, business managers should think in terms of a somewhat *centralized* system, which will minimize omissions of relevant and important information. Both planned and unsolicited marketing information can be handled and the intracompany flow of information facilitated. Some companies already have a degree of centralization in their marketing information system, but generally this is manifested only by a central marketing research unit, a central clearing house for decentralized marketing research units, or a company library.

The organization of a marketing information system that reflects the total information concept has two facets.

1. The marketing activity of an operating unit must be organized to: facilitate the determination of the information needed by managers;

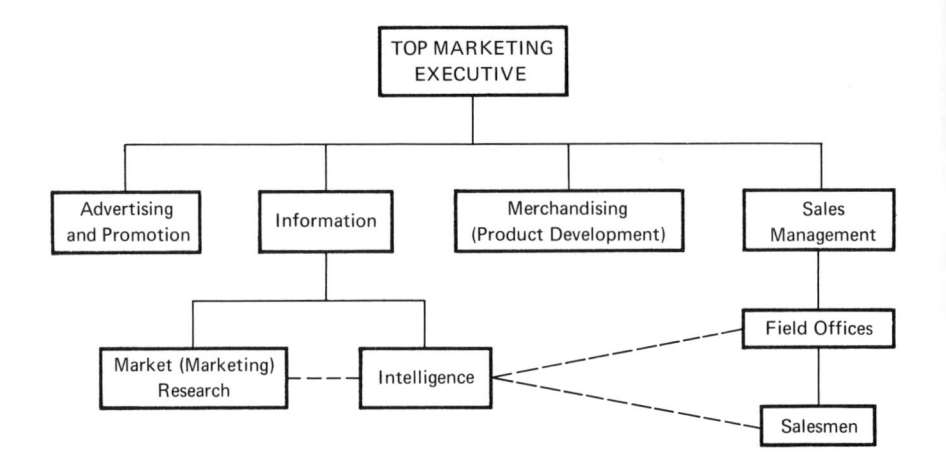

```
                    ┌──────────────────┐
                    │  TOP MARKETING   │
                    │    EXECUTIVE     │
                    └──────────────────┘
                             │
        ┌────────────┬───────┴────────┬──────────────┐
┌───────────────┐ ┌──────────┐ ┌───────────────┐ ┌──────────┐
│ Advertising   │ │Information│ │ Merchandising │ │  Sales   │
│ and Promotion │ │          │ │(Product Dev.) │ │Management│
└───────────────┘ └──────────┘ └───────────────┘ └──────────┘
                      │
              ┌───────┴────────┐
     ┌─────────────────┐ ┌────────────┐    ┌──────────────┐
     │ Market (Mktg)   │ │Intelligence│────│ Field Offices│
     │    Research     │─┤            │    └──────────────┘
     └─────────────────┘ └────────────┘────┌──────────────┐
                                           │  Salesmen    │
                                           └──────────────┘
```

Figure 1. **A Functional Marketing Organization Reflecting the Total Information Concept**

simplify the search for information by users; and effect the most efficient utilization of the information it receives.
2. There must exist a company information receiving, storage, and transmission system that enables information to move efficiently among the various operating or decision units.

In tackling these two facets, management should keep in mind that the marketing information system can be best integrated into marketing strategy when it is conceived and performed as an *intelligence operation* similar in concept to that operated by the military.

A highly simplified version of a typical functional marketing organization structured to reflect the total information concept is shown in Figure 1. In each operating unit an intelligence section—organizationally equal to the research section—is established for handling unsolicited information, while the marketing research section is concerned primarily with planned information. These two sections constitute the marketing information activity of an operating unit or company, whichever the case may be.[6] Thus, the marketing information department is an expansion of the typical marketing research department that will provide more timely and useful information to meet marketing decision makers' needs. This information department will perform the usual information activities of searching and collecting, processing (including evaluating), storing, dumping, and transmitting.

---

[6] The marketing information activity may be broken down into more specialized units than is shown in Figure 1, if the need for such specialization exists. For instance, an accounting data analysis unit may be established by those companies who believe that analyzing internal records is important enough to have a separate unit do the work.

It is not necessary that all companies organize their marketing information activity in the manner proposed.[7] In fact, for smaller companies this type of an organization may not be feasible. A marketing research activity may suffice. However, I do not mean that smaller companies should not be concerned with unsolicited information, but that smaller companies may not find it necessary to specialize their information activity to the extent of separating research and intelligence. Since such companies are likely to have a research activity, the scope of its operations can be expanded to include the handling of unsolicited information. In larger companies, on the other hand, it is desirable organizationally to separate the handling of planned and unsolicited information. When voluminous planned information is being collected, as is the case in so many companies today, the marketing research personnel have little time to concern themselves with unsolicited information. If unsolicited information is to be effectively utilized, a separate unit should be established to handle it.

Regardless of the specific organization arrived at, the major issue is that a business firm (or each operating unit of a large decentralized firm) should concentrate marketing information collection and storage at some central point where it will be readily available to all other parts of the organization. Concentration is also advantageous because a particular item of information, particularly unsolicited, can be evaluated in light of its relationship to other items of information. At times a specific item of information considered by itself may not appear to be significant, but, when combined with other items of information, it may turn out to be important.

Another advantage of concentration is that the field sales organization and the other functional departments, e.g., research and development, production, and engineering, no longer will have to determine which persons should receive specific items of unsolicited information. This job will be taken over by the intelligence unit. The intelligence unit also will handle the unsolicited information that the marketing research section develops in the course of acquiring planned information.

HORIZONTAL FLOW

Total System

So far the discussion on organizing a marketing information system has been concerned only with a single marketing organization. For those companies with a centralized marketing operation, no more need be said. However, companies with decentralized marketing operations need a company information organization which will facilitate the horizontal flow

---

[7] The other proposals are found in Kenneth P. Uhl, "Better Management of Market Information," *Business Horizons,* IX:1 (Spring 1966), 75–82; and Philip Kotler, "A Design for the Firm's Marketing Nerve Center," *Business Horizons,* XI:3 (Fall 1966), 63–74.

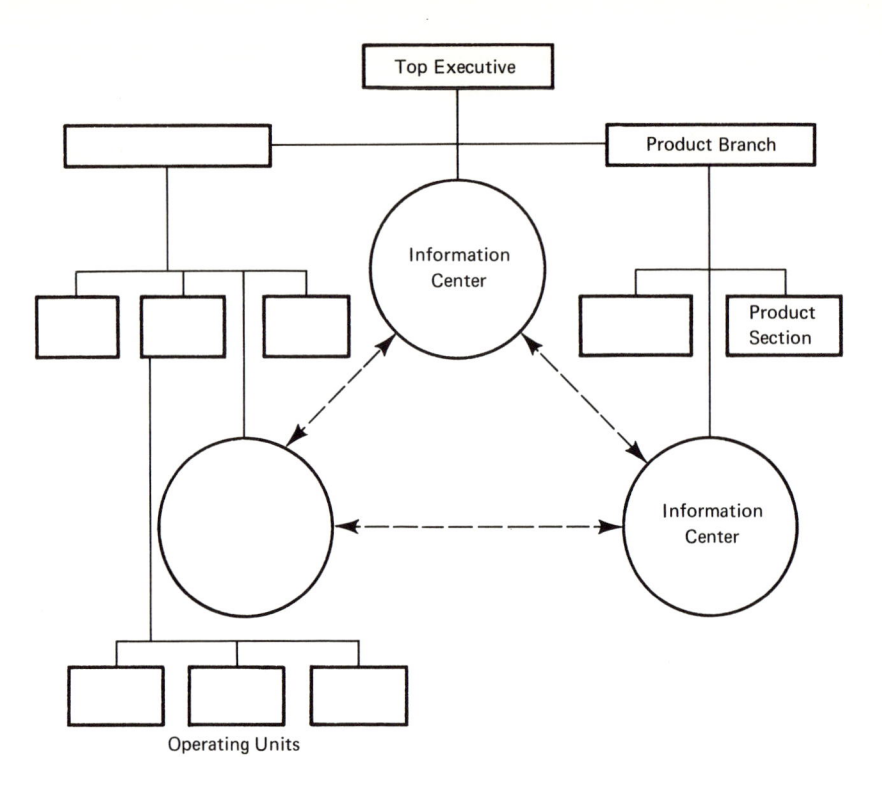

Figure 2. **Company Organization Structure Showing Centralized Information System**

of marketing information, particularly unsolicited information, between their various operating or decision units.

A total company marketing information system should be structured so as to overcome the previously mentioned problems existing in many business firms. Specifically, the information system should:

Minimize potential information users' lack of knowledge of the existence of information and its sources.

Minimize the lack of knowledge of possessors of information of who are the potential users.

Reduce the chance of distortion occurring during the transmission of information.

Minimize the amount of time it takes for information to flow from original recipient to final user.

These requirements can best be met by establishing a marketing information system that is separate from the regular operating organization.

There are many ways in which a marketing information system can be superimposed upon the regular operating organization. One such system for a typical company decentralized on a product basis is illustrated in simpli-

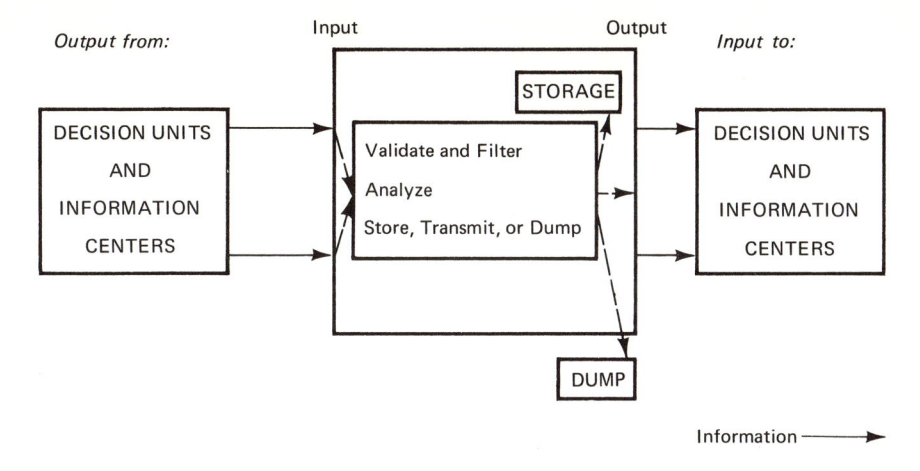

Figure 3. **Flow Diagram of Information Center Processing Information**

fied form in Figure 2. The various information centers of this system have no line relationships with the operating units of the company. There is, however, a staff relationship in that the information system acts as a service organization for the operating units by providing them with much of their information requirements. The major link between the central system and the decision makers in an operating unit is the marketing information department, particularly the intelligence section.

For most companies an individual information center will service at least one entire product section. Thus, in addition to the section management, a number of operating units will make use of its services. Whether the information centers service one section or a number of sections depends on the needs of a company.

Each information center acts as a complete input-output system, as shown in Figures 3 and 4. The inputs—which are outputs from decision-making units (branch, section, or operating unit) or other information centers—are either items of information or requests for information. Similarly, the output of a center is information—whether requested or automatically transmitted—and requests for information.

In the case of unsolicited information, the center handles each item in three stages (Fig. 3).

1. It acts as a filter and validates the information.
2. It analyzes the information and determines who in the company—decision-making unit or information center—might need the information.
3. It transmits the relevant information to potential users, stores it for future use, or dumps it out of the organization.

Information Flow and Decentralized Decision-Making **247**

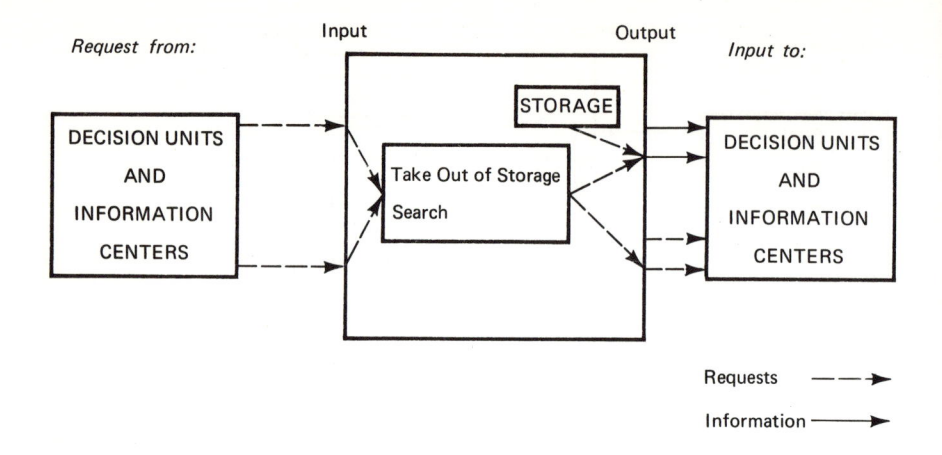

Figure 4. **Flow Diagram of Information Center Processing Requests for Information**

The procedure followed with respect to requests for information is somewhat simpler (Fig. 4). When a decision-making unit requests a certain type of information, the center:

1. Searches its own "storage pile" for all of the type of information requested.
2. Searches the organization by sending a request to the other units it services and the other information centers.

When another information center requests a certain kind of information, the procedure followed is a little different. In this case, the center receiving the request searches for any relevant information it has stored and also searches the decision-making units it services. There may be times in this type of situation when the information center will search other information centers, but this would be an unusual case.

A model of the functioning of the entire system is shown in Figure 5. While this is a simplified model, showing only two decision-making units and their respective information centers, the operation of the system would not be altered if additional decision units and information centers were introduced.

The system functions quite simply. Suppose Decision-Making Unit #1 has to make a particular decision and wants to obtain all of the information available in the company that would pertain to this decision. The decision unit would contact its servicing information center (Center #1) and request all the available information relating to the decision to be made. When Information Center #1 receives this request, it requests all available information from the other centers (in this case only Center #2) and supplies Decision Unit #1 with all of the relevant information it has stored. When Information Center #2 receives the request from Center #1, it sup-

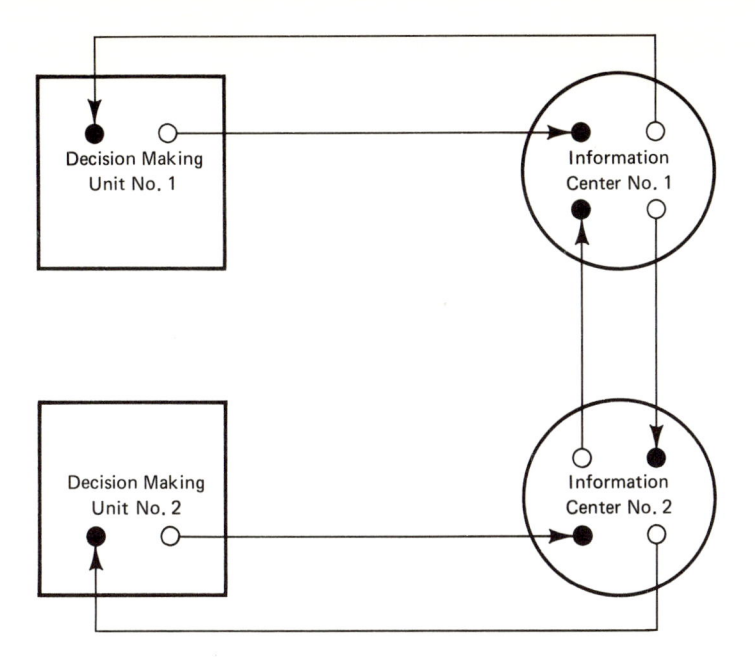

Figure 5. **A Model of the Functioning of a Company Information System**
(Solid dots are inputs; hollow dots are outputs.)

plies all the information it has stored and sends a request for information to Decision-Making Unit #2. Upon receipt of all the information Decision Unit #2 has, Information Center #2 sends it to Center #1, which then passes it on to Decision Unit #1.[8]

In some situations concerning requests for information, it may even be possible for all or some of the sources to bypass the information system and send what they have directly to the original requestor. For this to be possible, the sources must know which decision unit has made the request.

Now, suppose Decision Unit #1 has acquired an item of information and does not know what other decision units in the company might have use for this information. The item is sent to Information Center #1, which validates and analyzes it. If the information is relevant, Center #1 stores it, transmits it to Center #2, or does both. If Center #2 receives the information, it will process the information in the same manner as Center #1. If the information is relevant, Center #2 will store it, transmit it to Decision Unit #2, or do both.

---

[8] Rather than just sending all the "raw" information it receives, Information Center #1 may put the relevant information into a short, meaningful report that is then forwarded to Decision Unit #1.

Information Flow and Decentralized Decision-Making

In general, the functioning of this information system can be summarized as follows. The system is essentially a complex input-output system, comprised of decision-making units and information centers. These individual units are in themselves input-output systems. An output from both decision units and information centers can take the form of information supplied to some unit or center or a request for information. Similarly, an input can be either a request for information or an item of information received.

COORDINATED SUBSYSTEMS

Integration

As previously mentioned, an over-all company information system may consist of a number of more or less specific subsystems—individual systems to handle marketing data, financial data, personnel data, research and development data, or logistics data. These subsystems may be organized formally, e.g., the proposed marketing information system, or operated on an informal basis. If a company is to have an effectively functioning over-all information system, the various subsystems must be integrated and, thus, coordinated in some way. Moreover, any scheme devised for this purpose must be linked to top management.

Integration of the various information subsystems can be achieved by establishing at the top management level an *information services unit*. The information services unit will have the responsibility for operating and managing the over-all company information system, which in turn means having operating responsibility for each of the subsystems that is operational, e.g., the information centers comprising the marketing information system.

In some instances, the responsibility of the information services unit will be limited to operating the proposed information centers. That is, the information centers can be used as an integral part of all the subsystems, which means in effect that there is but one information organization within a company. Such an expansion in the duties of an information center, i.e., processing all types of business information rather than just marketing information, may be necessary to justify in terms of additional information made available at the point of decision, the potentially great overhead structure that might be involved in creating the information centers.

Because of the importance of information services, the head of this unit should report directly to the president or chief executive, in a staff capacity. Since the information services unit is designed to provide service to the entire company, it must not be part of the regular line organization. For instance, if a company has a staff-oriented service echelon at the level of top management, then the information services unit should be placed there, as shown in Figure 6. For those companies not having a services echelon, the exact placement of information services is not so easily prescribed.

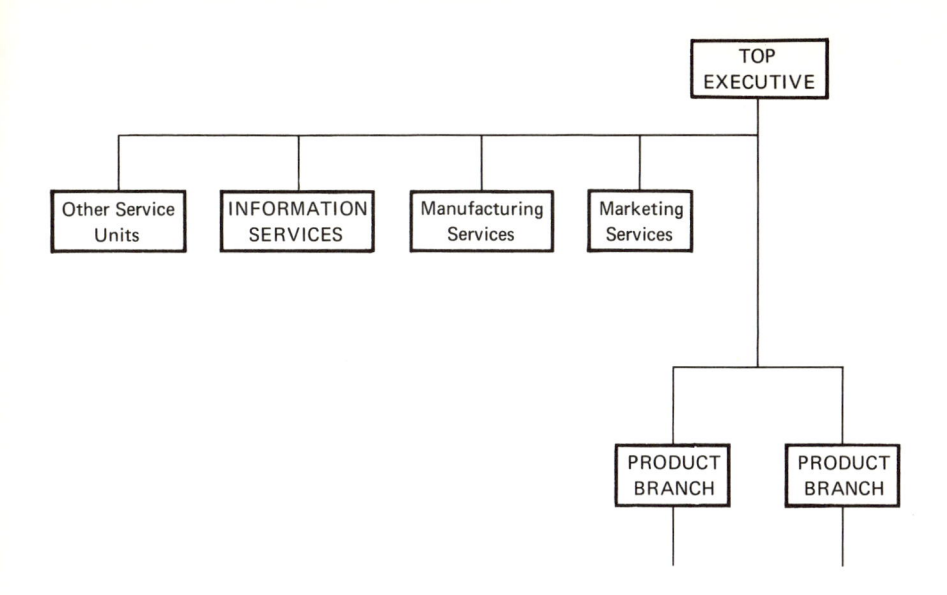

Figure 6. **Organizational Placement of Information Services**

Due to the diversity of company organizations, the only generalization that can be made is to re-emphasize that the information services unit should be so placed in the organization as to put its head on an equal basis with the other important second-level top management executives. In this way, top management will be linked directly to the information system of the company and will be in a position to receive reliable, firsthand information. Without this direct link, there exists the risk of vital information being misplaced, delayed, or, perhaps even worse, distorted. Just as importantly, the information possessed by top management can be more readily available to the operating unit decision makers. This is an important consideration, since in many instances top management represents a significant "external" source of information to an operating unit.

FORMALIZED SYSTEM

Conclusions

To a certain extent, a decentralized company can improve the efficiency of its handling of marketing information without formally organizing an information system by initiating two actions:

Training personnel in handling information.

Developing a formal search procedure.

However, these actions by themselves will have only limited effectiveness since available evidence suggests that in a typical company blockade points exist which impede the flow of information. Thus, a somewhat formal information system must be developed.

This article has presented a model of one such information system which may have more value as a conceptual foundation upon which a company can structure its own system than it does as a concrete proposal for a specific operational system. Regardless of the specific structure developed, any centralized system once fully implemented should minimize the amount of a company's total stock of usable information obtained by a transmission process and maximize the amount obtained through systematic "research" effort. Only in this way will decision makers be able to make their decisions with a minimum of uncertainty attached to the availability and relevance of potentially useful information.

In order to implement the proposed marketing information system, certain requirements must be fulfilled if this system or one based on it is to do the job it is designed to do. For instance, qualified personnel (information specialists) to staff the information centers must be obtained, and there is the obvious need for automatic data processing equipment, such as computers, random access memory storage units, and electronic transmission facilities, to process efficiently the voluminous information and request for information.

Finally, there remains the question of timing. The type of marketing information system proposed cannot be implemented at once, but must be phased into a company's operations over a period of time. How long a time should be planned for full implementation cannot be stated categorically, as this will vary with the over-all size of a company and the structure of the specific information system developed to meet its needs. One company may be able to fully implement this type of information system in less than a year, while other companies may need perhaps one, five, or even ten years to make their systems fully operational. To illustrate, the results of an information system study conducted for the government of the state of California recommends that the statewide information system proposed be phased in over a period of ten years.[9]

PATH SCHEDULING

Regardless of the amount of time it will take, implementation of a centralized marketing information system should be planned. Although there are many possible ways in which to prepare the plan, one form appears to be of great value—*critical path scheduling*. Thus, the general sequence and interdependence of the major phases of the information system development program can be easily identified.[10] The chart of the network will be useful to establish priorities in allocating funds if total funding

---

[9] Lockheed Missiles and Space Company, *California Statewide Information System Study*, July 30, 1965.

[10] For a more complete discussion of this technique, see Philip Kotler, "The Use of Mathematical Models in Marketing," *Journal of Marketing*, XXVII:4 (Oct. 1963), 40–41.

is not available at the outset. In the initial planning of the information system, critical path scheduling will enable a company to test alternative methods of realizing events by means of different resource combinations or of various techniques.

RECENT DEVELOPMENTS

Some companies already have developed more or less formal marketing information systems, and others are planning to do so. A study by Edward Brink of 1,000 large corporations in 1964 showed that 80 companies had established some kind of formal marketing information system and that a great number of companies had plans to activate such systems.[11] A specific illustration is the system developed by the Mead Johnson division of Edward Dalton Company.[12] Mead Johnson has a centralized marketing intelligence system that depends on coordinating and integrating the information system with the daily operation of the firm. This system is based on the decisions that are available to the people the system must serve. Thus, the system is geared to the information needs of individual decision makers.

Evidence such as this makes the future look encouraging. Undoubtedly, more business firms will take a close look at their own situation and institute whatever action is deemed necessary. However, the necessary starting point is to realize that their own management of information may not be as good as they *think*. This, of course, can be determined by an individual company only after it has thoroughly audited its existing methods for handling information.

21 Organization Structure and Its Underlying Theory of Buyer Behavior*

JOHN A. HOWARD

Changing technology—particularly that represented in our knowledge of buyer behavior and information systems—requires that marketing executive looks at current organization structures in new ways.

---

[11] Reported in "Marketing Intelligence Systems: A *Dew* Line for Marketing Men," *Business Management*, Jan. 1966, p. 33.

[12] *Ibid.*, pp. 32–34 ff.

*Reprinted from John S. Wright and Jac L. Goldstucker (eds.), **New Ideas for Successful Marketing** (Chicago: American Marketing Association, June 1966), pp. 87–92.

INTRODUCTION

The writer wishes to discuss a fact long true but only recently recognized. The fact is that the executives' theory of buyer behavior influences the nature of the organizational structure of their company. Only with the development of the computer, however, has this fact great significance. To lay a brief background for this discussion it is well to describe a way of looking at company organization.

EXECUTIVE THEORY OF BUYER BEHAVIOR

A company's organizational structure can be defined in terms of the flows of information that enable the company to operate. Specifically, these flows can be described by the usual paradigm of communications research: *Who* communicates *what* to *whom* and *when* through which *channel* with what *effect*. The central role of these information flows in a company is not at all obvious, however; and this is one of the reasons why the usual organization chart often hides more than it reveals about the real nature of a company.

Taking this view of company organization as a network of information flows as a background, one must analyze why these flows are what they are, which is another way of saying, "Why the organizational structure is what it is." Any company's organizational structure is the result of many forces, but one of the dominant forces is the way executives think. The way they think, in turn, determines the kinds and amounts of information they want in making their decisions. Normally it has been said that "An executive is a prisoner of his communication network." Now with the new computer technology his information network can be redesigned. Major organizational changes are in the offing.

One of the things that marketing executives obviously think much about is the buyer. The way they think about him determines the information they want about him. In fact, it seems that a greater emphasis upon thinking about buyers is the central characteristic of the marketing concept which has received so much attention.

Not only do executives think about buyers but they think systematically about buyers. Executives soon develop firm views about what causes buyers to behave as they do. These views imply that certain relationships exist. In other words, executives have a theory of buyer behavior. Anyone doing research on the executive decision process quickly finds, however, that executives do not generally articulate these beliefs with ease. The beliefs are implicit. Only upon repeated and insistent interrogation are they usually able to make their beliefs explicit.

Two developments have tended to place the executive in the position of having to articulate his theory of buyer behavior. One of these developments took place some years ago and the other is on the horizon. The first development is market research. It was adopted rapidly by industry after World War II. When they meet to discuss a market research report and they attempt to explain the findings, executives expose their beliefs about the nature of the buyers. The executive seldom has the time to participate in such meetings long enough to fully articulate his beliefs and his theory. By participating more in the original design of the study, however, he would be still more explicit. Unfortunately, one of the greatest weaknesses in rational decision in current marketing is that the executive who uses the report seldom participates in the study design where the decision is made as to what facts to collect.

Only when one looks to the future is it obvious how the executive's theory will shape company organization. Here we find that the second development which is a still more radical innovation than market—computer and its related paraphernalia—is clearly on the near horizon. First, the computer has removed some serious barriers to the use of normative decision models. In using normative decision models, General Electric is finding that automated marketing decisions are far more sensitive to errors in sales estimates than to errors in the other decision inputs such as production cost and the interest rate. Hence, in this way the computer is showing us how essential it is to reduce the error in our estimates of buyer behavior. Second, the computer has made possible the implementation of the concept of a *marketing information system*. What does one mean by a company marketing information system? It has at least two identifying characteristics: it is *centralized* and *continuous arrangement* for collecting market facts.

By examining these two characterisics of centralization and continuity, it will become more obvious why executives' theories of buyer behavior must now be laid bare. First, in the process of pooling the information collection activities of the marketing operation, each element of the operation such as advertising, distribution, market research, product development, sales and the like is placed in the position of having to defend why it wants some kinds of information and not others. The give and take of the negotiation process of working out this list of information requirements will inevitably give hints as to each executive's theory, and the more articulate executives will describe theirs in some detail. The executive's theory is probably most apparent when he is justifying the facts he wants than in most other circumstances.

Second, the continuity characteristic of a marketing information system requires that fact collection be far better planned than it now tends to be in the typical market research department which is so often deluged by *ad hoc* studies. If the system is to be useful, comparable data must be collected at regular intervals. Hence, a heavy investment is being made. In all areas of decision, the amount of money at stake strongly determines the amount of attention, thought and care given to the decision. Hence, the continuity characteristic will be a force requiring each executive to articulate his theory as best he can.

THEORY OF BUYERS AND INFORMATION FLOWS

The foregoing comments have implied that an executive's theory of buyers will shape the flows of information which are the structure of the company of organization. Let us now, however, be more explicit about the way in which this is so.

The implementation of a computerized marketing information system requires that all executives in the marketing operation of a company be willing to accept (to internalize psychologically) roughly the same theory of buyer behavior. Contemplating the installation of a marketing information system has a certain diagnostic value. For example, it implies that unless executives do have essentially the same theory the company cannot hope ever to *develop* and *execute* a coherent, unified marketing plan with or without a computer. A strong top executive may force the development of such a plan by sheer leadership; but unless his subordinates believe in it, they will not execute it as effectively. A corollary of this implication is that a company with a coherent, unified marketing plan is evidence that its executives do think alike and do hold to the same theory of buyer behavior.

The following illustrates the point of the consequences of a company's marketing executives holding different theories of buyer behavior. The example concerns the introduction of a new product in the package goods industry, e.g., General Foods, P. & G., or General Mills. Assume that the sales manager holds to the theory that the housewife has a simple information input system. For example, he believes that she is influenced simply in proportion to the brand stimuli that she is exposed to: the more shelf space devoted to a brand, the more likely she is to buy.

The advertising manager, on the other hand, having read some of the perception research holds to the theory that she has a very complex information input system. He believes that her attitude and values cause her to admit some information and simply not "see" (not perceive) other bits of information though they are directly in front of her on the shelf as she walks down the aisle of the supermarket.

A diagram will show the difference. Figure 1 presents a part of a theory of the process by which buying behavior is affected by marketing.[1] Here is the traditional hierarchy of awareness, knowledge, attitude, intention to purchase and actual purchase. To make it a meaningful and comprehensive analytic framework, motivation, and such inhibitory variables as price, level of availability in the retail store and the like must be added.

More important for the purpose here is the variable. Sensitivity to Information, because it distinguishes the sales manager's theory from the advertising man's theory. The principle underlying this variable is that as a buyer's attitude toward a brand becomes more favorable there is a feedback from his attitude to the buyer's perceptual process. The effect of this feed-

---

[1] For a complete theory of buyer behavior, see a forthcoming book by J. A. Howard and J. N. Sheth, *The Theory of Buyer Behavior*. For a summary of the theory see J. A. Howard, "The Theory of Buyer Behavior." Symposium on Consumer Behavior, University of Texas, April 18 and 19, 1966.

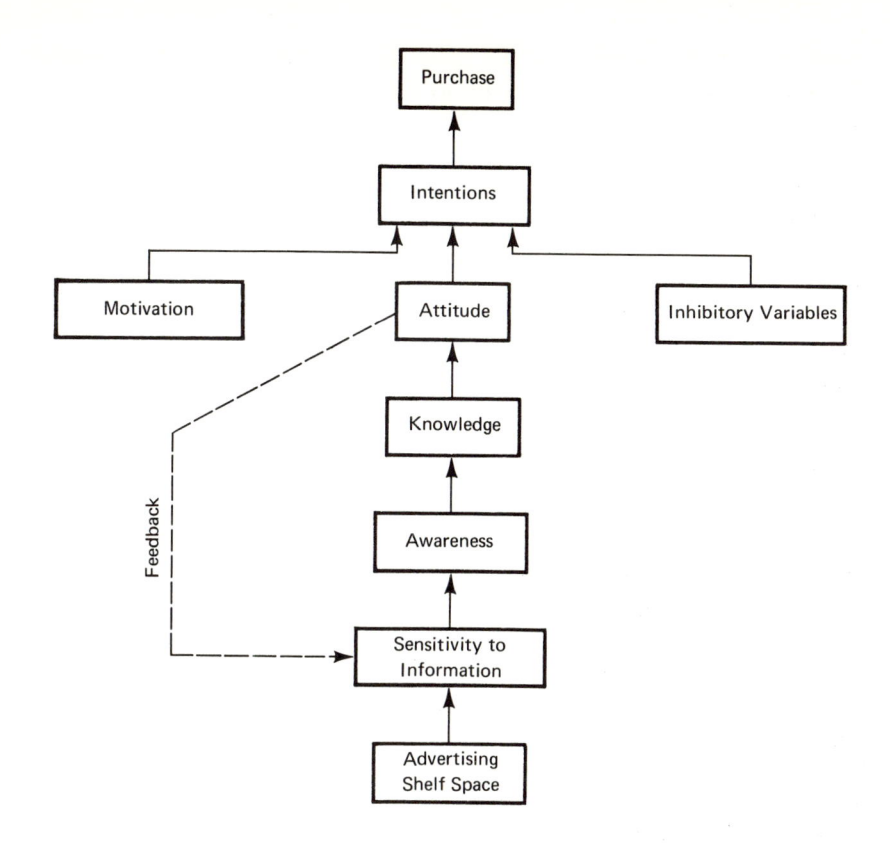

Figure 1. **Buyer Behavior**

back is to increase the probability that she will "see" (perceive) anything associated with the brand, such as a verbal statement, an ad, or a box on the shelf. This feedback is shown in Figure 1.

The sales manager does not believe that this variable exists; the advertising manager believes that it does. As a consequence the salesman will be much less sanguine than the advertising manager about the effects of advertising. Because of his belief in the variable, the advertising manager will argue that advertising has two effects. The first is the traditional effect. It causes the buyer to have a more favorable attitude toward a brand, which will increase the buyer's probability of purchase if she is exposed to the opportunity to buy the brand. The second effect is the more interesting one. The buyer has a greater probability of being exposed to the brand, that is, a greater probability of perceiving the brand when she is confronted with it physically in the supermarket.

The advertising man as a consequence of his theory will argue in a rational manner that relatively more money should be allocated to advertising and less to getting the product in to the supermarket. On the other hand, if both executives hold the same theory, that is, they both believe there is a variable called Sensitivity to Information which operates as described, they are far more likely to agree on a common marketing plan and to execute that plan in good faith rather than with some feeling that they have had something "foisted off" on to them.

A number of implications follow from the analysis here. A company's marketing operation can be organized more simply and its parts can work together far more smoothly if all executives hold the same theory of buyer behavior. Above all, there will be less latent conflict between the executive and his market researcher because the executive will fulfill his true role of being the formulator of the problem and leave the market research department free to collect the data that best measures the variables implied in the executive's formulation and free to develop the more basic theory that should underlie all of the company's market research. The elements of the marketing plan will be coordinated because all executives will be more inclined to think it is the sensible thing to do. There will be greater room for creativity. Finally, this common theory is essential to using the new information collection and processing technology most effectively.

CONCLUSION

It is well to cite some broader implications. First, the need and urge to have fully articulated and dependable theory of buyer behavior will be very sharp indeed. This need will force a high level of systematic scientific creativity on a broad front, the kind of creative activity which marketing as a field study has never before experienced. Second, there is the great task of retraining executives to think in these new terms. Third, for the past decade lip service has been given to the marketing concept. Now with a common theory of buyer behavior, the concept can be fully utilized.

A final implication is that we will be relatively ineffective in developing marketing information systems until there is also a far better theory of executive behavior. If there is to be one common model, questioning about the intellectual capacities of executives must be answered in order to know the kinds of models that executives can learn to think with. This last broad implication, however, is a topic for another paper.[1]

---

[1] See the article "Information Processing Model of Executive Decisions" in the next section of this book.

B The Implementation of Information Systems

Information Processing Model of Executive Decisions* — 22

JOHN A. HOWARD
WILLIAM M. MORGENROTH†

Company information systems demand an improved understanding of the nature of the executive's decision process. Above all his information requirements must be specified. The capacity to specify these requirements is the hallmark of the information-processing model. An example of the form of the simulation of a pricing decision process is presented here.

1. INTRODUCTION

Anyone attempting to construct a company information system quickly discovers that little is known about the precise nature of the executive decision process in spite of the plethora of management literature. Without the help of some general principles of the executive decision process the information technician—management scientist, market researcher, operations researcher, etc.—is seriously handicapped in determining the company's information requirements. It is not difficult when formal optimizing models can be used, but in many instances, perhaps even most, the information technician will find it necessary to work in terms of a much less general description of the decision process for which he is developing the information requirements. Further, we believe that largely to the extent he fully articulates his view (constructs a model) of this decision process he will be effective in carrying out his task. Hence, the type of model set forth here can be extremely useful to the large number of people who are now attempting to provide optimum information to executives.

---

*Reprinted from **Management Science**, Vol. 14. No. 7 (March, 1968), pp. 416–428.

† We wish to acknowledge our debt to the Ford Foundation for financial support and to express our deepest appreciation to Herbert A. Simon, Carnegie Institute of Technology, for his advice and encouragement.

Communicating with the executive in the attempt to specify his information requirements is a much more difficult assignment than is usually expected as every information technician quickly finds.

Much current discussion of designing information systems reveals a naive view of the difficulty of eliciting executive decision rules. It is our belief that serious mistakes are now being made in a too-ready acceptance of the executive's statement about how he makes his decisions and what information he requires. One need only recall the many footless scholarly debates that have ensued in economics about empirical pricing decision rules to disabuse his mind of this naivete.

Isolating the information required is complicated by the executive's view of the matter which usually reflects two contradictory attitudes. Since decision making has become second nature to him and he does it with such ease, to him the act cannot be very significant and he is a little surprised that anyone should be interested in knowing about it. On the other hand, he is quite sure that no amount of analysis will be able to reproduce it. His phrase is, "It is intuitive!" with the implication that it is innately unknowable, with the further implication that it is footless to attempt to specify the information he uses. Hence, he is typically not a very lucid source for a statement of the information that he must have to carry out his decision-making activities.

Information processing models provide a way to identify these information requirements. An essential characteristic of the models is that they specify the information used by the decision maker and what he does with it in order to arrive at a decision. The term "information processing model" is applied both to systems of artificial intelligence and to the description of human decisions.[1] We are concerned only with the latter here.

In the few instances where these models have been constructed, the results display a surprising degree of simplicity, a simplicity imposed by the limitations of man's intellectual capacity. It is sometimes asserted that the executive's inability to make extensive calculations is solved by utilizing the high-speed computer but this solution merely gives rise to still another problem which is to determine the optimum relation between the man and the machine (computer) in making the decision. It seems clear that to obtain this optimum man-machine relation and to meet the non-computational requirements of the decision such as the search for alternative courses of action and the sociological or organizational influences, a deeper understanding of human behavior in an organizational setting has become essential. It is our belief that the model presented here contributes to that understanding partly because it focuses on the organizational factors that underlie high level decisions. Further, models of this nature for the same

---

[1] For a discussion of the nature of information processing models and how they apply to human thought processes see (5).

levels in different organizations whose products compete in the same market might be compared for insights into differing strategies. Finally, models similar to this for adjacent levels of the same organization might be "hooked" together to simulate the organization's decision processes on a computer and the aggregate process could then be tested for its consistency with relevant company objectives.

The background of the study will first be presented followed by an exposition of the model and its terminology. The next stage is a careful discussion of how the model was validated ending with a summary of the conclusions of its significance and implications.

2. BACKGROUND

Here we describe the setting of and procedure used in simulating a pricing decision in a typical market: a few large producers along with a number of small ones, all selling a slightly differentiated product. The research was begun in 1959 and extended over a three year period of observation, interviewing and analysis in one company which must remain anonymous because of the sensitive nature of the data. The company is listed among the fifty largest manufacturing firms in the United States as measured by volume of sales. The product is one where the prices are frequently changed and are constantly visible enough to permit the documentation of the pattern of prices at any time. Further, execution of the decision follows the decision so quickly in this case that it is easier to infer causality. These factors all combined to facilitate the model building process.

A number of sources of information were used. Interviews with the decision maker came first. He attempted to identify the variables and to explain how they were manipulated. From the interview data the researchers constructed flow charts to describe the process. The flow chart was found to be a splendid vehicle for communicating to the executive how the interviewer interpreted his statements and what inferences had been made from these interpretations. The chart was also valuable in the analysis of the relevant communication networks in the organization.

Second, the executive was observed in the process of making decisions. This provided a check, for example, on whether the data that he allegedly used were actually available and on how they were transmitted and processed in the organization's communication system.

Third, records of past decisions and their supporting data were analyzed, and the resulting conclusions were reviewed with the executive. Because of anti-trust problems more detailed records of past decisions are maintained in the company than is probably true in most firms.

Fourth, the flow chart was tested against the recorded behavior of the decision maker and against the verbal statements of other executives at the same level, but in different regions of the country.

3. MODEL

Here we deal with the scope, structure, function and rationale of the model. The scope of the model provides some evidence of its importance as a description of decision activity. The executive estimated that the model incorporates about 95 per cent of the Company's pricing decisions. The model's output of price decisions includes all prices affecting less than a whole state. Price decisions involving a whole state or more are made at a higher executive level.

The reference marker's pricing actions play an important role in the structure of the model. "Reference marketer" is the label generally applied to the firm which has the largest share in that state. Although having the largest market share may have resulted from initial capture of and subsequent leadership in the market, a reference marketer may no longer be accepted by the other large firms as major initiator of price changes if it fails to interpret market conditions correctly. The reference marketer's price activity is watched by the other firms. This tendency for Company X to look primarily to the reference marketer for a stimulus to contemplate a price change as shown in the graphic description of the structure of the model in Figure 1 arises partly because the industry is made up of two distinct segments, a few large firms ("major") and several quite small firms ("private branders"). As will be explained later, the nature of the pricing behavior differs sharply between these two segments. In addition, Company X initially contemplates the price behavior of the reference competitor, but it as well as other large competitors acts with differing degrees of independence at different times. Company X quickly follows a price decrease by the reference marketer, but it follows his price increase more slowly.

For subsequent testing considerations it is important to distinguish between the structure and the function of the model. The *structure* of the model is a *set of rules* governing what actions are to be taken and as a consequence of the input of *certain pieces of information*. Obviously not all the objectively available information is used, which raises fascinating questions on the motivation underlying the decision to use certain pieces of information, and not others. These questions relate to problems of search: the search for alternative courses of action, the search for information about goals, and the search for information on the consequences of given actions for these different goals.

This structure has a *function* which is to generate the output of the process. The output is the decision which has a number of dimensions such as amount of price change, direction of change, and latency, the length of time that elapses between the triggering of the decision process and the actual decision.

The descriptive decision model derived from the research is shown in flow chart form in Figure 1 with price as its output. It depicts a sequential binary choice process. The cue or triggering element of the process is Box 1 in the upper left-hand corner of Figure 1, labeled "Watch P_{wilt}," which

Figure 1. **Model of Pricing Decision Process**

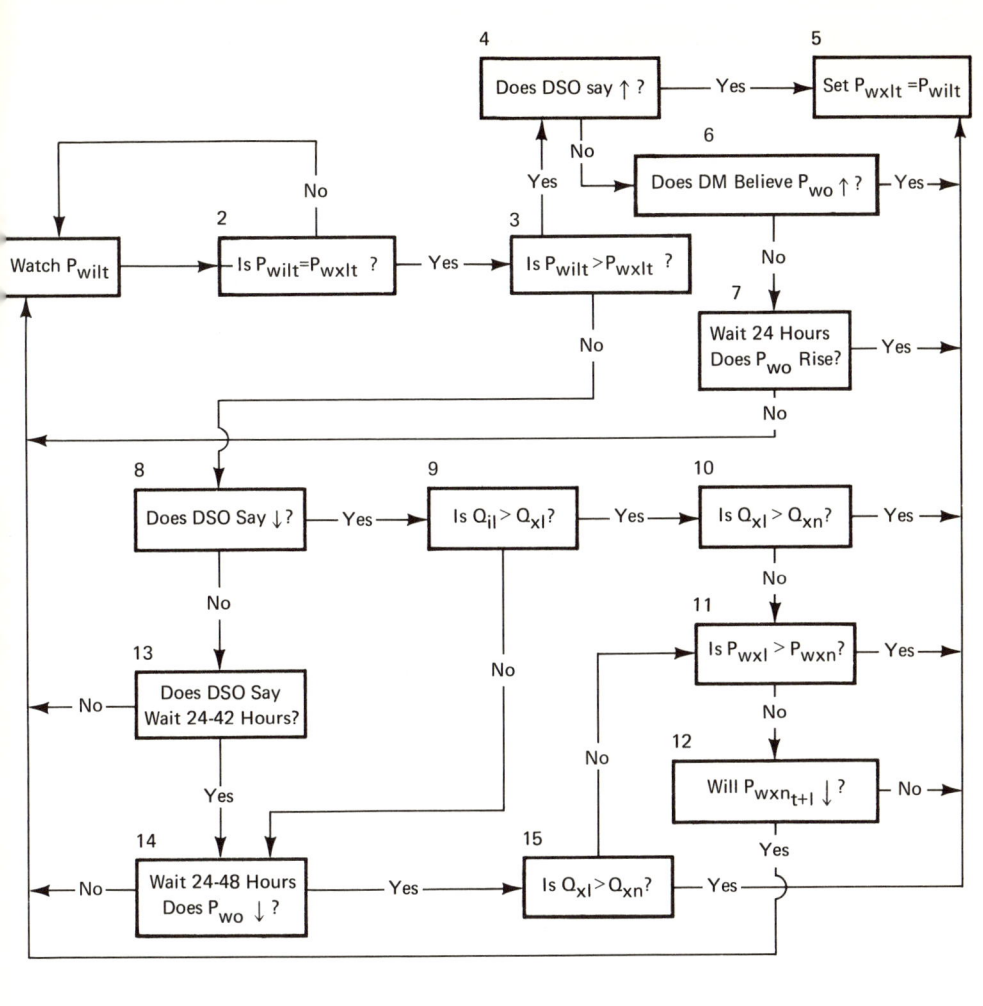

Symbols

- P - Price
- w - Wholesale
- x - Our Company
- o - Other Major Competitors in Local Market
- i - Initiator
- t - Time, at Present
- Q - Quantity, i.e., Sales Volume in Physical Terms
- l - Local Market Wherein Price Change Is Being Considered.

- n - Nearby Market with Funnel Influences
- DSO - District Sales Office (District Sales Manager)
- = - Is Equal to
- ≠ - Is Not Equal to
- \> - Is Greater than
- ↑ - Raise Price
- ↓ - Drop Price
- DM - Decision Maker

means, "Watch the wholesale (w price (P), of the initiator (I) in each local (l) market at each point in time (t)."

For administrative convenience the management of the firm divides the United States into geographic areas labelled regions, territories and zones,

Information Processing Model of Executive Decisions **263**

roughly aligned with population concentrations and structured by such criteria as natural geographic boundaries, roads and buying patterns. The zone is the smallest of the three units and is often termed "local market." Pricing activity is largely in terms of this local market unit and the decision maker focuses his attention upon it.

The direction of the price change, whether upwards or downwards, makes a great difference in the decision process. Figure 1 quickly reveals that upward price moves are much simpler than downward price moves. When Box 3 differentiates between the wholesale price of the initiator and that of Company X, it separates the model into two price directions: upward and downward. The upward move comprises only three steps, evidenced by Boxes 4, 6, and 7, before a decision is reached. The downward move may require up to 8 steps, as shown by Boxes 8 through 15.

This asymmetrical characteristic of the decision process serves to introduce the rationale for the structure. This asymmetry can be explained by the nature of the decision environment and by the executive's motivation: if all competitors follow, the nature of the market is such that it is always profitable to raise prices, since purchases of the generic product are relatively unaffected by price changes. In economic terminology, the market demand is highly inelastic in the short-term. If the executive's motivating criterion is profit, he will always desire a higher price if he does not lose market share in attempting to attain the higher price.

Profit, however, is only one of the organization's goals. Different levels of the organization have different goals. An interesting point is the nature of the goals at the next lower level, the District Sales Office which appears as "DSO" in Boxes 4, 8 and 13. In order to properly motivate the activities of the next lower level, the decision-maker strives to make decisions that are approved by that lower level (DSO). Much more important, however, is that the goals at the DSO and lower levels are biased against a price increase because the organizational incentive system is structured at these levels to favor volume of sales instead of profit. This point of view exists, because to the extent that competitors do not also decrease *their* prices, a price decrease is a way of increasing sales volume. Hence, if the lower level agrees to a price increase (Box 4) the higher level with its profit goal, "jumps at the opportunity" to raise the price. Where the lower level consistently fails to report competitive price increases in the field because of the conflict of goals, the executive can place his staff in the field to report directly to him and in this way temporarily correct the deficiency in his communication system.

When Company X is responding to the initiator's *decreased* price, the greater complexity of the decision process is a result of two elements. The first element is the relative strength of Company X versus that of the initiator as indicated by market share. If X's share of market is less, X is more inclined to follow in the price decline than to maintain his current price. Second, a distinction is made between the local market and the nearby market, the latter being the most significant adjacent market. The nearby market becomes relevant because a price decline in the local market may spread to the nearby market causing the prices of competitors there to decline. Like fighting a forest fire, efforts are directed toward "containing" the price decline. This tendency for a price decline in one market to drag down the prices in contiguous markets is called a "funnel" effect. The possibility of this dependent relation between the local and nearby market is a deterrent to price reduction in the local market. Hence, on a price decline, the influence of the lower level's bias in favor of price cutting is offset by (1) the complicating elements of intercompetitor differences in market share and (2) the distinction between local and nearby markets.

So far we have referred to only one dimension of the model's output, the direction of price change, but the distinction between decisions to increase price and those to decrease price introduces the latency dimension. The decision is made more rapidly on the upward movements in the sense that unless the others increase within 24 hours, X decides to do nothing, but when the decision involves a price decrease, X will delay as long as 48 hours before deciding to do nothing. The supporting evidence for this conclusion is from the thirty-one decisions shown in Table 1.

Company X's behavior differs, however, according to which competitor initiates the move. With respect to the reference marketer's nine upward moves, X's mean lag is three days and the median and modal lags are two days. For the reference marketer's eight downward moves, the mean lag is one day, the modal lag is either zero days or one day, and the median lag is one day. In short, Company X delays more in following the reference marketer up, than in following it down possibly indicating an attempt to steal the reference marketer's market, an attempt to avoid the loss of market share to a lagging competitor, or indicating goal conflicts between the reporting district, whose goal is mainly market volume, and division headquarters, whose goals include profit. Downward the lag is less, implying haste to avoid loss of market share, and loss of profit. On one downward decision [2] where the lag was four days, all the delay was in the district office.

The other majors originated ten moves: one up and nine down. These facts suggest lack of optimism on the other majors' part in initiating upward moves that others will follow. The solitary successful upward move was made simultaneously by four majors including Company X. On the downward moves the range in latency exhibited by X is impressive: zero to nineteen days. Over half the delay in the nineteen-day lag occurred in the district office. Apparently the remaining majors were reluctant to follow down.

When the private branders led with their one downward move [3] X and other majors were unwilling to follow. In the case of the three upward

---

[2] See No. 20, Table 1.
[3] See No. 19, Table 1.

Table I. **A Comparison of the Observed and Predicted Outcomes of Thirty-One Decisions**

Decisions	Box #3	Box #4	Box #6	Box #7	Box #8	Box #9	Box #10	Additional Elements of Decision	Box #	P.D.	O.D.
1	Y	Y							5	U	U
2	Y	N	Y						5	U	U
3	Y	N	Y						5	U	U
4	N				N			(13-Y)(14-Y)(15-Y)*	5	D	D
5	Y	N	Y						5	U	U
6	Y	N	Y						5	U	U
7	Y	Y							5	U	U
8	N				Y	Y	Y		5	D	D
9	N				N			(13-Y)(14-Y)(15-N)(11-Y)	5	D	D
10	N				N			(13-Y)(14-Y)(15-N)(11-Y)	5	D	D
11	Y	N	Y						5	U	U
12	Y	N	N	Y					5	U	U
13	N				Y	Y	Y		5	D	D
14	N				N			(13-Y)(14-Y)(15-Y)	5	D	D
15	N				Y	Y	Y		5	D	D
16	N				N			(13-Y)(14-Y)(15-Y)	5	D	D
17	N				Y	Y	Y		5	D	D
18	Y	N	N	Y					5	U	U
19	N				N			(13-Y)(14-Y)(15-N)(11-N)(12-Y)	1	=	=
20	N				N			(13-Y)(14-Y)(15-Y)	5	D	D
21	Y	N	Y						5	U	U
22	Y				N			(13-Y)(14-Y)(15-Y)	5	D	D
23	N				Y	Y	Y		5	D	D
24	Y	Y							5	U	U
25	Y	N	N	Y					5	U	U
26	N				Y	Y	Y		5	D	D
27	Y	Y							5	U	U
28	N				Y	Y	Y		5	D	D
29	N				Y	Y	Y		5	D	D
30	N				Y	Y	Y		5	D	D
31	Y	Y							5	U	U

On decision #19 no price change occurred because of danger of "funnel" effect.

Legend

P.D.—Predicted decision
O.D.—Observed decision
Y—Yes
N—No

D—Down
U—Up
=—No change
*—Numbers in parentheses refer to flowchart boxes.

moves by the private branders, X's lag averaged four days. How much of this delay was caused by the desire of the majors to discourage the private branders from cutting price in the future is not known.

A number of summary conclusions can be made. Although Company X's decision process is primarily that of a follower and the leader's move is normally duplicated, price differences do exist between the leader and X and these reflect the importance of organizational factors as they conflict with market factors in pricing. For example, time lags in downward price moves as compared to upward moves are caused by the conflict of different goals in the decision maker's goal hierarchy. The lack of symmetry of the model shows the relative greater complexity of the downward move compared to the upward move. Even though more complex, the downward move occurs more rapidly than the upward move when the reference competitor initiates the move, but this is not so when some other major company initiates the downward move. Company X will follow the private brander's up independently of the moves of other majors but it will not so follow a private brander down.

4. TESTING THE MODEL

Only when the model of the executive's decision process has been tested does it deserve the label "scientific." In this section the two test criteria are described, the procedure for applying each criterion is explained, some of the limitations of the procedure are set forth, and the results of both tests are summarized.

The research was carried out under field conditions and involved the observation of a single subject, both of which make the testing more difficult. Also, there are two features of the model to be tested: the structure (process) and the output (decision) of the structure. Traditionally we have tested only the output of a theory: how well the model's output predicts the executive's terminal behavior is taken as the measure of the adequacy of the theory. The rules (structure) implied in Figure 1, however, also represent behavior, both overt and ideational. For example, in Box 4 overt behavior is implied in contacting the District Sales Office for its advice about which action should be taken. Ideational behavior is implied in each of the boxes where the decision maker must make a judgment. Hence, even though the model appeared to predict the output correctly, the process (the rules and their sequence) could differ from that used by the executive in arriving at the decision.

4.1 Testing the Output

To test the accuracy of the model's output, a systematic, random sample of every tenth decision was taken from the files of the division of the company managed by the executive whose behavior was observed in deriving the model. The files containing the pricing decisions made over a six-year period were arranged in chronological order with the date that the decision was triggered serving as the specific ordering criterion. This sample yielded the data of 31 decisions shown in Table 1 which were used to test the model systematically. In addition, one hundred and thirty other decisions from three separate geographic divisions were used to test the model in a more casual way, which will be described subsequently.

The output test is presented in the last two columns of Table 1, in which P.D. refers to predicted decision, and O.D., to observed decision. The 31 decisions were inserted as the inputs and each consequent output is compared with the observed decision. The predicted decisions concerns only the price: whether it be changed to duplicate the leader's change or remain unchanged. No prediction is made of the amount of change nor the length of delay. The amount of change, because of tax reasons and custom, is always in standard units and almost always in terms of one unit at a time. The prediction of the amount would have contributed little. To predict the length of delay would probably have required the inclusion in the model of a much wider range of variables.

Each item in the predicted column (P.D.) in Table 1 is taken either from the Box 5 column (those cases in which Company X followed) or the Box 1 column (those cases in which Company X did not follow). Perfect agreement exists between the predicted and observed outputs as indicated in Table 1. Hence, the hypothesis that the model represents the executive's decision process is confirmed by the output test.

4.2 Testing the Process

If the model also describes the *process* used by the executive in coming to his decision, as well as describing his terminal behavior, our belief would be strengthened that the executive's behavior has been adequately explained. The reader will recall that the process is described by the model's structure.

Turing's test (6) has been suggested for testing the information-processing types of model. A rigorous application of Turing's test to the pricing decision would require comparing the protocols of the executive with the structure of a model that was inferred from some data other than the protocols. A protocol is the executive's description of the thinking process that he is going through in making the decision *as he makes the decision,* instead of a *post hoc* reconstruction. The protocol method of collecting data on ideational behavior has been called "the thinking-aloud technique." To the extent that these presumably independent descriptions of the process (the model and the protocols) are indistinguishable the model is an accurate description of the pricer's decision process.

Some aspects of the interviews taken in the study closely resembled protocols. The interviews were at first conducted in terms of questions, "How do you set prices?" As the research progressed, however, the procedure came to be more and more of the thinking-aloud technique, and specific decisions became the focal point of the interview as a means of illustrating the way in which the executive made the decision under certain specified conditions. Partially in this way, the general rules making up the process were elicited.

It is difficult to keep the protocols and model as distinctly separate in their origin as Turing's test implies. At a minimum, for example, discussion with the executive is essential to merely setting the limits on the general nature of the problem. From this point to extracting protocols is a matter of degree. Also, protocols may omit important details of the process. When the executive was asked to articulate the process, for example, he passed over a number of important rules that he was in fact using, and only when he was shown that logically he must be going through these additional steps did he become aware of this fact.

The procedure used here was to construct the structure of the model as shown in Figure 1 by inferring it from the interviews and then to test it against company records of the actual decisions. This method was facilitated because detailed data were recorded in Company X at the time of each decision and carefully filed.

These records contained much of the data specified by the model, such as the specific price set by the decision, the reference marketer's price activities, and data used as background, such as retail prices and the initial moves of the other majors and the private branders. Some data required in the model, however, were not in the records, such as market shares of the majors, location and price position of nearby markets, recommendations of the DSO's, and other elements of the telephone conversations of the DSO with the decision maker. These were obtained from the decision maker's memory.

When the data specified by the model are fed through the model box-by-box as shown in Figure 1, there is perfect agreement, which the reader can verify for himself by taking the information from the first ten columns of Table 1 and applying it to Figure 1. Hence the model is further validated, this time by the process test.

4.3 Inter-Divisional Comparison

Still another validating step was carried out in which the model was reviewed by the executives in three other regional divisions of the company. One hundred and thirty decisions were selected at random from the files of these three different geographic regions. This more casual method of testing had two phases. In the first phase the executives were asked to check the accuracy of the elements of the model including their order. Each of the three regional decision makers agreed that the model portrayed the process. In the second phase the interviewer used the model while the decision maker sat facing him with records taken randomly from the files. The interviewer asked the questions implicit in the model, and based upon the records and his memory the executive answered these questions. From the answers the interviewer predicted the price decision. Then, he compared the predicted price decision with the output recorded in the files, and finally, he checked the records for any data not represented in the model. In each of the 130 decisions the prediction was accurate. The executives expressed surprise that their mental processes could be so accurately and simply portrayed.

The purpose of this additional step was mainly to determine whether different decision-makers in the same company developed different decision processes to carry out their task of setting prices. This conclusion is particularly interesting because no effort at all, such as published standard operating procedures or training courses, had been offered by the company to insure uniformity among the decision makers in the different geographic divisions. A tentative conclusion, then, is that similar decision environments will produce essentially the same decision processes.

4.4 Summary and Significance of Test Results

Both the output test and the process test show perfect agreement between the model and the data. This conformity between theory and fact indicates that the model is a good description of reality.

The general significance of the test results is that they show it is possible to describe accurately an important, complex executive decision with a relatively simple non-optimizing model that in light of the organizational constraints upon decision probably represents fairly rational behavior. The fact that the model was constructed and in such simple form gives encouragement to the information technician that he can identify the current informational requirements of the executive, but that to do so is by no means an easy task.

Aside from testing, two other aspects of the research should be mentioned. First, throughout the discussion the "decision maker" has been referred to, but in fact he was two people: the chief executive for the geographic division and his price analyst. During the period of the study the analyst's position was a new position. He was more and more taking over the responsibility for pricing from the executive who had been doing it for many years. In addition, the analyst maintained the great amount of records required by the task. It was, however, an unusually close working relationship. The model was first inferred from interviews with the executive and then it was compared with the procedure elicited from the analyst. Neither at this time nor at any time during the research were there discrepancies between the executive's and the analyst's behavior.

Second, the point was made earlier that the executive articulated some of the steps in the decision process only when shown that logic demanded them. This suggests the obvious danger that the research process itself was an influence upon behavior, however, the model is validated by both tests, the output and the process test. That he was not aware of all the details of his behavior is not surprising. Under normal circumstances there was no need for him to articulate the process because it was never communicated to anyone except the price analyst and here communication was carried on over a long period on an intimate, face-to-face relation. Under these conditions errors in articulating the process to the interviewers could be expected.

5. Conclusions

This research provides additional evidence that it is possible to describe the decision process of a high level corporate executive making an important repetitive decision. The importance of the decision process is indicated by the magnitude of the price change, typically, five per cent or more with serious profit consequences, the amount of the actual time consumed in making a decision, and the number of decisions made annually. The assertion that the research offers evidence of our ability to describe such a decision process accurately is made with the same type of support that is accepted throughout science: the hypothesis was tested and confirmed. The simple model of the process is also plausible: the executive does not always follow, and whether he does or not, the decision is made on the basis of objective evidence.

A number of these studies can give us an understanding of the nature of complex behavior on which traditional research techniques in the main have faltered. The extent to which the findings can be generalized is open to question. The model, however, was tested against the behavior of executives of the same company in four different geographic divisions, although in only one was the analysis highly systematic. The probable error of a sample of four is high. It can also be argued, for example, that this decision, being highly repetitive, was atypical of the total activity of high level executives, but one who has done this type of research is impressed by the fact that when he first approaches the executive he is told how impossible it is to describe the decision process which is so terribly complex and intuitive. The experience persuades us that this sequential, binary choice process may describe a very wide range of the executive's activity. Two other studies (2,4), one of the department store buying and another of the decision to allocate advertising funds to advertising media, support this view; still another study (1) indicates that it is possible to similarly describe a more complex decision process, one in which the rules were modified depending upon the decision maker's estimates of the future state of the environment.

Our study also suggests how it may be possible with this type of research, to explicate the mechanisms by which decision makers generalize the behavior they have developed from one situation to new situations and from one type of decision to another.

In addition to the relevance of the model to an understanding of decision behavior generally, it has the obvious implication for company information systems of specifying an executive's information requirements. The simplicity of the model is encouraging to information technicians—management scientists, market researchers, operations researchers, systems people, etc.—faced with the task of specifying the executive's information requirements so that an adequate information system can be designed. It also offers a *general procedure* that the information technician can use in eliciting these information requirements.

The model has relevance to anti-trust. A safe conclusion from the study is that the major firms were inhibited somewhat by fear of anti-trust action from more closely coordinating their price moves with each other. In our opinion, however, it would be unwise to conclude that, even if they were permitted to collude, all price rivalry would be eliminated. Uncertainty about the future would cause some rivalry (3). Also, the presence of the small price-cutting firms sets an upper limit to industry price. The model also suggests a new defense against charges of collusion in price setting: models depicting strategies and behavior in the market for the accused firms might be constructed, tested and contrasted to reflect honest significant differences. This approach was being considered by defense attorneys in a different industry in 1964, when the government dropped the case.

The model has other implications that we do not develop but merely mention here. Organization theory, for example, is confronted with the crucial question of what determines the level to which authority becomes delegated. The model represents authority being exercised at one level and describes how it relates to the level above and to the level below. Economic theory takes as one of its central tasks the explanation of price decisions: the model presented here deals with a pervasive empirical pricing situation. Management science, with its emphasis upon the normative, needs a fuller understanding of the human and organizational limitations upon decision in order to develop more effective models of how the pricing decision should be made. Finally, the training implications of this type of model have not at all been exploited.

References

1. Clarkson, G. P. E., *Portfolio Selection: A Simulation of Trust Investment.* New York: Prentice-Hall, Inc., 1962.
2. Cyert, R. M., and J. G. March, *A Behavioral Theory of the Firm.* Englewood Cliffs, N. J.: Prentice-Hall, Inc., 1963.
3. Fellner, William, *Competition Among the Few.* New York: Alfred A. Knopf, 1949, Chapter 5.
4. Marschner, D. C., Quantification of Decision-Making in the Field of Advertising. Unpublished doctoral dissertation, Columbia University, 1964.
5. Reitman, Walter R., *Cognition and Thought.* New York: John Wiley and Sons, Inc., 1965.
6. Simon, H. A., and Newell, A., *The Simulation of Human Thought.* RAND Publication, p. 1734, June 1959.

23 Computers Begin to Solve the Marketing Puzzle*

Electronic data processing is furnishing the technique whereby "total systems" can be developed and implemented to provide fast, precise data for marketing decisions. Already, it is giving the buyer a new role; as it develops, it will transform the role of salesman and bring many other changes in retailing.

*Reprinted from **Business Week**, April 17, 1965, pp. 114ff. Used by permission of McGraw-Hill Publications Inc.

Routinely, every evening at J. C. Penney stores across the country, a chain of events begins that reflects the changing nature not only of retailing but of every other marketing practice.

The small, punched tickets that have been taken off merchandise sold during the day are dispatched to either New York City or Los Angeles. There the tickets, coded to describe the merchandise to which they were attached until it was sold, are fed into machines that transfer the information to punched cards. From cards, the data can be put on magnetic tape or fed directly into electronic digital computers.

The computers have been programmed to know what each store should stock of so-called "staples"—men's shirts, socks, ladies' hose, lingerie, and similar goods.

Every two weeks, a computer will match a store's planned stock level against merchandise sold in that store; and, when a store needs merchandise, the computer will send out an order to buy, along with shipping instructions.

Theory into fact. A retail store doesn't have to be as large as Penney—1,700 stores and $2-billion annual sales—to use computers in this way to control its stock level and ordering procedures. A score or so of stores around the country are using some variant of the system. In fact, some local chains, such as Woodward & Lothrop in Washington and Goldblatt Bros. in Chicago, use more complex and sophisticated systems to give them daily reports of stocks and sales.

In theory, it has always been true that a store's buyers could give management a daily report of stock conditions and what was sold the preceding day—just as in theory someone in almost any business gets the pertinent marketing figures every day. But as a matter of hard, cruel fact—as opposed to theory—this just hasn't been so.

The importance of what Penney and other companies are doing is simply this: They are turning the computer with its fantastic computational speed into a new marketing tool. It may be just a big adding machine, as is often said, but it adds at a speed that hardly gives a man a chance to have a second thought.

Legerdemain. A customer of Ownes-Illinois Glass Co. had that brought home to him recently. He had ordered some containers from O-I's Libbey Products Div., changed his mind, and called to cancel the order. He couldn't cancel; the shipment was already at his plant.

This disconcerting legerdemain was possible because Owens-Illinois is one of the hundreds of U.S. companies that are managing production, finished inventory, and distribution with a mathematical system controlled by computers.

O-I's data processing headquarters in Toledo (10 computers and 100 people) is connected by wire to 100 different sales and manufacturing locations. An order comes in, the computer determines whether the product ordered is in stock, indicates where it is, and sends a release and shipping order to the warehouse, or orders to a plant to make it.

What the customer who couldn't cancel was relying on is an order-shipping-billing procedure that is passing from the industrial scene. Normally, weeks elapsed between the time a salesman took your order and you got the shipment and the invoice. At Owens-Illinois, says Thomas H. Browning, manager of data processing, electronic data processing cuts the time to no more than 35 hours.

Over the wire. Helping to reduce the order-shipping-billing time is a system tying the computer that manages inventory to a data transmission network employing any one of a group of devices known as a Data-Phone. It is an adaptation of a normal telephone, and is used with what the trade calls a "terminal" (the exact designation varies according to who makes it).

Together they transmit voice and numeric signals. Instead of a salesman dropping around to fill out an order pad, orders are filed by punched card or tape over wires direct to the supplier's receiving equipment, where they are put into form to go into the computer.

At Beals, McCarthy & Rogers, Inc., a large Buffalo industrial distributor, the combination of computer-managed inventory and Data-Phone ordering in the past four years has meant a reduction of inventory of $200,000 and a sales increase of more than $2-million, according to Frederick L. Davis, the company's marketing manager. When you can know faster, and fill quicker, what your customers are ordering, you can carry a smaller stock.

It works if you're the customer, too. When you can get faster delivery you can carry a smaller inventory. Davis reports it is common now for his customers to do without general stores and tool cribs entirely. Normally, placing an order costs $15 and up; a BM&R customer has reduced this by 17%.

Taking over. The computer is flashing with dazzling speed across the panorama of marketing—which takes in the entire relationship between the designer of a product, the manufacturer, seller, buyer, and user.

Electronic data processing not only is managing inventory in nationwide chains of retail stores; it is telling large department stores which customers are the best prospects for certain merchandise, is "advising" a food company when to offer special "deals," is giving rifle-accuracy to the calls of an apparel manufacturer's salesmen, is forecasting crop yields for a canner, giving greater precision to the selection of media by advertising agencies.

There are still plenty of skeptics. A computer guided by programmers unfamiliar with the specific industry so thoroughly fouled up one heavy equipment maker's replacements parts production that it took two years to untangle. Most retailers, particularly supermarkets, are loath to use computers as anything but bookkeepers.

Too late? Strictly marketing uses of EDP, going beyond inventory management, are still uncommon in U.S. business. But those who have sampled its magic are convinced the hour is late for the laggards. In a shockingly matter-of-fact way, a department store man in an Eastern metropolis says: "Our competition is finished; they can't compete with us any more. They started too late with their [EDP] systems and now we are getting so much of the business they'll never be able to afford the system to do the job."

His competition is about as old, as well-established, and as outwardly prosperous as his own store. But in the age of the computer, the hands on marketing's clock are at half-past eleven—30 minutes before the witching hour. The use of EDP is about to become routine in many marketing operations which until now have defied systemization.

Only a year ago, Richard F. Neuschel, a director of McKinsey & Co., wrote in Marketing and the Computer:

> In none of the major functions of American business has the impact of the computer been so lightly felt as in marketing. Yet, in none of the major functions is its potential so great.

I. THE DATA COLLECTORS GO TO WORK

The potential of EDP in marketing is great simply because of a pervading belief that there are not enough good, hard numbers in marketing to make a fair-sized computer work up a mild sweat.

In the book, Decision Exercises in Marketing, Dr. Arnold Corbin, professor of marketing at New York University, Dr. George Blagowidow, and Dr. Claire Corbin, write:

> To many people, marketing ... is regarded as a business function in which most decisions are highly qualitative in nature and strongly rooted in intangible factors. ... Hence marketing decisions are often made on the basis of hunch, guess, or intuition, rather than on a rational analysis of the measurable relationships among the principal variables involved.

John F. Stolle, a Booz, Allen & Hamilton vice-president and specialist in operations research, comments that "marketing is the most difficult area to get quantification in."

You hear that strain throughout business: EDP, to do any good, needs hard data, tons of them, needs them fast—and there is a lack of data all through the marketing stream.

The automobile industry is about the only one that really knows who buys each of its products, where the customers live, and other useful bits of information about them. In contrast, another consumer goods manufacturer refused to advertise in Indianapolis because his records show no sales there; actually, his Chicago distributor serves Indianapolis retailers, but the manufacturer's own positive information about sales stops at the distributor level.

Bridging the gap. Yet, it simply isn't true that data do not exist in marketing; they exist in probably greater quantities than in any other business function. Until now there has never been a means to collect the information or to analyze it fast enough for it to be useful.

With the "peripheral" equipment associated with the computer—input-output devices such as the Data-Phone, tape, ticket and card readers, and high-speed printers, for feeding information to the computer and getting it out—the vast gap between collection of information and its analysis has been bridged.

Archibald J. McGill, an industry manager for the Data Processing Div. of International Business Machines Corp., figures that only 5% of the solution of what he calls the distribution problem is the computer, and 95% is the system. "Input-output devices are of more significance in distribution than the computer itself," he says.

There are computers whirring and blinking throughout U.S. business—for the accounting department. Now, with the input and output devices, the marketing department also is finding ways to get information for the computer to work on.

The Machine Knows What's in Stock

While the retailer is by no means in the van in the use of EDP, what's being done in stores around the country is exciting because it shows how much can be done.

You can see the future best, perhaps, at Woodward & Lothrop, Inc., in Washington, D.C. There, C. Robert McBrier, vice-president, finance, has installed what many authorities think is the most advanced EDP system in the country. Soon, Woodward & Lothrop executives every morning will get an 81-page report that, for each of the company's nine stores, will give the previous day's sales by store, by department, by dollar amounts, and a comparison with the previous year-to-date and the trend of sales. A record of sales for selected items will also be available.

The key to this astonishing flood of figures is a special cash register, for which McBrier designed the keyboard. There are eight keys across and nine from top to bottom, in addition to 13 control keys. The salesperson can punch in everything store management needs to know; every detail of every transaction is recorded on optical tape.

Each evening the information on the tape is read by an optical scanner and "exploded" into separate pieces for accounts receivable, accounts payable, inventory management, reordering and other store functions.

More and more. When additional equipment is received later this year and next, Woodward & Lothrop's system will include a direct connection from cash register to computer, a voice response from the computer when a clerk checks the credit standing of a customer, and even a daily report on the sales performance of each person on the selling floor.

Other big department store operations have many elements of what Woodward & Lothrop is doing; Joseph Horne Co., in Pittsburgh, is one step away from a voice response on credit authorization—the computer keeps up to date a list of accounts that, for one reason or another, should not be honored. Bullock's-Magnin Co. on the West Coast has its charge accounts so well organized they can be used for imaginative merchandising.

Goldblatt Bros., Inc., in Chicago, one of the most sophisticated EDP users in the country, even has a Data-Phone system to transmit daily sales reports of tapes from its 29 stores in the area to its State Street headquarters store.

Buyers' new role. Management's daily report of stock condition is already changing one hallowed role in department stores: the preeminence of the buyer. Since retailing began, buyers have been the leading figures, responsible for keeping their stores stocked with salable merchandise. But because of the enormous increase in the number of items a store now carries, the buyer has become too busy with a physical count of stock to try to know what the customer wants and when.

At EDP-equipped stores, management knows before the buyer does what's moving and what isn't. Some buyers find this disconcerting indeed. In the words of Jack Jacobson, Goldblatt's director of electronic data processing, they "don't trust computers and are not analytically inclined."

But others use the freedom EDP has given them to get out on the floor once more to see what customers are like. Jack Hanson, senior vice-president of Macy's New York, says buyers now have a chance to "get back into the market where they were 30 years ago, to get better prices and better merchandise."

Penney's merchandise planning and control manager, Emerson Tolle, sees another advantage to the end of physical stock-taking (Penney's counts stock only every quarter): "Instead of being under the counter counting stock, the sales clerk can be standing up taking care of customers."

Precise weapon. Putting accounts receivable—customer's charge account records—on the computer might seem to be only another accounting procedure. But it can be a merchandising weapon of profitable precision. Macy's has more than 1.3-million charge accounts on magnetic tape. Depending on what it is told to do, the computer will break up those accounts any way the store wants them—by alphabet, by house number, by size of average charge.

Not long ago Macy's had its computer print out a list of all charge customers of the Herald Square store who lived in four counties, and invite them to a special after-hours sale of furniture and furnishings.

The results can't be measured precisely because nothing like it had been done before; but compared with other special sales using radio and direct mail, the computer-based effort cost less and sold more.

Smaller Stock, but More Stores

In food retailing, the problems are different from those in a department store, and EDP has scarcely penetrated the retail end of food distribution.

For one thing, food retailing is about the most hidebound of all businesses dealing with the consumer. For another, a food store's after-tax profit is normally less than 2% on sales—so operators look at the cost of EDP and blanch. Yet, their low rate of return is in itself a reason to get involved with EDP; it offers opportunities for cutting costs and raising profits.

In food processing and warehousing, though, EDP has cut deep, mostly by use of an IBM-developed system known as Impact Inventory Management Program and Control Technique). All major food manufacturers, as well as other companies that sell through supermarkets—Scott Paper Co. and Procter & Gamble Co., for example—have data links between sales offices, plants, distribution and shipping points, and are managing production, warehousing, and shipping by computer-programmed economics.

Latest link. The newest trend is a data link between a manufactourer and a distributor for the automatic ordering of staple items.

This has barely started. Kellogg Co. warehouses are linked with warehouses of Safeway Stores, Inc., on the West Coast and of Wakefern Food Corp., a distributor for a group of New Jersey supermarkets. Pillsbury Co. has a similar hookup with Spartan Stores, Inc., a small chain in the Grand Rapids (Mich.) area—after having proved the procedure in experiments with Kroger Co. and Super Valu Stores, Inc.

Savings with this sort of system can be sensational; James Rude, Pillsbury director of information services and systems, quotes a Spartan official as saying the chain can save enough in lead time and storage to build another store.

There is no longer any question about the marketing power of a data link between supplier and customer. The clincher is what has happened in industrial selling.

Save Customers and Prepare for Systems

The data link between supplier and customer originated on the West Coast with Ducommun, Inc., an industrial distributor, about three years ago [BW Jul. 21'62p64]. It is now in use all over the country, but has reached perhaps its most influential and precedent-setting level in the Houston area.

"Ordermation"—a very well-suited term coined by Industrial Distribution, a McGraw-Hill magazine—was just beginning to be known in Houston when J. K. Bevel, purchasing agent at Hughes Tool Co., took a worry to Jack P. Cunningham, whose Cunningham Bearing Co. does an annual volume of about $1.5-million. Bevel wanted to cut down on the time his buyers were spending in placing repetitive orders, and thought an automatic ordering system would do it.

But he was aware of one danger: When you have a number of distributors in an area, each may use a different system; so a customer dealing with more than one distributor could wind up with a roomful of incompatible systems. Bevel warned Cunningham that, as a customer, he would use one data transmission system and expect his suppliers to conform. But that way, he pointed out, a single distributor could wind up with as many as 18 different systems.

Taking off. From this came the Houston Industrial Distributors Assn. With an IBM salesman coordinating the efforts—the IBM 1001 in conjunction with the Data-Phone is the common transmission device—the association now has 30 distributors "on line" to 10 customers. It will take 40 to 50 customers for the system to remain economically feasible. Cunningham hopes the idea "will really take off once the results begin coming in from the customers already participating."

Although the Houston operation is being studied by groups of industrial distributors in other parts of the country—and is bound to be a pattern—ordermation has not aroused universal enthusiasm. Distributors' reservations come mainly from unfamiliarity with EDP; some fear the system will make them lose contact with customers.

That fear is not shared by Owens-Illinois Glass Co.'s Thomas Browning. He asks: "How much does it mean, for example, if we can cut delivery time for a good customer from six days to one day? It may not mean much in one case; in another, it may mean that we have retained business that might have gone elsewhere. How do you measure that?"

Goal. The data link alone, of course, cannot make a radical cut in delivery time. It is an essential input, though, to a procedure that goes a long way toward the goal of building a "total information system." And that is the goal at Owens-Illinois, at General Mills, Scott Paper, Procter & Gamble, Hotpoint Div. of General Electric, and other long-time EDP users. Westinghouse Electric Corp. is one of the very few companies that already has a total system.

To such companies, inventory management, sales analysis, a rapid order-shipping-billing cycle, though rewarding in themselves, eventually become as routine as the coffee break. But they are a necessary preliminary to more complicated and challenging EDP work—getting the information to use in making the decisions that bring higher profits.

The ultimate question. There's an example of where this is heading in the Carborundum Co., which has been using computers for about 10 years and, says Group Vice-President Robert W. Lear, is "still experimenting." Carborundum, with more than 1,000 programs on computers, is ready for the next plateau, which is defined best by a series of questions Lear asked in a recent speech:

> Which of our districts, salesmen, distributors, customers, markets, and products are the real profit producers? How much does it cost to make a sales call? What does it cost to process an order item? If it's four bucks, can we afford to continue accepting five-buck or even twenty-five-buck orders without some kind of a surcharge or premium?
>
> What was the return on investment from our last promotion? Did we even try to calculate it? Which is more profitable—a direct

sale, or one through a distributor? Did our last price adjustment take into consideration the distribution cost for each item, or did we just study our factory gross margins and assume an arbitrary average for everything below the line?

Those questions get to the heart of the reason for using computers in marketing, for you can't answer them without getting data. Then, for the first time in marketing, management can ask the question: "What if . . .?"

II. MARKETING BY MATHEMATICS

Dr. Wendell R. Smith, president of the Marketing Science Institute, tells of a former business associate who constantly used computers to ask the question: "What if . . .?" He explained to Smith:

> I can ask the computer without starting a rumor. If I went to the controller and asked him what would happen to our profits if we dropped a certain product line, it would be all over the plant before lunch that we were getting ready to go out of that particular business.

Storage in a computer of mathematical models that simulate a market or that duplicate a marketing situation is perhaps the ultimate contribution EDP can make to marketing.

C. A. Swanson, manager of P&G's Data Processing Systems Dept., lists four things his company expects from EDP: savings of money, accuracy, speed, and "doing things not otherwise possible."

There is wide agreement that model-building and simulation is perhaps the most significant of those things not otherwise possible without a computer. As of now, an electronic digital computer is the only device that can handle variable on top of variable and give management a choice of alternatives while there's still time to make a decision.

Changing management. In a masterful little book, Mathematical Models and Marketing Management, published by the Harvard Business School last year, Prof. Robert D. Buzzell wrote:

> The model-builder offers a general, systematic approach to the analysis of management problems. To the extent that this approach is accepted and implemented, fundamental changes may take place in the practice of marketing management.

The biggest change that model-building is bringing about in marketing management is almost defamatory to mention: It is forcing management to plan, and to define its goals. To John Stolle, of Booz, Allen & Hamilton, one of the things that has slowed down the use of EDP and model-building in marketing is simply the fact that "it exposes the non-planners."

As Buzzell brings out, few developments in marketing have churned up so much skepticism and downright suspicion among marketing executives as model-building and simulation. The man who rose through the ranks from salesman to vice-president for marketing usually has little sympathy for the "fellow who's never met a payroll"—and into that category fall most of the mathematicians who are skilled at model-building and simulation.

But already models are regulating some marketing programs.

It's Better Than a Crystal Ball

Just about a year ago, Chrysler Corp.'s top management asked its planners the sort of question with which all marketing efforts must begin, for it was about the future.

"Can you tell us what the market for heavy trucks will be in 1970?"

The market analysis broke out the significant components of the heavy truck market for every year back to World War II. They determined the relationship of truck sales, by weight class, to population, national income, industrial production, and so on.

In about a month, they had a mathematical model—a simulation—of the heavy truck market. They found that of 36 variables in the model only about a dozen had substantial significance. Applying these variables in different combinations, they plotted the range for heavy truck sales in 1970.

Shortly afterward, Chrysler made an effort to merge with Mack Trucks, Inc., but was restrained by the Justice Dept.

What's new? There was nothing new in the Chrysler people's approach to the problem. Examination of past relationships—multiple regression analysis—is a standard statistical technique, and mathematical models are ancient.

The new thing was the speed with which the analysts were able to process an enormous amount of data and in only a month or so give management the information needed for a decision. That speed was due to the electronic computer.

Light on lamps. General Electric Co. (one of its divisions was the very first to put the computer to work on business problems, in 1954) has at least two models routinely assisting marketing management. One is in the Photo Lamp Dept. This division has 2,000 distributors, who customarily order in September (Christmas is the peak selling time for photo lamps) and pay in January.

The model is constructed on the assumption that each distributor has an interest problem; it takes into account 25 different types of distributors and interest rates and arrangements. It is designed to give answers to the question: What will happen if we let distributors delay payment—will they order more lamps?

At one of GE's heavy apparatus operations, a model is producing results that you'd expect only from a ouija board. This division sells on a

Computers Begin to Solve the Marketing Puzzle

bid basis, and the computer model is programmed to propose bids on the likelihood of what competitive bids will be. Says a GE man: "They have been amazingly accurate."

Routine. Simulation with computer models also is routine at all of the big package goods companies such as P&G, Pillsbury, General Foods, Libby, McNeill & Libby, and General Mills. Usually, companies such as these test in models the presumed results of price changes and promotions and what the probabilities are of competitive responses.

Producers of consumer durables use models to forecast sales. International Minerals & Chemical Corp. has a model of its complete agricultural chemical business (65% of the company's total volume), which has a strange cycle: Its year begins in July, but no fertilizer sales are made until the following spring.

Surprised admen. Models were at the root of all the hoopla in advertising agency circles a year or so ago about using computers to select media. The intention was to simulate a market area, then test the exposure gained by differing combinations of media buys. The problem, to a large extent, was proper data. The agencies didn't have it. Now they are collecting it—and are finding some strange byproducts.

At Leo Burnett Co., Inc., accumulation of demographic and economic data for one account showed a wide open area for a new product. At another agency, the collection of data showed that the agency's principal client should have very high on its magazine schedule one of the "confession" books. The magazine has never made a presentation to the agency —and the client is not yet ready to concede that his customers have such reading tastes.

The agencies are still far from satisfied with the data that can be obtained. The biggest hole is pointed out by Seymour Banks, a vice-president at Burnett: "What happens when people are exposed to an ad?" The agencies, meanwhile, are doing the best they can with what they have.

The top agencies all have simulation models; Norman Sondak, data processing director at J. Walter Thompson Co., says: "We continue to build models closer and closer to reality." And at several agencies, work is beginning on models that simulate test markets.

Bringing Marketing into Management

Advertising practitioners have always presumed that what they do is more art than science. So it may seem strange that all of the larger agencies now have people practicing operations research, which is presumed to be a science—the science of management. In reality it is not strange at all, for part of operations research deals with the weighing of alternatives— and the advertising man may have more numeric alternatives to deal with than anybody.

A media man with one ad and 30 media where he can spot it can be confronted with more than one billion combinations. The computer—that big adding machine—is the only way to run quickly through those combinations and weed out the obviously worthless.

What combinations remain are subject to management decision. The example used is in advertising, but it could just as well be in other marketing functions. Throughout marketing these days you are finding the computer used to weed out the obviously worthless things to do, leaving management with only a few alternatives to consider—sometimes, even, alternatives leading to a go or no-go decision:

What would be the returns now, compared to 60 days from now, on a cents-off promotion? Would it be more efficient to ship to Point A from Plant 1, or build a new distribution location to serve Point A and a potential future Point B? Would it be more economic to double our order for fast-moving baby food and receive shipments every other week rather than every week, even though it ties up more capital? Would it be more profitable to kill immediately Old Product, the life cycle of which is ending, and use the resources to push New Product harder?

Total. Decisions such as these involve determining the proper allocation of a company's total resources—in other words, operations research. Only now are the numbers so necessary for operations research being assembled for the marketing function, for only now is there a way to work with them: the computer. The more EDP sophistication pervades marketing, the closer a company moves toward a total management information system, toward true operations research. Says John Stolle, the OR man at Booz, Allen & Hamilton: "When we add marketing to our collection of trophies, we will be able to build models of total business systems."

It will still be some years before marketing's scalp hangs from the belt of the OR man, but the way marketing data already are being used indicates some changes the future may bring.

III. BIG BROTHER WILL ALWAYS WATCH

What's ahead for marketing because of EDP is summed up pithily by Michael H. Halbert, technical director of the Marketing Science Institute: "A man can no longer get away with the excuse 'We've thought about it, but we don't know how to get it.'"

Today, if "it" exists in numbers, or can be assigned numerical values, "it" can be used in an EDP system. What this means, explains Robert G. Dee, vice-president, marketing, at RCA Electronic Data Processing Div., is that in the future "marketing staffs are going to get a greater amount of direction, and get a better hit value for the money spent."

One of the first groups to feel the effects of this will be the salesmen—no matter what they sell.

Bobbie Brooks, Inc., Cleveland-based manufacturer of ladies' sportswear, presents a fairly common example of what is on the way. Each week, the salesman gets a report showing the current orders and past activity of the stores in his area. This tells him where he should be spending his time.

Bobbie Brooks also prints out a report of each salesman's results by style, color, and frequency of order. "By looking at the report," says Burton L. Kamberg, vice-president, "our supervisors can tell if a man has perhaps prejudged a garment and left it in his car rather than taking it into the stores." If he's taking Thursdays off, or avoiding certain stores, that shows up, too.

"The salesman gets used to living in a goldfish bowl," Kamberg says, "and we don't stress the Big Brother side of the computer, but the helpful side. It gives the salesman an excellent selling tool. He can, for example, tell his customers what styles are going best across the country, and help them in their purchasing."

Death of a Salesman, Birth of a Consultant

The computer not only is changing the selling function: it is going to change the salesman. He will have to know far more about merchandising than he does now; he will have to know far more about his customer's business and how it fits into an EDP system—already, some food companies report that their salesmen have had to show distributors how to fit new products into the IBM Impact system, which began with food distributors. In short, the salesman will have to be more of a consultant than ever.

Salesmen's week. Herbert M. Cleaves, senior vice-president of General Foods Corp., describes the week of a food salesman in the computer age—but it could just as well be any salesman:

Monday, the salesman calls on a major food chain, passes right by the buyer and goes to the chain's home economist to ask her support for a new recipe that will be used in a regional promotion. Next, he discusses details of the promotion's advertising program with the chain's advertising manager, and of store displays with the merchandising manager.

Tuesday, the salesman goes from store to store explaining the promotion to the managers and making suggestions for tie-ins and displays. Wednesday, he is in the chain's warehouse to learn how his company can pack a product differently to save the customer money.

Thursday, the salesman is back in the stores, to explain a new shelving arrangement his own company's market planners had worked out to solve a particular problem. The salesman spends all day Friday in his home office working with his district sales analyst on a presentation to a chain that does not carry his products.

The week has passed, Cleaves emphasizes, and the salesman "hasn't personally made a traditional sales pitch or taken an order." The orders have been transmitted electronically, "and his supervisor knows before he does how well his various marketing efforts are being translated into orders."

Eyes and ears. Data transmission devices cast a long shadow, blotting out the routine calls that salesmen have been accustomed to make.

So in the future the salesman who now spends a good part of his time writing orders is going to have to spend more time digging out new accounts, and ideas for new products.

He will have one other, potentially enormously valuable function. He will be his company's eyes and ears, its intelligence agent, in his territory, compiling information on market growth and development, competitive efforts, and everything his company needs to know.

Lots of Products and Plans for Retailers

In perhaps no area of marketing is EDP going to make as many changes as in retailing—which lags not only in use of EDP, but frequently in modern business thinking.

In a study of department store control systems, Douglas J. Dalrymple, assistant professor of business administration at the University of California at Los Angeles, found

> that a small minority of the merchandising executives . . . believed that stock turnover was an important control factor, but to most executives it was only a vague concept of secondary importance.

Yet, fast stock turnover was the weapon the discounters turned loose on department stores 15 years ago. The higher the turnover, the higher the profit on a constant amount of money used in the business.

But the computer is forcing retailers to become aware of the importance of stock turnover.

The EDP way. Stock turnover is usually about four times a year for general merchandise and about twenty times for dry groceries. There's a traditional way to turn it faster: Simply sell more without carrying a higher inventory. But it's a rare merchant who can do that.

The EDP way to get a higher turnover is by keeping such fresh data on sales that you know what's moving fast and what isn't, and by having a data hookup that will give you automatic replenishment of the fast-moving or high-profit items. In food retailing, one estimate is that a 24-hour replenishment cycle will reduce inventory by 30%, without creating out-of-stock situations that hurt sales.

In general merchandising, Seymour Helfant, head of the Small Stores Div. of the National Retail Merchants Assn., says he has reports of stores using EDP that lower their inventory by 25% and increase profits by 25%. And a specialty store that formerly turned its stock six times a year has added one full turn.

Analysis of information handled by a store's EDP system can also guide store executives in when, what, and how to promote.

Big and small. The benefits of EDP are not reserved for the big stores and chains. "Any retailer, regardless of size, will be able to be

Computers Begin to Solve the Marketing Puzzle

on-line to a big processing center," says James Hotchkiss, assistant director of product planning of National Cash Register Co., which probably has more experience than any other computer manufacturer with the problems of small retailers. NCR, of course, has data processing centers throughout the country [BW Aug.8'64,p66], as do GE, IBM, and other computer manufacturers. NRMA is sponsoring a cooperative processing center for small retailers.

An example of what a data processing center can do for small retailers is found at Santoro Management Consultants, Inc., in Houston. Santoro has 60 clients—whose volumes range from $50,000 to $500,000—for whom it provides a full package: budgets, advertising, merchandising, sales analysis and projection, inventory records. Says Mrs. Daisy Strother, of Fort Worth: "The service took the butterflies out of my stomach. We know which department is making money . . . our buying is controlled, dead merchandise eliminated and we have reorder money."

At present, most of the small stores mail or deliver tapes to the processing centers. But when Hotchkiss says small stores can be "on-line," he means a direct data link to some establishment using a computer. Once such a link is created, it will drive right through a barrier that (excepting, again, only the automobile business) still separates a manufacturer from sure knowledge of what's happening on the retail level.

A few months ago, B. S. Durant, president of RCA Sales Corp., did a little dreaming for a group of marketing executives. RCA, in common with other consumer electronics producers, is always in doubt as to how much of its product is in distributors' warehouses and how much is moving out of retailers' doors.

Durant began by conceding that a small retailer will probably never be able to afford a computer, "but he could afford a low-cost transactor of some type. . . . Before the dealer goes home at night, he would put the transactor device on standby. Somewhere along about a quarter after two, a central computer would interrogate the transactor and take from it the data covering the dealer's daily business transactions." Durant offered a new, and provocative thought: The independent distributor might have that central computer and be the retailer's data processing center.

If the distributor's computer could interrogate the retailer's transactor, then each night the manufacturer's computer could interrogate the disributor's computer. The next morning, the manufacturer's executives would have—for the first time in their experience—actual records of their product sales at retail the day before.

Gleaming vistas. This opens vistas that gleam so brightly that any marketing man has to shield his eyes to avoid snow blindness. New product performance could be gauged day-by-day and promotion money deployed for maximum effectiveness. A product that isn't going to make it could be withdrawn from the market before it hurt either profits or reputation significantly. When you know precisely what is selling where, and when, you can identify your customers, plan future promotions intelligently, simulate all sorts of situations.

You would even know enough to advertise in Indianapolis.

24 A Reporting System for Marketing and Sales*

LIONEL E. GRIFFITH

Properly constructed, a reporting program would generate information suitable for each level of management, some serving to assist in directing the main functions of the business and other information serving in the control of operations.

All businesses require information in order to achieve their objectives. This information may come from many sources. Some sources are external to the company—for example, in our business we require a knowledge of the female population because we are marketing products for this part of the population rather than the total. Other information a company uses is developed internally—that is, from data elements on records initiated by the company itself. Our purpose here is to examine some aspects of this kind of information, with only passing reference to information developed externally. We will discuss the "range" and "intensity" of the information we are obliged to develop and the responsibilities of the areas entrusted with the developmental work.

What do we mean by range? Marketing direction, to function properly, must have either insight or knowledge of the testing of products, the activity of accounts, the activity and distribution of products, and a host of other facts. If we have insight, we seldom need reports. Unfortunately, insight is so rare that we may as well dismiss the thought from our minds. Knowledge of a situation depends largely upon reported facts and requires a reporting structure to insure that the information collected is sufficient and produced at least cost in a systematic way. A well-designed reporting system for marketing and selling purposes would provide an accurate picture of each facet of the marketing and selling operation—from the way in which products are distributed as compared to the distribution of the buying population to the effectiveness of sales personnel in the selling job itself. A reporting system which allows for this would have an adequate range of information.

*Reprinted from **Control Through Information,** A.M.A. Management Bulletin No. 24, publication of American Management Association, Inc., pp. 17–21.

(text continued on p. 289)

Exhibit 1. **Tentative Range of Marketing and Selling Activities**

Activities	Elements Probably Involved in Measurement or Control of the Activity
Market testing	Testing of products at customer and consumer level. Test groups and control groups. External information on adequacy of test and analysis of test results.
Product activity	Measurement of product movement and activity with stores and consumers compared with goals or targets set. Territory, district, and regional movement. Comparisons of movement of the various styles.
Account activity	Knowledge of live and dead accounts. Reactivation of dead accounts still in existence. Comparisons with previous years of activity by product through outlets. Potential activity and quotas.
Advertising	Advertising media involved. Plans now operated by company within media and their cost in relation to sales. Comparisons of advertising costs by media in relation to sales. Effectiveness of the forms of advertising in relation to various products.
Promotions	Measurement of the effectiveness of promotions of the various products by region, class of trade, type of outlet, district, territory, and so forth. Measurement of promotion testing by independent and objective means. Measurement of promotion gimmicks upon cost of operations. Measurement of impact of kinds of promotions on consumer.
Contests for operators	Measurement of individual contests: operators, district managers, regional managers, and so on. Effectiveness of various forms of contests. Types of contests used in one's own and other industries. Comparison of contest results to forecast.
Experimental selling	Measurement of special selling plans involved such as the chain automatic merchandising plan (consignment selling). Design of the plan. Test group of stores and control group. Independent analysis of results of test.
Maintenance of territories	Report on territories not covered. Effect on sales. Turnover of operators by territory, district, region, and division. Number of territory changes. Effect on accuracy of reports incorporating comparisons involving territories, and so forth.

Customer service	Measurement of customer service drawn from customer correspondence and customer-operator contact, internal error situations, shortages in shipments, poor communications with customers and other factors which affect customer service, and of business lost—with the reasons given.
Forecasting	Effectiveness of forecasts—short term and long term. Forecasting techniques. Adequacy of methods and recording of results. Knowledge of forecasts of the growth of our industry. Population forecasts, national, regional, and others. Population movements. Forecasts related specifically to the company's buying population. Age groups. National and international considerations and effect on business.
Control of returns	Measurement of returns by reason. Returns history of company by product. Cost of returns problem.
Operator records	Reports assisting operator to maintain effective and accurate operator records, giving comparisons of volumes of business by product group and store with previous years. Call reports and comparisons with shipments. Analysis of store-inventory reports to give movement through stores or classes of trade.
Cost control	Development of budget reports to allow measurement of activities in terms of cost and cost control over them.

"Range" may be defined as the full extent of all selling and marketing activities existing for the specific purpose of furthering and expanding the profitability, size, or possibilities of the company. Exhibit 1 is a tentative range of marketing and selling activities.

What is intensity? In any reporting system for marketing, we are concerned with products, territories, salesmen, and so on. If we design a reporting system which allows us information, say, on the ten products we presently manufacture but not for the five products we propose to produce next year, we have failed to develop a reporting system with the necessary intensity. Lack of intensity of any data or information element implies a lack of elasticity or flexibility in our thinking.

Development of the range of the reports required and the intensity of the data within them is a prime responsibility of the marketing division. Important technological advances tend to extend both range and intensity as the years advance. For instance, the advent of television introduced a new medium into the advertising picture. Similarly, electronic data-processing techniques now allow information to be generated more accurately and in

(continued on p. 292)

Exhibit 2. A Reporting Work Sheet and Checklist

SECTION I
1. Is the report presently being prepared? Yes____ No____
2. What is the name of the report, or, if the report is new, what name do you propose?

   3. What is the purpose of this report?

   4. How have you accomplished your purpose without the report?

   5. How much in dollars is this report worth to you on a yearly basis?
      $_____

   6. How much is it now costing you per year to accomplish your purpose?
      $_____

SECTION II
   1. What reporting units are to be covered?
        a. Customer.   f. County.
        b. Customer group.   g. State.
        c. Territory.   h. Nation.
        d. Trading area.   i. Division.
        e. Television area.   j. Other.
   2. What types of data should be included?
        a. Orders received.   d. Unshipped orders.
        b. Shipments.   e. Advertising payments.
        c. Credits.   f. Other.
   3. How should the data be shown?
        a. In units.   d. By product detail.
        b. In dollars.   e. By product line.
        c. In units and dollars.   f. By product totals.
   4. What time period is to be covered? How frequently should the report be issued? What accumulative data are to be shown?

	Time Period to be Covered	Frequency of Issue	Accumulative Data
Daily	_____	_____	_____
Weekly	_____	_____	_____
Monthly	_____	_____	_____
Quarterly (cal.)	_____	_____	_____
Quarterly (fisc.)	_____	_____	_____
Annually (cal.)	_____	_____	_____
Annually (fisc.)	_____	_____	_____

   5. What comparative information is needed to make the report most useful?
        a. Previous history.

b. Pre-set goals, quotas, or standards.

c. Percentage calculations.

d. Other.

6. How soon after the close of the time period being covered is the report needed?

   _____ days after close of period.
   _____ weeks after close of period.

7. How many copies of the report are required, and who should receive them?

Copy number	Send to	Position
1		
2		
3		
4		
5		

SECTION III

If you can visualize the finished report format and would like to propose a specific layout of the report content, please show the format you prefer in the space provided here.

1. Salesman:

2. Customer:
   Type.
   Advertising agreement status.
   Buyer.
   Potential.

3. Geography:
   Territory.
   Trading area.
   TV area.
   District.
   Region.
   State.
   County.

4. Product:
   Product.
   Product group.
   Product line.
   Price.
   Units and dollars ordered.

(Exhibit continued on the following page)

A Reporting System for Marketing and Sales

Units and dollars shipped.
Units and dollars unshipped.
Units and dollars back-ordered.
Units and dollars deleted.
Units and dollars returned.
Units and dollars of sales forecast.

5. **Miscellaneous:**
Credit reason.
Invoice and credit memo number.
Orders canceled.
Promotion identification.
Birth rate.
Population movement.
Physical characteristics.

---

more varied forms than before. The construction of systems to produce the reports and the costing of them is a prime responsibility of the finance division (in some companies, an administrative services division). It is also a responsibility of this division to develop realistic reporting-program installation schedules and to develop at the least cost adequate machine and manual resources to do the job. If both marketing and finance do their jobs properly, then general management is in a position to determine the extent of the reporting program required in terms of the overall present and future requirements of the company in relation to objectives, resources, and cost.

We must develop a series of practical reporting programs at various expense levels, which will allow us a choice in terms of what is desirable from a cost viewpoint at any particular time. This will also permit us to select a better program for the time when the cost position allows this. Once we have done the difficult task of thinking out the "intellectual" aspects of the range and intensity of marketing information, we are well on the way to the solution of the problem of developing an adequate reporting program.

The extent to which reports are prepared to govern any element of the range must, to a large degree, depend upon the money we spend to maintain this element of the range. If we spend several million dollars on advertising and only thousands on the development of contests, we have indirectly indicated the relative value to us of reports in these two areas and the extent to which we should develop reports to control and guide our outlay. As a general rule—although this is not invariably the case—a more extensive reporting system is required to support and control the expenditure of large sums of money than of small sums. We should remember, however, that elements of the range that bristle with imponderables cannot readily be given a monetary value.

The design of each report format is a joint responsibility of marketing and finance. Since each report format will include basic static or fixed data —such as product number, territory, name and address of account, number of account, salesman, and many others—we are obliged to construct a list of all such data elements available from the present systems network. The degree to which we are required to extend the list in order to develop an adequate reporting system indicates the degree to which present systems and thinking are inadequate for generating the proper information to support the marketing effort. In developing the report formats, a work sheet and checklist is used. An example is given in Exhibit 2.

Data elements in the marketing and selling areas of the business include the following. This list is not necessarily complete but is used as an illustration.

1. *Salesman.*
   Salesman.
   Sales quota.
   Contest quota.
   Sample quota.
   Sample shipments.
2. *Customer.*
   Customer.

These are some of the basic elements of a designed reporting structure, suitable for application to any part of the business, although we have stated the prime responsibilities of finance and marketing in developing an adequate reporting program to support the activities of marketing and selling. Reporting programs are usually not thought out in this way but have been based on trial and error. Because of technological advances in the area of data handling and information development and the increasing volume and complexity of paperwork operations, which in essence are data and information, we can no longer follow an unsystematic approach. We must *design* a reporting system, regardless of the effort required, so that we will have a coherent, practical, least-cost program.

An examination of the usual reporting program does not seem to indicate that we have developed programs to measure and direct the activities of marketing and selling operations. We may be wrong in this, but until we have the assurance that it does form a part of a plan, we feel that a great deal of effort could be wasted. Even though we may not develop the perfect reporting structure, we will at least have a reasonable premise for the reports we produce in terms of cost. More significantly, we will be able to use the resources at our disposal with something approaching efficiency.

Reports are designed to identify action areas; to accumulate history for comparison purposes which may trigger action in the future; to allow comparisons to be made of performance to standards set with a view to doing something about the matter; to keep all elements of management informed of the size and nature of certain aspects of our business; to assess "error conditions" for size and to keep these conditions under control; to assist in forecasting the future so that we may take corrective action before problems become so severe that major surgery is essential; and for a host of other reasons. Properly constructed, a reporting program would generate reports suitable for each level of management, some serving to assist us in directing the main functions of the business and others serving as control devices over the domestic departmental resources needed to support given functions or subdivisions of the business.

25 A Corporate Information System for Distribution Management*

ALLAN D. DALE
RICHARD J. LEWIS

The relative inability to measure the efficiency, in terms of profit, of distribution decisions has been a constant thorn in the side of marketing. This article describes how the combination of information systems and accounting concepts should provide relevant measures for evaluating such efficiency.

THE NATURE OF INFORMATION SYSTEMS

Information systems are means, not ends, intended to provide clear and significant data. The ultimate uses (ends) of the information determine the design of the system (means). For instance, governmental information systems include those applied to population census, political apportionment, and unemployment calculation. Industrial information systems, crucial to evaluation and control of profit-making activity, involve location of plants, design of distribution facilities, and measurement of marketing efficiency.

Among the criteria whereby general information systems are evaluated are maximum usable information and flexibility; minimum cost, bias, and error; provision of flow data in space and time; geographical homogeneity of data; and compatibility of data with other information. These criteria admit interaction. For example, minimum bias and error require painstaking collection methods. Such collection methods are often time-consuming and therefore costly. Consequently, an attempt to minimize bias and error normally would be accompanied by increasing costs. What, on the other hand, are the primary requirements for "maximum usable information?"

1. The information-collection form should resemble, as much as possible, the final form in which the data are used.

*Reprinted from **Business Review,** Winter, 1964–65, pp. 11–22. Published by Center for Research, College of Business Administration, University of Houston.

2. The information collected should be the greatest consistent with the costs incurred and the ends to which the data are applicable.

If the data apply to many end uses, the information-system design approaches maximum flexibility and minimum costs. A general system may cost more than any one special system, but the general system is usually less expensive than the cost of *all* special systems that it replaces.

Primarily because of prohibitive costs, most information systems do not collect data continuously. Continuous information offers several unique advantages, among which perhaps the most important is to recognize trends as they occur. "Flow data" provide a motion picture of activities (profit-and-loss statement) rather than comparative snapshots (balance sheets). The snapshot approach, which gathers information at points in time, does not permit evaluation of activities occurring between those points.

Equally important as temporal flow data are their spatial (geographic) counterparts. Reporting the origins and destinations of inbound and outbound shipments enables management to discern changes in distribution patterns and to decide appropriately the location of plant and distribution facilities, modes of transportation, allocation of sales and promotional efforts.

A critical attribute of an information system is its provision of homogeneous (unbiased) geographic data, defining markets in compatible terms other than the political designation of cities, counties, states, and census tracts.

AN ANALYSIS OF SOME EXISTING INFORMATION SYSTEMS

Picadad

The PICADAD Information System is currently being used by the Bureau of Census for sampling bills of lading and then coding the information in terms of PI (Place Identification), CA (Characteristics of Area), and DAD (Machine Procedure for Computing Distance and Direction).[1] The place identification consists of a five-digit number which identifies the city or town and state of shipment origin and destination. The area characteristics are represented by a four-digit number showing the census division, the state, the city size, and area characterization as a Standard Metropolitan Statistical Area. This permits matching data from bills of lading with data from the Census Bureau's *County City Data Book,* which deals with counties, cities, states, and Standard Metropolitan Statistical Areas. The computation of distance and direction is accomplished through a latitude-longitude coordinate system; coordinates pinpoint the place as a point in space. The

---

[1] Donald E. Church, *PICADAD—A System for Machine Processing of Geographic and Distance Factors in Transportation and Marketing Data.* U.S. Department of Commerce, Bureau of the Census Preliminary Draft, Washington 25, D. C., June 6, 1961.

first four digits represent location in terms of miles north of a baseline that lies south of Texas. The last four digits are the number of miles west of a designated baseline.

PICADAD has many desirable characteristics of a general information system. When one considers the amount and types of data provided, PICADAD seems relatively inexpensive. Since the data are machine-coded and cross-referenced to census data, PICADAD provides highly compatible and useful information. Although the system is capable of providing temporal flow data, PICADAD is being used only to collect samples at various intervals. PICADAD also collects information on a geographic dimension. However, the unit of collection, limited to the various sizes of political subdivisions or a given point of latitude and longitude, inhibits flexibility. PICADAD can define a unique political area, but markets know no political boundaries.

Government Census Data

The federal government's huge program for gathering and compiling data includes the Census of Population, the Census of Housing, the Census of Agriculture, the Census of Business, and the Census of Manufacturers. A Census of Transportation soon will be added to this list. Although the cost of such data is very high to the federal government, the cost to private users is initially quite nominal. The expense may increase, when the firm transforms the data to meet its needs, e.g., when data needed by a firm are reported on the basis of states, while the firm's territories are defined in terms of counties. Since the federal government's units of collection are cities, counties, SMSA's, states, regions, and minor political subdivisions, the flexibility of data use is limited to these units. Considering the amount of data available in this form, it is not surprising to find most sales regions and territories defined on the basis of these political divisions. The greatest criticism of census data is its "comparative snapshot" nature. Not only are motion pictures of activities absent, but the "snapshots" are widely separated.

Input-Output Analysis

In 1947 the United States Department of Labor used an analysis in which firms were aggregated into industries. The purchases of each industry from every other industry were recorded. Each of these purchases was regarded as part of the output of the selling industry and part of the input of the purchasing industry; consequently, this method was called Input-Output Analysis. Ratios were computed between the output of an industry and each of its inputs. From these ratios, rough estimates were made of the effect on all industries of a given increase in sales of any one. For example, if consumers decided to increase their purchases of major appliances, the effects on the appliance industry and on all supplying industries could be traced. Input-Output Analysis exemplifies a highly specialized information system that is difficult to replace by a general information system.

Corporate Accounting Systems

A system of accounting used for determining profit or loss and income tax must, by the nature of its objectives, concentrate on the actual dollars exchanged and actual costs which required dollar outflows by the corporation. Due to this orientation, little is provided in the area of sales and distribution cost analysis. Such "costs" as special promotional allowances and discounts, or freight absorption, which result in a reduction in dollars received, do not appear as costs of making a particular sale. It is doubtful that anyone would argue that these are not costs, since the only reason for granting such concessions should be that the sale would not have been made without them.

Accounting systems provided temporal motion pictures of financial activities. Production cost accounting provides adequate spatial flow data; however, sales and distribution cost accounting provides little spatial flow data. In general, cost accounting adequately analyzes production costs; however, more attention to sales and distribution cost analysis is needed.

Sales Records

Although sales records, such as invoices, bills of lading, freight bills, sales slips, salesmen's reports, and inventory records, offer many data, if an attempt is made to aggregate them into a general information system, numerous problems arise. The total cost of all these reports reflects very high cost per unit of usable information. One of the main reasons for the high unit cost is the large amount of duplication of information among the reports. The combining of the data in these reports is extremely difficult due to the different bases of collection.

When estimating distribution costs within a sales territory, information is needed on modes of transportation used, distances shipped, origin and destination of shipments, the weight of shipments, the frequency of shipments, and handling costs. All of these data must be oriented toward the specific territory being analyzed. The firm is faced with a costly and time-consuming process requiring the sorting by geographical area and the merging of many department records.

The Proposed General Information System — GEMINI

The proposed general information system is based upon a grid superimposed over the entire United States. This system allows neutral identification with the defined area limited only by the size of the block within the grid.

History of Grid Systems

The Railway Express Agency Grid System. Apparently the first corporate use of a grid system for the United States was by the Railway Express Agency during the 1800's. The grid was composed of the one-degree lines of latitude and longitude which crossed the United States. These lines were renumbered and the new numbers used to provide a co-ordinate system for identifying any block within the grid. This simplified rate-making by reducing the number of rate base points from several hundred thousand points to nine hundred fifty-two blocks.

Corporate Grid Systems. In a speech before the National Freight Traffic Association, Mr. Gilbert P. Church, Assistant Director of the Traffic Department, E. I. DuPont, mentioned a grid system of identifying origins and destinations currently being used by his company.[2] From his remarks the DuPont system seems very similar to PICADAD. Mr. Charles D. Duffy, General Traffic Manager for the Westinghouse Electric Company, called for the development of a grid system for the solution of distribution problems in an address before Delta Nu Alpha transportation fraternity. He specifically mentioned that the system should have the following characteristics:

1. "Common languages that are common to all modes and all shippers for places (origins and destinations) and for commodities."
2. "The common language for place-names should have the following characteristics:

    . . . be a unique number of each specific pier, siding, municipality, etc.

    . . . have a logical sequence to perform one or more of the following functions: automatically identify state and county.

    . . . have a grid characteristic for mathematical solution of distribution problems."

Yaseen's Grid System. Leonard C. Yaseen, who developed this grid system, is a senior partner in Fantus Factory Locating Service. He uses his system to locate the center of markets for plant location. The following procedure is used in constructing the grid and calculating the center of markets for plant location:

1. First, a large-scale map of the market area to be serviced by the new plant is obtained, and an overlay is made on graph paper. (It is imperative that the number of squares per unit of measurement be equal in each direction.)
2. Customer locations (identified by code) are plotted on the graph paper according to their graphic position determined from the base map.
3. Horizontal and vertical axis lines are constructed with their origin as close to the lower left-hand corner as possible. The location of these lines with respect to the plotted points is immaterial, provided the entire market area is included within them. The graph now represents quadrant one of a Cartesian coordinate.
4. A uniform scale is laid out along the horizontal or "X" axis and the vertical or "Y" axis.

---

[2] Gilbert P. Church, "The Use of Computers for Improved Control of Transportation Costs and Service," an address before the National Freight Traffic Association, White Sulphur Springs, W. Va., June 3, 1963.

5. The number of distance units along the "X" axis and along the "Y" axis of each destination are found and then entered in a table.
6. An arithmetic mean is determined along the "X" axis by adding all of the distance units and then dividing by the number of points plotted. The arithmetic mean along the "Y" axis is determined in a similar manner.
7. That point located at the intersection of the mean number of units along the "X" axis and the mean number of units along the "Y" axis is the geographic center of markets. It is a "simple" geographic center in that each of the destinations has been weighted equally with no regard to the actual magnitude of tonnage to the individual point.

Yaseen then adds tonnages to the above calculations, arriving at a "weighted" geographic center of markets.[3]

The Proposed Grid System and Its Uses—GEMINI

The proposed grid system is basically a modification of the REA System. It begins with the one-degree latitude and longitude lines which cross the United States. Each one-degree block of latitude and longitude is then separated into two hundred and fifty-six sub-blocks. The number of sub-blocks is the result of dividing each degree of latitude and longitude into sixteen parts.

Since these blocks are derived from latitude and longitude lines, they are not squares but more nearly rectangles of varying sizes. The sizes of the sub-blocks vary from 4.3 miles by 2.9 miles between the 48th and 49th degree parallels to 4.3 miles by 3.9 miles between the 25th and 26th parallels. Since each of the original 952 REA blocks has been subdivided into 256 sub-parts, the new systems provides 243,712 unique block locations.[4] Once the grid system had been developed, the latitude and longitude numbers were dropped and a unique set of coding numbers for all the blocks was adopted. In addition to providing unique locational numbers for all blocks, the coding system also provides a Cartesian coordinate system for the measurement of relative location and distance. All of the points of origin and destination as shown on bills of lading, freight bills, sales invoices, and other corporate reports are identified by the code number of the geographic block involved. With this system, an "area" can be defined without the use of political boundaries, by agglomerating the specific blocks needed.

---

[3] Leonard C. Yaseen, *Plant Location* (New York: American Research Council, 1960).

[4] The grid block system described has been programmed for the Michigan State University Control Data 3600 Computer. It has been labeled as the MSU-GEMINI Information System, which emphasizes its uses in geographic market analysis.

GEMINI is designed as a general information system. Therefore its total cost should be less than the sum of the total costs of the special systems that it replaces. Otherwise, the system could still be justified if it provides significantly more useful information. GEMINI data are extremely useful because of the common coding system used in collection. GEMINI is highly flexible because it can describe any "area" in neutral terms and in any manner desired. For example, the coding system of the grid is used to identify the point of origin and point of destination of all the movements of a company's goods. Markets are then defined in terms of the sequence of blocks necessary to describe adequately the size of the company's sales operations in various areas. With GEMINI, markets can be identified primarily by the difference in the flows of a company's product mix into an area. This allows the market area to be defined without using political divisions. Therefore, the grid system permits a firm to define markets in terms of the actual area. A minimum degree of error is caused by the unit of description being rectangular, while the area described is irregular in configuration. An area can be redefined at any time desired simply by aggregating a new set of blocks. When the re-classification of an area becomes desirable, it is not necessary to change the reporting system since the data were originally reported on the basis of the small unique locational blocks. Flow information for distribution and sales analysis is provided by the electronic data processing of the coded information found on the bills of lading, freight bills, sales invoices, and other corporate reports. Since all of these instruments show the date and location of the activity involved, temporal and spatial flow data are provided. The use of this standard coding system results in complete compatibility of all internal information. The use of external data creates a problem; nearly all public data are reported on the basis of political divisions but the grid system is not oriented towards these divisions. This problem is partially overcome by the aggregation of the blocks needed to approximate the political division desired. Since political boundaries are normally stable, this task would only have to be done once for each political division desired.

SOME SPECIFIC APPLICATIONS OF GEMINI

A Model for Evaluation of Distribution Warehouse Location in Alternative Sub-Market Areas

One of the most important competitive tools is rapid delivery service. Often, delivery time becomes more important to a buyer than small price differentials. Knowing that this situation exists, the firm must ask itself: "How much additional cost can we afford to provide rapid, low-volume service to the buyer?" Before the firm can answer this question, it must know the cost of providing this service. A vital factor is the location of distribution warehouses within specific service (market) areas that will provide this service at a minimum cost.

In this model, the only service cost considered is that of transportation. The model should be most useful for a firm that has the following characteristics:
1. Few origin or production points.
2. Many relatively small volume customers.
3. Geographic and economic separation of customers into sub-markets.
4. National or large regional distribution of products.
5. Transportation cost a significant portion of total cost.

Although these characteristics appear to be highly restrictive at first glance, closer examination reveals that most medium-sized firms will fall within the restrictions of the model.

Given a transportation rate structure and historical spatial demand patterns, the model will solve for the maximum-service, minimum-transportation-cost warehouse locations within any qualitatively determined system of sub-market areas. The model also develops transportation cost approximations for each system of market areas.

Since market delineation is a function of many variables, no attempt is made to define the market area within the model. The market delineations are treated as exogenous input data.

An important feature of the model is its ability to compare the transportation costs of different systems of market areas, thus establishing cost approximations to evaluate various service levels.

This model is highly computer-oriented; many difficult, highly repetitive computations must be made. Hand computation would be so laborious that it would tend to discourage use of the system. One of these difficult computations is the computation of airline miles between the origin and destination of shipments. This airline distance is computed by using the grid coordinates of the origins and destination block of the particular shipment. Since these coordinates are in terms of degrees of longitude and latitude, a conversion formula given by C. A. Whinnen, in the Coast and Geodetic Survey Special Publication No. 238, issued 1947, is needed. This formula converts the latitude and longitude estimates obtained from the grid code numbers to statute miles. Once this conversion has been made, the actual airline distance is computed by using the formula for the hypotenuse of a right triangle.

The basic model has been programmed in FORTRAN for the Control Data 3600 computer. This program should be compatible with any FORTRAN compiler, if it has sufficient core memory.

The basic model requires only six types of input data:
1. Origin grid block of each shipment.
2. Destination grid block of each shipment.
3. Total weight of each shipment, in pounds.
4. Total cost of each shipment, in dollars.
5. Cost of carload or truckload shipments in dollars per hundredweight, to each warehouse location.

6. Grid block coordinates of each sub-market area.

Two basic assumptions are implicit within the model:

1. Transportation costs are a function of miles for all distances of over fifty miles.

This assumption is not unrealistic when shipment weights are in either less than volume (LTL, LCL) or volume (TL, CL), and are not mixed.

2. Air distances are proportional to road or rail distances. This is an untested assumption that appears in the literature. The proportionality multiplier is 1.15 for road miles and 1.25 for rail miles.

Once a period, perhaps the past twelve months, is selected to provide data, all shipments, which have been coded by grid blocks, are considered. Because this coding has been done, each shipment becomes available for input to the model. After the input of origin block, destination block, shipment weight, and transportation cost of each shipment, the first solution given is for the least-cost location of a warehouse serving the entire market. Once this location is known, the carload or truckload transportation cost to this block is entered into the model. This results in computation of:

1. Total present transportation cost.
2. Total transportation cost using the single-market warehouse.
3. Cost savings (loss) of using the single-market warehouse.

The next inputs are the grid block coordinates of each market area. These coordinates are the block numbers of the northwest and southeast blocks of each market area. All market areas must be rectangular, and all shipments do *not* have to fall within a market area. As many different combinations and configurations of market areas may be included within each market area as desired.

All of the inputs to the model are processed by electronic data processing to solve for the warehouse location with maximum service and minimum transportation cost. This is done for each system of combinations and configurations of sub-market areas within each market area.

With all new warehouse locations determined, the carload or truckload transportation rate to each new warehouse location must be input. Once these data are in the model, the total transportation cost of each market area, and of each system of combinations and configurations of sub-market areas, will be determined by the computer. Also determined at this time are total weight in each market and sub-market area, short haul transportation cost of serving each sub-market area, and identification of all output data by market and sub-market area.

As different market areas and combinations and configurations of sub-market areas are processed through the model, comparisons of total transportation cost may be made to the various service levels given by the systems of sub-market area warehouses.

This model is limited in application; it provides only transportation cost data. However, it may easily be extended to include handling cost, interest on inventory, and interest on warehouse investment. The inputs necessary for the addition of handling costs are the number of pieces per shipment and an average handling cost per piece, per move. Interest on inventory can be computed by imputing the dollar value of each shipment and calculating average inventories within the model, then inputing an average interest charge. Two inputs are needed to compute interest on warehouse investment, total cost of a warehouse at various volume levels, and interest charge based on cost of capital.

Once these additional data are introduced, the total cost of a system of sub-market area warehouses can be computed and compared to alternative systems.

Distribution Cost and Revenue Analysis

The information gathered on the basis of the grid system can be combined with that of an accounting system designed for the control of distribution activities. The accounting system is designed for the control of distribution activities by measuring the profit contribution of various combinations of marketing strategies used in each "market area" defined by the grid system. Donald W. Drummond presents an accounting system for the control of marketing activities.[5] He reports that the first year after inaugurating the system at Olin Mathieson Chemical Corporation, a 95% increase in net profits with only a 5% increase in sales resulted. This was accomplished without drastic reduction of selling costs or introduction of new products. It was accomplished because the analysis revealed situations and transactions which diluted the net profits. Although the article presents a complete model for marketing accounting, the only part used in this system is his concept of "the starting point for marketing accounting — 'gross sales,' " defined as the sum of the maximum dollars that could possibly be realized for each product sold.

With this figure as the starting point for a distribution accounting system, the procedure is as follows:
1. Subtract from gross sales the sum of the manufacturing costs up to the loading platform for all products sold. Manufacturing costs are defined as all costs incurred in producing the good until the good comes off the end of the line.
2. Subtract all physical distribution costs from gross sales minus manufacturing costs. Physical distribution costs include all costs of storage and movement incurred for the products sold, from the end of the production line to the buyer's location.
3. From gross sales minus manufacturing costs and physical distribution costs, subtract all selling costs. Selling costs are defined as all costs incurred to obtain, fill, and service orders, excluding time and movement costs.

---

[5] Donald W. Drummond, "A Marketing Yardstick," *Transportation and Distribution Management,* February, 1962, pp. 13–16.

4. The resulting figure is a measure of distribution efficiency in each geographic area.

When this system is applied to individual markets by product and by customer, etc., significant information can be obtained to measure distribution effectiveness. Such a system allows management to answer, "What is the difference in the profit margin obtained if I sell Product C in Market A rather than in Market B?" This is possible because the starting point, "gross sales," is defined as the highest dollar that could possibly be realized for each product. Therefore, the system does not start with a figure which was realized, but from one which could have been realized in the optimum situation, and thus accounts for opportunity costs as well as actual costs (i.e., the difference between selling the product in Market A, which produced only $1.75 in net returns, and selling it in Market B, which would have produced $2.00 in net returns). Using the highest price realized by a product in *any* market as the figure to be applied in *every* market forces the accounting system to indicate all the differences in every market in terms of differences in manufacturing, physical distribution, or selling costs. For example, if the highest price actually realized in any market for a box of cake mix was 47¢, then this is the figure used for every market.

GEMINI and Decision Making

The model for information gathering has two outstanding characteristics. First, it has a temporal dimension which allows data to be collected on a flow basis, providing all the advantages of decision making from flow analysis as compared with comparative statics. Second, it has a spatial dimension which allows consideration of a finite number of small areas rather than an infinite number of points in space. The impact of these two characteristics on distribution data and control of distribution activities has been illustrated.

One of the areas of concern in the field of distribution is the relative inability to measure the efficiency, in terms of profit, of decisions. The combination of the information system and accounting concept should provide relevant measures for evaluating such efficiency and improve distribution decision making.

26 "Some Day I'm Going To Have a Little Black Box on My Desk"*

Here is a description of how one firm has planned a market information system spanning the cycle from manufacturing to point-of-sale.

*Reprinted with permission of **Sales Management,** The Marketing Magazine, May 1, 1967, pp. 33ff.

Says Alfred di Scipio, group vice president of Singer Co. and head of its big Consumer Products Group (CPG). "It looks like a calculator, but with a TV screen and keyboard. By punching the keys in a pre-set sequence, I'll know immediately what took place in our four factories, seven warehouses, and 1,911 retail outlets yesterday. If we sponsor a TV spectacular Monday night, I'll have a good idea by Tuesday afternoon of the show's impact on sales. By tracking a new product, such as a low-price sewing machine, I'll know faster than ever before whether it's expanding our market or taking sales from costlier models.

Di Scipio may have to wait awhile for his "little black box," but when he gets it, he'll have a hot line to a total management information system (MIS). What put Singer's Co.'s Consumer Products Group, which contributed 64% of the company's $1 billion sales last year, on the road to MIS is an awareness that computers are the solution to management's spiraling need for better decision-making systems. Briefly, MIS pulls all the diverse functional areas of a business together, giving the marketer all the information he needs to run his operation.

Pinpointing the growing interest in MIS, di Scipio says: "In terms of managing a large, complex enterprise, a manager is only as good as the information he has available. The more complex and bigger an operation becomes, the higher the premium on the information's quality, timeliness, and refinement."

Three or four years ago, talk of a total systems approach was more fanciful than meaningful because the technology and the state of the art weren't there. Now, MIS looks attractive as a means of breaking the information bottleneck because of such technological developments as third-generation computers with their mass random-access memory banks for storing facts in a central location; time-sharing, which allows a multitude of chores to be carried out almost simultaneously; and remote terminal devices, which simplify data collection and give marketers push-button access to facts.

While no company can boast it has a full-fledged MIS, the few pioneers working toward this goal will enjoy a long lead-time in converting information resources into a powerful competitive edge.[1] That's because developing such a total systems effort is a long and tortuous effort. The rates of change in computer and communications technologies, as well as in the business environment, are so rapid that the problems themselves have shifted by the time a solution has been worked out. Thus, flexibility and experimentation are constant elements. Also, the forward planning must be enriched with a high degree of vision. "The important thing," says Sam

---

[1] Because information needs and problem types differ from company to company, there's no uniform approach to MIS. Alcoa's information network, which ties in company plants, sales offices, and subsidiaries, stresses message-switching. Direct access to computerized information via desk-top video consoles is a feature of the MIS used by IBM's data processing division. And RCA Sales Corp.'s planned MIS will have a headquarters computer query 82 distributors daily for sales information.

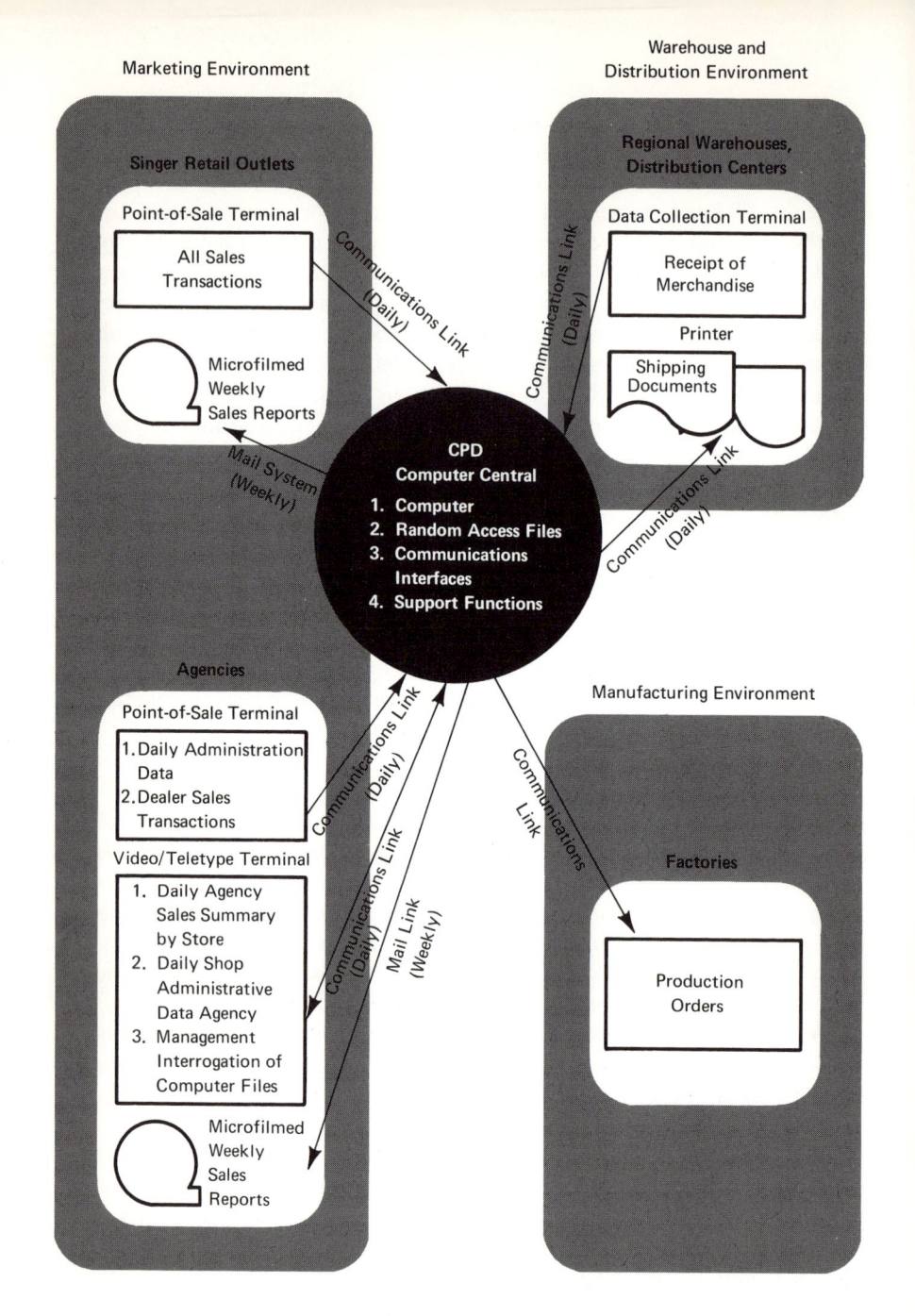

Figure 1. **Singer's New Management Information System**

Factories, warehouses, and retail outlets will be directly linked, via telephone lines, to the Consumer Products Group's computer center in Syosset, Long Island. Management gets an extra bonus because the system spans the product cycle from manufacturing to point-of-sale. The arrows show the principal direction of communications between the connecting points.

Harvey, head of Singer's corporate systems and development, "is to project as far into the future as possible as to where you want to be so that you can decide how to get there. Otherwise, if you don't know where you are going, and you get out to where you can take advantage of the new technologies, but haven't planned for them, you're in trouble."

A close look at how Single-CPG has gone about mounting its computerized information system turns up pointers for other companies, as well as several unusual features. In the first place, CPG's operations have a big potential for the ultimate in management information control. "Our system is unique," says Janet Norman, who as manager of advanced systems in CPG is responsible for designing the on-line phase of the network, "because division activities span the spectrum from factory to retail store, giving us a single entity for capturing data all the way from manufacturing to the point-of-sale."[2]

Second, CPG's MIS is well beyond the crawling stage. Accounting information has been completely overhauled and simplified; a sprawling network of 1,911 stores (including 1,453 division-operated Singer Centers, 38 leased departments, and 420 approved independent dealers) is integrated (logically, if not yet physically) with the central computer facility in Syosset, Long Island; management reports turn up information not heretofore available (such as effect of discounts on margins by product); and flash reports provide operating figures one week after the close of a period.

Third, Singer's Friden subsidiary (which specializes in data processing hardware, adding and calculating machines, and printing and mailing equipment) gives CPG a strong inhouse technical savvy for solving some very tricky MIS problems. As Miss Norman notes, "This availability of high-level talent in terminal equipment design within our own organization places us in a favorable position of being both potential developer and user of a data collection device tailor-made to our own terminal requirements."

A fourth element of CPG'c program is the carefully phrased advance planning, the teamwork, and the strong enthusiasm which carried the MIS through its *sturm und drang*. Jack McConnaughy, Jr., newly-named president of Canadian Co., who was CPG controller when pieces of the information system were being put together, recalls the "philosophy of operations" that guided the MIS builders. "We worked closely with headquarters and staff and invited corporate participation," he says. "Projections were carefully organized and their priorities set. We developed strong people because if, after studying a situation carefully, we felt we had to stick our neck out to get things moving, we did."

A final ingredient in CPG's formula was strong management support. Though he claims he is not wedded to computers per se, di Scipio is known

---

[2] While this gives CPG a built-in advantage, a few consumer goods outfits, such as Pillsbury and Bobbie Brooks, have linked their own computers with those of major distributors, giving them some insight into product movement at the retail end.

as a man with a talent for goading people into looking for new ways of doing things. One of the several bright young men president Donald P. Kircher brought in to remake the company, di Scipio put together a cadre of Whiz Kids who piloted the MIS through its birth pangs. McConnaughy was lured from Westinghouse, Sam Harvey from RCA, and Herman Bruning from ITT. Bruning is now controller with EDP activity under his wing.

If Singer-CPG is past the crawling stage, it took some doing to get there. Prior to 1960, when sewing machines racked up 93% of the company's corporate sales, manual accounting by the 32 then existing field marketing agencies provided the bulk of management's operating information. However, as the company, reacting to bruising competition from foreign sewing machines, began to diversify into product areas with healthier growth potential (see *Sales Management,* Sept. 20, 1963), the need to modernize the antiquated information base became more pressing. This was especially true in CPG because the wares vended in Singer Centers expanded to include home entertainment equipment, floor-care products, and typewriters, among others. In building an integrated management information system, two objectives were set: (1) provide a base for a greater degree of management control; and (2) pay for all changes and improvements out of current savings. In bringing this off, the program has gone through four steps:

Step One, from 1960 through Apr., 1964, saw the accounting previously done by the 32 agencies (there are now 25) consolidated into four regional centers, manual operations converted to punched cards, and the start of long-range planning pointing to a MIS. During Step Two, from May to Oct. in 1964, some 12 different sales forms at the shop level were consolidated into one report, data transmission over telephone lines between New York and the four centers was begun, and training programs for field personnel launched. The last aspect got special emphasis because, as many companies have learned to their sorrow, most computer problems are really people problems. McConnaughy points out that "every step we took had to be ratified by the field managers. They may not care if you're going to save a million dollars with a new system, but if you can offer them an incentive, such as a shorter order-replenishment cycle and fewer worries about inventories, then you're that much ahead of the game." At the same time, a systems and programming group was built and a long-range-systems study launched. Two main conclusions emerged from this study. First, to centralize management information and control at one point in the interests of greater efficiency and to take advantage of the changing relationships between data communication and data processing costs. Second, having centralized, to see how the information work load could be handled most efficiently, with special emphasis on the newer breakthroughs in the symbiotic computer and communications technologies. With the fundamental outlines of the emerging MIS taking shape, CPG moved into Step Three, from Feb. to Sept., 1965, when the four regional centers were consolidated into the central facility at Syosset, and more powerful computers were installed, making tighter management control and better standardization possible. CPG recently wound up Step Four, aimed at streamlining the centralized information system. Here, random-access equipment replaced tape files so that all files will be accessible from remote areas, and the most voluminous and widely distributed reports were recorded on microfilm directly off the computer. Forward planning for Step Five is now under way. Targets in this phase will include shop-data capture devices for recording and transmitting information to Syosset, direct interrogation of computer files by agencies and field management, and direct access of credit information from the stores.

Although CPG still has some way to go to reach a totally integrated on-line MIS, management is already getting solid payoffs. According to Miss Norman, some of the valuable information managers get now that was previously unavailable includes product profitability analysis, product mix analysis by type of salesman (inside versus sales rep), product combination matrix for product planning (that is, which combinations of sewing machine heads and cabinets, for example, are selling), accounts receivable with a customer matrix, territorial sales analyses using certain indexes developed by CPG, and more comparison-type data (budget versus actual results, year-to-date this year and last year).

CPG chief di Scipio says that "our accounting expenses per dollar of sales have gone down. Our business has gone ahead 30%, but actual dollars spent on accounting and EDP is the same as, or slightly lower than, it was three years ago. This means more margin and less expense per sales for us."

Looking ahead, di Scipio sees benefits that will move out from routine areas and come closer to the core of the management processes. Manufacturing schedules will be set more efficiently, he says, because the system will alert management as to how different sewing machine models are moving, making quicker adjustment of forecasts possible. More effective management of inventory is another glittering possibility. "Right now, we often have an inventory of a product that is 120% of what it should be," he says, "but 80% of the shops are out of stock because of maldistribution. When you think of the logistics involved in supporting almost 2,000 outlets, most of them relatively small, with 200 big ticket items and 5,000 small items, you can appreciate the difficulty of maintaining the proper balance. We can only achieve this by knowing what happened in the shops yesterday. So we are basing our whole forward inventory and distribution strategy on this use of the computer. This is very important to us in terms of return-on-assets and the cost of money."

With the basic building blocks in place, CPG is now fitting together the superstructure of its MIS. Future plans call for all stores to send data over telephone lines to Syosset within two years; factories and warehouses in two to five years.

Current development work pivots around collecting data in the stores and sending it to Syosset. Here, CPG and Friden are working toward a special point-of-sale device that could combine data collection and cash register functions. The nub of the problem is to come up with the kind of keyboard that would enable shop personnel to record, at the time of the sales transaction, any configuration of data that CPG may want for its MIS. If the two score a breakthrough in this area, the impact will extend beyond the shop floor. Internally, CPG could adapt the device for use at factory and warehouse levels so that the all-important merchandise coding will be uniform from production to final sale. Externally, considering the extensive R&D going on in this area by several companies, the device would be the kind of new product opportunity Singer Co. is looking for as part of its broad-based diversification program.

The data flow to Syosset will be speeded up by having the central computer query each store at night, taking in the information recorded at the point-of-sale that day. According to Miss Norman, this will slash the information turnaround cycle—the span between when a sale is made and when the manager gets a report—from the current 10 days to one.

Once the factories and warehouses go on-line with Syosset, and message-switching equipment is installed, CPG will have a stronger handle on inventory movement and production scheduling. For example, as the central computer is notified of sales transactions from the stores, it will scan inventory levels and send a release and shipping order to the proper warehouse. If the store orders can't be filled from existing stocks, factories will be flashed updated production schedules.

Now that CPG has demonstrated what a MIS can do, Singer is looking around to see if any of the other 192 market locations outside the U.S. can use the same kind of systems effort. A corporate systems and development department was set up under Sam Harvey, whose problems will be much more complex than those he confronted in CPG's program. While such problems as inventory control and production scheduling cut across all division lines, not all the market locations have the financial heft CPG commands. CPG was big enough to support a self-contained, first-class systems effort, but to duplicate the same program in a small country like Columbia, for example, would knock Singer out of business. Harvey's search for a solution strikes out in two directions. First, he says, "You look at the 192 different market locations that are involved and try to spot those areas and patterns of activity [such as the way inventory is kept] that are similar. Then you build support programs that can be pulled from large locations, or developed centrally with multiple installations across many locations. Of course, each location has some unique factors. Then it becomes a matter of tailoring the differences." Second, look at the new kind of equipment hardware coming out of the laboratories. "The technology of the industry is moving us to the time-sharing utility," he says. "As this applies to a worldwide company like Singer, it means that smaller locations that can't support their own systems effort will have terminals or satellite equipment which talk to much bigger centrally-placed computers, thereby spreading the costs over a wider base and gearing them to actual use."

While the technological artifacts of a MIS spark much of the excitement today, Harvey stresses that "the real objective of any information system is what the managers will be able to do with this type of control. When you consider the millions of bits-and-pieces of information a business generates each day, and the miles of paper it produces, its' impossible for anyone to keep up with it. The significance of a MIS is the ability of the computer to pull it all together and, under proper controls, ferret out the key-exception activity that requires management action. Of course, what is done with the information will always be a manager's prerogative, but its availability will give him a degree of control he never had before."

One can also point to the other side of the coin, which may be equally important as time goes on: namely, the computerized MIS will be a harsh taskmaster on poor managers. For with this informtaion power at their behest, managers will no longer be able to rationalize away the need for a decision on the grounds, "I don't have the facts I need."

C Problems With Information Systems

27 Keys to a Management Information System in Your Company*

ADRIAN M. McDONOUGH

Some of the problems that arise when management attempts to plan an effective information system are described here—along with suggestions on how to solve them.

The field of management information systems is so new, and is changing so rapidly, that it is impossible for anyone to really qualify as an expert. It is the very rate of change that causes many of our present difficulties.

The period in which we live always appears to us be the one in which the greatest changes take place. The present is no exception. Today we face a world where new philosophies and new technologies are being proposed, tested, and absorbed at a rapid rate. The growth of knowledge has reached a point where it has become a burden and, therefore, a challenge. This challenge is apparent when we consider the problems of organizing information to serve the appetites of all who would enlarge their personal knowledge. More specifically, in business and government organizations we see large amounts of manpower concentrating on the search for facts and upon the interpretation of these facts.

The opportunity thus arises for studying the productivity of knowledge and particularly the productivity of management information systems. Productivity has in the past been associated with physical production. The "Taylor Movement" in the United States and the "Stakhanov Movement" in Russia resulted in greater understanding of the problems of physical production. Factory jobs were carefully analyzed and improvements were made at every level of the conversion of raw material to finished product.

*Reprinted from **The Third Generation Computer,** A.M.A. Management Bulletin No. 79, 1966 publication of American Management Association, Inc., pp. 25–33.

Now there is a need for extending the concept of productivity to include all who work with facts and figures—those who collect, process, and interpret information. In the past such work has been treated as "nonproductive" labor. Today progress is increasingly dependent upon the efficiency with which we convert facts and figures into useful products as knowledge for management decisions.

The information in this paper is derived primarily from the work I have done in the field of information economics.[1] The work in information economics includes an exploratory attempt to define the problems of measuring productivity for "facts and figures" jobs. Facts and figures influence every administrative job from the lowest clerical positions to the top executive positions. Facts and figures influence the goals, the processes, and the results of all organizations. My approach, therefore, proposes that information be treated as a product and that both the values and the costs of information as a product be studied in the tradition of the scientific method. The ideas of information economics and management systems are presented with a hope that others will find them useful as they develop their own views of the productivity of information.

The title of my paper is "Keys to a Management Information System in Your Company." Keys, of course, are useless unless we can locate the right doors to unlock. Also, keys become obsolete when locks are changed. We must give due consideration to which doors we want to open and, especially, to why we might want to open them—and, remembering Pandora's Box, to why we might want to keep some doors closed.

The game of predicting what is going to happen in this field has been going on for some time now, and the stakes are getting higher all the time. This is apparent in the symbol of the third generation manager. We are no longer viewing data processing with a scope limited to machines and programming. Now the dimensions of the approach branch out to include all levels and specialties in an organization's list of positions. This means, of course, that not all of the locked doors are located in the machine room. We are now seeing that there are very few boundaries to where data processing might have an impact in an organization.

It is for this reason in particular that I have selected a few specific areas and will direct my remarks to them. These are areas that I believe should be of interest to the systems analyst, as well as to any manager who recognizes the importance of management information systems. I will comment on five locked, or at least sticky, doors that should be opened when seeking success in management information systems.

---

[1] McDonough, Adrian, *Information Economics and Management Systems,* McGraw-Hill Book Co., New York, 1963; and Adrian McDonough and Leonard Garrett, *Management Systems, Working Concepts and Practices,* Richard D. Irwin, Homewood, Ill., 1965.

If we are to get behind the locked doors, I propose that the following five are among the most important keys:

1. Surveillance.
2. Criteria.
3. Classification.
4. Documentation.
5. Boundaries.

It is my impression that each of these areas contains fundamental restraints to the development and use of effective management information systems. Our systems can be no better than the state of the art in handling these problems.

The First Key: Surveillance

Surveillance refers to all those activities by which a better perspective on an organization and its environment is obtained. It includes coverage of both external and internal situations. It includes immediate and longer-range circumstances. In effect, it can cover every aspect of an organization; but, practically, an organized surveillance effort must be very selective.

I believe it is useful to think of surveillance as limited to the search for major changes in the environment of a firm. Surveillance of the environment of a firm is made difficult by the very fact that its purpose is to bring out and highlight those factors which require management to make changes. The management that is demonstrating its ability in the face of change does so by devoting resources to a very selective surveillance of its environment. Such a management not only looks inward at its base of operations but also goes out into its external environment in order to get firsthand knowledge.

Surveillance can be very informal, but more and more organizations are providing formal arrangements for certain aspects of surveillance. The payoff here for management information systems is that good surveillance can provide the best guidance for what should be included in the formal information systems. This is especially so in situations where change is typical. Progress can be made only if good evidence of where we are and good statements of where we want to go are available.

Surveillance can be viewed as a level of analysis one stage ahead of the actual design of the information systems. A good surveillance program, in this sense, is insurance that good specifications can be set for keeping systems design up to date. We need a better framework in which to design and evaluate our management information systems. A good surveillance program is one of the keys to getting better design and evaluation.

Consider the reality of the world in which we live. What is stable? What is not subject to change? Certainly not our information systems! Attention to surveillance will prevent the development of rigor mortis in our systems. Today's systems design must include flexibility to accommodate future changes. A priority given to surveillance arrangements, at a minimum, can lead to the writing of better guidelines for systems success.

Let me go back over this point, because it is a difficult conceptual problem. Systems should not be designed in a vacuum. For any situation of significance a manager can ask, "What is it?" and, "What should we do about it?" At any point in time and experience, a first glimmer of a situation may appear. The difficulty is, of course, that the situation is rarely clear. In many business situations we are not sure of the factors, their significance, or their interrelationships. It is in the context of such vague situations that management problems are first identified and stated. This is the threshold level where the preliminary question is asked and the problem is stated for the first time. In the final analysis, no system can be evaluated except as it serves some purpose. The purpose can be spelled out only as we are able to provide effective surveillance of situations. We thereby obtain up-to-date descriptions of our information needs.

I am suggesting that more formal attention be paid to how our organizations carry out their surveillance activities. This will open the door to more concrete statements of the criteria with which information systems can be evaluated.

The Second Key: Criteria

Criteria, or measures of performance, have up to now been a rather academic exercise; this can no longer be the case. A major problem in government and industry is that we are spending fantastic amounts of money on systems and we do not know how to evaluate what we are getting for our money. We know what those systems cost, but we do not know what they are worth. Here is a real key to success in management information systems: concentrate on getting the real measures of the performance we should expect from our systems. This is the only way that I can see to do a better job in evaluating: (1) what the $5-billion computer industry is achieving and (2) what over half of the people who work for a living in this country are achieving. The information industry is at least this big, and it is growing every day. What are the results of all this investment, all this time-consuming attention to information? Again, the answer can be found only as we develop the analysis of criteria, the language in which we express values.

If we want to be able to evaluate the outputs of our systems we must be willing to spend more time and effort being specific about what we want from these systems. Getting to a better level of specifics requires that the managers themselves concentrate more on the formal expression of criteria involved in their jobs.

My assumption is that information systems serve managers in their job responsibilities. The reverse assumption, which is being made too often, is that the managers exist to serve the information system. It is because of this second assumption that we see so many conferences entitled: "The Impact of the Computer on Managers." The need today, however, is to look at the question of the "Impact of Managers on Computers." We are at a point where it is primarily the managers—not the hardware—that determine success or failure.

No matter how sophisticated the management information system is, it has to serve some level of management. The identification of the criteria appropriate to management at that level gives the best means to place values on systems outputs. Identification of criteria associated with various organization levels can provide a relatively crisp structure of an organization's decision needs. An approach that concentrates on criteria can get very close to spelling out the values that should be provided by a management system.

Much searching is now going on trying to find some way to put dollar values on information. I think that this is the wrong approach. We should be thinking in terms of the *real* measures of information values expressed in the criteria and units that fit the situation. Let me just note at this point that the Ten Commandments and man-made codified law provide important criteria for performance evaluation without using dollar units. In forcing our measures into dollar units, we may be distorting them to the point where they are useless. In budgeting, for example, the jump from the identification of problems to the assigning of dollars may take place too fast. We tend to focus on the dollar figures in the final budget rather than on the analysis at the level of spelling out problems and their related criteria. I suggest that the budget procedure is one good place to start finding and using better criteria for information systems.

When criteria are not clearly spelled out, it is necessary to make forced choices—that is, choices based upon hunch and intuition. The study of criteria is one of seeking gradual improvements that will reduce the dependence on hunch and intuition. When good criteria are available, management can have more confidence in the answers to its questions.

The environment of an organization as it generates problems is the prime reason for any work in management systems. Problems reflect from situations where opportunities may be obtained or where hazards can be prevented. From a given situation at a moment in time, an organization seeks to take actions that will increase its opportunities and at the same time to take actions that will reduce its hazards. As the organization moves through its environment, individual participants identify their place in the scheme of things. They consider their organization position level and the time dimension of decisions for which they are held responsible. It is at such a time that the individual uses his management ability to identify the problems on which he will work and, at least intuitively, starts to assign priorities to his problems. In so far as his opportunities and hazards are synchronized with those of the overall organization, he weights his problems by their importance to the organization.

When the individual recognizes a lack of consistency between his personal interests and those of the organization, he is faced with the forces of compromise. The scales of opportunity and hazards that he sets for himself will be balanced by the repercussions he can expect if he gets out of line with the best interests of the organization. In any case, if the individual is to make logical decisions and is to take logical action, he must be as explicit as possible regarding both his opportunities and his hazards. Again, he must select and express himself in statements of the prorities and criteria peculiar to his situation.

Criteria statements are logical extensions of initial problem definitions. They provide at least preliminary bench marks for testing the success of a project. Criteria are the English words with which we express the bases upon which we make choices. Any system that purports to aid decision making should be designed with conscious attention to criteria. Criteria become more meaningful when we are able to attach weights to the English words and thereby to make relative comparisons. This type of thinking is important in designing a system. It is especially important when attempting to set priorities among systems. Criteria statements can be quite useful when a management is attempting to compare and contrast projects and to set meaningful priorities.

Success in any job, at any level, must be measured against some set of criteria—some set of statements that separate the important from the unimportant. A manager in any job at any level has to:

1. Try to find out the criteria used by his superiors and, if appropriate, to help set such criteria.
2. Identify the criteria involved in his own job.
3. Provide criteria for subordinates.

Only as improvements are made at and among the levels of criteria is it possible to write meaningful specifications for the values that should come out of information systems. Criteria, I repeat, are the words in which values are expressed.

When I use the word "value," I am including two shades of meaning. The first is the type, or class, of what is being evaluated. This involves selecting the appropriate criterion. The second is the scaling, or attaching of a degree of importance. This involves putting weights on the appropriate criterion. To identify any value, therefore, a criterion must be selected and then a weight must be attached.

Criteria are necessary to spell out the responsibilities of a manager. They are, therefore, necessary in spelling out the information systems that must support the manager as he tries to carry out his responsibilities. It is for this reason that I define information as "evaluated data." This definition allows us to tie information values directly to the selection of the criteria for success of any organization.

If we want to be able to do a better job, we must be willing to spend more time and effort being specific about what we want from our systems.

This, in turn, may mean that we will have to cut back somewhat on the so-called total systems some of us are trying to build. There may not be enough resources to do a big and a good job at the same time. Getting to a better level of specifics requires that managers concentrate more on the formal expression of the criteria involved in their jobs.

Only as we make progress in expressing criteria in the job context can we expect to be able to attach values to our information systems. In a changing world, problems will change; and we must expect job content and systems content to change. Attention to the level of criteria can facilitate the implementation of such changes. No matter how sophisticated the management information system is, the manager must attach his values if he is, in fact, to have a job. Identifying criteria is a major part of his job.

The Third Key: Classification

Classification is another key area that is holding up progress in information systems. All information systems depend on classification, yet we really have very little knowledge about how to build good classifications. Work in classifying anything is tedious, and most people shy away from such work.

The importance of classification in information systems is, however, gradually being recognized. Classification is the very beginning of the organization of facts and information. Without classification there can be no information systems. Unless something is first classified it is impossible to measure it. With bad classification even the most powerful management science techniques can be made ineffective. It is time to look at the problems of classification more carefully.

The decision to establish a business class, or to use an existing class, is the threshold at which we determine that a certain factor cannot be ignored. The identification of a factor as significant is the justification for including that particular factor. The recognition that classes should be selected carefully is a major step in minimizing the detail in an organization's systems.

There has been a tendency to build data processing systems upon existing classifications. Now we find that we have large investments in programming using these classifications. Such classifications are usually oriented toward use in quite separate functions of the business. Now we want to get integrated usage from our systems. If the classifications are not integrated, how can we expect to get integrated results from the systems?

We do not want *all* the facts—we want very selected facts. A selected fact is information. Selection should start with the classifications from which we build our systems.

Classifications are the building blocks of representations. These blocks can be big or small, gross or detailed; it is the critical job of the developer to match needs with an appropriate coverage of classifications.

A classification is a grouping of items of similar characteristics into classes or sets. This is not, however, a sufficient definition, for it ignores the need for identifying what we mean by similar characteristics. Further, it ignores the needs to treat differences as well as similarities. Let us look at this point more closely.

An overall classification development requires consideration of both differences and similarities. Similarities are sought so that they can be brought together in one place and worked on with a relatively uniform approach. Differences are sought in order to recognize when different treatment must be applied to the classes. A class, therefore, represents a grouping within which the subclasses fit together in relative harmony. These subclasses have meaning in the sense that they form the class as a whole. Contrasts of classes, however, emphasize the need to identify differences and the significance of these differences.

This running back and forth between similarities and differences plays an important part in the development of a useful classification system. The fundamental idea is that classifications are built to facilitate decisions. Decisions involve both the making of comparisons for similarities and of contrasts for differences. In a good classification system, certain significant comparisons and contrasts are already built in.

Consider the mass production approach now being applied to the development of centralized data banks. If these banks are built before the classifications are carefully studied, they may simply turn into massive collections of unusable equipment. Data collection can become even more expensive and the results can become utterly useless. Classifications are very much involved in the quality control aspects of producing information products.

The Fourth Key: Documentation

Documentation is a real key today for those who are trying to keep track of all the details involved in the development of information systems. By documentation, I mean a recorded set of evidence showing the characteristics of some part, or all, of a management system. As our systems get larger and more complex, we are being overwhelmed by the expanding amount of detail. If we cannot keep track of what is in our existing systems, how can we ever make comparisons between existing and proposed systems?

Documentation of a system, or parts of a system, can be done in a careless or in a careful manner. In some cases, scratch pads and all other working papers are thrown in a file drawer (or perhaps a wastepaper basket). At the other extreme, every detailed decision made is carefully reviewed, indexed, written up in some standardized manner, and filed for easy retrieval. Both extremes are rare; actual practice is usually somewhere in between.

"Documentation" as a term is usually reserved for describing work at the levels of systems design and computer programming. It is here that we see explicit flow charts, programming instructions, and computer-run manuals. I include other areas when I use the term documentation. One of the big areas where documentation needs to be improved is in those stages before systems design. In particular, I am referring to the needs for providing much better analysis and documentation of the specifications of information requirements. Only as these requirements are carefully chosen and documented is it possible to formfit the design of the system to individual managers' needs to know. Typically, information requirements will be expressed in the vocabulary of the manager's field of specialization, and this is just the way it should be.

Systems design is not the first step in the development of a management system. Unless the steps of problem definition and determination of information requirements are carefully documented, the stage of systems design may start with no clear-cut objectives—and this happens too often. What happens is that the systems designer, by himself, creates *his* problem definition and *his* view of the information requirements.

I believe that more formal pressure is being placed, and rightly so, on managers to provide the specifications for what they want out of information systems. This, of course, is where many of our programs for management information systems run into difficulty. It is not easy for a manager to spell out the information requirements of his job. Yet, if he does not, who can? If he does not, how can we expect better information? The frustrations existing here represent a key restraint to improvements in our systems. We are starting to see increased attention being paid to getting managers to become converts to information systems. This is anything but a simple problem. Flag waving and statements that the manager is responsible for setting his information requirements are not sufficient to get results. Managers must be given help in defining their information needs. An organized effort in a company documentation program can be a good start in helping managers to express their needs.

A documentation program in a company can serve as a rallying point for gradually improving the effectiveness of management information systems. Documentation touches every level and every specialty in an organization. The variety of "languages" used in operating a business can cause confusion and consequent inefficiencies in operations. Documentation, at a minimum, highlights these problems. It gets them out in the open where something can be done about them.

Consider the possibility of having a manager's information "menu." This would be an organization's documentation of what can be available in existing information systems. The availability of a menu makes it possible to identify the set of choices for the manager and guides the systems designers as improvements are suggested. The menu of information available that can be served to managers can be viewed as the documentation of the important systems in the organization. With the information menu available, both the manager and the systems designer have a positive basis for discussing systems requirements.

There is a major need to have available much better means whereby the content in management systems can be identified and analyzed at various levels of detail. Progress in documentation will aid in the following situations:

1. Where add-on systems are being proposed.
2. Where systems are to be dropped.
3. Where the effectiveness of a given system has been challenged.
4. Where cross-relations within and between systems are to be studied.
5. Where audits of any nature are to be performed.
6. Where a new management technique has become available and consideration is being given to changing systems to exploit the improvement.
7. Where an approach is needed for penetrating parochial defenses of decentralized systems by reducing some of the barriers of complexity behind which parochial interests can hide.

Present methods for handling these problems are quite inadequate. At best they depend upon a voting process used by experienced people in the organization. More formal rules and techniques are needed to reinforce the judgments of these experienced people. There are just too many detailed pieces involved in systems content to make much progress without some sort of an organized approach to improving documentation.

The Fifth Key: Boundaries

Boundaries represent the last key area that I will discuss. Here, I am afraid, we are being misled by all this talk about "total systems." The present quest for total systems should be recognized as a hazardous quest for the ideal. If the use of the term "total systems" leads to the impression that it is simple to integrate systems—or if it is only a merchandising slogan—then the term should be discarded. It is better to think of a system as being made more complete or more comprehensive. The question, "Should certain systems be integrated?" is just as important—if not more important—than the question, "How can these systems be integrated?" When nature puts certain odd systems together the result is often a freak. Managers and systems designers must guard against integrated but freakish systems.

As we try to increase a system's scope, or take on larger problems, there are compounding complications that set up restraints. We should recognize these complications and build our systems accordingly. Total systems are not good in and of themselves. In the production environment we had something like a total system years ago when one very large motor would drive many machines through a series of belts. Then it was found advantageous to set up separate systems with individual motor drives on machines. It was only when we were able to conceptualize the overall relationships of individual machines that we were able to move to integrated production systems, and even now this covers only a small percentage of our physical productive capacity.

A significant area of systems design is the setting of boundaries in which systems can operate with some measure of self-policing. The setting of boundaries is a key part of any problem definition. In practice, problem definitions are usually developed to the limits of comprehension of those involved in their design and utilization. We cannot design systems boundaries that go beyond our ability to define our problems. At some point things go out of focus and out of control.

We must not let the drive for progress put us in the position where we make promises that are impossible to keep. Too often I find false fronts on the stores that are peddling total systems. These merchandising outfits worry me, but it is their customers who buy the panaceas that worry me a lot more. A concentration on the problem of boundaries can quickly demonstrate the need for clear separation of systems.

Notice how the four areas that I discussed earlier all lead up to this problem of setting boundaries for separate information systems.

Surveillance, or lack thereof, sets limits to how well we see many of our most critical problems. Surveillance, therefore, greatly influences how many missing parts there may be that are not yet subject to integration through the systems approach.

Criteria must be available if we are to make decisions about the value of the services provided by an information system. Systems integration should take place only when we can meaningfully relate the criteria in the enlarged scope of the problem we have defined. In general, as we extend the boundaries of our analysis, we must be prepared to develop more explicit criteria.

Classification I described as the first level of organization of facts and information. Inadequacies and inconsistencies in our classifications are major restraints to our attempts to take on larger systems.

Documentation involves getting good descriptions of our problem definitions, of our information requirements, and of the logic of a system which can meet these requirements. The amount of effort now going into the seeking of better methods of documentation indicates that we are having a terrible time describing what already exists in our present systems. Note that many times we do not really tie separate systems together. In fact, we often cannot describe what exists and we start all over again trying to get the new and larger system.

In the area of management information systems the big challenge now is to tie systems content to job content. We are back with the emphasis on organization problems and are asking, "How can authority be balanced with participation?" We are starting to think about ways to relate the talents and the techniques available in an organization.

Talents are recorded in the minds of managers, and techniques developed by talented managers can be recorded in systems. Thus, one of the challenges of talented people is the need to provide good techniques. Such techniques are then put to use to make easier the handling of the organization's recurring problems. In simplest terms, a good technique records the use of good talents. The talent is built into a technique, applied as a system, and used over and over again.

A manager who believes that he can run his job without systems is mistaken. A systems specialist who assumes his system can run the organization is mistaken. The emphasis should be on the extension and blending of management skills. A management should think of its systems, as well as its personnel, as being skilled. Skills in this sense can be built into a system.

This skill conversion is a vital link between the interests of the manager and the systems specialist. It is in this area of relating the manager's job content and systems content that I believe big payoffs can be achieved. The keys to this problem are improvements in the areas of surveillance, criteria, classification, documentation, and boundaries.

All things are somehow connected. There is, theoretically, in the ultimate, a wholeness. The basic fact is, however, there are so many things and, therefore, so many connections that man can work forever and yet discover only a small part of what there is to be known. I recommend the incremental approach to getting bigger and better systems.

Some Organizational Problems Which Arise as the Result of Large-Scale Information Systems*   28

EMANUEL KAY

When installed, large-scale systems will intensify organizational problems. One way of avoiding this is for users to play a larger role in the planning of the system. Users tend to leave too much of the installation of the system to systems specialists.

INTRODUCTION

During the past several months, I have had the opportunity to look at several large-scale information systems and to identify some of the organization problems associated with their development and implementation.

This afternoon I would like to describe some of the things that I have seen. Specifically, I would like to describe the organization problems related to the implementation of large-scale logistics systems, i.e., systems which support a manufacturing delivery schedule. Under these systems, the manufacturing organization develops and commits to a schedule to meet the requirements of customers. The manufacturing organization places material

---

*A paper presented to the 13th International Meeting of the Institute of Management Sciences, September 6, 1966. Reproduced with permission.

requirements on in-house component shops and on the purchasing organizations. These organizations in turn review and negotiate this schedule and commit to it. The purchasing organization places orders with outside vendors and these materials enter the plant through a receiving area, are inspected, and placed in the manufacturing inventory. As part of this process, the finance organization is notified of the receipt of acceptable material and they in turn pay the vendors. The systems associated with this process attempt to provide an integrated flow of information (status reports, inventory levels, efficiency, vendor/in-house quality, documentation to support payment to vendors) to help assure that the material requirements of the schedule are met. In general, these systems result in the following:

An increased flow and availability of information.

Shorter feedback cycles on material status.

Information being available to more people.

Less opportunity for individuals or organizations to review and adjust data in advance of release.

Greater visibility of performance (errors become obvious much sooner).

Greater difficulty (in terms of time/source documentation) to backtrack and to correct errors.

Greater interdependence of organizations involved in the system.

As the result of the implementation of large-scale logistics systems of these types, organizations are faced with a number of problems which probably existed before but now are intensified and highlighted by the operation of the systems. In addition, there are some new problems which they must solve.

MAJOR PROBLEMS

1. The System Is Integrated But The Organization Is Not

Management information systems are concerned with work functions/information flow and cut across traditional organization boundaries. Various organizations involved in the system typically try to maintain their traditional methods of operation; they tend to react defensively to those aspects of the system which challenge their usual methods of operation. In some instances, traditional organization prerogatives are affected by information systems, e.g., initiation and control of work within the organization, reporting of organization results, goal setting.

Specifically, I found the lack of integration between organizations in various systems:

1. Organizations were concerned only with their own part of the system. The various organization segments did not see themselves as part of a larger system and were not concerned about its overall success. This was true particularly at lower organization levels.

2. Organizations did not adapt themselves to the requirements of the system. In many instances relatively minor organization changes or changes in responsibility would have improved the system operation. Many organizations either did not see the need to adapt or in some instances showed marked unwillingness to make necessary changes. In general, the overall systems were jeopardized because the various organizations did not or would not look beyond the goals and values that normally guided them. What this means is that they refused to accept and adapt to the new goals and values of a multifunctional information system.
3. The amount of conflict between organizations went up, particularly in those cases where the inputs from one organization resulted in high error output to other organizations. In these cases, there was considerable back-biting and finger-pointing as well as numerous memos being written for the "file" to later prove that one was correct.
4. Systems performance in these instances was poor and it took unusual efforts to get improvement.

In order to solve these problems, we found it valuable to use an objective, disinterested party to diagnose various situations and to start the corrective procedures. We found that this person required a broad understanding of organizational processes and group dynamics as well as individual behavior. This person was not a member of the systems organization, nor was he a member of any of the organizations involved in a system. The initial reason for bringing together the organizations which were part of the system was the errors that were being generated. Typically, errors created considerable hostility toward the system and generated a considerable amount of negative feelings between people. Each organization was approached and asked to describe problems they faced in operating its part of the system. The errors which affected them were identified, as well as the source of these errors. When this was done, it became clear that every organization was generating errors which affected every other organization. Procedures were set up to provide the organizations with a list of the errors which they generated. Representatives from the various organizations met to review the errors and to discuss ways of reducing them.

Initially, these meetings were quite emotional and negative, but after several sessions, a more positive tone prevailed. The positive element took over when the representatives of the various organizations began to realize that they were tied together by a common system and that they now had a common goal, i.e., the successful operation of the total system. At this point, cooperative effort increased and numerous proposals were made, debated, and agreed upon within the group to reduce errors. Types of solutions which typically evolved as a result of these discussions were organization changes of a minor and major nature, system changes, and more direct communication links between various people in the system regardless of the organization of which they are a part, to facilitate system operation.

Some progress was made as a result of these actions, but at best it must be regarded as a "clean-up" effort. The after-the-fact effort, I found, was a poor substitute for proper preparation, particularly by the user, to operate and maintain a system. At a later point in this talk, I will describe in more detail the responsibilities of user organizations in this regard.

2. What Jobs/Organizations/Skills Will Change As A Result of Information Systems

One of the questions raised most frequently in systems efforts has to do with the impact of information systems on such things as job content, organization structure, and skill requirements. A sampling of opinion and a cursory review of the literature in this area does not show any consistency as to the change effects of information systems. On the one extreme, we hear prophecies of revolutionary changes in the management and control of a business, while at the other extreme we see some empirical studies which suggest little or no impact.

Our experience to date does not enable us to make any direct contributions in this area. My own bias is not to look at a system in terms of what does or does not change, but rather to look at it in terms of (a) what should change, and (b) what are the factors which facilitate or impede the necessary changes. In order to reflect this perspective, I have found it valuable to ask the following kinds of questions:

> How many different functions/organization units are involved in the system? Will it be contained within one organization/one function or will it cut across a number of functional organizations.
>
> To what extent will the system generate new documents and new information? Will the new system change the usual work flow? What will be the input point/output points?
>
> How many people are in the group(s) using a new system? What is the range/variety of skills required of the people who will be using a system? What are the current skill levels?
>
> How "old" is the current system? To what degree is it manual or computerized? How long have the current incumbents been in their jobs and using the old system?
>
> What is the source of the motivation to change the "old" system? Systems people? User dissatisfaction? Higher management? Reorganization? What about the current way of doing things? Do people like/dislike?

I think we should avoid getting locked into an argument as to whether information systems will result in a lot of change or little or no change. To me, this type of debate would be almost meaningless because the amount of change would depend almost entirely on the system you are designing and the situation in which you are installing it. I think the focus should be on the objective we are trying to achieve through the design of an information system and how we get from here to there.

3. The Effect of Systems Errors

The existence of errors in a system, regardless of their source, will ruin a system and significantly reduce the credibility of systems effort. This may appear to be a strong statement, but it is one that is confirmed (to me, anyhow) every day. Errors and the need to correct them rapidly cause frustration, hostility toward the system and systems people, poor relationships between organizations linked into the system (backbiting, finger-pointing), and in some instances a feeling of helplessness and wanting to give up. I cannot stress strongly enough the need to keep systems error-free (not always possible) and to correct errors as rapidly as possible and in a way that does not cause individuals to become defensive.

In one of our systems, we had an intolerable error rate which resulted in poor systems performance, very negative relationships between organizations involved in the system (everyone blaming everyone else), very negative attitudes toward systems people (everyone blaming them and the system), and a defensive attitude on the part of the systems people (they blamed the users). We found that we were able to significantly reduce errors (from an error index of 100 to an index of 15 in six to eight weeks) by taking the following steps:

1. Creating an positive climate for learning by establishing a learning period. During this period, the objective was to learn from past mistakes and to eliminate errors. People were assured that they would not be reprimanded for their errors.
2. Sorting out errors by type, i.e., users and system.
3. Providing help to users to reduce their errors; correcting the system where needed.
4. Providing feedback on error performance to people/organization units so they could see where to focus their efforts and to enable them to see their progress.

This approach took people off the defensive and focused attention and resources in those places where the errors were being generated. This error reduction program not only improved the performance of the current system, but made it possible to more smoothly introduce more advanced systems in this area.

Again, I would like to point out that there is nothing more demoralizing to a work group than to be confronted with a new system which (a) has a large number of error messages, (b) to be blamed for making the errors, and (c) see no way out of the problem. Error control must be a top priority item in implementing and operating any system.

4. Relationships Between Systems Designers and Systems Users

In our organization, the efforts and the outputs of the systems designers are increasing rapidly. Our systems effort is centralized in one organization and the systems people have the opportunity to look into every aspect of the organization's operations. Centralization of systems people has several advantages.

1. It enables systems people to look broadly at the business and to design systems which cut across a number of functions when this is necessary in order to design a good system.
2. It enables systems people to commit some part of their resources to the development of their art.
3. It enables design and implementation of systems which are integrated in the true sense of the word, i.e., common data bases, common interfaces and common hardware.

Centralization of systems efforts can, however, lead to certain imbalances, particularly in the role played by the user. It is to these imbalances that I would like to address myself in this section, and particularly to the responsibilities of the user in the development and implementation of an information system.

My observations have led me to believe that users play too passive a role when the systems effort is centralized, i.e., the users tend to leave too much of the job to the systems people. I also feel that many of the after-the-fact system problems which I have described above could be prevented by a more active role by the users. I see the responsibility of the user organization during the development and implementation of an information system as follows:

1. The user must commit some resources in his organization to act as an interface with the systems organization. The individual or individuals designated must have sufficient knowledge, authority and prestige to enable him to act for the user organization and to make decisions about the proposed system. These people must be good enough to command the respect of systems people and to influence their own organizations in regard to system characteristics. The user organization is responsible for making sure that systems people understand their needs and requirements. To do this, they need one of their best men in place to speak and to negotiate for them.
2. The user organization should be held responsible for developing the organization and jobs that will be needed to facilitate the operation of the proposed system and which will derive the benefits from the investment that is being made for them. I have seen a number of instances where the user organization does not consider its organization and job problems until after the system has been imple-

mented. At this time these problems become quite evident and also quite difficult to manage. I am convinced that many of the organization and job changes required by a system can be anticipated relatively early in the design of a system. Clearly it is the responsibility of the user organization to anticipate these changes and to take appropriate steps.

3. The user organization must develop a plan for taking the system over and effectively implementing and operating it. Here again I have found user organizations to be remiss in their responsibility. The tendency has been to put the responsibility for implementing a system onto the systems people. Systems people can and should contribute significantly to this effort but a system will only be effective if the user organization has a plan for making it work.

4. The user organization must provide a plan to assure accurate input data for the system after it has been implemented. Many systems that I have seen either fail or have their effectiveness materially reduced because of poor control over input data. There is nothing more frustrating to system users, particularly in a multi-function system, than data which are full of errors. Here again I believe that high error input can be avoided if a plan is developed to prevent it. Systems people can make important contributions in this area but it is up to the users to take the necessary steps that will give them and others accurate data.

You will notice that I have stressed responsibilities of the user organization. I have done this because I feel that this is the area that needs the emphasis. The things I have stressed are well within the capability of business organizations as they are the things they do normally to prepare themselves for other costly investments, e.g., new manufacturing equipment. Information systems are not always as tangible as manufacturing equipment but they do cost as much. They warrant the same level of preparation on the part of potential users.

SUMMARY AND CONCLUSIONS

Large-scale multi-functional systems highlight organization problems which always have existed. The usual problems of cooperation and interdependence between line organizations, information errors, organization change and relationships with staff or service organizations are intensified because of the characteristics of information systems, e.g., greater visibility of performance, low tolerance for errors, significantly shorter reporting cycles. In order to gain the benefit from management information systems, *user* organizations must assume greater responsibility for the overall planning, introduction and operation of these systems.

29 The Total Systems MYTH*

W. M. A. BROOKER

The author raises questions about the value of the total systems concept. He claims that the basic error in the concept is the assumption that this approach is the most important one. He outlines an alternative approach in which system theory plays only an auxiliary role.

The purpose of this article is to examine critically the value of the total systems concept and to make predictions on the effects of its application. As is implied in the title, the author does not regard the concept itself as having the practical value claimed by its followers. On the other hand, the belief in this concept is a powerful motivating force among those who have accepted it as a frame of reference.

Why and what is untrue about the total systems concept? The basic error in the total systems concept is the assumption that the total systems approach is the most fruitful; that systems analysis in any situation is the most powerful kind of planning that can precede planned and profitable change for a company.

This article will discuss the foundations of the systems concept, the value of this concept and the limitations of its application. These limitations amount to an inadequacy as to the totality of pervasiveness of the approach, notwithstanding its value in an auxiliary role. We shall then discuss the requirements of an overall approach and outline an alternative in which systems theory occupies a significant but auxiliary role.

FOUNDATIONS OF THE SYSTEMS CONCEPT

The foundation of the systems concept seems to rest on the work of Von Bertalanffy, who apparently coined the term "general systems theory." Hall, who is referred to by Bertalanffy, defines the system . . . "a set of objects with relationships among the objects and among their attributes. Objects are simply the parts or components of a system."[1]

More specifically, systems are defined in terms of flows. According to Forrester: The business system is . . . "a system in which the flows of information, materials, man-power, capital equipment and money set up

---

*Reprinted from **Systems & Procedures Journal,** July–August, 1965, pp. 28–32.

[1] Arthur D. Hall, *A Methodology for Systems Engineering,* Van Nostrand, Toronto, 1962, p. 60.

forces that determine the basic tendencies towards growth, fluctuation and decline."[2]

The flows of business system, according to Optner, are in the form of a closed system which . . . "can be defined as one which is free of variation or disturbance . . . the concept of the black box"[3] of which the basic model is thus:

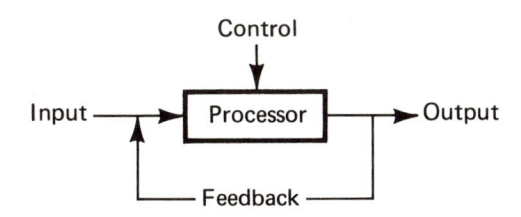

```
                    Control
                       ↓
    Input  ───▶ ┌───────────┐ ───▶ Output
                │ Processor │
             ┌─▶└───────────┘──┐
             │                 │
             └──── Feedback ───┘
```

In its business form, this model becomes:

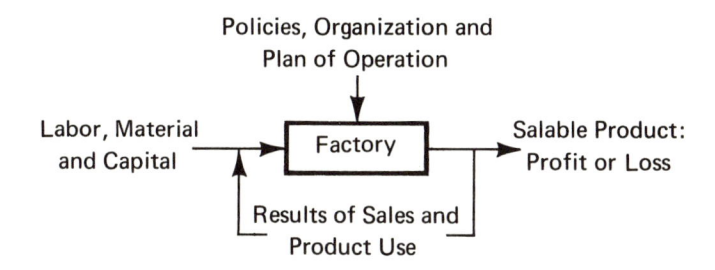

```
            Policies, Organization and
                 Plan of Operation
                        ↓
  Labor, Material   ┌─────────┐   Salable Product:
  and Capital  ───▶ │ Factory │──▶ Profit or Loss
               ┌───▶└─────────┘──┐
               │                 │
               └ Results of Sales and ┘
                   Product Use
```

An advantage of the systems approach is that it focuses attention on broader issues than may be contained in a single department. This is because of the emphasis on inputs and outputs. What goes on *inside* the black box is of secondary importance. Naturally this has a healthy effect on any departmental narrowness of viewpoint.

The second advantage of the systems approach is that it aids in the formulation of purpose or objectives for a particular department or operating area. The reason for the existence of any operating area can very neatly be expressed in the formula:

$$P = O - I$$

where P is purpose, O is output and I stands for input.

---

[2] J. W. Forrester, *Harvard Business Review,* July–August, 1958, p. 52.
[3] Stanford L. Optner, *Systems Analysis for Business Management,* Prentice-Hall, pp. 3–15.

A third advantage of the systems approach is that it can sometimes be related to decision making. Forrester, for example, in his model for industrial dynamics (below), shows information flows controlling valves in material and money flows.[4]

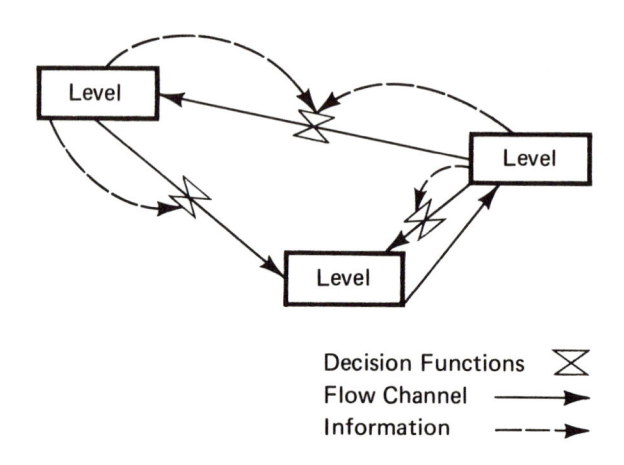

```
        Level
                          Level

              Level

        Decision Functions  ⋈
        Flow Channel        ⟶
        Information         ⇢
```

Forrester, incidentally, develops this theme very well in demonstrating the effect of varying sales volume on inventory levels.

DISADVANTAGE OF THE TOTAL SYSTEMS APPROACH

The author's main quarrel with the approach is that many of the followers of systems theory seem to have translated *general* systems into total systems; they give the impression that if systems are omnipresent they must somehow, like God, be omnipotent. General systems theory is a valid field of inter-disciplinary study. Those who profess general systems theory realize its limitations, which are not recognized by those who take the *total* systems approach. As an example of an understanding of the limitations of the approach, let's refer again to Hall. Following his definition of a system quoted on page 28 of this article he continues:

"Systems may consist of atoms, stars, switches, springs, wires, bones, gases, mathematical variables, equations, laws and processes.[5]

Nowhere in this list does he refer to businesses or people; nowhere in his book does he suggest the use of systems engineering models in business.

Bertalanffy remains conservative:

---

[4] From J. W. Forrester, *Industrial Dynamics*, John Wiley & Sons, New York, 1961, p. 67.
[5] Hall, *Ibid.*, p. 60.

332 The Emergence of Marketing Information Systems

> General systems theory in its present form is one—and still very imperfect—model among others. Even then, this organismic picture would not claim to be a "nothing but" philosophy: it would remain conscious that it only presents certain aspects of reality . . . but never exhaustive, exclusive or final.[6]

In contrast is the Forrester definition quoted above. Later, in his book, he says:

> Industrial dynamics models in their purpose and origin will be . . . similar to models of engineering systems . . . concentration must be on those factors that determine the characteristics of information feedback systems—structure, amplification and delays.

Even more ambitious is Wiener:

> It is the thesis of this book that society can only be understood through a study of the messages and the communication facilities which belong to it. . . .[7]

THE ERROR IN THE "TOTAL" APPROACH

In a nutshell the objection to the "totality" of systems approach is that there is an assumption that this approach is the most important one.[8] This assumption is translated into practice by writers who define the role of change agents such as systems analysis in terms of the total systems concept.

In term of this concept, the role of the change agents is to design the business system in terms of *flows* of information, materials, money and people, and to persuade members of the enterprise to adopt the system or sub-system so designed. The author has never come across a situation where this has actually been achieved nor has he read an account of where this has been done. This may be coincidental or it may be because of the following:

1. The total systems approach in business makes no attempt to explain, predict or understand why the human members of the business system act the way they do. It is concerned with components of a business system in the same way as communication theory is concerned with electronic components in a communications system,

---

[6] Bertalanffy, *General System Theory—A Critical Review*, Yearbook of the Society for General Systems Research, Vol. VII, 1962, p. 10.

[7] Norbert Weiner, *The Human Use of Human Beings—Cybernetics and Society*, Doubleday-Anchor, New York, 1954, p. 16.

[8] The reason for the error lies in what the author calls the Magical Fallacy.

but it offers little or no understanding of those components either as individuals or as members of business organizations.
2. If it cannot explain the way things are, the total systems approach cannot be expected to explain the way things are going to be. Insofar as the total systems approach is weak analytically with regard to the most significant aspects of the business system (viz., the people), it must also be weak in predicting future developments with regard to people.

ILLUSTRATIONS OF THE MYTH

In order to demonstrate the points we have been making we are going to discuss two articles, both heavily influenced by the total systems concept.

The first is "Analyzing an Overall System" by Charles J. Berg.[9] Early in his article he defines a business system as a:

> ". . . set of policies, rules, and procedures which defines the actions, responsibilities, and authorities of all elements of a business organization in the day-by-day conduct of its normal activities."

This is all-encompassing, and justifies us as classifying it as being an wholistic or total approach. How does Mr. Berg use it? The core of his article is concerned with the stepwise "analytical technique for defining our present position and for use as a systems reference point. Step One is the use of the conventional flow chart of the existing system, with each step analyzed and measured showing the amount of time, money and physical distance required in each processing component. It is not unusual to find at this stage that unnecessary transportation, time and money are incorporated into the system. Step Two relies on the information previously produced, but it is a modified form of the same information. This is the input-output analysis chart. This technique clearly depicts the multitudinous uses of various data. Generally it can be stated that where many inputs are used to devise many outputs, potential systems improvements are of a high order. Step Three is to relate the present system as described in steps one and two above into financial terminology. What lines on the statement are affected and what are the potential improvements available? Step Four is the allocation of people responsibility for the planned systems improvement, along with specific financial objectives to be attained. Step Five is to accomplish the improvements resulting from the analysis of the above information."

Diagrammatically Berg expresses his approach as shown in Figure 1.

But the author does not fulfill his promise. In terms of his own definition of a business system his analytical technique is mainly concerned with "procedures and actions." He refers to policies, rules, responsibilities and

---

[9] *Systems and Procedures Journal,* November–December, 1963.

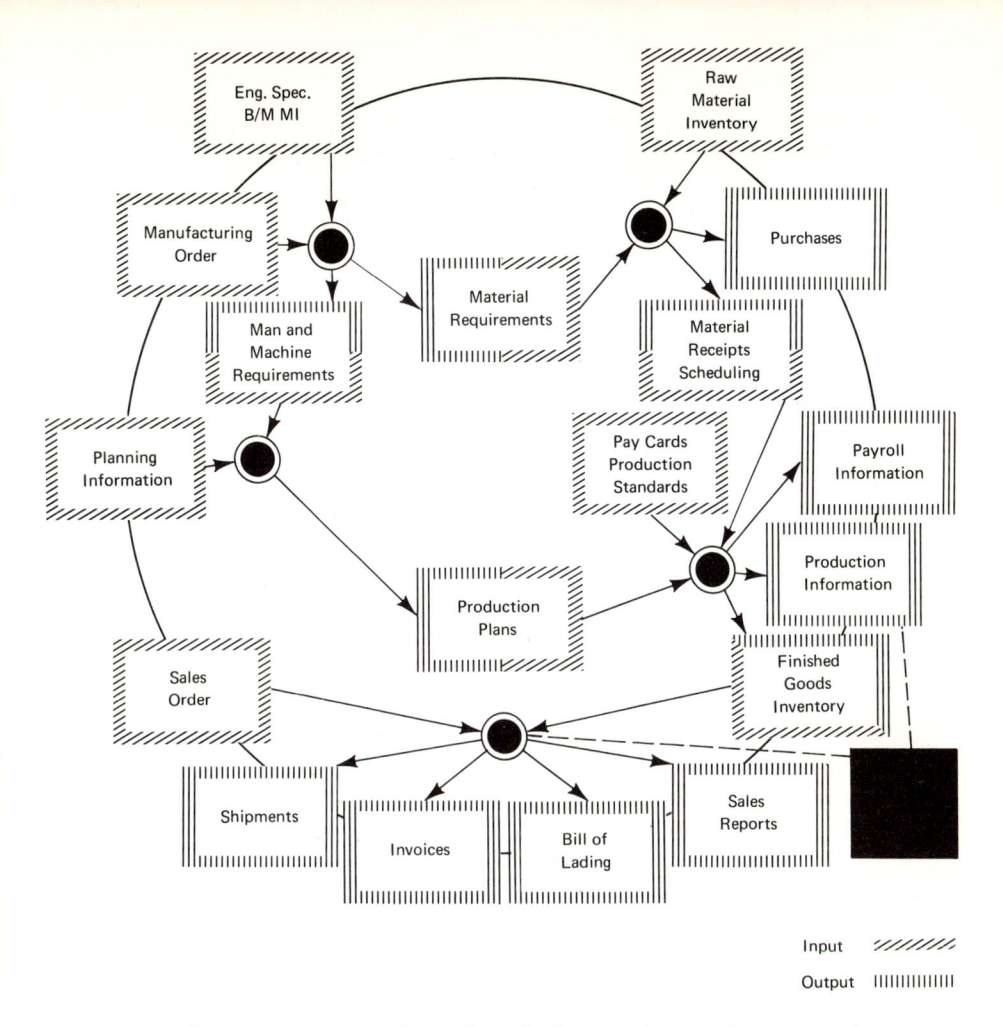

Figure 1. **The stepwise analytical techniques shown here are too narrow to fulfill the promise evident in the definition of total systems.**

ONE: If you have a manufacturing order and this is combined with an engineering specification, bills of material and manufacturing information, these can be combined and materials information, manpower and the facilities required can be determined.

TWO: With material requirements being compared to raw material inventories, purchases and material receipts schedules can be derived.

THREE: Returning now to the manpower and facilities requirements, combining and comparing this with planning information, we can evolve specific production plans.

FOUR: Material receipts schedules and pay cards, along with production standards and the production plans, can be integrated to produce payrolls, production data and finished goods inventory.

FIVE: Coordinating the information of a sales order with that of the finished goods inventory, we can produce shipments, invoices, bills of lading and sales receipts.

SIX: Finally, we can build management decisions into the system which are necessary to operate it most effectively.

authorities *of all elements of a business organization* in his definition of a business system quoted above, and says precious little about them in his analytical technique. Under which of his stepwise analytical techniques could one consider the following problems which have to be considered in any business organization?

What business should we be in? For example, should we diversify our operations, or consolidate? Should our business be divisionalized along product lines, customer grouping, or geographic areas? Should our engineering function be centralized or decentralized or along some combination of both?

In fact these problems cannot be subsumed under the techniques proposed because they are too narrow. The promise of total systems—evident in the definition—remains unfulfilled in the proposals for its creation.

Similar objections come to mind with a second article by Dr. R. L. Martino.[9] But in this case the gap between promise and proposal is even more blatant. The promise lies in the title: "The Development and Installation of a Total Management System."

Most business people are inclined to accept the simple motion that management is concerned with governing and controlling of the activities of a company, somewhat analogous to the executive branch of the government of a state. To enlarge "management" to "total management system" emphasizes the pervasiveness of the phenomena and also its completeness and orderliness. This promise is not borne out by the following:

"*. . . The primary objective in developing a total management system should be the production of detailed up-to-the-minute summaries of the past and the use of these summaries to project future activity. In essence the functions of a total management system are: (1) To predict; (2) To compare the prediction with actual results; and (3) To produce the deviations between the predicted and the actual.*"

In other words, the total system conceptualizers, when they really get down to it, talk of designing flows of information to enable management to do its job better. Martino represents this diagrammatically in Figure 2.

The figure shows what management does with various kinds of information. In Martino's model, management *itself* is not part of the total management system, for nowhere is there any phase where management looks at itself or the organization of which it is a part. It is as though management were something like the driver of a car, detached; as though, like a car driver, management made the decisions, the "system" carried them out.

Factories, warehouses and saleshouses and other industries, services, utilities—whatever the business exists for—consists of much more than Management itself, however, is not part of the total management system, for nowhere is there any phase where management looks at itself or the organization of which it is a part.

[10] *Data Processing for Management,* April 1963, p. 31.

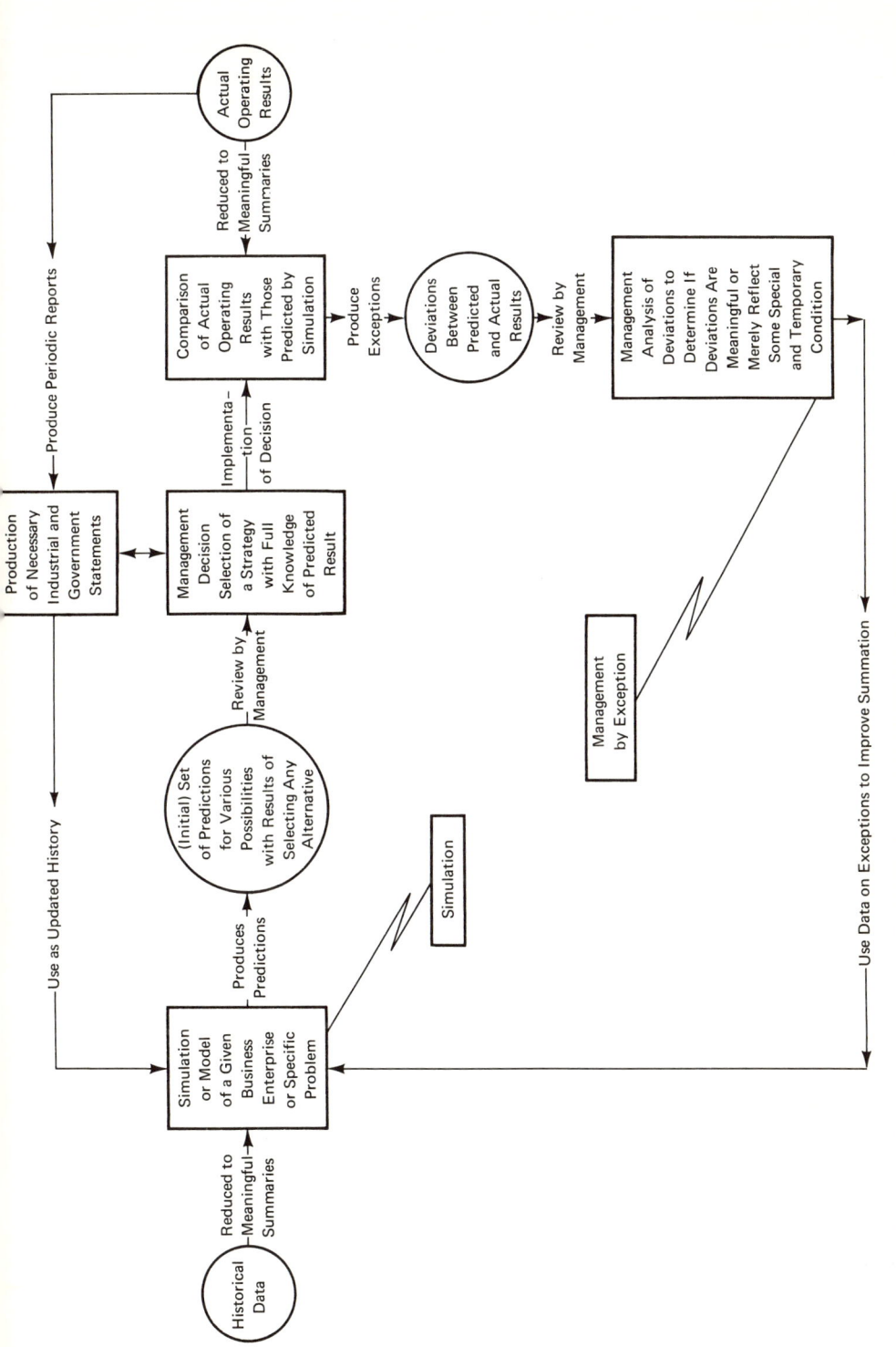

Figure 2 **shows what management does with various kinds of information.**

information handling systems glorified into some state of "totality." Just as a map of a country may cover the whole of it, it is not a "total" depiction of it, because in a country there are other dimensions and features that cannot be shown on a map. Similarly, in a business there are other dimensions and features which cannot be subsumed under the kinds of total systems we have been discussing.

REQUIREMENTS OF A GENERAL BUSINESS THEORY

What, then, are the theoretical requirements of change agents in business? The following thoughts are offered as criteria for basic theory:

A. Understanding for Action

1. It must be capable of understanding current problems of business. Therefore,
2. It should be capable of realistic predictions on consequences of proposed actions.
3. It should provide a basis for establishing direction for proposed change.

B. Basis for Theoretical Development

An acceptable basic theory should be broad enough to include other more specific theories. If, for example, we reject total systems theory as a basic tool, the basic tool we do adopt should be capable of covering the valuable aspects of such a theory.

OUTLINE OF A BASIC THEORY

What follows is a skeletal account of a theory which meets these requirements:

1. A business is primarily a social human group. The machines, however vast, are originated by and operated by human beings. Therefore, the theoretical basis should be human oriented.
2. There are three aspects of human groups which are important to the understanding of a business. They are objectives, or purpose; activities, or the actual work performed; and relationships which include cooperative and functional as well as the ever-present man/boss relationship. In addition, there are three corresponding concepts pertaining to the individual: values, status and activities.
3. The basis of the approach suggested is, first, that there are certain desirable or healthy conditions for these group and individual aspects, particularly in their relationship to one another. Second, it can be assumed that these conditions do not necessarily apply at at all times. Third, it is suggested that the lack of desirable conditions applying will lead to the occurrence of certain defects or symptoms. Fourth, the approach envisages the use of various techniques to reveal these symptoms. Fifth, it is suggested that the symptoms can be used to identify the *causes* of malfunction, and

sixth, that planning and executing projects which rectify causes are the proper work of systems analysts, or other change agents, in business.
4. The activities of business are only one of many aspects. Only when this aspect is viewed against its proper background of group purpose (or objectives) and structure, and individuals' values and status, should it be elaborated into a "totality" of system.
5. It is entirely possible to make use of the valuable aspects of systems theory (discussed in the early part of this article) within these other concepts, but then the systems aspect is no longer "total" but ancillary.

A PROPOSED ROLE FOR SYSTEMS ANALYSIS

How can the role of the systems analyst be met in view of these criticisms? The senior systems man in a company may be analogous to a cabinet minister in charge of communications (embracing, for instance, tele-postal-road-rail and air-communications). A minister of communications is concerned with the development of channels for the transmission of information in whatever form. Similarly, the VP of communications with a firm should be concerned with the development and maintenance of communication networks which best achieve company, and divisional if necessary, purpose(s).

This is far reaching in that it would be extending throughout the whole but it is not wholistic or "total" in the Wiener or Forrester sense. Systems departments, therefore, are not analogous to the management of a *real* whole (e.g., a company, a plant or a division).

Let us again take a geographic analogy. All the cities in North America are connected by a system of roads, but urban development—as in the case of corporate development—means working with the wholes in the situation.

City management and development undoubtedly requires auxiliary and parallel development and modification in the road system, and occasionally cities have to adjust to a road development program under the control of a wider authority which constitutes a natural whole,[11] such as a state government.

Roads in this way are analogous to the communications networks of business. Corporations as natural wholes are composed of other, smaller wholes (divisions, operating departments, staff functions, etc.), and the role of management is the continuous mutual adjustment of these parts to one another in order to achieve company goals. This process of continuous adjustment requires the continuous development of new communications transmittal, reception and storage, and it is the role of the systems analyst to carry out this development.

---

[11] J. C. Smuts, *Wholism and Evolution,* Compass Books, New York, 1961.

Sometimes, as in the case of a city having to adjust to the road development by a wider authority, the natural wholes (e.g., divisions, departments) within a company have to adjust to the communications system imposed upon them by the company as a whole.

The total systems concept implies—indeed some of its exponents, as we have seen, are quite explicit—that the communications system is the basis for understanding and changing society, or the micro-society that the corporation forms. This is not true; the systems concept is not that "total."

D The State of the Art

The Marketing Executive and Management Information Systems* **30**

ARNOLD E. AMSTUTZ

This paper discusses the characteristics of successful management information systems in use by operating and policy managers concerned with the marketing function. A four-part framework for evaluating information systems is suggested and representative systems are examined within its context.

INTRODUCTION

This paper is concerned with the present state of the art in market oriented management information and control systems and the impact of these systems on policy and operating management. As such, this discussion will be narrowly focused. Normative questions of what management should or should not expect or obtain from an information system will not be considered.

Objectives

The two major objectives of this paper may be simply stated as:
1. To identify relevant characteristics of successfully implemented management information and control systems.
2. To evaluate the impact of representative systems on the managements they were designed to serve.

The Process of System Evolution

It is seldom possible to impose a pre-packaged information system on a management group. There are no generalized management information systems. Each company's management has unique information requirements; a unique perspective on the environment within and outside of their firm; unique priorities; and a style of management which is the

---

*Reprinted from Raymond M. Haas (ed.), **Science, Technology, & Marketing** (Chicago: American Marketing Association, Fall, 1966), pp. 69–86.

unique product of the particular personalities making up the management group. Successful system development is a matter of evolution. Effective management systems will evolve over time as management and system specialists learn to communicate, structure problems, and achieve a joint focus on increasingly broad information needs.

The process of designing and developing a management information system to meet the requirements of a particular management's decision style makes significant demands on management time and thought. If the resulting product is to be compatible with management's perspective, priorities, and systems of measures, management's models of the decision environment must be made explicit and used as the basis of system design. In addition, management must evaluate the implications of alternative system structures in terms of criteria which only they can supply. Intelligent choice between alternatives must be based on management's understanding of the implications of available structures. In order to achieve understanding the manager must take the time necessary to become familiar with the management implication of basic system design concepts.

DIMENSIONS OF EVALUATION

No two managements have the same information needs. As indicated earlier, the characteristics of systems developed for different managements are as different as the managers' personalities, the problems they face, and their approach to the complex art of management. Despite these differences it is possible to identify sets of dimensions for use in evaluating specific systems and isolating similarities and differences between systems. Fgures 1 and 2 illustrate four such dimensions.

Information Recency

The first dimension, information recency, refers to the time lapse between occurrence of an event in the environment and inclusion of data describing that event in the system. This may range from several weeks in the case of certain market developments to a few hours or minutes for automated inventory control.

Information Aggregation

The second dimension, information aggregation, describes the detail with which information is maintained in system data files. Inventory control systems in which information regarding product components or sub-assemblies is maintained at the item level are representative of relatively disaggregated (micro) data maintenance while industry market share statistics of the type developed through trade associations are representative of highly aggregate (macro) measures.

As illustrated in Figure 1, there is normally a relationship between level of aggregation and the time delay involved in incorporating associated data in the system.

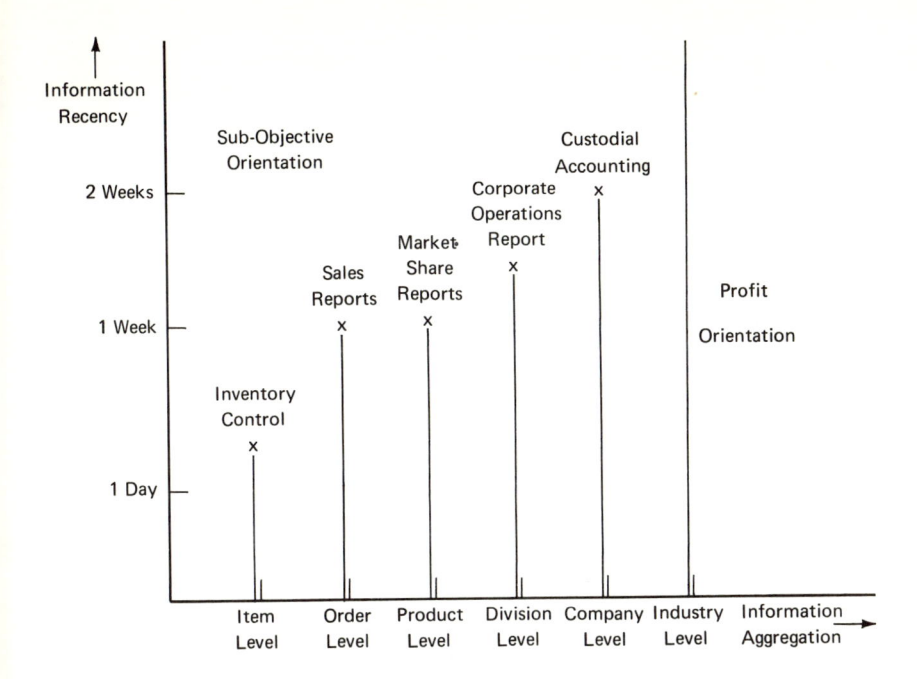

Figure 1. **Basis of System Evaluation—Dimensions 1 and 2**

Analytical Sophistication

The third dimension, analytical sophistication, refers to the sophistication of models or structure encompassed by the system. As illustrated in Figure 2, the lowest level of analytical sophistication is that required to identify a particular file and record. At this level it is only necessary for the computer to retrieve the specified record and display the information which it contains. The second level of analytic sophistication information which it contains. The second level of analytical sophistication involves aggregation—gathering together numbers from within one or more records to produce a total or sub-total. At the third level the computer may be programmed to perform arithmetic averaging or to compute differences. The fourth level, logical analysis, introduces the use of classification schemes through which various types of data are aggregated within sub-sets or conditionally segmented.

At the fifth level of analytical sophistication statistical analyses may be employed to develop extrapolations from historic data, statistical best estimates, analyses of variance, or trend estimates.

The term learning is used in Figure 2 to indicate adaptive system processes through which the computer is programmed to modify parameter values or model structures on the basis of experience (data inputs received) over time.

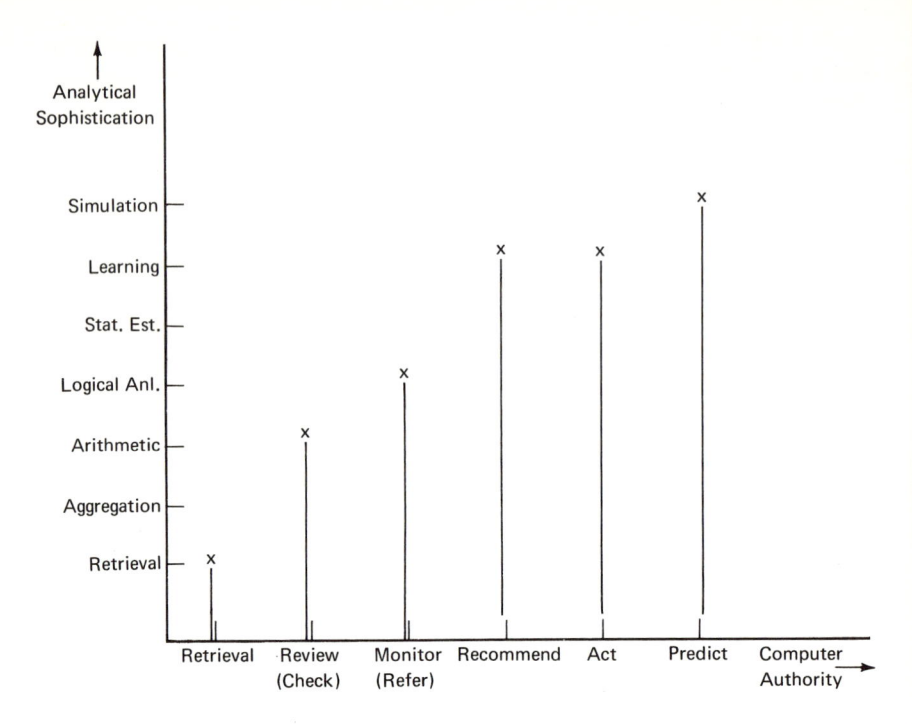

Figure 2. **Bases of System Evaluation—Dimensions 3 and 4**

At the most advanced level of analytic sophistication, simulation, models on which the system is based constitute an artificial environment paralleling real world markets referenced by the information systems. The manager's perception of the environment has been explicitly modeled to a sufficient exent and detail to justify the assumption that the models making up the simulated environment duplicate in all relevant aspects the response pattern of the real world environment monitored through the information system. Inputs to the information system are directly related to process variables in the simulation models. At this stage in development the system provides management with the capability of testing proposed policy and strategies in the simulated environment; choosing between alternatives on the basis of resulting output; implementing the policies in the real world environment; and evaluating the effectiveness of implemented plans through the information system. The manager references the simulated environment to ask "What if?" and the information system monitoring the real world environment to determine "What is?".

Computer Authority

The final dimension of system evaluation, authority delegated to the computer, is closely associated with the system's analytical sophistication. Management is more willing to delegate authority to sophisticated systems and, conversely, as management places greater demands on an information system, a greater level of analytical sophistication must be embodied in the system structure.

At the lowest level management may delegate to the computer authority to retrieve information from specified records and files—entrust to the computer system processes associated with identification and retrieval. Once a retrieval capability has been established it is usually a short step to the next level of computer authority. Recognizing that the computer has access to all records in the file, management concludes that while the computer is "looking at" the contents of each record it might as well check the reasonableness of record content to insure against gross clerical errors. At this stage the computer is delegated a supervisory function checking on human personnel responsible for input.

As management comes to accept computer review for purposes of error detection, they normally begin to think in terms of other functions which the computer could perform "while looking at all those records." It follows quite naturally to have the computer perform additional analyses on records already being reviewed and to refer for further review and action situations meeting criteria established by management.

Management frequently finds that certain classes of monitor output are consistently subjected to additional analyses to determine whether or not action is warranted. In such situations it is natural to suggest that the computer be programmed to perform the additional calculations in order to add a recommendation for action to the monitor report.

As management gains experience with computer based recommendations they may find that in most situations they are able to implement computer recommendations without further investigation. Criteria may be modified to isolate non-typical cases requiring additional review. The computer is then given authority to take action on the remaining cases in which its recommendations are a valid basis for action.

The hierarchy of Figure 2 suggests that delegation of authority to predict involves a higher level of management dependence on the computer than authority to act. While the models on which the computer bases its action normally involve prediction, the potential impact of computer based prediction is often greater than computer action. Computer originated actions may adversely affect the firm's position at a point in time. However, actions relate to the operating sphere while predictions are the basis for planning. Thus, inaccurate prediction may have a damaging effect on the firm's activities for months or years while erroneous actions can be corrected in days or weeks.

The chance for successful computer based prediction is ironically reduced by the very nature of management-computer interaction. Since predictions are often based on relatively sophisticated models, management is frequently hesitant to accept the computer's prognostication until they have gained experience with the system and had an opportunity to "see how well it does." With the passage of time management's satisfaction with predictions which are verified by subsequent experience increases. However, as time passes the modeled environment may change—the original models may become less and less applicable. Finally at that point when management is ready to take action based on the computer's predictions, the models may be completely outdated and no longer accurately represent the decision environment. When this happens the stage is set for disillusionment or worse. It is considerations such as these which argue strongly for management involvement in the system design process, familiarity with system structure, and understanding of models on which system decisions and predictions are based.

CHARACTERISTICS OF SUCCESSFUL SYSTEMS

While specific functions performed by successful systems are as varied as the managements to which they contribute, four common characteristics of successful systems, or perhaps more correctly the environment in which successful systems operate, can be noted.

1. The system is founded on management's conception of the decision environment.
2. The user-manager understands the system structure.
3. The system is based on disaggregated data files.
4. System development has proceeded to increasing levels of sophistication through a process of gradual evolution.

Management's Conception of the Environment

If a system is to provide meaningful information to a particular management it must reflect that management's priorities and provide information of a type and in a form which is assimilable in the context of existing management decision processes. In most situations this requirement specifies that the information must be selectively generated—management is simply incapable of assimilating reams of paper—and must be based on accepted measures—output must relate directly to management conceptions of processes occurring in the monitored environment.

In order to meet this requirement an information system must be based on explicit models of the environment provided by management. In most instances management's initial system definition is stated in qualitative "business terms." Before meaningful specifications can be established this frequently vague and ambiguous initial statement must be refined and restated in explicit terms. Factors considered relevant in the decision environment must be defined and differentiated from those to be excluded.

Management Understanding

Management must be involved in this quantitative specification of system boundaries. They must understand and accept the conceptual structuring of system requirements in terms sufficiently explicit to define the measures and analytical procedures to be encompassed by the system. If this level of communication is not achieved, it may be impossible for those concerned with system formulation to develop a system which will be used.

But, it may be argued, this means involving management in wholly unacceptable detail. "Management is appropriately concerned with the big picture. It is unrealistic to expect them to become involved in questions of measurement." The response to this objection is to reiterate the area of eventual system application—matters of company policy. It is difficult to conceive of a point in the decision-making process at which involvement is more warranted than in insuring precise description of the decision structure—unambiguous system specification.

The process of explication often uncovers the not altogether surprising fact that various members of management have different implicit conceptual models of the decision environment. Making these models explicit removes the ambiguities which permit vague words to mean different things to different people. Alternative representations are proposed and necessitate the creation and validation (or rejection) of more than one model.

As with any other specialized tool the information system must be carefully designed to meet the specific requirements of the craftsman who will use it and the user must understand its function and capabilities. There is no such thing as a generalized information system. It is difficult to conceive of a more specialized and highly segmented market than that for management information. The products which have gained acceptance in this market have been one of a kind special orders produced with careful attention to the needs and preferences of the ultimate user.

The Disaggregated Data File

At the heart of every successful information system is a disaggregated data file—a file in which information is maintained in detailed time sequence as it is generated. As new inputs are received they are maintained along with existing data rather than replacing or being combined with existing information. As a result, structural biasing through aggregation which destroys much information value is avoided.

The disaggregated customer file contains the name, address, demographic, and financial experience records for particular consumers. Each transaction is recorded in chronological order in the file so that at any point in time it is possible to recreate the company's interactions with each consumer over time. In a similar manner the product file is organized to reference a detailed chronological sales record.

The importance of a disaggregated file rests in part on the evolutionary process through which successful information systems develop. Although an information system may initially be designed to perform strict limited functions, as management gains experience, these functions change. If data are initially structured (aggregated) to meet first stage requirements, later modification of the system's functions necessitates costly file reorganization.

The existence of a disaggregated file facilitates system evolution. Given access to detailed chronological data, the manager is able to test new concepts and ideas against historical data asking the question "what would have happened if we had used these criteria in our monitor system—performed this analysis to isolate actionable situations?" In the first stages of system development it is simply impossible to anticipate the direction of later advancement. Aggregate data files may preclude highly profitable system modification. The disaggregated data file provides the flexibility which is the prerequisite of intelligent system evolution.

Design for Evolution

Successful information systems are designed to permit expansion and change. As indicated above, the disaggregated data file is a key element in system flexibility. In addition, data files must be designed to permit expansion. Variable, rather than fixed record length file structures and self-expanding file constructs are basic to the well planned system.

As management gains experience in working with well organized and accessible data they become increasingly interested in and prepared to use more advanced analytical procedures. The system's analytical structure must not preclude this advancement. Programs must be organized to permit experimental use of new techniques as well as the permanent incorporation of additional capabilities as part of the standard system configuration.

EXAMPLES ILLUSTRATING BASIC CONCEPTS

The remainder of this discussion will be devoted to examples illustrating system concepts associated with the management impact of information systems. On a previous occasion, the author presented a paper to the American Marketing Association describing a basic marketing information system developed for use by a small electronics company introducing a new product to a difficult to define market.[1] A relatively simple retrieval system that performed basically repetitive clerical operations and data organization was reviewed. Building upon this earlier work, consideration in the balance of this paper will be given to the impact of system conversion to on-line operations and the introduction of monitor, advisory, and decision making functions. The impact of real time information acquisition and micro-analytic simulation will also be considered.

An On-Line Management Information System

The term "on-line" relates to systems in which direct man-machine communication is made possible by the use of remote access consoles through which management may interrogate or, given appropriate

---

[1] "A Basic Marketing Information System—A Case Study in the Economical Use of Computerized Management Information Systems," A Talk presented to the American Marketing Association Meeting in Dallas, Texas, June 16, 1964.

programs, interact with the computer. The point of origin device is generally a teletype or comparable typewriter based machine, however, in some more recent systems, video display consoles utilizing a television-like display unit in lieu of paper output have been employed. The use of television displays facilitates the rapid presentation of extensive displays. In most instances the manager using a display unit of this type has the option of obtaining hard copy through ancillary printers.

The on-line system may directly parallel the off-line or batch process system with the remote access console serving the same function as the card reader or input tape unit in the batch system—communicating to the computer the desired report format and source references. With the introduction of direct access the problem of communication language must be considered. The language problem is obviated in batch processing since clerical personnel code requests for card input. It is, of course, possible to continue using the card code structure on-line. The manager requesting information must then type onto his console the same information punched in the batch process request card. Since card codes are designed to be economically communicated and directly read by the machine, this coding procedure requires that the manager work in terms of numeric code structures. While not an impossible requirement, this type of communication can be very frustrating.

Simpler communication is frequently achieved through the use of control words or function keys. In this case the manager uses a function specifier such as CHART, DISPLAY, or CALCULATE to indicate the action to be taken by the machine or presses a "function" key which generates the desired process code. The function specifier is then followed, usually in relatively strict format, by a series of nouns and adjectives indicating the data source on which the desired report is to be based. The statement "DISPLAY BRAND X SALES, 6/1/61—12/31/61, DOLLARS, UNITS, MONTHLY" is representative of this type of request.

From the executive's point of view, the easiest form of communication is achieved when the machine can be programmed to accept "free form English language requests." The language is never totally free form in that the machine has a limited vocabulary—it is assumed that the person communicating with it will limit himself to a pre-determined set of topics. In the absence of strict formatting, there is a danger of ambiguity leading to misunderstandings between manager and computer. However, proper preparation of report formats insures that the manager is made aware of that which the computer thought he wanted. If the report content indicates that the computer is "confused," the manager restates his request using a different word order or a more explicit statement. With experience, the manager learns to avoid ambiguous expressions. In the interest of efficiency, he is apt to develop the habit of communicating with the machine in relatively strict format despite the "free form" capability.

The output illustrated in Figure 3 was obtained via an on-line console (in this case a teletype machine) interrogating the retrieval system. In this

Report Distributor Activity from Sept. 1965 thru October 1965
Sales and Estimated Profit

	Sep	
DISTRIBUTOR 1	1170.53	399.95
DISTRIBUTOR 2	649.63	238.77
DISTRIBUTOR 3	755.08	284.51
DISTRIBUTOR 4	1066.97	348.56
DISTRIBUTOR 5	541.01	197.43
	Oct	
DISTRIBUTOR 1	990.63	327.04
DISTRIBUTOR 2	567.18	186.53
DISTRIBUTOR 3	707.95	218.86
DISTRIBUTOR 4	850.51	297.83
DISTRIBUTOR 5	520.11	189.10
READY		

Figure 3. **On-Line Output—Example 1**

instance the manager has typed the request, "REPORT DISTRIBUTOR ACTIVITY FROM SEPTEMBER 1965 THROUGH OCTOBER 1965." The computer has interpreted the word "ACTIVITY" to mean "sales and estimated profit." This definition is consistent with management's emphasis on providing profit computations whenever sales figures are given.

Figure 4 illustrates a second request and the corresponding computer response which demonstrates another aspect of system design. Although not evident to the reader unfamiliar with file content the interrogation requesting "company" information in fact provided data applicable to only one region of the firm's operations and a limited portion of the product line. Through the use of a password convention the system had previously established the identity of the inquiring individual. The information displayed in response to the word "COMPANY" was at the highest level of aggregation to which this individual had access on the basis of pre-determined priorities. In this instance the figures relate to the regional level for those product lines which are the legitimate concern of the individual originating the inquiry. This type of security control insures that each individual using the system will have access only to data which is relevant to him. Through the use of aggregation structures which interpret limiting words such as "company" in context of a need-to-know hierarchy the system designer may insure that, once correctly identified by the computer, the president making a request for "value of company inventory" will receive actual balance sheet figures while the custodian making a similar inquiry will be given the value of janitorial supplies on stock.

A Monitor System

Without expanding the system's capability measured in terms of the first three dimensions of evaluation, management may elect to grant

Ready
Report Company Quarterly Sales, Profit from First 1965
Thru Third 1965

	Sales	Gross Profit
QUARTER 1	149660.55	34184.92
QUARTER 2	114589.05	28875.66
QUARTER 3	73799.81	21130.12

READY

Figure 4. **On-Line Output—Example 2**

additional authority to the computer by developing programs which enable it to monitor the content of all accessed files. In taking this step, management is delegating to the computer authority for review and referral. The information system is used to implement a policy of management by exception with the computer directed to review all relevant data and refer to management only those situations which meet previously established criteria.

Installation of a monitor system introduces a new class of management problems. Policies must be formulated for computer implementation. Vague descriptions of "the sort of situation we are looking for" must be reduced to explicit definitions of that which will constitute an exception appropriate for referral. These specifications must indicate the data to be reviewed, frequency of review, and criteria of selection.

Figure 5 illustrates one type of monitor report obtained by adding those capabilities to the retrieval system. This report indicates that the computer has encountered a situation in which a statistically significant, adverse sales trend has been established in one outlet of a particular distribution channel class while other outlets in that same class are showing a favorable trend.

Monitor Report

PRODUCT —
BASIS — DOLLAR SALES TREND
DATES COVERED — 01/01/64 — 0/08/64
CHANNEL — ELECTRONIC SUPPLY.
OUTLET —
AVG. CHANNEL SALES 800. PROFIT 250. TREND +46.
THIS OUTLET   210.   62.   —34.

Figure 5. **Sample Monitor Output**

The Advisor Function

If management is willing to go beyond the specification of criteria for referral and establish procedures to be followed when specific situations are encountered (e.g., write a letter, schedule a salesman call) the computer may be programmed to recommend an appropriate course of action. System expansion to encompass this function implies movement along two of the previously specified dimensions. Additional authority must be delegated to the computer system and, in most instances, more complex analytical programs must be developed and tested. The implications of alternative policies are frequently examined by using historical data to establish the recommendations which would have been generated had each policy been implemented during a past time period.

The Decision Function—Direct Computer Action

Once management gains sufficient confidence in the quality of computer based recommendations they may extend the authority granted the computer one step further along the delegation dimension illustrated in Figure 2. The computer may be permitted to take the recommended action (e.g., write the letter or send the order) subject to intermittent review by supervisory personnel.

From a systems standpoint, differences between the advisory and decision making functions are small—it is as easy to program the computer to write a letter or to generate a report indicating that a letter should be written. However, from management's point of view, the relative impact of the computer is greatly increased once it is given the authority to act on behalf of the company. There is great solace in knowing that someone with whom we share human sensitivities is going to determine whether or not action should be taken. Management has an at-times justified fear of what an unattended computer might do if left to its own resources.

Successful implementation of decision systems is a result of management understanding of the procedures controlling the computer's action and careful specification of the precise level of authority granted the computer—the specific situations in which it is permitted to take particular actions. In some situations management requires approval by supervisory personnel of computer based actions involving a commitment of resources above a certain level or the generation of communication beyond a specified point. In all instances, management establishes orderly review procedures to be followed as part of a continuing assessment of computer based actions. Just as policies implemented by human subordinates are reviewed to determine their continuing applicability, it is necessary to insure that models governing computer actions continue to be applicable to changing market conditions.

Learning Through Simulated Experience

Given access to a detailed disaggregated data file and a flexible program structure, management is able to test the effect of alternative analytical approaches under historical conditions—to determine what would have happened if a particular decision procedure had been employed during the period of simulation.

In simulating past conditions, the computer at the point of decision, has no more information than it would have had were it making its decision at that moment in the then existing environment. Data following the point of decision are totally unavailable and the system must function on the basis of analyses of conditions existing at the decision time and historical records of conditions which prevailed prior to that time. As the computer moves through simulated time, information becomes available only when it enters the simulated time period when the information was generated. Through this process, years of hypothetical operating experience may be simulated in a few months of research. Following extensive testing of alternative criteria, the decision procedures which yield the highest performance in terms of previously defined measures are implemented in the operating system.

Real Time Data Acquisition

The concept of real time process control is not new. It normally involves a situation in which some aspect of the production process is to be monitored to determine whether or not specified conditions are being met; evaluated to determine whether corrective action is required; and, when required, modified to establish the desired conditions. The basic elements of a real time system are:

1. A means of sensing the environment.
2. A conditional referral procedure.
3. A feed-back mechanism permitting the environment to be changed.

The development of real time information systems has not been simple. Although the basic concepts of real time process control are, at first blush, applicable to information system design, conditions motivating real time management information acquisition are not always clear.

At the present time, managers are faced with hardware capabilities which greatly simplify real time access. Rapid data acquisition has improved the quality of airline reservation services, inventory control, and environmental surveillance systems. There is, however, a natural temptation, aggravated by the pressures of computer salesmen, to apply the real time capability in situations where there is no need for real time data acquisition. Movement in the direction of real-time processing is along the information recency dimension of Figure 1 in the direction of shorter time lags between event occurrence and system notification of the event. More rapid file updating is not necessarily harmful. However, the emphasis on recency created by the real time capability can cause management to give undue attention to recent events while ignoring more significant long term trends. It is ridiculous for a management to be concerned, for example, if sales in a particular region between 10 o'clock this morning and 2 o'clock this afternoon are off by 5% from sales during the same period last week.

Simulation-Based Information Systems

Systems discussed in the preceding sections have, for the most part, been based on relatively simple arithmetic or statistical models relating limited data from the market place to a single, dependent, performance measure. Since the planning and implementation of marketing programs involves the coordination of many types of management activity, information systems have been designed to make use of micro-analytic behavioral simulations of the market environment. Two characteristics of the marketing decision structure strongly motivate the use of simulation based systems.

1. Controlling conditions in the market are a function of complex human behavior and responses.
2. Management must influence actions and responses in the market through persuasion since they are unable to exert direct control.

Management information systems based on micro-analytic market simulation generally focus on the processes through which management attempts to influence behavior in the market. The models on which such systems are based encompass detailed representations of retailer, distributor, salesmen, and consumer and industrial purchaser behavior as well as competitive interactions in the environment external to the firm.

The data files associated with these information systems encompass measures of the extent and nature of inputs to the market environment generated by the company and its competitors. The objectives in developing a simulation based information system are to achieve an artificial (model based) environment structured to accept inputs of the type monitored by the information system, and to generate outputs comparable to those obtained from the real world environment.

Figure 6 illustrates the structure of a simulation based information system. Inputs from the market environment are reviewed and formatted by a pre-processor system before being transferred to the master data file. The data file serves as the reference source for the information system and provides the historical data base for simulation model initialization.

Management has the ability to interrogate the data file directly and obtain responses following procedures comparable to those associated with the basic retrieval system discussed earlier. This set of interactions is noted by A in Figure 6. Management's use of the simulation model as a basis for testing proposed programs is illustrated by the interaction set indicated by B. Proposed plans are inputted to the information system which establishes hypothetical conditions for runs of the simulation model. Results obtained in the simulated environment are transferred to the information system which formats them for presentation to management. Following this process, management is able to evaluate the conditional results of proposed programs using the same procedures and equipment employed to assess the current state of the market through traditional interrogation.

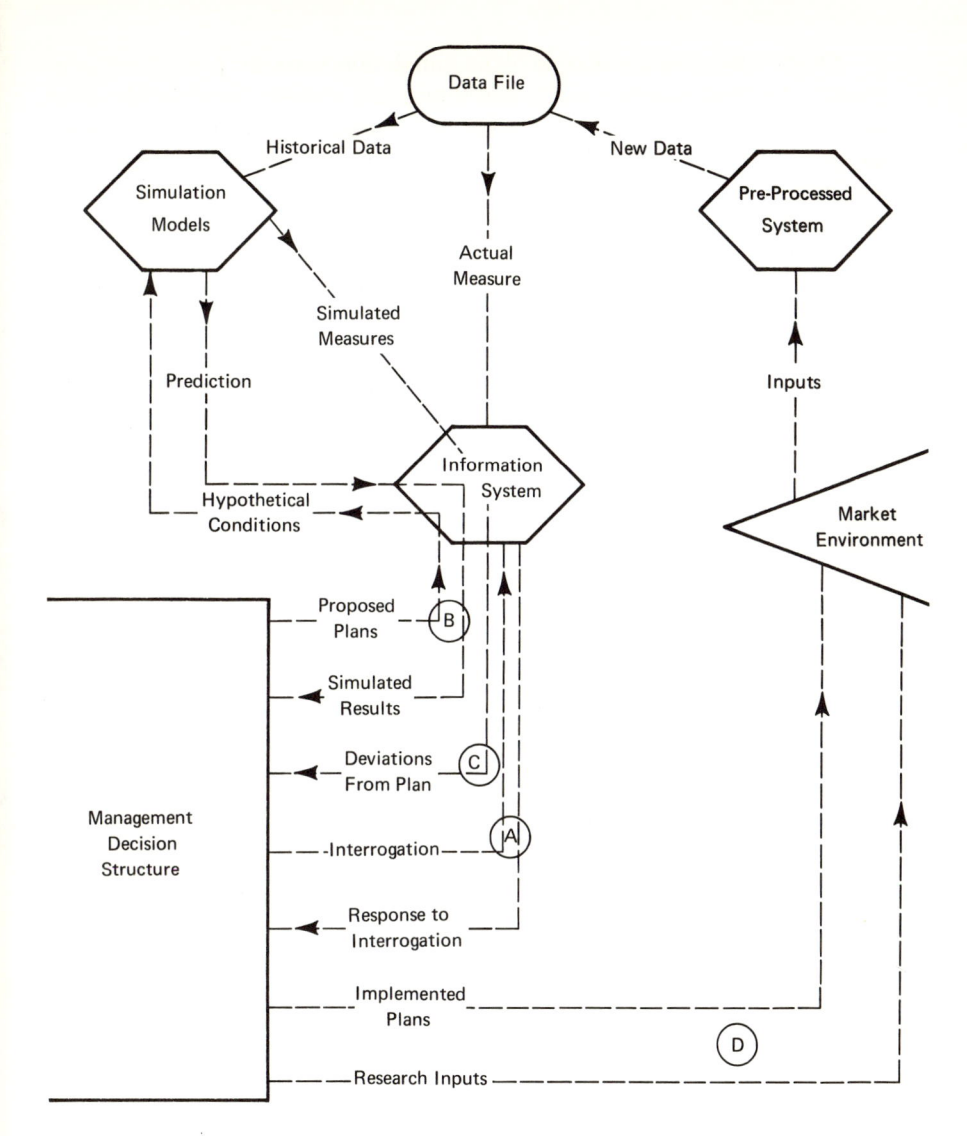

Figure 6. **Simulation Based System Structure**

Once a program has been finalized, the proposed plan is established as a reference, and simulated measures based on the plan are generated for use by the monitor sector of the information system. As the plans are implemented in the market environment, actual measures of market performance are compared with simulated measures indicating the expected results of planned implementation. Significant deviation from plans becomes the criterion for monitor referral to management as indicated by C in Figure 6. The information system may be used to evaluate the results of research activities as well as operating plans, as indicated by D.

The Marketing Executive and Management Systems

Development of a micro-analytic simulation involves procedures comparable to those followed when developing less complex models. However, due to the structural detail, the extent of management involvement required in order to achieve the pre-conditions of successful system implementation are greatly increased. Model development begins with management's definition of system scope and the objectives to be achieved through system use. Initial specifications establish boundary definitions for the simulated environment. As the development process continues, increasingly detailed descriptions of behavior within key sectors of the environment and interactions between sectors are established. Models are designed to facilitate the simulated generation of measures referencing key backlogs, delays, and transfer points at which the rate of product, information, or value flow may be monitored. Key decision and response elements are identified and factors influencing these processes are delineated. Hypothesized relationships between inputs and observable behavior are formulated in terms of measurements which permit validation of the model against data from the real world. Once validated at the function level, decision and response formulations are combined in a simulation structure encompassing artificial populations exhibiting actions and responses covered by these formulations.

The behavior of population groups within each simulation sector is described by accumulating simulated individual behavior. Population behavior may be summarized in terms of the proportion of purchases allotted to each brand (brand shares), changes in population attitude distributions towards brands, or any other measures encompassed by the real-world information system. Once the simulation models have been validated to management's satisfaction the simulation structure may be used to produce outputs over time comparable to those received as input from the real world market environment.

SUMMARY

This paper has examined characteristics of successful management information systems in use by operating and policy managers concerned with the marketing function. It has focused on the attributes and impact of representative systems. Four dimensions of information systems evaluation have been suggested: (1) information recency, (2) level of information aggregation, (3) analytic sophistication, and (4) degree of computer authority. Representative systems performing retrieval, monitor, advisory, and decision functions have been examined in the context of this dimensional framework. Management implications of on-line, real-time, and micro-analytic, simulation based, system structures have also been discussed.

Marketing Management and the Computer* 31

Electronic data processing (EDP)—a rousing success in accounting, inventory control, and distribution—may be the new key to successful and creative sales management. Here are the important advantages, and disadvantages, of measured markets and men in the computer age.

Early next month a Honeywell 1800 computer at General Mills headquarters in Minneapolis will start augmenting its 9 a.m. reports to divisional sales managers with a projection—updated daily—of each division's end-of-the-month sales totals, by brand.

At Chemstrand's Management Information Center in Greenville, N. C., an IBM 1410 keeps track of some 1,500 fiber and fiber-related products, following their use through seven different buying levels right down to the consumer.

Starting with the premise that "the computer is here and you'd better get used to it," top management of Pillsbury Co. recently devoted the lion's share of a seven-city sales meeting marathon to a rundown on the systems planned for the company's fifth computer—a GE 635 due to arrive in January. Explained vice-president and national sales manager Dean Thomas: "Salesmen are creative and smart, but slow; the machine is fast, but dumb—and we're teaming them."

Thomas Who had just been through the company's top management indoctrination on IMPACT (Inventory Management Program and Control Technique), is not put off by the insiders' joke about a skeptic who asked a computer, "Is there a God?", and was told with electronic certitude, "There is now!" Rather, he typifies the growing group of sales executives who are discovering the potential of "the beast" for sales management—a potential which Pillsbury views in terms of turning its salesmen into marketing advisors to their customers.

For the computer, it seems, only scratched the surface of its potential in accounting, distribution and inventory control. Now—especially with the advent of the third generation of computers—more sophisticated uses of electronic data processing are helping management determine exactly where they should be selling, and to whom; how salesmen can most profitably spend their time; what's likely to be important to a company and/or its customers five years from now; and what would happen if strategy B were used instead of strategy A.

---

*Reprinted with permission of **Sales Management,** The Marketing Magazine, August 20, 1965, pp. 49–60. Appearing also in **Sales Management's** "The Computer in Marketing."

Mechanization of records is, perforce, the first step, the base on which the measure of markets and men must rest. Says Dr. Joseph N. Froomkin, marketing administrator of IBM's Data Processing Division, "The only way you're going to be able to do better next year is by analyzing what's happening this year. Eventually, a firm should run a balance sheet, by sales territory, calculating profitability of that territory on a weekly, monthly, semi-annual and annual basis. If properly utilized this can give you profitability, share of market and growth of market, so you can estimate marketing and marketing expense on a viable basis."

Setting up the base for such programs can be an agonizing procedure, however. One marketing executive who has lived with a computer for several years, working out all the painstaking details of a complex information system, talks bitterly of midnight appointments with "the machine," of nerver-racked associates and near marital casualties. He calls the computer "an idiot that offers no companionship to soul or body."

As such, the computer must be used by men with creativity. Properly used it can be a tool that supplies the information for new dimensions in marketing planning, at all levels—from the field salesman who can know more about his customers and his own most profitable use of time, to the sales manager who has increased time and knowledge with which to manage, to the top corporate decision-maker who can base marketing strategy on a more realistic consideration of alternative actions.

One of the pitfalls is that the maneuverability of data may result in an overdose of averages that hide the variances management should be looking for. Says IBM's Froomkin, "The computer allows you to get away from the average sale, the average salesman, the average cost, to determine marginal salesmen and marginal costs. In considering a plan to extend a sales territory, for example, too many firms assume they have salesmen of equal ability. A much finer breakdown could be based on past performance, experience, even character of the territory. This would gradually improve the allocation of salesmen.

"Most successful companies have little to gain by changing everything around," Froomkin continues. "Through sophisticated analysis they can see where a few more drops of sales blood in one area or another can bring increments of profit."

Throughout, EDP should be a matter of starting with the results you want and working backwards. The biggest danger of a computer system, according to William H. Israel, who played a major role in the development of Chemstrand's Greenville information center, is that it gets to "feeding on itself, massaging the same data seven times around from the middle." It is up to the marketer, therefore, to work closely with his systems people in determining what information he really needs in order to make informed decisions.

The following reports of several of the nation's top-ranked computer users show some of the "actionable" sales and market analyses being developed today:

HONEYWELL: What Our Business Is, and Where

The more marketing and sales management learns to capitalize on the computer as a business tool, the better Honeywell will like it. And vested interest was doubtless one factor in the company's decision two years ago to set up a pilot study on the use of EDP in industrial sales management —which has information needs totally different from those of the consumer field.

Because of the variety of end uses and diversity of customers likely for a single industrial product, the industrial challenge to EDP is more often based on the measure of total markets than on fast tabulation of daily transactions. Honeywell's Micro Switch Division, selected for the company's pilot study, is a classical case in point. The division has over 100 salesmen working with more than 300 distributors to sell 14,000 different small electric switches to a broadly diversified list of OEM customers.

"Just finding out what our business is is a major undertaking," says John K. Lincoln, the division's general sales manager. "But not until you know what it is, and where, geographically, can you begin to measure the effectiveness of your distributors and find out whether they, as well as your salesmen, are in the right locations. Then, given two or three years to develop customer histories, you can get a measure of trends and growth in a given industry."

In setting up a base to plan its EDP system, the Micro Switch Division first assigned SIC (Standard Industrial Classification) codes to all its customers. Separating these codes in 250 different groups by combining compatible classifications according to product use, the division was able to assign broad segments of the business to its market development managers. "This way we could find out where we were in the appliance field, for example," Lincoln explains, "and where the market had been. We could compare our own projections with those of appliance manufacturers to see if in five years, say, we'd be doing what it seemed they would need done."

By identifying customers by industry, by state and county, the division could apply such data as the Buying Power Index (Sales Management's Survey of Buying Power), with other weighted indices to establish the high points, geographically, of a given market. For example, if the plastics industry looked bright for Switches, the application of these indices could be used in conjunction with SIC to determine area by area and city by city where sales effort should be concentrated for prime profitability.

For their part, the salesmen are called on to help develop customer histories and to report on the major end uses of their products for clarification of coding. Their call reports, which have been redesigned for computer use, also cover the amount of time spent on a call, the reason for the call, and the result. Digestion of this data, from all the salesmen, gives a further indication of the most effective targeting of sales effort. This is used as a support for salesmen rather than to evaluate their performance—"That's up to their branch managers who have the full measure of performance," notes Lincoln. "We're not trying to measure how good a man is but what he is doing, versus what he could do."

The Micro Switch Division is still some distance from the full objectives of the information program it is setting up. Says Honeywell's market development department manager E. A. Starkey, "We haven't scratched the surface yet in establishing market potentials and setting objectives against them." But for the first time the division's sales managers are completely aware of what's going on in their areas. Quarterly reports sent from divisional headquarters in Freeport, Ill., which show how and where the salesmen are spending their time in relation to the dollars they're bringing in, have replaced volumes of uncoordinated records kept previously. According to Starkey, "The managers have been given more time to manage and the salesmen are being helped to spend their time more meaningfully."

As to distributors, the development of customer histories has put Micro Switch in a better position to assist distributors in determining what they should be doing for customers or prospects. Says sales manager Lincoln, "We expect to carry this forward, in the near or far future, to the point where we can provide inventory control for distributors through the computer. This would include inventories for new products and new markets, so we'd actually be giving better service to customers, through distributors."

The division's major goal with EDP is to do a better job of forecasting, based on accurate measurements of total potential, and to integrate marketing planning with product planning. In advertising, more precise identification of markets has already pointed up the areas where the division should be advertising—and will be next year. "Ultimately," says John Lincoln, "we hope to relate customers' inquiries to advertising and by establishing a relationship between what people are asking for and what we're telling them to buy, find out more about where we're wasting money and where we should spend more of it. But in setting up the computer as a business tool you can only take one step at a time."

PILLSBURY: From SOAR and DOAR to COAR

The tremendous potential of Pillsbury Co.'s EDP system stems from the collection of input data—both the type of data and the manner in which it is collected. In three branches of the Grocery Products Division, salesmen are mark sensing their call reports—using special computer data sheets that are mailed into Minneapolis headquarters each night and electronically recorded the next morning by an optical scanner.

The big words are SOAR (Store Objectives and Accomplishments Report), DOAR (Direct Objectives and Accomplishments Report) and COAR (Consumer Observation and Analysis Report). What they could add up to is the kind of Nielsen-like reporting system considered the ultimate in the grocery field—a combination of sales reporting and in-store checking that will give a realistic picture at the retail level.

The program now being tested is based on 324 items of basic sales information—18 breakdowns for 18 product categories—backed by the re-

> ## The Ideal System
>
> Using the computer in sales management means no more, or less, than building an effective management information system. Its contribution is thus directly related to management's ability to determine exactly what information is needed. In a recent talk on "Conceptual Models for Determining Information Requirements," Arthur D. Little consultant James C. Miller noted that an ideal management information system would do at least the following:
>   1. "Provide each level and position of management with all the information that can be used in the conduct of each manager's job."
>   2. "Filter the information so that each level and position of management actually receives only the information it can and must act on."
>   3. "Provide information to the manager only when action is possible and appropriate."
>   4. "Provide any form of analysis, data, or information whenever it is requested."
>   5. "Always provide information that is up to date."
>   6. "Provide information in a form that is easily understood and digested by the manager."
>
> Finally, according to companies that are attempting to build such information systems through EDP, they can only succeed if management is totally committed.

ports of managers or other observers checking in-store impact, frontings, shelf position, displays, and competitive displays. How often the retail check must be made, how many stores must be included to make the survey valid, and whether it will be conducted by managers or by a separate group of field surveyors are questions still unanswered, but Pillsbury hopes to have the program operational in two years.

"Once we've collected this information we can begin to experiment with the reorganization of salesmen's time," says Donald Berry, sales analyst working on the program. Basically, what the company is doing through EDP is setting up 50 branch offices as independent units and profit centers that can concentrate on local problems.

Pillsbury has 16 different classifications of salesmen, based on whether they sell to chains or independents, large or small wholesalers or retailers, chain headquarters or their retail stores, and so on. The men have assigned call frequencies based on store size. Some sell full lines; some, split. "We've already found out their coverage is far less regular than we had assumed," Berry notes. "This system will show them how close they're coming to filling their assignments, and show the managers what the variations are so they can be fair to the men in changing coverage patterns. Eventually, it should take us to the development of ideal coverage."

Besides tightening supervision of salesmen by figuratively putting their managers right out in the field with them, the system is expected to lead to a realistic allocation of time and expenses on which branches can more accurately measure profitability.

GENERAL MILLS: Daily, a Projection of Trends

Every zone, regional and district sales manager in General Mills' Grocery Products Division starts his day with a teletype report on what happened in his area the day before. Beyond the record of orders placed and cumulative totals by brand, he's given progress percentages to compare with percentages of estimated sales achieved and with the comparable progress percentage of the previous year.

In a month or so, individual brand progress will be even more completely spelled out by a tabulation—updated daily—of what the current sales trend indicates for the end-of-the-month total. The pace of Cheerios sales, for example, will be shown in current sales figures, current projection of monthly total vs. the monthly total projected the week before, and how the current projection for Cheerios shapes up against the programmed total and the year-ago total.

This, however, is just the beginning. By next June, the company hopes to have operational a complex system that will analyze "problem" products, monthly, in terms of current profitability and projected annual profit-and-loss compared with operating target. Starting with a breakdown of profit-and-loss by individual product, the system will show cumulative profit, whether it is above or below target and if below, how much below, and whether the current trend is better or worse than previously reported and for how long the trend has existed. In addition to the division's major ten products, which will be reported to the general manager whether or not they are problems, individual product data will be shown only for problem products on the top-level summary report.

A similar report, also being programmed to start next summer, will break down the nature of individual product problems in each region according to whether they are lack of delivery volume, rate of profit margins, overspending on consumer advertising and promotion, overspending in trade and price activation, etc. While 1700 profit breakdowns will be held within the computer memory, only "exception" items requiring attention will appear on management reports.

In the area of marketing planning General Mills wants a better picture of what's happening to its products at the retail level. Current records stop at the distribution level, and the company feels taking its information system one step closer to the consumer would bring a more realistic yardstick for the planning of regional consumer advertising.

Systems work is also under way to provide improved data to evaluate trade promotion expenditures. "Our approach to this will be simple," says assistant controller H. R. Sutter. "We want to know whether we have attained sufficient net added deliveries for each promotion to each account to pay the cost of the promotional expense. Evaluation of the results must also consider competitive activity occurring simultaneously."

CHEMSTRAND: On the Road to Disciplined Marketing

Chemstrand Co. (a division of Monsanto) has what is probably one of the most advanced management information systems in existence today. Its four-year-old Greenville, N. C., Management Information Center has been the model on which other such centers aimed at the "total information" concept—the centralized collection, storing and processing of all company data—are based. In what was a revolutionary move, Chemstrand has grouped some of its key manufacturing, marketing and financial management in Greenville, geographic heart of the textile market and digestive center of its information system. Reports that need to be brought to the attention of top management are usually restricted to exceptional items and summaries, and thus constitute a program of management by exception.

"For years this kind of centralization was considered a revolutionary concept," reports William Israel, manager, market forecasts and analysis, "and it's still a step of the future for many major corporations." Israel explains that Chemstrand's program grew out of the use of the computer to optimize production and inventory, and the realization that, since marketing overrode these areas, "we had to optimize that, too. What we're trying to do," he points out, "is to discipline marketing so it can lend itself to more scientific analysis."

The current EDP series breaks down roughly into four categories:

1. *Detailed sales analyses*—by product, by category of product (encompassing some 1500 fiber and fiber-related sub-products), by sales district, type of mill, type of process and end use. The use of Chemstrand products is analyzed all the way down to the consumer. In fibers, this can mean up to seven levels of buying—including the spinner, fabric manufacturer, dyer, cutter, distributor, retailer and end-user. Tire yarns are sold direct to manufacturer or wholesaler; carpet yarns, to mills.

Chemstrand sends approximately 20 different reports monthly, along with appropriate summaries, to its "working marketing groups." For example, product sales directors receive analyses of the sales pertinent to their particular operation; top management officials get more concise summaries, flagging the areas that may need their attention. The company's 80 salesmen receive monthly summations dealing with their individual customers, products, and product uses, which they are required to edit to keep history straight. Thus if a customer buys 250,000 lbs. of yarn for women's slips and then decides to use a large part of it for inner linings, editing corrects the record for both markets. This control system is maintained by the company's merchandising people, salesmen, and a group of specialists in the field who devote all their time to following the end use of individual sales.

2. *Consumer analyses*—reports of what's going on at the retail level are gleaned from diaries Chemstrand buys showing the purchases of 7500 households representing the market, nationwide, in such characteristics as geography and social, economic and educational levels. Transferred to EDP cards and then analyzed for current buying trends, these consumer purchasing records are especially useful to merchandising and advertising planning.

3. *Industry analyses*—based on data collected by survey people in the field. Chemstrand keeps a close record of what competitors are doing with their products. A survey of the broad woven industry, for example, would collect data on all end uses and what's being done by every factor in the field. Analysis comparing current trends with history would then be used as an aid to both technical and marketing planning.

4. *Forward planning*—short-, medium-, and long-term forecasting. Chemstrand attempts to predict the levels and turning points for about 50 national economic indices, by the month, for two years ahead, basing its projections on typical operating cyclical patterns adjusted by trends and seasonal effects. A similar technique is used to forecast company sales and economic and sales series for the textile industry and for end-use industries.

In addition, five-year forecasts for industry, company, and end-user sales are made annually, and the end-user predictions compared with those made by consultants and market surveys. Short-term projections for about 400 individual products are based on weighted averages of current and past sales data (arrived at by techniques such as exponential smoothing and adaptive control).

All these, and other programs not yet operational, are part of a long-range plan to build an econometric model (a mathematical model based on the different forces operating in the economy) of the textile industry—both U.S. and worldwide. "It will take many years," says Israel, "but we're making everything fit as we go—every analysis fits into a notch in the overall program. When we're finished we'll have a miniature textile industry on which to judge the effects of alternative actions at the time of decision-making. At that point we'll have the opportunity for totally optimized marketing."

LEVER BROTHERS: Knowing What You're Doing Right

Since the first installation of electronic data processing equipment at Lever Brothers, in 1956, EDP has grown from a tool for the simplest kinds of sales and customer-movement analyses to a centralized program in control of all daily transactions. With the addition of magnetic tape processing three years ago, the system has resulted in tangible savings (based on 1960 operations) ranging up to $500,000 annually.

Far more important, however, the magnetic tape system has allowed Lever Brothers to integrate its data processing with a data communications network—joining plants, warehouses, and district sales offices for almost instant communication of data, and allowing the company to centralize many of its processing systems.

Lever Brothers' electronic data processing, or LB/EDP as the program is called, is being aimed at creating a complete EDP data center. Imbued with the total system concept in its communications, Lever Brothers is looking—albeit far into the future—to integrated data processing (IDP), to the day any company operation can be programmed as part of a larger network of company activities.

Currently the heart of the system is order processing. In order to reduce paperwork of its salesmen, Lever Brothers uses an order form that covers all pertinent information on merchandising, out-of-stocks, and so on.

From the data collected, LB/EDP produces 2500 different pages of daily reports, 3,000 pages of weekly reports, and 40,000 pages of monthly reports. The system provides brand management at Lever House headquarters with daily tabulations for each brand and size by geographic district, and, turning the information around, gives daily breakdowns by brands to sales management in each district. Reports include the daily activity, week to date, and promotion period (salesmen's call cycle, usually about four weeks) to date, as well as percentage of quota achieved vs. percentage of promotion period elapsed.

As Milton Uscher, assistant comptroller, methods research, describes it, speed is more important than sophistication of analysis. For a highly promotional company such as Lever Brothers, it's necessary to know, fast, what's going on in the field. "On promotional items and new products, sales management must know movement day by day in order to change plans and allowances," Uscher points out. "Unlike Rheingold ['We must be doing something right'], when we do well we know why."

Another important aspect of LB/EDP is measurement of performance shown in weekly reports to district sales offices. Each district includes up to seven sales areas; each area has about five or six salesmen. Quotas, by individual brands, are assigned centrally to district offices and subdivided for each area. A Monday-morning package of reports to district sales offices shows (1) year-to-date totals and weekly averages vs. those of the previous year, (2) percent of current quota achieved, (3) current weekly totals and amount of deals this includes, and (4) current promotion period totals, total period quota and percent of quota achieved. In addition, a Weekly Sales Forecast Analysis compares sales by pack and plant area to prior sales forecasts.

Monthly market zone reports are used to compare brands by zones, districts and regions—and zones, districts and regions by brands. For these Lever Brothers uses county figures on population, income, households and buying power from Sales Management's Survey of Buying Power to create 51 market zones which are then built up to the company's district breakdowns. For each brand an index is formulated from a comparison of percent of total nationwide sales each zone accounts for vs. the percent of total households included.

Monthly reports on 3,000 key customers are available the first week of the new month—20 days earlier than before Lever Brothers added its magnetic tape system. These reports show records of the last four months and indicate how an account has done in comparison with the previous year on a year-to-year basis. They also show what percent, item by item, the account has taken of the total Lever Brothers' market zone volume, and how this percentage has changed since last year in comparison with the market trend in general. These reports are used by salesmen as a guide for providing customers with a relative measure of their performance.

Despite the seeming abundance of LB/EDP reports and analyses, Lever Brothers is attempting to restrict them to an "actionable minimum." Looking ahead, Milton Uscher talks of a management information system that will integrate Lever Brothers' sales data with records that go right down to the consumer. "One of these days," says he, "we'll be able to put Nielson or similar statistics into the computer and get a decision-making tool that's far broader than one restricted to our own sales data."

RCA: The Touch of Gold

Radio Corporation of America is comfortably in the vanguard of computer-oriented firms in the utilization of sales analysis by product, by territory, comparisons with quota, and the like. But it is distinctly ahead of other leaders in its introduction of the profitability factor in such analyses, a feature which stems in part from its use of distributors rather than direct salesmen in several major divisions—including the RCA Victor Home Instruments Division (TV sets, phonographs, radios). Beyond this, the company is outstanding in its use of EDP to establish an information flow that correlates all the functions of an operating division.

The vehicle for this is MIDAS (Management Information and Data Assembly System), a concept developed by the division's data processing group that includes all current and planned EDP projects, and is aimed at an information flow that integrates financial and sales planning with product development, and ties planning to operation and distribution.

Take the area of planning. RCA's production planning is dependent on sales forecasts, but both sales plans and production systems are analyzed by financial's Gross Margin system as part of the development of divisional sales cost and profit factors—which, in turn, form the basis for top-level divisional and corporate planning. The emphasis on gross margin, therefore, makes profitability a key factor in the evaluation of performance vs. goals.

Among the sales-related programs used by the Home Instruments Division:

A Sales Planning Program, determining the quantities of each model to be offered to each distributor, is created for the division's major model introduction dates. In brief, requirements for individual distributors are determined from the distributor's past sales history, and his acceptance of past plans, modified by statistics on his market area and by RCA's share in that market area. Requirements are then used against planned total production.

The Gross Margin Planning System is designed to help management evaluate sales or production plans, both long- and short-range. Input data includes unit information, selling price, cost and factors of cost, factors of loading and other related variables—adding up to some 100 variables. The system can be used to determine gross margin for individual models or for families of products, expressed in dollars per unit or as a percentage of change from a predetermined base.

The system is the basis for reports on unit sales analysis, sales plan analysis, and product mix analysis (evaluation, by time period, by family and line for a particular plan, the sales dollar, factor cost, loadings, loaded and unloaded gross margin).

The Sales Production Inventory System, still in the planning stage, is designed to evaluate a specific sales plan in terms of production and tooling capabilities, manpower requirements and gross margin produced. Among other benefits, it's expected to provide a basis for product planning, plant analysis and forecasting.

At the other end of the sales cycle, distributor progress is evaluated by such analyses as (1) a weekly Sales Planning Program Status Report showing total commitments, sales, shipments and balances for each model and distributor; and (2) a report showing sales percentages and weeks' supply on hand for each product line.

The market research department has developed a monthly Dealer Sales Report showing sales by product, by dealer county area and by distributor. What the Home Instruments Division wants to do now is carry the analysis one step further—right into the marketplace, with consumer analyses. RCA is experimenting with different ways of getting dealer feedback, such as representative retail sampling reports on the last and next to last model set (or any make) sold, and the time elapsed since the last sale. The problem is getting the data in time to act on any trend indications. But the area is deemed important enough that D. J. McCarthy, the division's manager of market research, recently proposed that all the firms in the industry work together towards educating their respective dealers to feed back such retail trends.

Looking ahead, one of the planned projects for MIDAS involves construction of an econometric model for forecasting industry sales. The model would assist in determining cyclical, seasonal, secular and random effects in past industry sales, after which these data will be individually analyzed and forecast and summed up into a single forecast of industry.

In particular, the division's information system is being keyed to improved accuracy and timing of forecasting—giving management the means to know, for example, where the market will be in five or ten years, and the predicted moment and speed with which a market change such as the mass move to color TV will occur.

Through integration of the various programs in MIDAS, its creators hope to improve forecasting and model building to the point where consideration of multiple choices becomes routine to management planning.

Bruce G. Curry, manager, RCA staff data processing systems and administration, concludes that "the key to scientific management is getting management to consider alternatives."

32 The Corporate CIA—A Prediction of Things To Come*

WILLIAM R. FAIR

One aspect of corporate intelligence coming more and more into focus today is the necessity to analyze competitors carefully with a view to finding weaknesses which can be capitalized upon. According to the author, a likely consequence of this development will be the growth of covert activities of a kind which are at least distasteful, probably immoral, and possibly illegal.

THE ISSUES

Shortly after World War II the government of the United States found it advisable to create an entity for which there was no precedent in the country's history. The duties of this entity, which was given the status of a separate administrative agency responsible directly to the National Security Council, are to collect, screen, collate, organize, record, retrieve and disseminate information germane to the security of the country. There were, of course, several antecedent organizations, both within and outside the military structure, whose duties were similar, but all of these lacked the stature, resources, and recognition accorded the new arm of government which was called the Central Intelligence Agency or, for short, CIA. This was the first time that our country felt it necessary not only to centralize the intelligence function, but to announce to the world that it had done so. The thesis of this paper is that large corporations soon will find it necessary to adopt a similar policy for approximately the same set of reasons. In particular, I predict that within five years the gathering of intelligence as currently practiced by governments in both military and diplomatic affairs will become a formal, recognized activity in corporate management.

Given that this prediction is lent any credence at all, a large number of complex issue can be raised and I can deal only with a few that strike me as

*Reprinted from **Management Science,** Vol. 12, No. 10 (June 1966), pp. B-489 B-503.

being most interesting and pressing. Four reasonable points of view that one might adopt in response to a prediction of this kind have been suggested and attention is directed in part to each. Probably the largest group of readers will be those who react with not much more than passing interest. The second group will have their curiosity (scientific or otherwise) aroused and will consider pursuing the activity professionally. A third group will think of a corporate CIA as a possible means of gaining competitive advantage. The fourth group will become concerned with how the potential ill effects of corporate intelligence activity can be controlled. My own position on the matter is something of a mixture of the last three points of view. As a scientist, understanding an organism as complex as a rival corporation is a great challenge and there is the added attraction of possible material as well as intellectual reward. As a businessman, I am completely convinced of the value of knowing my competitors better than I do. And as a citizen, I feel that serious thought should be directed to the question of how we are to avoid the socially undesirable consequences of intelligence activity.

There is room, then, for many positions, but the first concern is that of establishing whether or not there is something worth taking a position about. With no pretense of doing more than scratching a surface, I propose to touch on the following:

First is an outline of the role of a corporate CIA stating how it could fill a gap in the coverage of staff specialists who have made their place in corporate management.

Second is an argument that economic, technological and moral conditions of today are conducive to the emergence of such a development.

Third are some observations from which one could reasonably conclude that corporate intelligence is already an important activity that lacks only formal recognition and a methodology of its own.

Fourth is a set of guide lines for conducting a corporate intelligence activity.

Fifth is a discussion of the central task of the corporate intelligence function and its relation to other corporate features.

Sixth is an exposition of the scientific, legal and moral consequences of increased emphasis on intelligence activities.

WHY A CORPORATE CIA?

Turning, then, to a primary issue, one could reasonably ask, "Why should there be a corporate CIA?" Hasn't there already been a proliferation of staff specialists, each claiming the ear of the decision maker and each justifying his salary or fee on the basis of producing reports rather than a salable product? To answer this question fairly requires a look at history and an appreciation of the common characteristics of all staff work. (My usage of the word "staff" is strongly influenced by military practice which tends to make a sharp distinction between those who plan and advise and those who act and bear direct responsibility.)

There is a class of simple, well-delimited situations wherein there is no reason whatsoever to do other than concentrate in a single brain the activities of exploring alternatives and reaching a decision. In this simple kind of situation the cost of communication with all its ramifications of establishing common concepts and language far outweighs the expected cost of error due to misassessment or miscalculation on the part of an individual. The essence of such a situation is captured in the aphorism, "Too many cooks spoil the broth." But as soon as one becomes concerned with situations which are even slightly complicated, the balance tends to shift the other way rapidly, i.e., the totality of thinking and acting must be shared by two or more individuals. The reason for the shift is twofold. First, the reliability of conclusions drawn from a single individual's conceptual and computational capacity decreases rapidly as complexity increases. Secondly, and more important, when a situation is consciously conceived as being complex, it is likely that there is a high payoff from arriving at the correct conclusion. Said another way, it would seem that human beings do a reasonably good job of conceptualizing situations with a degree of complexity appropriate to the level of importance of the decision at issue. This is far from a universal and anyone could find counter examples by the score. None the less, I propose to proceed on the thesis that the argument is substantially valid.

We are led then to consider possibilities for the division of labor. One obvious way is the partnership idea wherein responsibility and decision making are shared equally among several people. This works after a fashion in a few business enterprises, but on the whole is a comparative rarity. Historically, it has been a failure in government. On the other hand, there are many examples of successful collaboration of staff advisors and responsibility bearing executives. In fact, the whole notion has been institutionalized in governmental, corporate and many other forms of organized activity. The point to be emphasized is in part obvious; namely, that staff study activity has proven its worth by standing the test of time; in part, less obvious, that it is of value only in complicated situations; in part, not so obvious at all, that the complexity which necessitates staff work also limits its utility.

Complexity can derive from many sources and it is usually treated in a non-precise way not dissimilar to the numbering scheme which consists of one, two, many. The kind of complexity of interest here is that which permits a large number of concepts to be justifiably defended as representing a situation in question. Thus, a business enterprise of any size can be represented in a variety of ways, each of which is useful for one purpose or another, yet none bears much resemblance to another. For example, the legal counsel can and probably will regard a corporation as an entity which engages in conflicts of interest with other corporations while, incidentally, manufacturing and selling something along the way. The corporate controller will tend to think of the enterprise as an acquirer and distributor of cash and the means whereby the cash flow is generated will be of lesser interest to him than how much will arrive when. Similar arguments can be presented for the points of view of the corporate economist, the industrial engineers, the systems and procedures people, the organization analysts, etc. The observation that numerous staff groups and points of view exist need not be belabored, but it is important to note that these viewpoints and their adherents arrived on the scene at different times and survived for excellent reasons.

To be more specific, consider the recent history of three activities which either have become or are in the process of becoming entrenched in corporate organization. Probably, the least well established group are the long range planners. The detail of their proposed and actual functions are not yet firmly established, but it seems clear that their claim for existence rests on the mismatch of the time scales of other corporate planning activities to those of real life. It is easy to be sympathetic with this stand because institutionalized planning mechanisms, such as the annual budget, are clearly too narrow in both breadth and time horizon to serve well all the purposes to which they are put. Another staff group, the market researchers, have been recognized longer and, at least in part, have justified their claim that it is worthwhile both to measure aspects of the consuming public and to attempt to understand the mechanism whereby purchase choices are made. Both satisfactory measuring processes and the desired understanding seem very elusive at this point in time (as attested by articles in various marketing journals). None the less, confidence resides in the attitude that some understanding and predictability is better than none and it's worth the cost. The third group is in one sense the oldest and in another the newest. If data processing is taken to be an outgrowth of the function of bookkeeping, it is the oldest staff activity. On the other hand, the advent of computers has so changed the function that it is probably preferable to consider it as something qualitatively different. The genesis of this new activity is abundantly clear—a technological revolution in information handling has taken place and there is no choice but to respond to it. It is a matter of record that corporate organizations have responded at an astounding pace. Data processors tend to bemoan their fate of having to court recognition, but adherents to almost any other discipline can observe how attention catching gadgetry helps bolster their case.

In at least these few instances, then, staff functions have been developed in response to a perceived need or opportunity for conceptualizing the world in some particular way. The reality is hopelessly more complex than can be dealt with completely by an individual attempting to govern a large organization, so opportunities arise for those who are willing to devote effort to a particular aspect of the whole. However, these occasions present only opportunities, not guaranteed winning ploys. A number of circumstances must coexist before emphasis on a particular aspect is economically justified. Or, put another way, there are a vast number of models of any real situation which could be created, but only a few will produce more than their cost. The central thesis of this paper is that a particular class of model shortly will be recognized as having a payoff-cost ratio larger than one and that a recognizable activity will grow to exploit the opportunity.

THE ROLE OF A CORPORATE CIA

By definition, a corporate CIA is an activity devoted to gathering information and making models whose center of attention is the competitor. "Center of attention" in this sense is exemplified by the flow of money in accounting models, by the flow of goods in inventory models, by the presence of conflicting goals in game models, by a queue in waiting line models, and so on. Model types which have appeared in the literature have a "sine qua non" which types them. The center of attention is characterized by relatively realistic description, but completeness and accuracy tail off as one looks away from this focal point along any dimension. Thus, a model produced by a corporate CIA might well include facets of the competitors' production systems, but it would not normally make reference to the corporation's own equipment. Again, observations might be made from which the competitors' personnel policies could be inferred, but the company's own policies would not normally be explicitly introduced. This is not to say, of course, that the company's own policies are not excellent candidates for investigation. Rather, the intent is to make an explicit demarkation of the province of the corporate CIA and to differentiate it from the spheres of operations analysts, market researchers, industrial engineers, legal counsel, etc. The province of the CCIA (an abbreviation used hereafter) will include research, design, production, personnel, sales, corporate development, etc., etc., but always of the *competitors' organizations*. This restriction of the center of attention to the competitor is *the* defining characteristic of the activity whose emergence I predict. It is also a self evident distinction from any staff activity currently given widespread, formal recognition in business practice.

The military parent of this idea, of course, is anything but new. Gathering of intelligence about the enemy is probably just as old as warfare. References to what are now unmistakably classifiable as intelligence activities appear throughout recorded history. Looking back not too far, for instance, cases can be found of kings acting as their own intelligence gatherers during purportedly friendly visits to other lands. But this rather ineffective method necessarily gave way to delegation of the task to others who were better equipped by reason of mobility and obscurity. Gradually the process was refined to the present state of the art. The current status of intelligence activity in the U.S. Army, which is nearly on a par with operations, logistics and administration, is indicative of the status corporate intelligence activities eventually will be accorded. Furthermore, it is likely that a parallel distinction of approximately equal sharpness will be made to the current separation of operations and intelligence in the military organizations.

WHY A CCIA NOW?

Turning to the second phase of this discussion, the question at issue is why a development of this kind of activity outlined should take place now. The first argument concerns a necessary but insufficient influence; namely, that it is now within known technology to produce models of the competitor which will "pay for themselves." There are three relevant aspects of current technology, each of which has undergone violent change in recent years. The first, and most obvious, is the development of computers which provide capacity to store and retrieve information at far lower cost than heretofore possible. The second, and less well publicized, development is that of various devices used to gather information. It is now quite difficult to evade a clever and persistent eavesdropper who uses suitable mechanical aids. The third development, not well understood at all, is that of conceptual models which are useful in dealing with truly complex situations.

The reduction in cost of storing and retrieving information made possible by use of a computer is a subject that has been dealt with at length from a number of points of view. Studies and manufacturer's literature show that the cost can vary over a very large range depending on the frequency of access, time delay of response, the amount stored, etc. But analysis of even what is probably a "worst case," i.e., using a commercial data processor not designed specifically for information retrieval, indicates that information handling cost is not the dominant influence that it has been in the past.

Recent developments of sensory devices for information gathering, though startlingly successful, are known to relatively few people, or at least this was the case prior to the publication of "The Naked Society" by Packard. "Bugging," wiretapping, long distance photography, and the like, are certainly not new, but technical developments, particularly in the direction of miniaturization, have tremendously increased capability for obtaining information that someone else would prefer to conceal. Rather than take space here to, at best, scratch the surface of a complicated topic, it seems preferable simply to point to the technical characteristics of miniature tape recorders, directional microphones, telephone conversation recorders, etc., that are readily available to any purchaser. Packard notes these in some detail. He also recounts cases such as the successful bugging of the U.S. Embassy in Moscow which reinforces the credibility of claims for the technical aids. Ultimately, information can almost always be gained by the seeker; the defender can at best impede the operation and make it costly. The importance of sensory device development lies in the fact that it sharply reduces the cost of accessing hidden information (provided, of course, that the seeker does not restrict the means he uses).

The third kind of technical development, that of models which can cope with complexity, is both the most difficult to describe and the most difficult to justify as having occurred. The problem is not one of justifying the need for a suitable class of models since we now require a variety of models to describe a business *from the inside*. The task of capturing aspects of value from the outside is obviously much more difficult. Rather, the requirement seems to be for a long digression on the applicability to intelligence models of the modes of thought of cyberneticians, learning machine designers, and students of self-organizing systems. Since this discussion properly belongs to a later section of this paper, it seems best not to pursue the issue at this point.

The second basic argument for the development of CCIA in the next few years rests on the thesis that companies will achieve much greater understanding of the magnitude of effects that stem from the actions of their competitors. At present, there is neither a high level of such understanding nor much effort expended to increase it. And so long as one is surrounded by a kind of multivariate chaos, or at least feels that this is the case, there is little motivation to sort out the causes of exogenous events. But there is reason to suspect that the current state of affairs is only in local equilibrium and that as understanding of internal relationships is increased, ability to sort out such causes will also increase. A natural consequence is further allocation of effort to isolate them. Carried to a logical conclusion, critical positive feedback will ensue and drive the whole system to quite a different point of equilibrium wherein all contenders (perhaps better named as survivors) will have a much more thorough understanding of both their own and their competitors' operations. Obviously, this will not happen overnight particularly since the current situation is sub-critical and moving toward criticality at an apparently slow rate. On the other hand, the consequences of positive feedback are notoriously rapid and one can easily misestimate the timing of events by failing to recognize the inadequacy of simple extrapolation.

The effort necessary to carry out CCIA activities will, of course, have to come from somwhere. But, here again, there is an influence, namely automation, which will tend to make resources available. Perhaps I should emphasize now that this whole essay is presented on the basis of prediction, not advocacy. It seems entirely reasonable to react with dismay to a suggestion that the activities in question, which may include spying, will absorb energies released from productive labor. But in the absence of other factors, which for the most part have yet to appear, the course of events predicted seems inevitable.

The basis for this claim becomes more apparent if the global point of view is abandoned and the situation is examined from the viewpoint of an executive who carries the ultimate responsibility for the success of his organization. To take an extreme case, assume that his product rests on a very fast changing technology like solid state electronics. He may adopt a common strategy and seek success simply by attempting to produce better products or lower priced products than his competitors. That is, he can base his claim for survival on having a more technically capable organization than his competitors. But what are the odds of being that much better or faster in developing products than the competitor? Current events are demonstrating that they are not high. Suppose, however, that he must bet a substantial share of his development resources on a particular device. How much is it worth to him to know what his competition is doing in the same field? My guess is lots. The simple fact that a financially and technically stronger competitor is researching a particular area may well be enough to cause our executive to drastically shift his emphasis. This case, of course, typifies the kind of situation wherein the role of intelligence is familiar and uncomplicated. The existence of a highly critical item of information is a given condition and the problem is to find it. In such a situation, we could criticize the executive only if he failed to pursue the needed observation.

It seems reasonable to believe that he will see the situation in approximately the same way. He may do no more than peruse appropriate technical journals for clues. He may only tell his people to keep their eyes open at technical meetings. Or he may take some more overt step like trying to hire a knowledgeable employee of a competitor suspected of pursuing similar research. If he is even more aggressive, he will start some covert operation such as buying knowledge from a competitor's employee or planting an agent on the competitor's staff. Clearly, at some point the actions become both morally and legally indefensible, but this condition is irrelevant to the point that a good executive will indeed conduct an intelligence operation of some kind when faced with such a situation.

At the other end of the spectrum is the case where the technical base of operations is quite stable and well established. Interestingly enough, a number of obvious candidates fail to meet these two criteria. For example, steel and glass making are going through substantial technical changes. The environment of sugar refining has been upset by Cuba's political development. Traditional building materials and methods are changing, etc. Perhaps the best example of enterprice is not too affected by technical change is money lending. But even here there is strong motivation toward increased attention being given to what competitors are doing.

Consider the problem of the chief executive officer of a bank in maintaining and increasing the fortunes of his organization. Little, if anything, in his sphere of interest changes as fast as electronic products. Furthermore, his alternatives are circumscribed by governmental regulations. Yet, the fact remains that some banks prosper and grow at a rapid pace while others fail to survive and end up as the junior element in a merger. It is clear that the time scale of events is substantially different from that of the electronics world and it appears that critical elements of information are less likely to exist. On the surface, it would appear that an intelligence activity would offer little prospect of being effective. But one needs only to look beneath the surface to find that such is not the case. "Looking beneath the surface" means no more than formulating more sophisticated models of competitors' activities than conventionally done and using these models to find the binding constraints on competitors' activities. That some are growing and prospering while others are not is readily observable, but the underlying reasons for this behavior are not at all clear. The competitor is indeed a suitable subject for detailed observation and research. Its complexity, however, precludes a high level of understanding when the only resource allocated is part of the time of individuals who have other more immediate responsibilities.

INTELLIGENCE ACTIVITY ALREADY AT WORK

The third major argument of this paper is that one could reasonably reach the conclusion that corporate intelligence activity lacks only formal recognition and its own methodology. This may well be held to be self-evident, but a few illustrations will at least indicate the range of evidence which is quite large.

Some examples are:

1. The Macy shopping team introduced during the era when the store featured "6% less for cash."

2. The Wall Street Journal advertisements which feature the useful intelligence that bank officers gather for their customers.

3. The Honeywell "200" computer, a perfect example of a machine that was built to supplant a competitor's product. When a company writes and advertises a program to "liberate" the customer from his supposed bondage, there can be little mistake about intent. It might be argued that this course of action required "intelligence" only in the IQ sense, but analysis of the situation, particularly with reference to timing of the new product, suggest either good intelligence or very good luck.

4. The corporation whose successful formation purportedly is based on the "theft" of $10,000,000 worth of research. Assuming that this is an accurate picture of the facts, and some knowledgeable observers do, the group who seceded from their employer to form the new corporation most certainly conducted an intelligence activity from a very privileged position.

5. The widely publicized case of recent date centered on the manufacture and sale of antibiotics. There are charges and counter-charges now being reviewed in the courts, a ring of drug secret thieves has purportedly been exposed; there is evidence of collusion leading to price fixing on government sales, and so on.

6. A final case which needs only be mentioned here since Time Magazine reported on it in some detail. This is the apparently well established practice of the automobile manufacturers spying on each other for styling information.

This list could, of course, be extended to almost any length desired, but lengthening it would simply reinforce a belief that a wide variety of activities which can properly be labelled "intelligence gathering" do go on. On the other hand, the list neither confirms nor denies my conjecture that few of these actions have been taken as a result of, or in conjunction with, the development of a formal model. Just as any organization plans with or without a long range planning staff and operates with or without an operations analysis staff, so it gathers intelligence with or without a formal staff charged with gathering it. About all that one can be sure of is that any careful analysis that may have been done so far is well hidden. The change to be expected is one of giving more recognition to the need for formal intelligence analysis and more recognition to those who will make the analyses. Groups will be given opportunity to make specific hypotheses about competitors and will be assigned well defined responsibility to perform the intelligence gathering tasks necessary to confirm or deny them.

THE FORMATION OF A CCIA

The current situation seems analogous to that of about 1950 with CCIA activity playing the role of operations research. At that time, a few people felt that models useful for controlling operations could be developed by a staff with a particular background and training (that of science). "Useful" in the sense used meant ultimately "more than effective enough to pay for their cost." This feeling was a hypothesis rather than a result of much demonstrable evidence; consequently, advocates had to plead for a chance to demonstrate their case. The same may reasonably be expected by would-be developers of intelligence models. Such a person is in the position of asking for appreciable resources to research an admittedly very complex phenomenon and he cannot in honesty guarantee success in any particular instance. Operations research grew slowly as a result of being a gamble in the earlier days and the same sort of influences will slow the development of the CCIA. There is an important compensating influence, however, in that operations analysts have demonstrated the power of the formal model in internal business operations. It would seem a substantially lesser job to demonstrate that formal models will work well on a different scene.

At this point, it should be clear that a CCIA has been defined in such a way that "cloak and dagger" operations are a relatively small part of the whole. It would be foolish to ignore the potential of such activities, but they become important only after the criticality of some item of information has already been established. A "fishing" expedition carried on covertly will probably be very expensive simply because the bulk of what is uncovered is apt to be of very limited use. Or, put another way, there is so much less expensive information which goes undigested and unused that intelligence money is better spent trying to make sense of what is available without resorting to covert methods. To the extent intelligence work is limited to this kind of activity, moral issues are largely irrelevant and one is free to consider the scientifically interesting aspects.

Assuming for the moment that life is so simple, the following guidelines may be useful if one chooses to create a CCIA or to work with one:

1. Recognition should be given to the fact that most scientific work requires a continual interplay of data gathering and model making. Some people tend to "ivory tower" hypotheses and then check them with data. Others prefer to gather data more or less haphazardly and then ruminate over it until a model emerges. There can be no hard and fast rule to choose

between these two approaches, but since some data will likely be expensive to get, the chances are that the first approach will be preferred.

2. An aspect of operations research that is, or at least used to be, strongly emphasized is that the analyst should build normative models. The precept for the intelligence modeler is the opposite; namely, to build descriptive models. This suggestion stems from the apparently useful maxim that responsibility for operations and intelligence should be separated. It is likely that one will need all his resources to predict the behavior of a competitor and that he will hopelessly overload and bog down if advice on operational decisions is added to an already complex task.

3. Intelligence model builders will be well-advised to adhere strictly to the operationalist philosophy of Bridgeman. The first question an operations analyst should ask is "What decision am I trying to influence?" The first question the intelligence analyst should ask is "What can I observe and hopefully measure?" The intelligence modeler must be at least as operational in point of view as the operations analyst.

4. The CCIA will be at least as needful of team effort as OR at one time was held to be. It is not nearly so clear in 1964 as it was in 1954 that team efforts are effective in operations research. But, whereas OR efforts have tended to become more specialized, hence, less requiring of broad background, the intelligence modelling activity will have as its sphere at least one whole corporation (a competitor's) in all of its complexity.

5. Successful CCIA operations will be observed to be pack-rat like in their clinging to data. The maxim to be followed in assessing the utility of saving data will be, "When in doubt, save it." It follows that the CCIA will develop and use a whole spectrum of file types which will probably vary from computer disks with millisecond access to unsorted garbage with access time measured in weeks. For some unexplained reason, many people fail to recognize that the access time-cost of storage tradeoff extends over a very large range and they tend to err either by keeping too much in high cost form or throwing away beyond retrieval that which could and should be kept at very low cost. A successful CCIA will not make this error.

6. A corollary to care in storing data will be care in classifying data prior to storage. This is not the place to delve into the relationships of classification technique, concept formation, case of retrieval, etc. It is worthy of note, however, that associative processes of thought and data handling will be important, at least until the earliest stages of ignorance are past. It may also be the case that an efficient associative memory device (content addressable) will provide the impetus necessary to stimulate CCIA activity.

Aside from these more or less specific guidelines there are some broader observations which are in part prediction, in part recommendation, in part speculation, and on the whole reflective of the author's personal preference and prejudice. The observations can be summed up with the statement that insofar as intelligence models are concerned (and probably much more broadly), the people who call themselves cyberneticians are on the right track. There are a number of reasons for this belief among which are their strict adherence to operationalist philosophy, their willingness to deal with very basic and, hence, general concepts (e.g., states, transitions, homeostasis, etc.), and their explicit recognition of systems which are complicated beyond hope of complete description with currently available tools. But the most commanding aspect of their point of view is the important place given to the notion of survival of an organism. A corporation can usefully be viewed as a very complex organism which has the need to survive above and beyond the need for profit, growth, and other goals attributed. This is not a new idea, but it has not as yet been a very important one. Given a sufficiently higher level of understanding of how one corporation can cripple another, it becomes paramount. The relevance of cybernetic to this kind of situation is very nicely summed up by Ashby, who notes that cybernetics and game theory can be viewed as the foundations of a theory of "How to get your own way." One can hardly disagree with his remark that few subjects are richer in application.

THE TASK OF A CCIA

Earlier in this discussion, a CCIA was defined as an activity charged with modelling the competitor. But, just as one can build many models of a corporation centered on internal activities, so can one build many models of the opposition and there must be some basis for choice. The central task of a CCIA is to model the opposition, but how? Here again, cyberneticians suggest a most useful mode of thought in that they direct attention to searching for constraints or rigidities. The view taken is that if one is going to control a many variable organism (the competitor), he must be prepared to cope with a variety of responses from that organism. He must match variety with variety. But it is readily observable that an organism does not respond with all possible combinations of all variables. There are always some combinations of variables which are forbidden, that is, there are some constraints which restrict an organism's behavior. When one finds such constraints he can control the organism with far less resource than would otherwise be necessary. This might seem to say very little more than that one should look for behavior he can predict. Regular behavior does not, however, imply that it is preserved by anything more permanent than custom.

To be more concrete, one might find (if he went looking) that the competitor's sales manager in the Northwest is weak, or that there is a bottle neck in a certain production process, or that there is a severe imbalance in the age distribution of their executives or that the top management habitually over-corrects when it encounters a transient. Each of these action limiting conditions and the myriad of others that might exist are removable at some cost in money and time. But, until they are removed they provide opportunity for exploitation. To be still more specific, consider the possibilities of discovering constraints on either side of some corporate duties that have existed or could exist. To name a few:

1. Schenley vs. Seagram in liquor.
2. Lever Brothers vs. Procter and Gamble in soap.
3. Hertz vs. Avis in rental cars.
4. Boeing vs. General Dynamics in the TFX situation.
5. New York Central vs. Pennsylvania RR.

This list, too, could be expanded greatly, but the suggestion is probably sufficient. No doubt the most obvious constraints of each of these organizations has been exploited by its competitor without the thought being given the name. But it seems likely that there were and are other constraints of a more subtle character that have gone unnoticed through lack of analytical effort.

The central task of a CCIA can then, to real advantage, be limited to the building of models which will identify and demonstrate limitations on the actions of competitors. This leads to the question of "What next?" Appealing again to the military model, the indicated next step is integration of intelligence with operations. This can be done in varying degrees of formality ranging from parallel briefing of the top executive to formulation of some higher level model. The process cannot be pursued in detail here; the important point is that the CCIA delivers only a component to some strategic decision maker who will then decide what to do. If a high degree of control has been gained over a competitor, the actions can be taken which will cause him to react in a predictable way. Such an action will give the intelligence analyst a particularly good opportunity to test his understanding, but such tests will be, at most, ancillary to the main purpose of contributing to the welfare of the analyst's organization. There is a certain "with, but after" role that intelligence plays vis-a-vis operations in the military and a carry over to the CCIA seems likely. In short, the CCIA as visualized, is very specifically *not* the strategic decision element, but only a servant of it.

THE NEED FOR CONTROL

At this point, it is worthwhile to reiterate that the comments immediately preceding have been made within the assumption that one could restrict his interest purely to the scientific aspects of intelligence work. Another way of stating this assumption is that a solution to the moral and social problems raised has been taken as given. The fact of the matter is that no such solution exists at present. If one looks to the law, the Sherman Act, the Robinson-Patman Act, and the present vigilance of the Justice Department are somewhat reassuring. We have at least in part responded in the past with governmental regulatory action that has curbed the most severe concentrations of power. This suggests that if the least desirable outcomes of corporate intelligence work becomes prominent, we may again be resourceful enough to restore some sort of sensible balance. We are ill advised, however, to rely on mere optimism.

It may be held that it is "scare thinking" to suggest that possible controlling actions be investigated now. But perhaps a few examples of current practices will be persuasive to the contrary. An unimportant, but illuminating, case was mentioned in front of me recently. It seems to me that an executive had the chore of "enticing" (his word) executives from competitors to fill out his staff. He mentioned that there was an agreement among members of his industry not to "pirate," but he was either ignoring it or he had somehow convinced himself that this case was different. The legal and moral status of the agreement itself is worth questioning, but, bypassing that issue, consider the effect of greater knowledge on the problem faced by my acquaintance. So long as he had only a very dim idea of the effect on his competitor's losing a key employee, he could retreat behind euphemisms and avoid direct confrontation of the issues. But, assume that he is informed that a prospective "piratee" is indeed vital to the success of the competitor as he might learn with better intelligence work. His thinking now has to go deeper and he will consider the likelihood of breaking up the coalition represented by the no-pirate agreement, the likelihood of reprisal, etc. He may choose to abide by the agreement and forget the candidate, which is certainly a stabilizing action. But he may choose the reverse with full knowledge that it was his complete understanding of the consequences that led him to his decision. He will then value information about his competitor more, presumably spend more on it and take further steps of a destabilizing nature. His competitor who lost the man will likely take an equivalent set of actions, thus moving even further from the present equilibrium.

The case of the electrical manufacturers trial and conviction of conspiracy has been by now well publicized. There seems no doubt whatsoever that a dozen or so manufacturers of heavy electrical equipment met, formed a coalition, and parcelled out the total business available in a way specifically designed to circumvent the competitive bid system. Apparently, not all members were faithful to the group at all times, but the coalition was at least in part successful until it was discovered. In this case, the actions taken were not at all in the grey zone of the law. They were well in the black and they constitute demonstrable evidence that some people will ignore the social consequences of their actions even at the risk of imprisonment.

In another case, a very senior executive of a very large company was confronted with the fact that his sales people were making delivery promises of a few days' delay when the production facility could not possibly do better than a month's delay. The decision made was that completely unrealistic promises should continue to be made and the comment justifying the decision was, "We can't afford to get religion until our competitors do. . . ." In short, the staff was told to deliberately lie to its buying public.

The conclusions that I believe are worth drawing from these examples and many others like them are:
1. There is no reason to believe that a simple appeal to conscience and social values will be effective in a system where competition is a dominant feature of the environment.
2. Detailed knowledge of the competitor will, in most cases, tend toward actions which are destabilizing, i.e., the strong will grow stronger and the weak weaker.
3. The "rules of the game" are inadequately drawn up currently and this favors the group with the most flexible conscience.

As further verification that the problem of control is a real one, ask yourself whether or not you would engage in the following practices, and, if not, how you would control them:
1. You are offered the opportunity of recording all telephone conversations without your callers knowing it.
2. You are asked to "bug" the hotel room of a competitor.
3. You are asked to note during a technical meeting "field trip" as much as you can of a competitor's equipment.
4. You are asked to design a method to confuse the results of a competitor's test marketing experiment.
5. You are asked to try to hire a competitor's employee.
6. You are asked to be a covert agent spying for company one while purportedly working for company two.
7. You are asked to research the personal history of all members of the competitor's executive group.
8. You are asked to develop a model of the competitor with full knowledge that some of the data will come via means of which you disapprove.

A very few experiments have indicated that a wide variety of attitudes exist toward this set of questions. Assuming the results are valid, they reflect the most perplexing question that can be raised with respect to the development of CCIA activity. The question is, "How can a basis be stated both for what a CCIA should and should not do and for what it will and won't do?" One can appeal to social values for an answer or, perhaps, to definitions of personal privacy that one thinks should limit permissible intrusions. But the grey areas are very large and it seems possible to construct a counter example to almost any broad statement. A reliance on existing law, for example, appears to permit actions which most people regard with at least distaste. This situation may well change as new law is evolved to meet recognizable new conditions, but this entails an appreciable period during which the issue of how one will behave toward his competitors must be resolved on other grounds.

A TENTATIVE CONCLUSION

A tentative conclusion is that *no* general basis for behavior will be found in the sense of a rule or code. Rather, the whole pattern will evolve as a series of ad hoc decisions specific to individual situations and that the result will be a very broad spectrum of behavior. This exists today in the form of unwritten "gentlemen's agreements," in the refined competition of professionals who agree not to criticize each other, in the rougher competition of the used car industry, and on through the no-holds barred tactics used to dominate illegal activities such as gambling or sale of narcotics.

In a sense, then, the future is likely to resemble the past in that the one who plays the game the roughest will make the rules. His opposition will have to respond in kind as soon as any practice becomes effective. But this very characteristic suggests that the kind of equilibrium that the United States and the USSR now have may emerge. That is, it will become quite important not only to have retaliatory power, but to make it known to the opposition that this is the case. It will thus become advanageous not only to model the competitor and know his weaknesses, but to let him know that such work is being done. Hopefully, he will respond by behaving within the existing ethics of the business in question, either because he accepts them as desirable, or from fear of touching off a series of mutually damaging actions.

It may seem, in part, an inconsistent argument to suggest that a CCIA will emerge because it can gain competitive advantage and then to suggest that potential advantages will not be capitalized upon for fear of encouraging mutual loss. Actually, the process anticipated is one of moving from a set of current equilibria to a new set of equilibria where each organization will know its competitors' capabilities far better than it does today. Relative positions will change in the transition; gains and losses will be incurred depending on who moves first, how well and how fast. But new equilibria will evolve as dictated by law or mutual agreement. Hopefully, these new equilibria will be typified more by competitors having the capability to behave in a socially undesirable way than by actually behaving that way.

A SUMMARY

To summarize briefly, the arguments presented herein are as follows:

First, there is, at present or will be very soon, a coexistence of the technical capability, the manpower and the motivation for corporations to know their competitors better. This confluence of necessary ingredients will find expression possibly accompanied by covert activities we would prefer not to have.

Second, the emergence of this kind of activity will present an opportunity for fascinating scientific work, but it should not be approached with the expectation that proverbial scientific detachment from consequences can be maintained.

Third, unevenness in the rate of gaining understanding of competitive relationships will yield advantage to those organizations which move first and fastest. Pioneers in the creation of CCIA's will take a gamble with moderately long odds against early success, but with a high payoff in the long run.

Fourth, undesirable invasion of privacy and waste of resources may very well result from increased activity in the intelligence field. The probability of such eventualities is high enough to cause concern now. Appropriate rules and definitions of terms will be hard to find, but they will have to be found lest the communist caricature of rapacious capitalism begins to be more nearly a fact.

33 How To Build a Marketing Information System*

DONALD F. COX
ROBERT E. GOOD

The benefits of marketing information systems are still unproven. Yet marketing men in many large corporations are enthusiastic about the promise of the computer-based, advanced marketing information system.

Recently the marketing vice president of a company whose sales volume is $350 million asked, "How should we go about developing a marketing information system? I don't mean one that will keep track of orders and shipments, but a system giving our marketing managers information that will help them make better decisions about pricing, advertising, promotion, product policy, sales force effort, and so forth."

He asked the question of us because, since early 1966, we have been studying the attempts of 15 major U.S. corporations to develop a sophisticated marketing information system, or MIS. We have talked with executives at companies such as Chemstrand, Coca-Cola, General Electric, General Foods, IBM, Lever Brothers, Pillsbury, Schenley, and Westinghouse.

Although this field is relatively new, most of the technical aspects of developing an MIS are no longer an obstacle. Nevertheless, few companies are very far along in taking advantage of an approach which, its users agree, has great potential.

In this article we will attempt to provide some guidelines which might help answer the inquiring marketing vice president—and others with similar questions. First we will present a brief review of some of the characteristics and advantages of a sophisticated MIS, and of the current "state of the art." Then we will identify some of the key decisions which must be made by top management in the MIS development process. In each case we will present

*Reprinted from **Harvard Business Review**, Vol. 45, No. 3 (May–June 1967), pp. 145–154.

	TYPICAL APPLICATIONS	BENEFITS	EXAMPLES
CONTROL SYSTEMS	1. Control of marketing costs.	1. More timely computerized reports.	1. Undesirable cost trends are spotted more quickly so that corrective action may be taken sooner.
	2. Diagnosis of poor sales performance.	2. Flexible on-line retrieval of data.	2. Executives can ask supplementary questions of the computer to help pinpoint reasons for a sales decline and reach an action decision more quickly.
	3. Management of fashion goods.	3. Automatic spotting of problems and opportunities.	3. Fast-moving fashion items are reported daily for quick reorder, and slow-moving items are also reported for fast price reductions.
	4. Flexible promotion strategy.	4. Cheaper, more detailed, and more frequent reports.	4. On-going evaluation of a promotional campaign permits reallocation of funds to areas behind target.
PLANNING SYSTEMS	1. Forecasting.	1. Automatic translation of terms and classifications between departments.	1. Survey-based forecasts of demand for complex industrial goods can be automatically translated into parts requirements and production schedules.
	2. Promotional planning and corporate long-range planning.	2. Systematic testing of alternative promotional plans and compatibility testing of various divisional plans.	2. Complex simulation models both developed and operated with the help of data bank information can be used for promotional planning by product managers and for strategic planning by top management.
	3. Credit management.	3. Programmed executive decision rules can operate on data bank information.	3. Credit decisions are automatically made as each order is processed.
	4. Purchasing.	4. Detailed sales reporting permits automation of management decisions.	4. Computer automatically repurchases standard items on the basis of correlation of sales data with programmed decision rules.
RESEARCH SYSTEMS	1. Advertising strategy.	1. Additional manipulation of data is possible when stored for computers in an unaggregated file.	1. Sales analysis is possible by new market segment breakdowns.
	2. Pricing strategy.	2. Improved storage and retrieval capability allows new types of data to be collected and used.	2. Systematic recording of information about past R & D contract bidding situations allows improved bidding strategies.
	3. Evaluation of advertising expenditures.	3. Well-designed data banks permit integration and comparison of different sets of data.	3. Advertising expenditures are compared to shipments by county to provide information about advertising effectiveness.
	4. Continuous experiments.	4. Comprehensive monitoring of input and performance variables yields information when changes are made.	4. Changes in promotional strategy by type of customer are matched against sales results on a continuous basis.

Exhibit I. **Benefits Possible with a Sophisticated MIS**

a distillation of the experience of the companies studied as an aid in making these critical management decisions.

WHAT IT IS AND CAN DO

An MIS may be defined as a set of procedures and methods for the regular, planned collection, analysis, and presentation of information for use in making marketing decisions. This of course is a step beyond logistics systems, which handle inventory control, orders, and so forth.

It is desirable first to differentiate between the two major components of such systems—*support systems* and *operating systems*. Support systems include those activities required to generate and manipulate data—i.e., market research and other data gathering, programming, and data processing. Operating systems are those that use the data as an aid to planning and controlling marketing activities.

This article is concerned mainly with the development of three types of marketing operating systems—those designed for control, for planning, and for basic research. In Exhibit I we summarize some of the applications and probable benefits of each type of system (assuming increasing degrees of sophistication) and present examples of systems now operating. The following are examples of marketing systems we have observed, with some of the advantages the companies claim for them.

1. Control Systems

These provide continuous monitoring (sometimes through exception reporting) and rapid spotting of trends, problems, and marketing opportunities. They allow better anticipation of problems, more detailed and comprehensive review of performance against plans, and greater speed of response. For instance:

IBM's Data Processing Division has developed an MIS which district sales managers can interrogate through a time-sharing computer terminal located in an executive's office. A manager punches a typewriter-like keyboard and receives an immediate print-out of information such as:

> Sales (or rentals) to date—broken down by product code, type of customer, and branch making the sale.
> Sales in relation to goals.
> Combinations of information which relate to sales, customer classifications, product codes, and so forth.

The data are current to within three or four days, allowing the manager to keep up to date on marketing problems and opportunities and on progress in relation to goals.

Schenley has installed the so-called SIMR (Schenley Instant Market Reports) system which allows key executives to retrieve (via video display desk consoles and printers) current and past sales and inventory figures for any brand and package size (or combination) for each of 400 distributors.

SIMR furnishes information in less than one second after a query, compared with many minutes or even hours under its former computer and manual system. Furthermore, since the computer does the calculations, managers have great flexibility and near-instant speed of response in making many types of comparisons of sales and inventory positions, such as:

How a brand is doing in any size or in all sizes in any market or in all markets.
How a distributor is doing with a particular brand.
How a bottle size is doing by distributor, state, or region.
How a market is doing by month or has done since the end of the previous fiscal year.

"We can get answers literally while we are still formulating the questions," states Bernard Goldberg, president of Schenley's marketing subsidiary. "Needed information is available so quickly that it helps us think."[1]

2. Planning Systems

These furnish, in convenient form, information the marketing executive requires for planning marketing and sales programs. At least three major consumer goods producers, for example, are developing "data books" for product managers. The books bring together the basic information a product manager needs to formulate annual marketing plans and to "replan" during the course of the year. Putting the information into one book, rather than in a welter of reports, not only saves time, but it also enables all product managers in a group or division to base their plans on the same data. Consequently, their superiors are able to review comparable information quickly when considering the plans for approval.

At a more sophisticated level, planning systems allow simulation of the effects of alternate plans so that the manager can make a better decision. For instance:

Pillsbury's system enables marketing managers to obtain sales forecasts for each of 39 sales branches, supported by varying levels of trade promotion. The marketing manager asks the question, "What will sales be in each branch if we spend x dollars on trade promotions in comparison with .75x dollars and with 1.2x dollars?" Pillsbury does not claim that the system is perfect—it is obviously no better than the assumptions on which the simulation is based—but it has had a surprisingly good "batting average" in accuracy. It has great value to marketing managers because it allows them to look at alternate plans in each of the 39 sales branches; this was never feasible before.

A large pharmaceutical company has developed an even more complex model. The company has programmed an artificial panel representing the

---

[1] *Industrial Data Processing Applications Report* (S_3), Business Publications International, Division of OA Business Publications, Inc., 1965.

nation's population of doctors. Every week the company simulates each doctor's prescription decision for every patient he "sees." (Commercial research services are available which provide information on the incidence of symptoms of illness and the "patient mix" of the various medical specialists.) The doctor considers the symptoms "presented" by each patient and decides whether to prescribe a drug and, if so, which type and brand. His decision is based on factors such as his experience with the drug, current attitudes, exposure to the advertising of various brands, exposure to detail men, and word-of-mouth information from other doctors. The simulation even includes a "forgetting routine" which causes a doctor to forget from time to time some of the information he has acquired.

While the company does not disclose how the simulation model is being used, it certainly is capable of generating extremely sophisticated marketing planning. For example, marketing managers can test the effects on share of market and sales of variations in amount, type, and timing of advertising and simultaneously test the effects of variations in frequency of detail men's calls. On a broader basis, the system can be used to screen a number of alternative marketing programs to select the most promising ones to be actually test marketed.

Perhaps the ultimate in sophistication is a marketing planning system which reviews alternatives, then actually makes decisions and takes action. Thus, several large retailing organizations have developed systems that review sales trends and inventories and then place orders for merchandise.

The most advanced unit of this type we have seen is not a marketing system; rather, it buys and sells securities in a stock brokerage house. Still in the future are marketing systems that decide the amount and timing of advertising and price promotions in each of several dozen sales districts.

3. Basic Research Systems

These systems are used to develop and test sophisticated decision rules and cause-and-effect hypotheses which should improve ability to assess effects of actions and permit greater learning from experience. For instance:

A large consumer goods company is developing an MIS which, among other things, stores in computer memory the characteristics of each advertisement run (color versus black and white, nature of illustration, amount of copy, and so forth) and readership and attitude change scores for each ad. The purpose is to be able to relate ad characteristics to effectiveness measurements under different conditions and with different types of consumers by systematically studying "experience."

Most companies find it difficult to relate advertising to sales because there are so many important "uncontrollable" variables which are nearly impossible to take into account in an unsophisticated MIS. One large consumer goods producer has developed an MIS which for the first time allows the company to collect, store, and retrieve advertising, sales, and other marketing data at a level of detail which makes possible much better controlled studies of the relationship of advertising to sales.

CURRENT PROGRESS

The examples which we have presented probably represent the most sophisticated types of MIS now in existence. While we have not surveyed the 500 largest corporations in the country, we have screened more than 50 companies and have reviewed more than 100 current articles on information systems. As far as we have been able to determine, the current state of the art is something like this:

> Very few companies have developed advanced systems, and not all of these are in operation. Some might even best be classified as subsystems, since they relate to only a portion of the marketing decisions made.
>
> Some companies, perhaps 15, are actively upgrading their systems to a high level. Of these, about half seem to be progressing well; the others have been much less successful.
>
> Many other companies are contemplating plans to develop sophisticated systems.

The reasons why marketing systems have not developed to the same extent as, say, production, logistics, or financial systems are not "technical." Marketing research technology (data gathering), computer technology (data handling), and analytical procedures (e.g., mathematical model building) are all sufficiently advanced to permit companies to build effective marketing systems.

Although insufficient time has elapsed since the installation of most advanced marketing information systems to allow a precise assessment of benefits, the users of sophisticated systems with whom we have talked are virtually all very enthusiastic about their systems, even though many see room for improvement.

DEVELOPING THE SYSTEM

Because many of the technical problems of developing sophisticated support systems have been solved and many users are gratified over the results, why are there so few advanced marketing information systems in operation? And why have some companies succeeded more than others in realizing the potentials of the MIS?

One characteristic of the more successful companies is striking. In every case, at least some members of top management have seen the promise of the technique and have viewed its development as a top management responsibility. They have devoted a great deal of time, thought, and effort to guiding (and sometimes actually protecting) the development process. Unfortunately, it is widely believed that the job of building an MIS can be turned over to a technical staff group. This has not proved to be the case.

Information systems are not merely technical appendages (developed by technical people) that are easily meshed with most existing marketing planning and control systems.

The best way to show why participation of top management is necessary is to pose five key questions which must be answered in the process of instituting a sophisticated MIS. In our opinion, each is a management question:

1. How should we organize to develop a better MIS?
2. How sophisticated should our marketing systems be?
3. What development strategy should we follow—do we attempt to build a "total" system in one move, or in stages?
4. What should be the major characteristics ("macro specifications") of our system?
5. How much should we spend on developing and operating an MIS?

While the field is too new to permit comprehensive and conclusive statements about all its aspects, we can present some guidelines and working hypotheses that are worthy of management's consideration.

Readying the Organization

The starting point in organizing for MIS development is not the establishment of a marketing systems group. The starting point is a review and appraisal of the entire marketing organization and of the policies that direct it. As James Peterson, vice president–grocery products marketing at The Pillsbury Company, pointed out to us:

"We realized we couldn't develop a marketing control system until we had clearly and sharply defined the responsibilities of our marketing managers. If the system was to measure their performance against plans, we had to specify precisely what each man was accountable for."

Some companies, for instance, have failed to decide whether a product manager is accountable for unit sales and market share, for sales revenue, for marketing profit, or for net profit. Until responsibilities and spheres of activity are clearly defined, it is virtually impossible to build a marketing control system. In fact, specification of who is accountable for what automatically determines many of the control system's characteristics.

Management must next decide how to organize MIS development activities. Our observations show that this is a much more complex problem than might be assumed. Sophisticated systems require the coordinated efforts of many departments and individuals, including:

Top management.
Marketing management, brand management.
Sales management.
New products groups.
Market research personnel.
Control and finance departments.
Systems analysts and designers.

Operations researchers, statisticians, and model builders.
Programmers.
Computer equipment experts and suppliers.

The contribution of each group of course depends on its specialized talents and interests in the system. Programmers cannot define managers' information needs, and managers usually cannot program. No one person knows enough to accomplish all phases of MIS development.

Furthermore, sophisticated systems do not fall into a company's traditional data handling domains, such as the market research department or the accounting and control department, because an essential feature of a good MIS is that it integrates and correlates marketing and financial data.

Many companies we have observed have not really come to grips with the difficult problem of providing the organizational arrangements and leadership necessary for successful MIS development. They have not answered the question of who is responsible for MIS design, planning, and development. Why is there a leadership vacuum? Partly because top management does not fully appreciate the requirements and implications of the MIS, and partly because it has an understandable reluctance to disturb entrenched and powerful departments.

The approaches which have been tried in an attempt to solve the problems of organization and leadership can be characterized as:

"Clean piece of paper" approach.
Committee approach.
Low-level approach.
Information "coordinator" approach.

"Clean Piece of Paper" Approach. This involves drawing a new organization chart. The argument goes that the financial and accounting departments and market research departments have developed as much from growing data gathering and processing capability as in response to management information needs. In the pre-computer era, it was rarely possible to correlate marketing and accounting data in a sophisticated manner and on a regular basis for presentation to management. Now it is possible, but the marketing data are supplied by one set of departments and the accounting data by another. In the absence of coordination and compatibility, line management must often do its own correlating. Therefore the "ideal" procedure is to abolish the traditional information gathering and processing departments and establish a management information department.

While this may represent an "ideal" solution, it is not feasible in most companies. Traditions and positions are too well entrenched. Furthermore, it would not solve all the problems. For one thing, it would not ensure the development of an MIS geared to management needs. For another, no management information department could supply all of the data the system needed, such as reports from the field sales organization.

Committee Approach. Some companies have established MIS committees. They are excellent vehicles for communicating points of view and for joint learning and sharing in the experience of developing an MIS. They can create shared awareness of compatibility and coordination problems and of the need to resolve them.

The committee approach alone, however, is not the answer. Because meetings and committee assignments consume time, it is difficult to involve busy line managers. Furthermore, it is not easy to get anyone to carry out assignments in addition to his regular job. Finally, a committee of peers, chaired by a peer, is not always able to exert the leadership which may be required. Committees of this kind simply lack "clout." And at times clout may be the only thing that will accomplish necessary changes.

Low-Level Approach. Some companies have assigned the task of MIS development to a junior member of the market research department—often as a part-time assignment. This reflects a total lack of understanding of the difficulty of the task, and the outcome is predictable. The man, no matter how clever he is, lacks the time and the clout to overcome the organizational and psychological barriers he encounters. Such an assignment has led to the resignation of more than one bright young research man.

Information "Coordinator" Approach. Some companies, while retaining traditional departmental boundaries, have appointed a top-level executive to the post of information czar or "coordinator," sometimes called "director of marketing systems." We have observed that men who are capable of understanding both management information needs and systems problems can make substantial progress in MIS development in this position—*when* they enjoy top management support. But it is a delicate position; one coordinator we know preferred not to have any formal title until, after a year, he had established good working relationships with the various departments. Furthermore, even a sensible and sensitive information manager must establish organizational lines that encourage the coordinated efforts of the affected departments and divisions of the company in the design and the accomplishment of the MIS plan.

For many companies this approach has the best chance of success. We suggest that management designate the director of marketing systems as a "prime contractor" who develops MIS plans and specifications, and coordinates and reviews the work of the various "subcontractors" or suppliers contributing to the program. Such a prime contractor-subcontractor approach has proved in military and civilian applications to be effective in handling projects or tasks that require the utilization of many talents and capabilities, not all of which exist in the department or organization directly involved.

For the prime contractor to be effective he must have cost control. It is therefore advisable to use an interdepartmental billing system. The prime contractor is responsible for the overall budget, and negotiates with users (marketing managers to determine their information needs and to obtain from them the funds required to develop and operate an MIS that would meet these needs. He also arranges to compensate the various supplying departments, such as the systems group for programming, for their services.

Management must also determine the prime contractor's organizational location. It is essential that he represent the department or division which will use (and pay for) the MIS. For a variety of reasons, not one of the companies studied having a central or corporate systems department (responsible for support systems) has designated that group as the "prime contractor" for operating its MIS. They view the corporate systems group as an important supplier of technical advice and of programming and data processing services for the marketing departments. But in the large companies, at least, final authority and responsibility for MIS development, where such authority has been designated, generally rests with the marketing department.

Of the several arguments for this practice, the most important is that the expertise of corporate systems groups is usually in support systems (programming and data processing). Effective development of marketing planning and control systems requires a management, rather than a technical support systems, orientation. Furthermore, effective MIS can be developed only by people who understand users' problems and who can be responsive to users' needs.

How Sophisticated?

Someone must decide on the level of sophistication of the MIS to be developed. This decision should, of course, be based on a review of the company's needs and the costs of meeting them.

Equally important, the abilities of managers must be considered. To develop and use effectively some of the more sophisticated systems that have been described, managers must be able to:

Define specific information needs.
Develop analytical approaches and models.
Make explicit their planning, decision-making, and control processes and procedures.
Interpret and use sophisticated information.

One of the characteristics of the more advanced MIS is automation of certain aspects of the marketing management process. But it is first necessary to make the process explicit. For instance, to develop exception-reporting systems, managers' exception or "control" criteria must be articulated. Simulation models cannot be built into the system until managers have spelled out the characteristics of the different elements of the company's marketing system (consumers, distributors, competitors, and so forth) and have attempted to define how these elements interact.

If a company already has a well-articulated set of decision rules as to what constitutes an "execution," it would not be difficult to build an automated exception reporting system. Such a system could be developed, for the marketing manager who says,

> I always like to know about all situations in which sales, profits, or market share are running 4% or more behind plan. Furthermore, in any exceptional cases I also require the following diagnostic information: prices, distribution levels, advertising, and consumer attitudes.

The problem is, as has been well documented in a Marketing Science Institute study,[2] that many marketing managers, particularly those at the operating level, do not use explicit planning and control systems. They do not make their decision rules and exception criteria explicit. In short, they are not equipped to contribute to the development of a sophisticated MIS, nor are they comfortable with it once it is operating. Though related to research information, their decisions often are highly intuitive. The problem seems less severe at higher management levels, partly because top management control systems are more explicitly articulated than those at the operating level.

System-Manager Balance. It is important that a balance be maintained between management sophistication and MIS sophistication. As a company upgrades the latter, so must it raise the former.

In a "steady state" (before anyone tinkers with the marketing system) there usually seems to be a correspondence between management sophistication and information quality. Managers usually get the quality of information they ask for. Though they may complain of a lack of good information and blame one or more of the information supplying departments, questioning often reveals that in most cases they have not been asking for better information in any specific way.

If, as we have suggested, the two "quality levels" are roughly in balance, what happens when only the level of information quality is raised significantly? Our prediction is that this would not lead to better decisions. In fact, the reverse may be true, as the result of the confusion and resentment generated by the manager's inability to deal with the more sophisticated information.

Information quality can be upgraded much more rapidly than management quality. It is easy to throw the management system out of balance by installing a sophisticated MIS, but there seems to be little point in doing so. A more positive approach is to develop a master plan for improving the system, but make the improvements gradually—say, over several years.

---

[2] D. J. Luck and Patrick J. Robinson, *Promotional Decision Making* (New York, McGraw-Hill Book Company, Inc., 1964).

Marketing control systems like Schenley's or IBM's, described earlier, are easier to develop and use than those like the pharmaceutical company's simulation-based planning system. So a company might first install a marketing control system and subsequently, as managers gained experience in using it, develop advanced planning systems.

"Complete" Systems

While an attempt to develop a highly sophisticated "total" marketing system at the outset has a high probability of failure, it *is* desirable to build a complete subsystem at one time—even if it is only a part of what will eventually be the company's total system. To illustrate:

A company develops a first-rate exception reporting system that will quickly present "exceptional" sales results to the marketing manager. Very likely he will be faced with more problems than ever before, because of the system's ability to monitor large amounts of detailed information. It will be difficult (and dangerous), however, for the manager to act on this information. Before he can take intelligent action, he must also know whether the deviations from plan are the result of deviations in sales effort, of unusual competitive activities, or of other factors. To be complete, therefore, the system must also include a diagnostic procedure.

"Macro" Specifications. Apart from decisions on the general characteristics of the system to be used, the company must determine the overall or "macro" MIS specifications. Besides the type of system to be developed, the most important considerations are the nature of the data bank, the form and the method of data display and presentation, and computer selection.

We should, however, underscore here the necessity of ensuring the participation in these decisions not only of top management but also of the line managers. In most cases we have studied, and in all of the least successful instances, the marketing systems developers have failed to involve line managers in the process of developing macro specifications. In many cases where systems developers have made the effort, they have found it difficult to elicit the views of busy line managers in the brief periods available in typical interviews or meetings. The systems developers subsequently present the managers with a fait accompli—which may or may not work.

A more effective approach is to involve the managers in an extended session, lasting days if necessary, in which a consensus on overall MIS specifications can be reached. In these sessions the group should develop flow charts of the "system"—or total environment in which the company operates—and designate critical decision points, identify the information they require for planning and controlling marketing (or other management) activities, and make cost/benefit analyses of alternative designs before agreeing on one design. This approach not only helps ensure a system that is keyed to management's needs, but also allows management to defer a decision on the size of the MIS development budget until it has assessed the alternative systems.

"Micro" Data Bank. Perhaps the most essential element in upgrading a system is a bank or file based on disaggregated or "micro" data. These are data recorded and stored in the lowest level of aggregation and detail—such as the size, price, time, and location of a single purchase of a product.

As Professor Arnold E. Amstutz of M.I.T. has commented:

> At the heart of every successful information system is a disaggregated data file. . . . As new inputs are received they are maintained along with existing data rather than replacing or being combined with existing information. . . . The existence of a disaggregated data file facilitates system evaluation. . . . In the first stages of system development it is simply impossible to anticipate the direction of later advancement. Aggregate data files may preclude highly profitable system modification. The disaggregated data file provides the flexibility which is the prerequisite of intelligent system evolution.[3]

In designing the data bank it is important to provide for common denominators in different sets of data, so that the correlation and analysis potential of the MIS can be realized. This means that such elements as the geographic, time, and responsibility boundaries of different types of data must be compatible to permit meaningful comparisons.

A disaggregated data bank gives the system the flexibility required for future upgrading. The alternative is to try to anticipate all possible future uses of the system and to agree on aggregated units (like aggergating all package sizes of a brand), aggregated time periods (a week, month, or quarter), and aggregated geographical areas (sales territories or regions).

Management must weigh the greater cost of a disaggregated data bank against the possibility that future conditions or new insights may call for analyses which are precluded because the data have been aggregated. Since most people who have participated in MIS development admit that they are unable to foresee all important management information needs, and since most current systems are likely to evolve to increasing stages of sophistication, the prudent decision would be to develop a disaggregated data bank —*if* the company can afford it.

Presentation and Format. Developing a sophisticated MIS involves resolving the matters of what information should be presented, how it should be presented, and to whom.

One important aspect of this question is the degree of executive-system interaction desired. At the extreme of "distance," executives receive information in the form of regular reports. With somewhat closer but not complete interaction, the manager can make special requests for information

---

[3] "The Marketing Executive and Management Information Systems," in *Science, Technology and Marketing,* 1966 Fall Conference Proceedings of the American Marketing Association, p. 76.

from the data bank. At the extreme of "closeness," the manager con obtain almost instantaneous computer response with a time-sharing or on-line system. Consider Schenley's experience:

> Schenley has installed a vido display and retrieval system. Of interest is the fact that the new system carries little new information; indeed, the same data were generated previously in the form of computer print-out. The information in paper form, however, was too voluminous and unwieldy to use. What the new retrieval and presentation system has achieved is simply to make data much more usable for management.

On-line systems such as Schenley's have a tremendous advantage in speed of access to information. Critics of these systems argue that managers do not need to know what happened as of the close of business yesterday.[4] This may be true. But there are benefits in being able to receive split-second responses. A manager's willingness to formulate questions and get data on which to base decisions may depend on the ease and speed with which he can retrieve answers from the computer. Although it is too early to tell whether the cost of this capability can be justified, large companies should seriously consider experimenting with this type of system.

Computer Selection. The computer requirement for a company's MIS will, of course, depend on the system's performance specifications and the decisions management has made on each of the preceding design problems. While technical help is necessary in the decisions on equipment, management has the responsibility for making certain that the hardware chosen will meet the MIS needs and specifications at the time of installation, which may be some years away. In this respect, managers should recognize that they probably will learn many new ways to use the computer, such as new marketing planning, control, decision, and research applications, given some experience with an improved MIS. So even with the most careful planning, demands for computer capacity are likely to expand faster than anticipated.

Cost and Value

It is difficult to generalize about how much an MIS will cost—or how much it will be worth. Usually there is not a large increase in data gathering costs, since many companies now have available to them much of the raw data required. Cost increases result from data storage and transforming the raw data into useful information. It is extremely difficult to determine MIS development costs, since many companies lack accounting arrangements, like interdepartmental billing, which allow them to keep track of the total cost of the manpower contributing to the program.

---

[4] See John Dearden, "Myth of Real-Time Management Information," HBR May–June 1966, p. 123.

On a "best estimate" basis, we are aware of simple or partial systems which have cost only a few thousand dollars. At the other extreme, one complex marketing system we know of must have cost several million dollars. A large company with sales in the $500 million range should expect to invest several hundred thousand dollars (plus equipment charges) to develop a relatively sophisticated, computer-based MIS. And development costs will not end there, since after the first stage is operational, it is probable that management will want to upgrade the system continually.

If top executives authorize expenditures of this magnitude, they are likely to want a justification of the value of the system. Usually, computer-based information systems, such as those used for accounting, have been justified mainly on the ground that they reduce personnel and other administrative costs. Few advanced marketing information systems could be justified on the basis of cost reduction.

However, that test alone is not appropriate for an MIS. The main purpose of an MIS is to help the marketing manager make more profitable decisions, not to reduce data handling and paperwork costs. So an MIS should be evaluated in terms of its estimated effects on marketing efficiency.

Determining how much an MIS could increase marketing effectiveness is not an easy task. The involvement of management in developing overall specifications should help in making an estimate, however imprecise, of system benefits. In addition, the decision on a budget for MIS development need not be made in a single giant step. Rather, it is possible to attain system sophistication in discrete increments, involving a series of smaller budgeting decisions and cost/benefit evaluations.

CONCLUSION

Marketing men in many of the large corporations we studied are almost uniformly enthusiastic about the promise of the computer-based, advanced MIS. Relatively few such systems are now operating, however, and many companies have had indifferent success in deriving benefits from them.

In the more successful companies, the following patterns have been evident:

The development of the MIS has been viewed as a management responsibility, including both top management and operating line management.

Formal organizational lines have been drawn to provide leadership in use of the technique—usually including the appointment of a high-level information coordinator or "prime contractor" who develops plans and coordinates the efforts of the departments involved.

The prime contractor reports to the user group, such as the marketing department, rather than to the central systems group.

Line managers participate in developing overall specifications for the MIS.

The sophistication of the system is balanced with that of the managers who use it.

Systems development typically proceeds in manageable stages, rather than in attempts to develop "total" systems at once.

The system is based on a disaggregated data bank which allows managers to retrieve analyses in the form they want without having to specify all their information needs in advance.

Investments in systems development and operation are justified not on the basis of cost reduction, which is often irrelevant with the MIS, but on an estimate of the system's ability to help managers make more profitable marketing decisions.

It is evident that a good deal of faith is required to make substantial investments in the MIS—whose benefits by and large are still unproven. Yet more and more companies are demonstrating their faith. And some of the pioneers already claim their faith is justified.